# OBJECTS OF CULTURE IN THE LITERATURE OF IMPERIAL SPAIN

*Edited by Mary E. Barnard and Frederick A. de Armas*

Collecting and displaying finely crafted objects was a mark of character among the royals and aristocrats in Early Modern Spain: it ranked with extravagant hospitality as a sign of nobility and with virtue as a token of princely power. *Objects of Culture in the Literature of Imperial Spain* explores how the writers of the period shared the same impulse to collect, arrange, and display objects, though in imagined settings, as literary artefacts.

These essays examine a variety of cultural objects described or alluded to in books from the Golden Age of Spanish literature, including clothing, paintings, tapestries, playing cards, monuments, materials of war, and even enchanted bronze heads. The contributors emphasize how literature preserved and transformed objects to endow them with new meaning for aesthetic, social, religious, and political purposes – whether to perpetuate certain habits of thought and belief, or to challenge accepted social and moral norms.

(Toronto Iberic)

Mary E. Barnard is an associate professor of Spanish and Comparative Literature at The Pennsylvania State University.

Frederick A. de Armas is the Andrew W. Mellon Distinguished Service Professor in the Humanities, Spanish Literature, and Comparative Literature at the University of Chicago.

# Objects of Culture in the Literature of Imperial Spain

EDITED BY MARY E. BARNARD
AND FREDERICK A. DE ARMAS

UNIVERSITY OF TORONTO PRESS
Toronto Buffalo London

Toronto Buffalo London
utorontopress.com

Reprinted in paperback 2022

ISBN 978-1-4426-4512-7 (cloth)
ISBN 978-1-4875-4769-1 (paper)

Publication cataloguing information is available from Library and Archives Canada.

We wish to acknowledge the land on which the University of Toronto Press operates. This land is the traditional territory of the Wendat, the Anishnaabeg, the Haudenosaunee, the Métis, and the Mississaugas of the Credit First Nation.

University of Toronto Press acknowledges the financial support of the Government of Canada, the Canada Council for the Arts, and the Ontario Arts Council, an agency of the Government of Ontario, for its publishing activities.

Canada Council for the Arts
Conseil des Arts du Canada

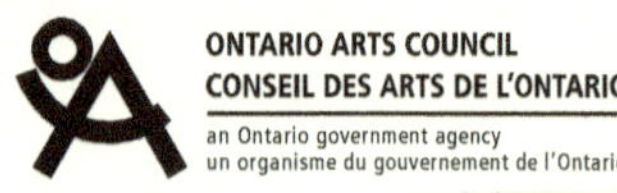


Funded by the Government of Canada
Financé par le gouvernement du Canada
Canada

# Contents

**Part Two: The Matter of Words**

# Illustrations

**Chapter 1**



**Chapter 3**



**Chapter 11**



**Chapter 13**

## Chapter 14

# Preface

This collection is about objects that are described or alluded to in books, objects like clothing, paintings, tapestries, playing cards, enchanted heads, materials of war, monuments, and books themselves. The notion of objects within books, and of books within objects, had a lasting currency. According to ancient texts, Alexander hid the Homeric *Iliad* under his pillow, wanting to emulate the feats of Achilles and Ulysses. Legend has it that when he found a luxurious chest among the booty taken from King Darius, he ordered the *Iliad* to be placed within it. This second tale became so popular in the Renaissance that a grisaille painting, *Alexander the Great Places Homer's Iliad in Safe Keeping*, appears in Raphael's *Stanza della Segnatura* at the Vatican (Jones and Penny 1983, 74). The painting, which allows us to "view" the moment in which the book was placed in a magnificent coffer, was, in turn, the subject of an engraving by Marcantonio Raimondi, the famous popularizer of Raphael during the Renaissance (Shoemaker and Brown 1981, 10). These two objects, book and coffer, continued to live through painted and engraved images as well as in written texts such as Cervantes' *Don Quixote* (de Armas 2007, 27). Like the *Iliad*, the objects discussed in *Objects of Culture* pass through many hands, being valorized, hidden, collected, and exhibited for a variety of reasons. The journeys of these textual objects can tell us much as to what was valued and what was shunned, what held power and what subverted it in imperial Spain.

## 1 Recovery of a Material Past

The production of goods in all forms permeated the cultural life of early modern Europe (Jardine 1996). Collecting and displaying finely crafted objects was a mark of character and taste, and a sign of "magnificence." Indeed, the ceremonial show of material treasures ranked with extravagant hospitality as a "hallmark of noble virtue" and as a token of "princely power and status" (Swann 2001, 16). The monarchs of imperial Spain shared that disposition, and became dedicated collectors. The itinerant court of Charles V (r. 1516–56) carried in its train sets of tapestries for public display during his travels, while his Titians performed a similar service in his palaces, an ostentatious self-marketing learned from his grandfather Maximilian (Silver 2008). Philip II (r. 1556–98) amassed a collection of relics that revealed the pious side of his character (Lazure 2007), all the while keeping a private collection of erotica hidden behind curtains at the Pardo, consisting notably of several Titians, including a Venus and a Danaë. Philip III (r. 1598–1621) likewise was an energetic collector of paintings of the premier artists of his day and of other luxurious objects that comprised one of the largest collections of its kind (Schroth, Baer, et al. 2008). His *valido* the Duke of Lerma (1603–36), chief architect and procurer of works of art, amassed a huge personal collection of tapestries, jewellery, reliquaries, and foreign and domestic glass and ceramics. Thirteen recently discovered household inventories list his enormous private collection, numbering between 1500 and 2747 paintings, which hung in his various residences (Schroth, Baer, et al. 2008, 88). Lerma stood as a mirror of royal tastes and aspirations in acquiring and gifting cultural objects. It is a tribute to his ambitions that he commissioned a palace larger and more magnificent than the Escorial, and more suitable to display his unrivalled collections of art and artefacts. But Philip III was not to be challenged on that score, and the duke fell from royal favour. Only kings and emperors could play the game of cultural superiority against each other.

Philip IV (r. 1621–65) is well known for favouring the paintings of Rubens, Poussin, and especially his court painter, Diego Velázquez. Indeed, it is said that the visit of Charles, Prince of Wales, to Madrid in a quixotic knight errant effort to woo the infanta María "was the culminating experience in his education as a collector," as a junta was organized to guide Charles and his entourage "through local collections" (Brown 1995, 33, 35). Instead of a promise of marriage, the prince left for England with a treasure trove of art works, the most important being gifts from the king: Titian's *Pardo Venus* and *Charles V with a Hound* as well as Veronese's *Mars and Venus* (Brown 1995, 37). But Philip did not surrender his favourite paintings, and he soon acquired many more, especially by Velázquez, whose *Surrender of Breda* (1634–5) held a privileged place in the Hall of Realms of the Buen Retiro, the pleasure palace built by Philip IV in the 1630s on the outskirts of Madrid.

Like the palaces and collections of the Duke of Lerma, the Buen Retiro served as a prism through which to view the royal court and, more generally, the cultural and political doings of imperial Spain. In their classic study, *A Palace for a King* (2003), Jonathan Brown and J.H. Elliott sought to recapture the material and cultural life of the Buen Retiro. Through a comprehensive study of the great central hall, the Hall of Realms, and its paintings, which are the only objects to survive from the complex of palace buildings and grounds, Brown and Elliott recovered a rich court life saturated with objects, mostly paintings, prints, tapestries, sculpture, furniture, and the related trappings of a powerful monarch. With the Buen Retiro serving as the architectural frame for the objects commissioned, collected, and displayed within it, the royal court can now be understood as a complex melding of place, events, and objects with which it was identified. No less grand than Fontainebleau, Versailles, or the Pitti, the Buen Retiro and other stately houses and palaces of the Habsburg kings of Spain – the Escorial, the Alcazar of Madrid, the Pardo – were well appointed to guard the cultural objects acquired by the royals, with court theatre and political intrigue vying for attention with patronage and collecting. The monarchs of imperial Spain, from Charles V through Philip IV, surrounded themselves and their courts with cultural objects in a manner unimaginable by their predecessors, and their collections, both for public display and for private contemplation, rivalled or surpassed those of other European monarchs of the time.

## 2 Writers of a Material World

The writers of imperial Spain, we argue, were just as deeply implicated by the production and circulation of material goods as were the royals and aristocrats who consumed them and shared the same impulse to collect, arrange, and display those objects, though in imagined settings. Indeed, this impulse extended to the colonial world and back.[1] The transmutation of objects of culture into the realm of the imagined may be seen as a metaphorical instance of what Stephen Greenblatt calls the human touch, the moment when objects are moved, mutilated, or broken, when they are taken away from their original placement and relocated to a new site (1991, 44).[2] In collections of art objects, for example, each item is labelled and explained through brief textual summaries to aid the viewer in understanding the object's significance and function. Writers performed a similar manoeuvre as they wrote objects into their texts, which were stocked with paintings, tapestries, books, clothing, armour, and other artefacts of the time as well as Roman antiquities, which had become coveted objects recently unearthed in Italy (Barkan 1999). The essays in this volume explore some of the ways in which those objects "performed" as literary artefacts, for they are more than bibelots strewn about for decorative or rhetorical purposes. The essays engage what might be called an archaeology of real and imagined objects in order to understand the various ways in which writers of sixteenth- and seventeenth-century Spain appropriated those objects for their own aesthetic, social, religious, and political purposes.

Our second avenue of inquiry is the role of the material objects themselves as carriers of culture and as agents of disruption. In this sense, we are interested in what Greenblatt calls resonance: "The power of the displayed object to reach out beyond its formal boundaries to a larger world, to evoke in the viewer the complex, dynamic cultural forces from which it has emerged and for which it may be taken by the viewer to stand" (1991, 42). How did objects of diverse provenance (books, pyramids, paintings) acquire new meaning within new contexts, both in Spain and in its overseas possessions? How were some objects (books of hours, musical notations) used to perpetuate certain habits of thought and belief, whereas others (food, clothing, and instruments of war) challenged accepted conventional social and moral norms? And how did these objects serve to enhance and authorize the author, and/or create wonder in the reader through the excesses of writing and collecting? In sum, we examine both the function of cultural objects and their circulation and re-purposing within the various realms of imperial Spain.

## 3 Our Cabinet of Curiosities

Anthony Grafton has observed: "A network of museums ... grew up across Europe in the later sixteenth and seventeenth centuries. From Oxford to Vienna, from Naples to Nuremberg, kings and merchants, doctors and professors set spaces aside for collections of the wonderful works of nature and art" (1998, 14). We envision this volume as a *Wunderkammer* or a *camerino* much in the spirit of those who created their private cabinets of illustrative exotic curiosities, for we imagine the writers of imperial Spain as metaphorically collecting and displaying all manner of objects for the delectation of readers and viewers. Although Greenblatt notes that the wonder cabinets were "at least as much about possession as display" (1991, 50), he reminds us that an important aspect of viewing the objects was to create "reports" in order to explain what had been seen, and the significance of the objects on exhibition. Writers of early modern Spain likewise "report" real or imagined objects and collections in written texts, which we have here placed on exhibition in separate essays that can be viewed as rooms in an early modern museum. And like the actual objects in a cabinet of curiosities, these imagined curiosities are not mute items on display; they are evoked as active, discursive participants in narrative performances.

It is well-known that not all early modern museums survived. Some were absorbed while others were scattered. The Accademia dei Lincei in Rome obtained Gianbattista della Porta's substantial collections by promising him "that donating his museum to the academy would ensure his fame." Indeed, his bust as well as those of the Roman nobles Federico Cesi and Galileo Galilei "looked down on the giants of antiquity" (Findlen 2000, 171). And yet, this was not to be. This collection, as well as that of Cardinal Pietro Bembo, was scattered through the antiquities markets. The transitory nature of collecting inspired Federico Borromeo, founder of the Biblioteca Ambrosiana in Milan (1609), "to continue the project of writing the museum" in order to preserve it. "Borromeo wrote that the ancients had commemorated their cultural monuments in writing in order 'to let them live a double life'" (Findlen 2000, 176).

This was the double life followed in Spain not only by royal collections, but also by the famous museum of the *curioso* Vincencio Juan de Lastanosa (1607–82), whose treasures are evoked in Baltasar Gracián's allegorical novel *El Criticón*. In his palace, works of art by Rubens, Titian, and Tintoretto vied with some seven thousand tomes on alchemy, astronomy, botany, mathematics, and many other topics. Indeed, art vied with the natural sciences as coins and ancient weapons could be seen together with exotic plants, magnificent sculptures, and delightful gardens. Lastanosa was conscious of the need to reproduce some of his objects, not only in writing but through illustrations. Of that twin enterprise, John Slater concludes: "What is particularly helpful about Lastanosa's book … is the way in which he sifts apart and then juxtaposes the conflicting tendencies in Baroque historiography into, on the one hand, a graphic naked series of engravings, and on the other, their corresponding texts" (2008, 41).

In our collection, objects lead a double life: material and textual. In this sense, this museum of words contributes to the increasing scholarly interest in the material culture of imperial Spain, displayed to us in the essays collected by Enrique García Santo-Tomás (2009) and in monographs by Encarnación Juárez Almendros (2006) and Laura Bass (2008). García Santo-Tomás's volume includes a multiplicity of objects – carriages, *bodegón* painting, textiles, tobacco, and more – in an attempt to understand the formation of identity and the culture of consumption (2009, 20–2). Juárez Almendros focuses on garments in autobiographical writings and Bass on portraits that circulate in dozens of dramas and which serve, among other things, "as tokens of love, objects of jealous passion, and icons of royalty' (2008, 1). In our collection, objects of art, power, and the quotidian predominate, be they paintings, tapestries, edifices, monuments, food, talking portraits, or books as amulets. Our emphasis is on writing as a way of preserving and transforming these cultural objects as they "resonate" in their performative roles.

## 4 The Essays

The essays in Part One, "Objects of Luxury and Power," examine how familiar material objects function both in structuring narratives and in animating their arguments. In "Gifts for the Vicereine of Naples: The Weavings of Garcilaso's Third Eclogue," Mary Barnard follows recent scholarship that restores the role of tapestries as the most iconic of objects, along with paintings, commissioned and displayed by aristocrats in the sixteenth and seventeenth centuries. She analyses Garcilaso's four discursive tapestries woven by nymphs as lyric versions of actual tapestries, which circulated as artistic commodities within an aristocratic culture of consumption. Placing those tapestries within a vibrant gift-giving tradition, Barnard shows how the poet constructs an elaborate, self-referential stage for imagined material objects that are collected, gifted, and displayed to great effect: they serve at once as celebratory presents for María Osorio Pimentel, as items of social networking, and as the locus for inscribing the poet's identity as friend, flattering courtier, and skilled verbal craftsman. The complementarity between writing and weaving reveals the poem itself as a fabric in its various functions as text, textile, and networking, all connected to the enterprise of fabric-making in cloth. Like the emperor Charles V, who carried an extravagant collection of tapestries to enhance his authority and prestige, Garcilaso crafted his lyric tapestries to celebrate both the vicereine and himself.

Marsha S. Collins reminds us of the importance of spatial context – here a palace and a cave – for the display and performance of material objects. In "Artful Edifices and the Construction of Identity in Montemayor's *Diana* and Lope's *Arcadia*," she explores how Montemayor crafted an intricate and sumptuous imaginary palace to frame his pastoral, in effect transferring the classic rural background into a building filled with chambers and all manner of manufactured artefacts. In essence, architectural space displaces nature's realm as the setting for pastoral narration. Just as portraits in the *comedia* could move from static accessory to active narrative participants, so could pastoral with its attendant myth and metamorphosis unfold within constructed architectural space in lieu of nature's space. Lope's cave, on the other hand, retains a nature-like space for his narrative, but it too is filled with cultural objects – a pyramid, a magnificent marble tomb, a steel box for preserving books and a culture of learning – that elicit powerful visual imagery in the *Arcadia.* Here again the material not only intrudes into traditional narrative forms, it shifts the storytelling from untroubled rural pastoral scenes into a more visually complex world of the late sixteenth century.

Miguel de Cervantes used playing cards and paintings as similar visual cues in *Don Quixote.* Frederick A. de Armas in "The Artful Gamblers: Wagering Danaë in Cervantes' *Don Quixote* I.33–35" turns to *El curioso impertinente*, arguing that the characters in the tale could be portrayed as gamblers: theatrical gamblers who create new roles to win or accomplish their desires; and artful gamblers who prize works of Italian Renaissance art concealed within the text and even model themselves after these paintings. Indeed, de Armas asserts that the tale conceals an ekphrastic moment in Terence's *Eunnuchus*, and that the painting exhibited therein is key to understanding the interpolated tale: it represents the myth of Jupiter and Danaë, a tale that circulates not only through the antique play and Cervantes' novel as an ekphrasis, but also through the recollection that Titian's Danaë was exhibited in what some have claimed was an erotic *camerino* by Philip II and his successors.

In "The Things They Carried: Sovereign Objects in Calderón de la Barca's *La gran Cenobia,*" María Cristina Quintero examines how stage props – sceptres, crowns, thrones, and books – were as critical to the performance of the *comedia* as the script itself. As theatre became more elaborate, she contends, visual devices became more prevalent and carried more of the performance's meaning. In *La gran Cenobia*, with its positive and negative exemplars of monarchy, and gendered struggle for power, she finds Calderón acting as a master manipulator of stage objects. Visual cues take on new meanings as the playwright constructs and interrogates political power before the very eyes and conscience of the audience, including the king himself. In this instance actual material objects are scripted as dramatis personae in their own right.

Tapestries and paintings were primarily handcrafted objects made to be hung on walls, where their fixed scenes could be admired. But, as Christopher B. Weimer explains in "Beyond Canvas and Paint: Falling

Portraits in the Spanish *Comedia*," portraits in the *comedia* could assume far more active, nonconventional roles, as lifelike surrogates for their absent subjects. These stage portraits not only engaged viewers directly with their eyes, but they could also enter the scene to participate in the representation. In one case a fictive portrait, crashing to the floor, even attempts to change the script. In another case, a declaration of eternal love addressed to a portrait, standing for the deceased, evokes the mystical language of love, with the portrait, by allusion, serving as a performative religious object. Far from being inert, imagined painted portraits – ostensible static set pieces – could participate in their own drama, usually for beneficial effects.

The essays in Part Two, "The Matter of Words," address the relationship between material objects and conceptual investigations, specifically relating to sound, vision, time, memory, and space. How is sound materialized in writing? How are the hours of a Christian's day, a typical medieval episteme, translated to the indigenous peoples of the new world? Is memory best preserved in a monument or in a poem? Like the Buen Retiro palace that occasioned musical and cultural performances, the cultural products analysed here – musical scores, books of hours, picaresque novels, and buildings – occasioned transactional performances in writing.

In "Book Marks: Jerónimo de Aguilar and the Book of Hours," Heather Allen shows how a medieval religious episteme introduced into the New World became an ambiguous agent of empire. The book of hours serves as a useful example of how material objects circulated far beyond the area of their intended use, and how a familiar object, re-contextualized, acquired new meaning. Aguilar appears in multiple histories of the conquest written by a variety of authors from Spanish and *mestizo* backgrounds. In the stories she examines, literacy and its material manifestation – the book of hours – fulfil specific roles according to each historiographer's goals. She argues that although we might expect a rupture between Western and indigenous concepts of literacy, the authors do not, in fact, structure their arguments along ethnic lines. To the contrary, they restructure their ideas to incorporate elements of literacy from the other's culture, moving into flux what were once static cultural beliefs and attitudes towards reading, writing, and texts.

In "Embodying the Visual, Visualizing Sound in Sor Juana Inés de la Cruz's *Primero sueño*," Emily L. Bergmann finds that musical notation pervades the language (sound) and composition of *Primero sueño* at the same time as the visual (a pyramid) invokes a range of graphic images imposed on time and space. It is not the transposition of the objects themselves (as in the first set of essays) that strikes us here, but rather the incorporation of structured sound itself within the language of the text, and within images that resonate with the scientific discourses of the time. Instead of staging objects, Sor Juana processes them by absorbing sound and extending the parameters of their epistemology.

Edward H. Friedman focuses on the materiality of words themselves in his "Picaresque Partitions: Spanish Antiheroes and the Material World." Indeed, words mirror the quest for acquisition by the picaresque characters, a quest that often ends in failure. While words and objects are at odds, so are the protagonist and the authorial narrator. While Pablos hides behind words, Quevedo puts words on display. And yet, Pablos's words are also a display, attempting to wrest free from the adornments of an author that would contain him, as the *pícaro* seeks to become more. But the narrator keeps him tied, leading him to fail miserably – overreaching and descent to criminality being the two main paths. While objects of worth and power remain elusive, the beauty of language as object glitters as it attempts to divert the reader from Pablos's being. He is in the end, more than an object, but a being of value in spite of his criminality.

While Friedman's Pablos stays in our memory, Robert ter Horst addresses the long-standing question of whether memory is best preserved by architecture, that is, materialized space, or by poetry, written memory. In "Francisco de Quevedo and the Poetic Matter of Patronage," he situates Quevedo within a long continuum from antiquity to the seventeenth century in which poets addressed, and attempted to combat, the power of buildings to serve as repositories of memory. The palace of Philip IV, the Buen Retiro, with its multiple buildings and gardens, became an aspirational model for the nobles of the royal court, who built their own extravagant residences – trophy estates – as manifestations of their power and as material bases for their future lineages. These "theatres of ambitions" later expired, noted Quevedo the poet, and a palace without life became a mausoleum. Only a poet's words could adequately capture and preserve the memory of great men and great deeds. But for that, as the ancient poets had recognized, a poet needs a patron to furnish the requisite *otium*.

The essays in Part Three, "Objects against Culture," consider the use of material objects to subvert or counter the dominant culture. Food, clothing, and war material are eminent tools for disrupting and challenging the conventional and normative, that is, the prescribed stasis of the times. Cultural objects are subversively upturned in order to question existing hierarchies, as in the consumption of food, in a prayer inscribed on a paper amulet, or in the proper role of clothing for its producers and consumers.

In the same manner a cultural icon (the head of Orpheus) might materialize in a new context, and the machines of war could occasion a reexamination of ethical questions pertaining to war, its conduct, and its effects.

Carolyn Nadeau's "Transformation and Transgression at the Banquet Scene of *La Celestina*" takes the banquet as the site of contestation between the proper and transgressive rites of conduct and consumption. The table, etiquette, service, seating, and dress all define the norm within an accepted social hierarchy, but it is food and drink that most occasion conversation, which can disrupt the staged banquet scene as it extends to topics beyond the meal itself. Even more disruptive are the subsequent recollections and dissections of the choreographed banquet scene, whose foods and formalities are seen to encode gross social inequities. The carefully structured banquet thus stands both as the epitome of an ordered social scene and as the symbol of a society in need of reordering.

A sixteenth-century *Oración de la emparedada* (*Prayer of the immured woman*) recently discovered hidden in a wall near the border of Spain and Portugal, like other kinds of prayer books, was believed to convey apotropaic power through its recitation, as well as the materiality of the text (a paper amulet) carried on or bound to the body. In "The Prayer of the Immured Woman and the Matter of *Lazarillo de Tormes*," Ryan D. Giles studies the connection between this heterodox textual amulet and the 1554 *Lazarillo de Tormes*, a prohibited book that was not only stowed away in the same hidden stash as the *Oración*, but also recited by the rogue's first master in an early edition of the proto-picaresque masterpiece. Giles's essay considers how the contents of this prayer relate to the practice of immuring heretical women and other transgressors during the Inquisition, and how the efficacy and material presence of the *Oración* exert an ironic, proleptic force over the course of his narrative, with its prophetic structure and dishonourable outcome.

The third essay in this section is by Luis F. Avilés, who examines the ethical issues enjoined by war, its technology, and its material consequences in his "War and the Material Conditions for Suffering in Cervantes' *Numancia*." The Numancians, about to be defeated in war by an irrational Scipio, decide to destroy all their personal possessions before their capitulation. Against any hope of survival, they distance themselves from their material objects by their only possible act – destruction. Only bread retains its value for the famished and doomed. The devaluation of cultural objects has its analogue in relations among the survivors: the violence and destruction of war changes fundamentally how one thinks about worldly goods, about craftsmanship and beauty, and about the very carriers of "culture." Cervantes' powerful drama, written in an age of abundant worldly goods, poses the ultimate question of how our identities are dependent on the cultural objects we gather around us or, under certain conditions, dispensed with as superfluous.

Timothy Ambrose in his "The Goddess, Dionysus, and the Material World in *Don Quijote*," weaves together three very disparate objects – an enchanted head, a painting by Titian, and a labyrinth – in order to bring to light mythical mysteries in Cervantes' *Don Quixote*. These mysteries have to do with the ancient Great Goddess and the god Dionysus. Guiding us through Sierra Morena as labyrinth, a place beholden to Ariadne, a name for the ancient goddess in Crete, we encounter the Mountain Goddess. Illuminating Ariadne's encounter with Dionysus at Naxos and then revealing the enchanted head as that of Orpheus, priest of Dionysus, Ambrose shows the many links between Dionysus and Don Quixote, and between the god and the Great Goddess of old. Objects in Cervantes' novel, then, point to the antique and they in turn question the culture of imperial Spain where the goddess has been relegated to the imaginative labyrinth of a madman's mind. And yet, it is Dulcinea, the woman of the madman's dreams, a woman that can be seen as a new Ariadne, who has dominion over the labyrinth of the mind and of the narrative.

The volume closes with clothing since it, too, both encodes and challenges a stable, hierarchical social organization. In Goretti González's "Dismantling *Sosiego*: Undressing, Dressing, and Cross-Dressing in Mateo Alemán's *Guzmán de Alfarache*," sartorial fashion and expectations serve to mask Spain's dire economic circumstances, which were bizarrely attributed to clothing itself, that is, to cross-dressing and sartorial effeminacy. Alemán thus depicts a different Spain from the somberly clothed nation of *sosiego* of Boscán and Fernando de Herrera. Alemán's Guzmán cleverly alters his attire in negotiating an ever-changing discourse of identity, using his tailored garments to enter the picaresque underworld, where clothing is freely employed to create and dissimulate identity. Guzmán's persona is not so much reflected in his clothing as obscured by his frequent undressing, dressing, and even cross-dressing. Just as the prescribed rite of eating encodes both order and contestation, clothing in its various permutations simultaneously encodes both acceptance and subversion of the sartorial order.

We would like to thank our research assistant, Felipe Rojas, from the University of Chicago for his invaluable assistance in editing this volume. We also wish to express our gratitude to Martha Roth, Dean of Humanities at the University of Chicago, and to Henry Gerfen, Head of the

Department of Spanish, Italian and Portuguese at the Pennsylvania State University, for their generous support with this project. Finally, we thank the two anonymous readers for their wealth of information and detail on material culture.

## NOTES

1 For those interested in cartography, scientific instruments and other transatlantic materials, see Padrón (2004), Portuondo (2009), and Bleichman (2011).
2 The field of English studies has been very influential in the study of material culture. The interested reader might wish to consult de Grazia, Quilligan and Stallybrass (1996), Fumerton and Hunt (1999), Jones and Stallybrass (2000), and Orlin (2000).

## WORKS CITED

Barkan, Leonard. 1999. *Unearthing the Past: Archaeology and Aesthetics in the Making of Renaissance Culture*. New Haven: Yale University Press.
Bass, Laura R. 2008. *The Drama of the Portrait:Theater and Visual Culture in Early Modern Spain*. University Park: Pennsylvania State University Press.
Bleichman, Daniella. 2011. *Collecting across Cultures: Material Exchanges in the Early Atlantic World*. Philadelphia: University of Pennsylvania Press.
Brown, Jonathan. 1995. *Kings & Connoisseurs: Collecting Art in Seventeenth-Century Europe*. Princeton: Princeton University Press.
Brown, Jonathan, and J.H. Elliott. 2003. Rev. of 1980. *A Palace for a King: The Buen Retiro and the Court of Philip IV*. New Haven: Yale University Press.
de Armas, Frederick A. 2007. *Quixotic Frescoes: Cervantes and Italian Renaissance Art*. Toronto: University of Toronto Press.
Findlen, Paula. 2000. "The Modern Muses: Renaissance Collecting and the Cult of Remembrance." In *Museums and Memory*, edited by Susan A. Crane, 161–78. Stanford: Stanford University Press.
Fumerton, Patricia, and Simon Hunt, eds. 1999. *Renaissance Culture and the Everyday*. Philadelphia: University of Pennsylvania Press.
García Santo-Tomás, Enrique, ed. 2009. *Materia crítica: Formas de ocio y de consumo en la literatura áurea*. Madrid / Frankfurt: Iberoamericana / Vervuert.
Grafton, Anthony. 1998. "Believe It or Not." *New York Review of Books* 45 (17): 14–18.
de Grazia, Margreta, Maureen Quilligan, and Peter Stallybrass, eds. 1996. *Subject and Object in Renaissance Culture*. Cambridge: Cambridge University Press.

Greenblatt, Stephen. 1991. "Resonance and Wonder." In *Exhibiting Culture: The Poetics and Politics of Museum Display*, edited by Ivan Karp and Seven D. Lavine, 42–56. Washington, DC: Smithsonian Institution Press.

Jardine, Lisa. 1996. *Worldly Goods: A New History of the Renaissance*. New York: W.W. Norton.

Jones, Ann Rosalyn, and Peter Stallybrass. 2000. *Renaissance Clothing and the Materials of Memory*. Cambridge: Cambridge University Press.

Jones, Roger, and Nicholas Penny. 1983. *Raphael*. New Haven, CT: Yale University Press.

Juárez-Almendros, Encarnación. 2006. *El cuerpo vestido y la construcción de la identidad en las narrativas autobiográficas del Siglo de Oro*. London: Tamesis.

Lazure, Guy. 2007. "Possessing the Sacred: Monarchy and Identity in Philip II's Relic Collection at the Escorial." *Renaissance Quarterly* 60 (1): 58–93. http://dx.doi.org/10.1353/ren.2007.0076.

Orlin, Lena Cowen, ed. 2000. *Material London, ca. 1600*. Philadelphia: University of Pennsylvania Press.

Padrón, Ricardo. 2004. *The Spacious Word: Cartography, Literature, and Empire in Early Modern Spain*. Chicago: University of Chicago Press.

Portuondo, Maria. 2009. *Secret Science: Spanish Cosmography and the New World*. Chicago: University of Chicago Press.

Schroth, Sarah, Ronni Baer, et al. 2008. *El Greco to Velázquez: Art during the Reign of Philip III*. Boston: The Museum of Fine Arts.

Silver, Larry. 2008. *Marketing Maximilian: The Visual Ideology of a Holy Roman Emperor*. Princeton: Princeton University Press.

Shoemaker, Innis H., and Elizabeth Brown. 1981. *The Engravings of Marcantonio Raimondi*. Lawrence, KS: The Spencer Museum.

Slater, John. 2008. "From *Historia naturalis* to *Historia au naturale*: Lastanosa and the Naked Truth." In *The Gentleman, the Virtuoso, the Inquirer: Vincencio Juan de Lastanosa and the Art of Collecting in Early Modern Spain*, edited by Mar Rey-Bueno and Miguel López-Pérez, 30–46. Newcastle: Cambridge Scholars.

Swann, Marjorie. 2001. *Curiosities and Texts: The Culture of Collecting in Early Modern England*. Philadelphia: University of Pennsylvania Press.

# PART ONE

## Objects of Luxury and Power

# 1 Gifts for the Vicereine of Naples: The Weavings of Garcilaso's Third Eclogue

MARY E. BARNARD

In sixteenth-century Europe, tapestries were markers of wealth, status, power, and cultivated taste. More expensive to produce and more prestigious than paintings, these "woven frescoes" were at once signs of splendour and artistic commodities that circulated within an aristocratic culture of consumption. Their dazzling scenes commemorated notable deeds from a distant past, like Alexander the Great's conquests, and more recent ones, like Charles V's victory at the battle of Tunis (1535). They retold all manner of tales – mythological, religious, historical – and they could serve as purely decorative objects. Whether they hung in the chambers of kings and nobles or in public arenas, tapestries played a prominent role in the art, propaganda, and ceremonies of church and court.[1] In this essay I examine the tapestries woven by nymphs in Garcilaso's Third Eclogue as lyric versions of the figurative tapestries of the period and as objects that, like many actual tapestries, served as gifts for social and political networking with patrons and powerful others, in this case María Osorio Pimentel, vicereine of Naples, to whom the poem is dedicated.[2] What makes these lyric weavings so striking is that they appear *en abîme* within a poem itself conceived doubly as a fabric: as an interweaving of textual fragments from ancient and contemporary Italian works, and as a text on paper [carta], a sheet of matted fibre on which the poet's quill [pluma] inscribes and thus preserves the memory of María.

In an age thoroughly imbued with the dynamics of networking, making and maintaining social connections "became something of an art" that deeply implicated the self (McLean 2007, 4). Perhaps no one understood that better than Baldassare Castiglione, papal nuncio to the Spanish court (1524–9), whose book of manners, *Il Cortegiano* (1528), was translated into Spanish by Juan Boscán with Garcilaso's polishing touches and prologue (1534). Castiglione reveals elegantly the interplay between the art of networking and the construction of the self. His courtier, far from autonomous, shapes an identity through masks donned in staged public performances while interacting with those in high position (1959, Book 2). Garcilaso, an equally keen observer of social manoeuvrings and gift-giving in his own circles, figures himself in the eclogue as grateful friend and flattering courtier, but also as a skilled verbal craftsman of four sumptuous tapestries for the vicereine, whose court at Naples had sheltered him during his exile from the imperial court (1532–6).[3] The poet's luxurious gifts in turn figure María as a discerning member of a literate culture.

## Tapestry Culture

In the heartland of tapestry production in the Low Countries and northern France skilled artisans crafted the most expensive and highly sought weavings in silk, silver, and gold thread that circulated throughout France, England, Italy, and Spain.[4] They were an ideal medium of ostentation to parade monumental images of ancestors, military campaigns, and historical or mythological figures with which a patron wished to be associated (Campbell 2002, 15). The most affluent patrons commissioned sets of related tapestries, called "chambers," which typically covered a room's interior walls from floor to ceiling. An engraving by Frans Hogenberg, ca. 1558, *The Abdication of Charles V* (see fig. 1) shows how a chamber of tapestries set the stage for that historic event: Charles is surrounded by his heraldic devices – most prominently the stag – and behind him hangs his coat of arms, below which is inscribed "Carolus Caesar." Marketing visual imagery for propaganda, just as his grandfather Maximilian had done so successfully in his own time, Charles exploited the symbols embedded in the tapestries to enhance imperial authority on behalf of his son Philip and his brother Ferdinand, who would carry Habsburg rule forward.[5]

As a member of Charles's court, Garcilaso would have been familiar with these imperial trappings, especially when displayed conspicuously on festive occasions at home and abroad, notably during the emperor's coronation by Pope Clement VII in Bologna in 1530, which the poet witnessed. At a time when royal households itinerated for seasonal and political reasons, tapestries became the ultimate transportable emblem of wealth and power, as essential to a Christian prince as his portable altars. An inventory taken in 1544 of Charles's Removing Wardrobe, as portable tapestry collections were called, listed fifteen sets comprising ninety-six tapestries, the most prized being the spectacular nine-piece chamber, *Los Honores*

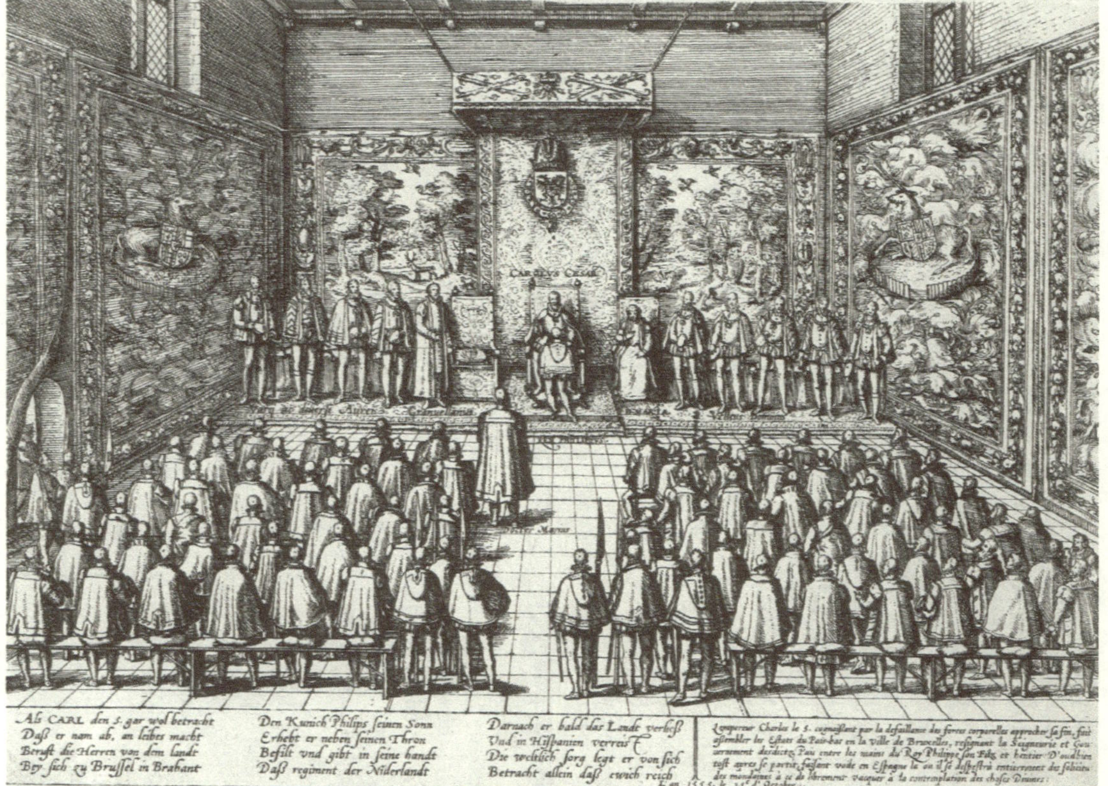


Figure 1 *The Abdication of Charles V* from *Events in the History of the Netherlands, France, Germany and England between 1535 and 1608*. Impression of an engraving by Frans Hogenberg, ca. 1558. The Metropolitan Museum of Art / Art Resource, NY.

(1520s), an allegorical celebration of Habsburg values and a kind of "mirror for princes" because of its moral content (Delmarcel 2000). The seven-piece *Battle of Pavia*, commemorating Charles's victory over Francis I (1525), remains one of the most important chambers in the imperial collection (see fig. 2). For the wedding of Prince Philip to Mary Tudor (1554), Charles sent his twelve-piece *Conquest of Tunis* tapestries to hang in Winchester Cathedral. That formidable set, a visual tour de force, celebrated Habsburg prestige and magnificence. But if the display of tapestries indexed a ruler's status and authority, the lack of tapestries reflected just the opposite. When in 1527 Stephen Gardiner, bishop of Winchester, visited Pope Clement VII, then in exile in Orvieto following the sack of Rome, it was the absence of tapestries that first drew his attention. "Before reaching [the pope's] privy chamber," he reported, "we passed three chambers all naked and unhanged" (cited in Campbell 2002, 4). Living within bare walls, the pope was as undressed of authority as his chambers were of tapestries.

## Nymphs' Weavings

The eclogue's four discursive tapestries, like a chamber of actual hangings, are linked by style, iconography, and subject matter – the violent loss of a loved one and an abandoned, grieving lover in the mythological tales of Apollo and Daphne, Orpheus and Eurydice, Venus and Adonis, and the pastoral story of Elisa and Nemoroso. They recall the decorative hangings known at the time as verdures and now often called millefleurs. Characterized by foliage arranged in "repeating patterns of flowers and plants, enlivened with animals and figures in more elaborate pieces," they made up the majority of tapestries in quotidian use, particularly in private, intimate settings (Campbell 2002, 24). The *Diccionario de Autoridades* fittingly offers the plural "verduras" for these designs: "Llaman en los paises, y tapicerías el follage, y plantage, que se pinta en ellos" [Called in paintings (of villas, country houses, or countryside) and tapestries the foliage and plants that are painted in them]. Garcilaso plays with the technical term in the singular "verdura" to describe the stylized, bucolic setting of the banks of the Tagus, where the nymphs execute their craft:

Cerca del Tajo, en soledad amena,
de verdes sauces hay una espesura
toda de hiedra revestida y llena,
que por el tronco va hasta el altura

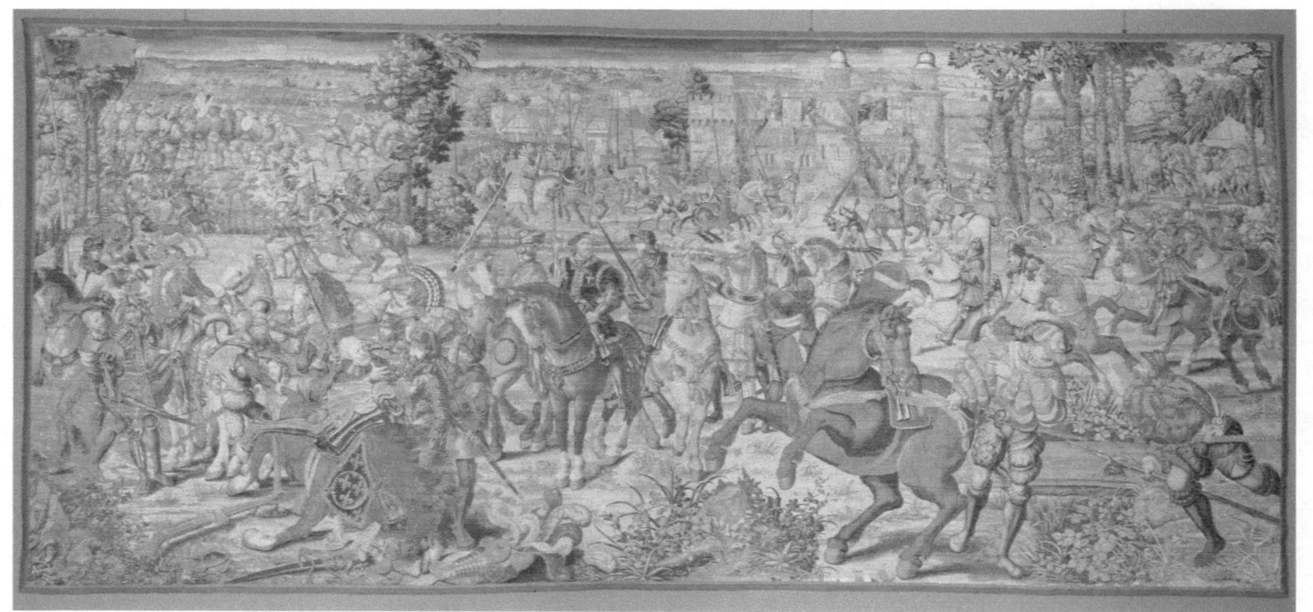

Figure 2 *Surrender of Francis I* from the *Battle of Pavia* tapestry series. Bernaert van Orley, woven in the Dermoyen workshop. Brussels, ca. 1528–31. Wool, silk, and silver. Museo Nazionale di Capodimonte, Naples. Erich Lessing /Art Resource, NY.

y así la *teje* arriba y encadena,
que'l sol no halla paso a la *verdura.*

[Close by the Tagus, in pleasing solitude,
there is a stand of willows, a dense grove
all dressed and draped with ivy, whose multitude
of stems goes climbing to the top and *weaves*
a canopy thick enough to exclude the sun,
denying it access to *green leaves* below.] (57–62, my emphasis)[6]

"Verdura" is joined by the metatextual "teje," by means of which nature weaves its own thick, complex patterns. The ground is covered with flowers: "el suave olor de aquel *florido suelo*" [the subtle scents arising from the *flowery field*] (74; my emphasis). "Verdura," "teje," and "florido suelo" announce a kinship between the textual setting and actual millefleurs tapestries, presaging the plant and floral weavings fictionally destined for María's quarters: the snake that bites and kills Eurydice lies hidden in the grass and flowers [entre la hierba y flores escondida] (132); the blood oozing out of Adonis's chest, torn open by the boar's tusk, turns red "the white roses that beautified that spot" [las rosas blancas por alli sembradas] (183); and a decapitated Elisa, metaphorically echoing the floral setting, "cuya vida mostraba que habia sido/antes de tiempo y casi en flor cortada" [whose life has clearly been cut short before its day,/just as the bud was coming into flower] (227–8), appears in a flowery spot (229), lying among the blades of green grass (231–2).

Millefleurs were eminently suited for a vicereine in accordance with contemporary tastes in weavings, their place in private vs. public spaces, and in certain cases gender-based themes as the following anecdote suggests. When Philip the Fair and Juana of Castile visited the Château de Blois in 1501, they found it filled with tapestries and cloths of all types. Louis XII had hung his *grande salle* with *The Destruction of Troy* and his dining room with *The Battle of Formigny*, scenes celebrating military events, much like Charles V, who displayed tapestries to reflect his imperial status and magnificence for political purposes. By contrast, the queen, Anne of Brittany, had her private quarters at Blois hung with tapestries akin to millefleurs, depicting "beasts and birds with people from distant lands," while her daughter Claude had her room hung with "a very beautiful bucolic tapestry filled with inscriptions and very small figures" (Guiffrey 1878, 67). At Naples the palaces of the vicereine and her husband were richly decorated with hangings, including millefleurs according to an inventory taken in 1553.[7] When the ambassador from Mantua, Nicola

Maffei, visited the capital in 1536, he found the walls of Castel Nuovo covered with tapestries: "tapezarie fine et bellisime et vanno attacate fin alla volta delle camere" [elegant and most beautiful tapestries were hung up to the vaulted ceilings of the rooms] (cited in Hernando Sánchez, 1993, 51). Most likely the vicereine did needlework – a sister art to weaving – much like her contemporaries Catherine de Medici in France and Mary Queen of Scots, who typically went about their stitching while engaged in conversation (Jones and Stallybrass 2000, 153). We would expect the vicereine to share a bond with Garcilaso's nymphs, who had previously appeared in Sonnet 11, "labrando embebescidas / o tejendo las telas delicadas" [bowed over your embroidery, / or toiling at the weaver's delicate art] and taking pleasure in one another's company, "unas con otras apartadas / contándoos los amores y las vidas" [sitting in little groups apart / making your loves and lives into a story]. A millefleurs tapestry dated circa 1520, now at the Musée de Cluny (see fig. 3), offers a splendid pictorial play *en abîme* illustrating how aristocratic ladies pursued their favourite activity: one is embroidering a millefleurs scene, while another is carrying skeins of yarn and a convex mirror, which reflects the very setting that is the subject of the embroidery.

Garcilaso knew that according to conventions of tapestry making, only the highest level of craftsmanship and the finest materials, gold being the most luxurious and expensive of threads, were worthy of a vicereine. His nymphs fabricate tapestries from the riches of the Tagus River, transforming nature into culture by turning its grains of gold and aquatic plants into thread, and by colouring their yarn with the purple dye of its shellfish:

Las telas eran hechas y tejidas
del oro que'l felice Tajo envía, […]
y de las verdes ovas, reducidas
en estambre sotil, cual convenía,
para seguir el delicado estilo
del oro, ya tirado en rico hilo.
La delicada estambre era distinta
de las colores que antes le habian dado
con la fineza de la varia tinta
que se halla en las conchas del pescado.

[The fabric of the cloth that they were weaving
was made from gold the happy Tagus gives, […]
and also made from the strands of green waterweed,
converted into a fine warp [yarn], which serves

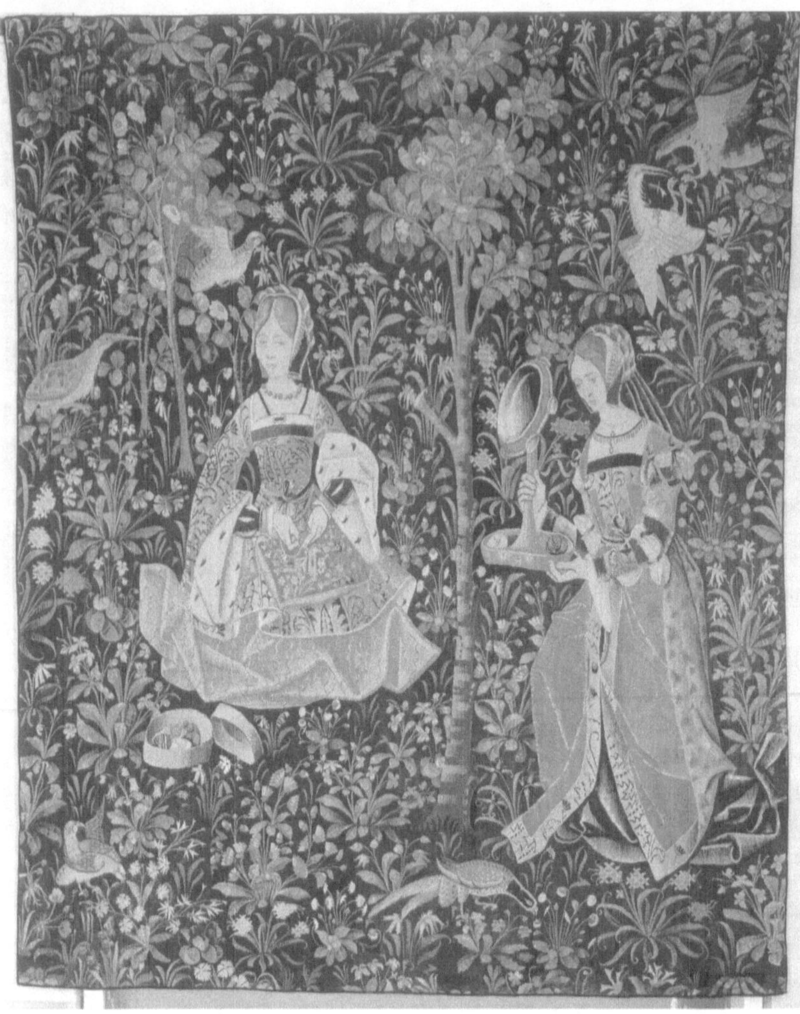

Figure 3 *The Seignorial Life: Embroidery*, ca. 1520. Southern Netherlands. Wool and silk tapestry. Musée National du Moyen Age-Thermes de Cluny, Paris. Réunion des Musées Nationaux / Art Resource, NY.

to complement the delicate style that's bred
from gold spun out into a precious thread.
The threads they worked were delicate and fine,
subtly coloured with many tinctures,
using the various shades one can obtain
from their origin in shells of the sea's creatures.] (105–6, 109–16)

The gold of the Tagus was legendary – it is mentioned in Pliny's *Natural History* and cited by Ovid and Martial, among others (Morros 1995, notes to vv. 105–8, pp. 229, 518) – but purple dye (the most desirable being from Tyre) was no doubt added by Garcilaso to glorify the fertile river. The poet likens the artistry of the weaver-nymphs to that of the ancient Greek artists Apelles and Timanthes (117–20), a comparison justified by the coupling of painting and weaving: "lo que pinta / y texe cada ninfa" [what each nymph paints and weaves] (117–18, my translation).[8] The term "pintar" [to paint] appears here as a Latinism, according to Leo Spitzer, since "*pingere* was used in Latin also of embroidery" (1952, 246). Erwin Panofsky notes that in sixteenth-century Latin the terms *pingere*, *pingi*, and *pictus* refer "to a graphic representation, drawing or print, in contradistinction to a sculpture or metal" (1951, 34, note 1). If we follow Panofsky's lead, "pintar" (placed alongside "texer") draws our attention to the cartoon, a drawing used in the weaving process. Joseph Campbell alerts us to its meaning: "Full-scale colored version of the intended designs that weavers copy during weaving. Generally painted on linen until the late fifteenth century. From the early sixteenth century on, cartoons were painted mostly in body color on paper" (2007, 397). Garcilaso does not mention a weaving technique, but we may suppose that given their mythological origins, his nymphs did not use cartoons as guides to weave their pieces.

Beyond dexterity in weaving (vv. 122, 145–6, 169–70), it is their use of perspectivism that serves as a touchstone of the skill of these artisan-weavers, who are well-versed in Renaissance artistic codes:

Destas historias tales varïadas
eran las telas de las cuatro hermanas,
las cuales con colores matizadas,
claras las luces, de las sombras vanas
mostraban a los ojos relevadas
las cosas y figuras que eran llanas,
tanto, que al parecer el cuerpo vano
pudiera ser tomado con la mano.

[Such are the varied stories that were told
in the fine tapestries of these four sisters,
who joined their colors in an artful blend,
with highlights that from the empty shadows
brought forward, as if standing in the round,
objects and figures that were flat and so
you'd think that empty forms were solid and
could actually be taken in the hand.] (265–72)

Perspectival depth, achieved through chiaroscuro to produce a sense of three-dimensionality, was a valued technique for oil paintings and tapestries alike. Giorgio Vasari, writing from his experience as a tapestry designer, has this much in mind when he describes what was required: "[F]or pictures that are to be woven ... there must be [a] ... variety of composition in the figures, and these must stand out one from another, so that they may have strong relief, and they must come out bright in coloring and rich in the costumes and vestments" (1996, 2.571). In the eclogue's tapestries, shaded colours ["con colores matizadas"] converge with bright highlights ["claras las luces"] – Vasari's "bright in coloring" – to provide an arresting visual display for the vicereine.

## Tapestries as Gifts

By virtue of their portability and splendour, tapestries made for convenient, lavish gifts. When Don Juan's widow, Margaret of Austria, left Spain in 1499 she reportedly took not only her own collection of tapestries but also twenty-two others as a parting gift from Juan's mother, Isabella of Castile (Sánchez Cantón 1950, 91, 108–9). We may suppose that these hangings had a diplomatic as well as personal value. Isabella had arranged the marriage of Juan to Margaret and of her daughter Juana to Maximilian's son and heir, Philip the Fair, for a double wedding celebrated in 1496. Aware of the need to reaffirm her political alliance with Margaret's father, she found the ideal objects for gift-giving in her large collection of tapestries, acquired through inheritance, purchase, commission, and as gifts (Sánchez Cantón 1950, 89–150, Junquera 1985, 22–5, and Junquera de Vega 1970, 16–22). Garcilaso surely must have witnessed the ritual exchange at court of weavings, needlework, paintings, medals, and precious items such as gems and jewellery. The tapestries of his Third Eclogue belong to this culture of aristocratic gift-giving and networking.

If a soldier and courtier like Garcilaso could not have afforded such an expensive material gift, an inspired poet could "weave' a set of tapestries worthy of the wife of his patron and protector, Pedro de Toledo, viceroy of Naples. Fernando Bouza documents the early modern practice of gift-giving as a way of keeping friendships and as a sign of deference, a social custom that was defined as "service': "Generosity was a virtue to be displayed at all times by the [courtier], who, devoid of self-interest … generously *served* those whom he regarded as his equals or friends or those to whom he was indebted: his superiors or others who had rendered him service with the same generosity" (2007, 153; emphasis in original). Located at the intersection of history and fiction, art and court society, Garcilaso's cloth gifts were tokens of friendship and gratitude for the vicereine, and for her husband, who (with his nephew Fernando Álvarez de Toledo, Third Duke of Alba) had successfully convinced the emperor to trade the poet's exile on an island in the Danube for exile in Naples; there, Garcilaso moved easily in aristocratic and intellectual circles, making friends with the likes of Bernardo Tasso, Luigi Tansillo, and Giulio Cesare Caracciolo, and attending the exclusive Accademia Pontaniana. Pedro also recommended Garcilaso for the post of chatelain of Reggio, which Charles readily granted.[9] But, as Sharon Kettering points out, the notion of "service" in the giving of a gift, ostensibly a "courtesy" freely offered by the donor, was a "polite fiction" (1988, 135). Something of what Marcel Mauss observed about gifts in archaic societies – items of exchange requiring reciprocity – applies here, for Garcilaso's tapestry gifts were not totally disinterested. In theory, according to Mauss, gifts are "voluntary, [but] in reality they are given and reciprocated obligatorily." Apparently gratuitous, they call for a return (1990, 3).[10] Garcilaso's verbal weavings are as much tokens for the future as gifts for past hospitality and protection, a gesture from the nimble-minded courtier to noble friends to keep him in their thoughts for when he might need them again. Within the fiction of the text the tapestries function as a site of exchange procuring a return: his gift for new favours. And of course these magnificent presents would enhance his status and prestige at the Neapolitan court.

## Intimate Bonds

Gift-giving functions as a highly personal transaction between Garcilaso and the vicereine, creating an intimacy that further ingratiates the poet to her and reaffirms their friendship. Mauss writes that a gift bears the "soul" or "spirit" of the giver, the *hau* in Maori gift rituals – "to make a gift of something to someone is to make a present of some part of oneself … In this system of ideas one clearly and logically realizes that one must give back to another person what is really part and parcel of his nature and substance, because to accept something from somebody is to accept some part of his spiritual essence, of his soul" (1990, 12). If we demystify the magical quality of Mauss's gift exchange, we might say that Garcilaso's "hand made" gift did indeed embody him, for his tribute to María bears the craftsman's artifice as a seal, an "imprint" of his identity. The symbolic link between the giver and his gift creates in turn an intimate bond between the courtly giver and his aristocratic recipient.[11] Garcilaso's gifts to María sent in 1536 from Provence, where he wrote the eclogue while "maestre de campo" [aide de camp] of the emperor's troops facing the army of Francis I, recall the "portrait" letters of the period. In his study of letter-writing customs of the European nobility, Fernando Bouza notes that for those separated by long distances, a handwritten letter was "a second-best substitute for private conversation," and that customarily a portrait accompanying the letter as a gift served as a "personal contact" to reaffirm a relationship (2007, 154). Bouza cites the letter and self-portrait that Philip II sent to Francisco Barreto as thanks for his support in capturing the rock of Vélez de Gomera in 1564. "I did not know how to pay and thank you," writes the king, "but by sending you a portrait of myself on a chain in order that I be bound to you every day of your life, for whatever you wish" (2007, 151). The gesture of sending a letter and "himself" in a portrait makes the king's presence "doubly felt" (2007, 154). Garcilaso's poem sent from a great distance is a kind of letter (as I explain below), containing his personal imprint within verbal tapestries so that he will "be bound" to the vicereine.

Inscribed within the fourth tapestry woven by the nymph Nise is a snapshot of special significance: the topography and cityscape of Toledo, "la más felice tierra de la España" [the happiest region of the whole of Spain] (1995, 200), where Garcilaso was born. The famous Tagus ["el claro Tajo"] (197), reified through ekphrasis, is pictured bathing the land, circling the mountain on which the old buildings of the imperial city stand majestically:

> Pintado el caudaloso rio se vía,
> que, en áspera estrecheza reducido,
> un monte casi alrededor ceñía […]
> Estaba puesta en la sublime cumbre
> del monte, y desd'allí por él sembrada,

aquella ilustre y clara pesadumbre
d'antiguos edificios adornada.

[The mighty river in her picture's seen
reduced at this point to a rocky narrows,
surrounding almost on all sides a mountain [...]
Perched on the lofty brow of the great hill
and scattered down its slopes on every side,
was that incomparable and weighty pile,
with many an ancient edifice supplied.] (201–3, 209–12)

The celebrated river irrigates the countryside "con artificio de las altas ruedas" [with the ingenious aid of water-wheels] (216). If not a self-portrait, Garcilaso sends the next best thing, a poignant material recollection of a place of origin. And more poignant still, now that both he and María are in foreign lands fulfilling Charles's calling, the poet in the emperor's army on the field of battle in Provence, the vicereine at the Neapolitan court in service to the imperial administration. That bit of nostalgia was announced in the eclogue's dedicatory stanzas, where Garcilaso tells María about his longing for the homeland and for all that he holds dear, revealing early in the poem, albeit obliquely, his desire to connect with her at an intimate level: "la fortuna ... / ya de la patria, ya del bien me aparta" [fortune ... now separates me from my country, now from all that is good and safe] (17–19, my translation).

## The Poem as Fabric: Weavers and Writers

Roland Barthes's well-known observation that "etymologically the text is a cloth; *textus*, from which text derives, means 'woven'" (1979, 76), resonates in the eclogue with an almost literal sense: the nymphs are weavers, as is the poet, who "weaves" with words. This complementarity, anchored in the poem on the word "texer" [to weave], echoes an ancient link between text and textile. "[B]y the first century BCE [*texere*] no longer meant simply to weave or braid but could also mean to compose a work. From the first century CE on, the word *textus* took on its modern sense of 'written text,' yet it remained common in the lexicon of weaving: *textor* (weaver) ... *textum* or *textura* (fabric or textile)" (Chartier 2007, 86). In the eclogue, "texer" appears both materially in the making of each tapestry ("lo que pinta / y *texe* cada ninfa" [what each nymph paints and weaves]) (117–18) and metaphorically in the speaker's scriptural weaving, which combines pieces from ancient texts with fragments from contemporary Italian works to compose stories in the vernacular.[12] A dramatic example is Eurydice's death, where Garcilaso transforms and expands in implicit competition clipped renditions of scenes from Ovid and Virgil with re-writings of images from Ariosto's *Orlando furioso* and Sannazaro's *Arcadia* (Barnard 1987, 318–19).

John Schied and Jesper Svenbro write about this cross-cultural appropriation in Roman literature in terms of a textual "weaving" applicable to the eclogue:

> When Catullus writes his poem on the wedding of Peleus and Thetis, his "weaving" has meaning connected to the occasion of the poem and the symbolism of the nuptial fabric, of course, but inevitably the poem-fabric also becomes a fabric on an "intercultural" level. It is a place where two cultures meet. And here, it is as if Catullus were using a Greek warp – the traditional basis for his poem – into which he introduces his own Latin woof, as if the best text were made of a Greek warp and a woof of Latin words. (1996, 145)

The nuptial fabric, a coverlet placed on the marriage bed of Peleus and Thetis, is inscribed with the story of Theseus and Ariadne (Catullus 1988, 64.50–264). Like the coverlet, the nymphs' tapestries serve as a thematic occasion and symbol of the eclogue's own textual fabric, the point at which cultures meet, a warp of Graeco-Roman mythology and Italian subtexts intersecting with a weft of Castilian words. Texts and textiles naturally call forth the instruments and the "authors" that produce them: the poet "weaving" his intercultural discursive cloth with a pen parallels the nymphs "writing" stories with a shuttle as pen.

In the sixteenth century, the needle was the primary female tool for composing narratives in fabrics, needlework being a sign of aesthetic virtuosity and even a way of making political statements, while the shuttle belonged to the exclusively male world of industrial production in tapestry workshops (Jones and Stallybrass 2000, 148–71, 94). The eclogue's weaver-nymphs who "write" their stories with shuttles thus belong to a wholly literary tradition, a product of an ancient textual memory. They find precedents in the lovely Virgilian naiads of *Georgics* 4, who appear "spinning fleeces of Miletus, dyed with rich glassy hue" (1998, 334–5). Filódoce [Phyllodoce] and Climene [Clymene] are cited here by name (336, 345).[13] Ovid's *Metamorphoses,* a popular exemplar for literature and textiles in the sixteenth century, offer even closer antecedents, Philomela and Arachne, who narrate their stories with the shuttle as pen. The Ovidian tales, like those told by the eclogue's nymphs, are violent narratives, and distinctive in that the mythological weavers, like the naiads, are eminently skilled. Philomela is raped by her brother-in-law, the Thracian king Tereus, who cuts off her tongue with his sword to silence her. Her tongue "faintly murmuring" on the dark earth (1984, 6.558) signals her alienation from speech. Weaving a tapestry for her sister Procne to read, a victim becoming a master in her telling, she chooses materials that represent the brutality of her rapist and her bloody mutilation: "She hangs a Thracian web [*barbarica* tela] on her loom, and skillfully weaving *purple* marks [*purpureas* notas] on a white background, she thus tells the story of her wrongs" (1984, 6.576–8; my emphasis). Lydian Arachne, for her part, after challenging Pallas Athena to a contest, weaves tales of deceit and seduction committed by the gods against mortals. Like the goddess, she works warp and weft with "well-trained hands" (6.60), deftly blending threads of gold (6.68) and Tyrian purple with lighter colours (6.61–2), details that resonate in the fabrics of the eclogue's nymphs. Arachne's tapestry is "flawless," but she is punished for her presumption. Pallas strikes her with a shuttle and then, in pity, transforms her into a spider, the very emblem of her delicate art (6.129–45).

Garcilaso's mingling of ancient and contemporary cultures, connecting as he does the world of luxurious textiles with classical myth reimagined within a court setting, finds a suggestive pictorial analogue a century later in Diego Velázquez's recreation of the myth of Arachne in "Las hilanderas" (The Spinners, ca. 1655–60) (see fig. 4). In the painting's foreground appear humble spinners working their wool.[14] But what interests me here is the courtly scene in the brightly lit background, where Arachne and a helmeted Pallas Athena, similarly dressed, stand centre stage in front of a tapestry and, anachronistically, they are in the presence of three seventeenth-century aristocratic women in elegant clothing. The tapestry, which portrays the rape of Europa (one of the "celestial crimes" woven by Ovidian Arachne in her own tapestry), is a copy of Titian's painting of the same subject, housed at the time in the royal collection at the Alcázar (Brown 1986, 252). Jonathan Brown notes that the tapestry is a homage to Titian, the favourite painter of Charles V and Phillip II. By "quoting" Titian, Velázquez celebrates painting as the noblest and most transcendent art: "Titian is equated with Arachne, and Arachne could 'paint' like a god" (Brown 1986, 253). Arachne, however, does not "paint"; she "weaves" like a god. If the tapestry is a homage to Titian the painter, as Brown suggests, it is a more distinctive homage to Arachne the weaver, who within Velázquez's painterly fiction weaves her loom like Titian paints his canvas,

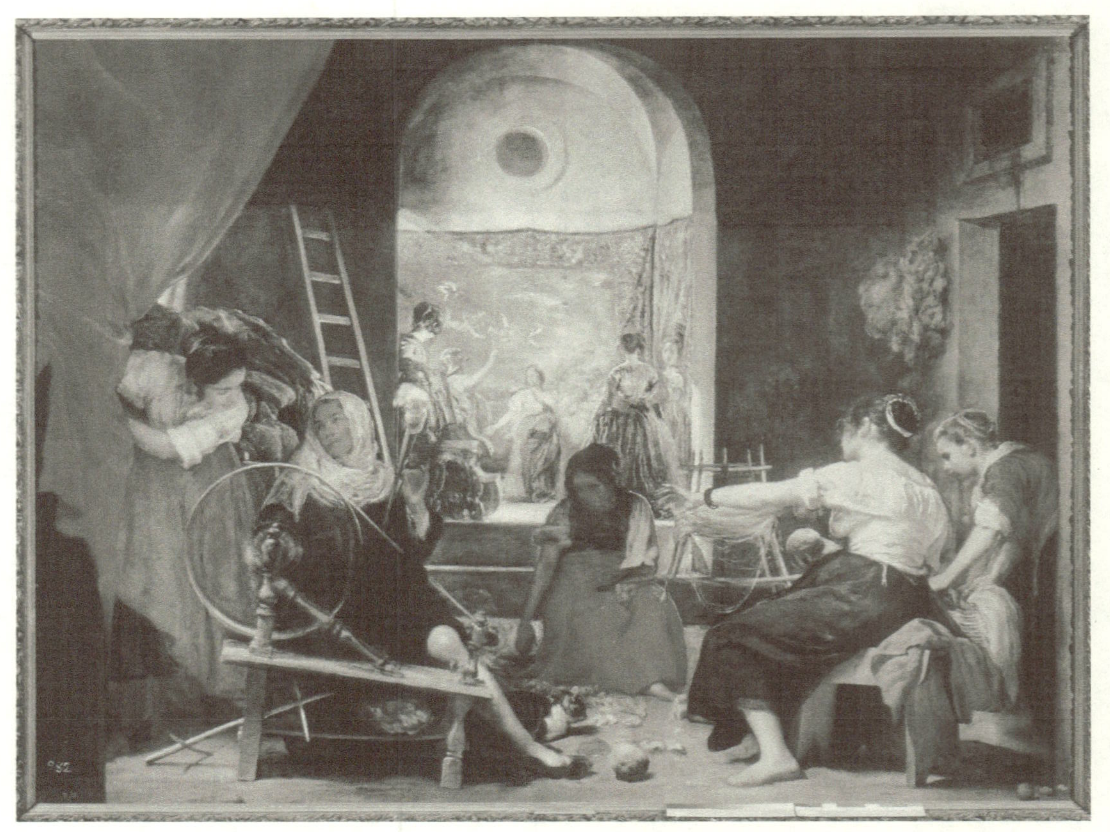

Figure 4 Diego Velázquez, *Las hilanderas*, ca. 1655–60. Museo del Prado, Madrid. Scala / Art Resource, NY.

implicitly with equal skill, reminiscent of Garcilaso's weaver nymphs whose own artistry [artificio], as noted above, is celebrated by its identification with that of the Greek painters Apelles and Timanthes. Velázquez stages "[Titian's] design into the more luxurious and costly world of textiles. Velázquez himself was keenly aware of the significance of textiles and of other costly goods in the production of the court and the courtier" (Jones and Stallybrass 2000, 102). The painter captures a social scene that could well have been the vicereine's own at her Neapolitan court. A magnificent chamber of tapestries covers the walls (only the Europa and a strip of another hanging are visible) and the three finely dressed noblewomen admire the display, two of them chatting as in a typical court event. The vicereine, an admirer of tapestries and perhaps a collector in her own right, belonged to this world of luxury and magnificence, and by extension to the practice of the shuttle as a metaphorical pen. But, as we see next, she belonged also to the world of the actual pen and its special fabric, paper.

## Pen on Paper

The eclogue's dedication is a rich discursive space containing another type of fabric and another occasion for praise and networking. Despite the poet's Orphic voice celebrating the vicereine in two lines inspired by Virgil – "mas con la lengua muerta y fria en la boca / pienso mover la voz a ti debida" [for with the tongue cold and dead in my mouth / I aim to raise the voice I owe to you] (11–12) – it is the poet's pen and its fabric, paper, that will record both voice and María's fame. In the Virgilian source, *Georgics* 4.523–7 (1998), Orpheus's head, torn from his body by the Maenads, floats down the Hebrus River, "its voice and death-cold tongue" singing the name of Eurydice, who was lost to the underworld. Recast in Garcilaso's vernacular, the Latin fragment is animated for the self-representation of the lyric voice as an Orpheus figure and for a celebration that calls into action a magical act of memory. The tongue that gives birth to song belongs to the son of Calliope, the muse who possesses the gift of song, and the daughter of Mnemosyne, goddess of Memory. The new Orpheus in his own katabasis will use his voice to still the waters of oblivion, the river Lethe, in order to keep María's presence alive in historical memory:

> libre mi alma de su estrecha roca,
> por el Estigio lago conducida,
> celebrando t'irá, y aquel sonido
> hará parar las aguas del olvido.

> [my soul, when freed from its narrow prison
> and ferried over the waters of the Styx,
> will sing of you, and the sound it gives out then
> will turn back the flood tide of oblivion.] (13–16)

The poet further promises María that Apollo and the muses will bestow on him "ocio y lengua" [leisure (otium) and a tongue] to praise her (29–31, my translation). But María's memory will be preserved not by the tongue, the instrument for composing song, but by pen and paper, the authorial tools for textual production. Garcilaso mentions in a typical *recusatio* how the duties of the soldier take him away from celebration through pen and paper: "y lo que siento más es que *la carta* / donde *mi pluma* en tu alabanza mueva, / poniendo en su lugar cuidados vanos, / (fortuna) me quita y m'arrebata de las manos" [and what troubles me most is that the page (paper) / my pen ought to be filling with your praise / (fortune) snatches from my hand … / replacing it with unprofitable cares] (21–4, my emphasis). But *carta* and *pluma* already had appeared implicitly at the beginning of the dedication, where the poet turns to epideictic, the rhetoric of praise, for an encomiastic "ilustre y hermosísima María" [illustrious and most beautiful María] (2). María, the wife of an eminent imperial official, was important in her own right in carrying the lineage of the marquisate of the Osorio Pimentel. Her official title was Marquise of Villafranca del Bierzo, which she brought to the viceroy by marriage. The pen is mentioned once again in the memorable "tomando ora la espada, ora *la pluma*" [taking up now the sword and now *the pen*] (40, my emphasis) in the field of battle, where Garcilaso writes his textual gift to María. The self-conscious staging of pen and paper ("carta" means paper, according to its Italian or Latin etymology [Morros 1995, 225]) against song and voice illustrates what Roger Chartier sees as a major concern of the period, the desire to record what was in danger of obliteration:

> [S]ocieties of early modern Europe … preserved in writing traces of the past, remembrances of the dead, the glory of the living, and texts of all kinds that were not supposed to disappear. Stone, wood, fabric, parchment, and paper all served as substrates on which the memory of events and men could be inscribed. In the open space of the city or the seclusion of the library, in majesty, in books or in humility on more ordinary objects, the mission of the written was to dispel the obsession with loss. (2007, vii)

Understood in this context, Garcilaso's written word rescues the vicereine from the instability of commemoration through voice and song.[15] Her memory is materialized, inscribed by the author's quill on the surface of the paper – a kind of fabric made from linen and cotton rags – then printed in the ubiquitous chap-books [pliegos sueltos], and ultimately in a book.

The tension between oral and written discourses reminds us that the lyric speaker is the product of a written culture. And if *he* is a writer, the vicereine is above all a reader, and if *carta* is understood to mean letter as well as paper, the eclogue acts as an epistle, sophisticated and erudite in its classical import, sent from afar to be read in the privacy of her chambers. Placed in the world of learning and the pen, where she is lauded for her beauty and high worth [valor], María is also praised for her "ingenio" [ingenium] (3–4), meaning here intelligence and excellence of mind, traits customarily reserved for men, as in "hombre doctor y de ingenio agudo" [a learned man of acute intellect] (*Diccionario de Autoridades*). This is not the first time that Garcilaso flatters a woman for her intellectual acumen. In his letter-prologue to Boscán's translation of Castiglione's *Il Cortegiano*, he similarly flatters Jerónima Palova de Almogávar, following the example of Giuliano de' Medici, who in his defence of the *donna di palazzo* [the court lady], calls on her to assume the virtues of the male courtier, among them wit and "knowledge of letters" (1959, 3.211). Garcilaso praises Jerónima's courtly virtues, including her intellectual qualities: the poet assures her that the book she convinced Boscán to translate is worthy of being in her hands ["merece andar en vuestras manos"] (Boscán 1994, 75), that is, it is worthy of being read by her, its success now guaranteed by virtue of her very reading.

Garcilaso's praise runs counter to the conduct manuals that advised women to shun learned texts and the pen in favour of religious books and the needle as signs of virtue. In his *Árbol de consideración y varia doctrina* (Tree of consultation and varied teaching, 1548), the canon Pedro Sánchez writes about this feminine ideal of behaviour: "She should pray devotedly with a rosary and if she knows how to read, she should read devotional books and books of good doctrine, for writing must be left to men. She should know how to use a needle well and how to use a spindle and distaff, having no need for the use of a pen" (cited in Bouza 1999, 60). Garcilaso distances himself from this type of moral preaching as well as from counter prescriptions of court poets like Ariosto who, seeking patronage from noblewomen, reversed the preference for textiles over writing in his *Orlando furioso*, praising instead "the women poets of Italy for leaving 'the needle and the cloth' for the fountain of Aganippe on Parnassus, proving that Italy could produce more poets like Vittoria Colonna" (Jones and Stallybrass 2000, 142). Garcilaso does a double turn. While placing María as participant and spectator in the nymphs' world of the needle and the shuttle, the poet locates her as well in the erudite world of the pen, as a reader for a distinctive act of networking. If we recall Barthes's observation, mentioned above, that "etymologically the text is a cloth" (1979, 76), and that networking in its own etymology points to the enterprise of fabric-making in cloth – "work in which threads ... or similar materials are arranged in the fashion of a net; especially a light fabric made of netted thread" (*OED*) – text, textile, and networking become fused for a celebratory inscription of the writer as a poet-craftsman, and in his flattery and praise of the vicereine, he joins Castiglione's courtier as a skilled performer of court manoeuvres. In writing his tapestries, Garcilaso celebrated himself no less than Charles V in the tapestries that celebrate his triumph at the Battle of Pavia (1525) or the Conquest of Tunis (1535), where as a participant in the campaign, the poet may well have witnessed the artist Jan Cornelisz Vermeyen drawing scenes that would serve as the basis of cartoons for these hangings.

## A Precarious Figuration

Garcilaso's reassuring identity crafted in artifice and networking within a tapestry culture, however, is not the whole story, for the violent narratives complicate the configuration of an identity based squarely on these cloths as gifts. Another poetic self emerges: a vulnerable one centred on "lengua," Orpheus's tongue, the bodily organ that is the locus and emblem of voice and song. Speaking from a severed head swirling down the Hebrus, Orpheus's tongue stands for both the power of voice and its fragility. Thus its restaging in the eclogue, as the lyric I appropriates it to become an inspired verbal artist, involves a double movement: the tongue that sings María and the tapestries also conjures up an act of precarious voicing that culminates in the fourth tapestry, the scene of the decapitated Elisa and her epitaph, written by a mourning nymph on the bark of a poplar tree, whose letters speak on her behalf, "que hablaban ansí por parte della" (240):

> "Elisa soy, en cuyo nombre suena
> y se lamenta el monte cavernoso,
> testigo del dolor y grave pena
> en que por mí se aflige Nemoroso

y llama: 'Elisa,' 'Elisa'; a boca llena
responde el Tajo, y lleva presuroso
al mar de Lusitania el nombre mío,
donde será escuchado, yo lo fío."

["Elisa am I, and to my unlucky name
the cave-infested mountain echoes and moans,
witness to the grief, the overwhelming pain
Nemoroso must suffer on my account:
'Elisa,' he calls out, and 'Elisa' again
Tagus intones, as it rushes swiftly on,
bearing my name to the Lusitanian sea,
to where it will be heard, I can safely say."] (241–8)

The pastoral convention of carving letters on bark shares in the practice of carving inscriptions on funerary monuments designed to preserve the memory of the dead in stone.[16] The eclogue's epitaph, incised on wood as if on a tombstone, preserves the memory of Elisa in a public space, addressed to a literate pastoral community, the shepherds being, as the genre dictated, courtiers in disguise. If the memory of the vicereine is directly inscribed and preserved on paper [carta], that of the dead Elisa is inscribed and preserved on multiple surfaces: the epitaph's words are carved on wood and recorded by Nise on cloth, in the manner of a tapestry's cartouche, which the poet transcribes onto paper. And yet, encased *en abîme* within these material objects, Elisa's voice, which had been ventriloquized by the epitaph's "speaking" letters, betrays a profound fragility as it recedes into a polyphony of voices, with first the mountain, then Nemoroso, and finally the Tagus echoing her name. Elisa's name becomes a disarticulated utterance mirroring her decapitation. Orpheus's decapitation by the Maenads and their scattering of his body parts, present subtextually, strengthens the sense of violence and vulnerability. Chartier argues that one of the missions of the written is to preserve "remembrances of the dead" (2007, vii), as is the case here. Nise's purpose in weaving her tapestry is to make known Elisa's "lamentable cuento" [dreadful tale] (257) on land and beyond:

quiso que de su tela el argumento
la bella ninfa muerta señalase
y ansí se publicase de uno en uno
por el húmido reino de Neptuno.

> [she had planned that the subject of her tapestry
> would single out the beautiful dead nymph,
> so that from mouth to mouth the news relayed
> should fill the humid realm where Neptune reigned.] (261–4)

What is "published" in the tapestry – and recorded by the poet – is not only the news of Elisa's death, but the loss of a beautiful woman through violent death: the decapitated body of the delicate nymph lying like a white swan among the grass and flowers (229–32).

A fragile, personal lament is thus projected through the mediating screen of the tapestry, a space where figures take on bits of discourse, which stand for a disguised lyric self-reflection. In the eclogue, Garcilaso offers María another memorable gift, a vulnerable self, the voice of loss, now encased in a lovely weaving: an intimate gesture from a soldier skilled with the sword that decapitates and a poet whose pen captures decapitation intrinsic to both war and eros.

## NOTES

1 On Renaissance tapestries, see in particular Campbell (2002, 2007), Delmarcel (1999, 2000), Thomson (1973, 189–276), and Balis, et al. (1993).

2 On the identity of María, see Keniston (1922, 255–8).

3 Garcilaso was sent into exile for having acted as a witness to the marriage of his brother Pedro's son to Isabel de la Cueva, heiress of the Duchy of Alburquerque. The duke and other members of the family opposed the marriage. Charles sent a *cédula* (4 September 1531) from Flanders to the empress urging her to prevent it. It was too late. Garcilaso was finally punished and sent to an island in the Danube, but later was allowed to serve his exile in Naples. For further details, see Keniston (1922, 103–16) and Morros (1995, xxxiv–xxxv).

4 Spain had a thriving industry of fine cloth weavings in silk, gold, and silver threads (especially in Granada, Toledo, Cordoba, Seville, and Valencia), as well as embroidery in particular for the nobility and church. Toledo at one point had thirteen thousand *telares*. However, there was no significant tapestry industry that could compete with the Flemish and the French until the establishment of the Real Fábrica de Tapices (first known as the Fábrica de Tapices de Santa Bárbara) by Philip V in the eighteenth century (Sánchez Cantón 1950, 105, and Junquera 1985, 49). For details on the tapestry

industry in Spain, see Junquera (1985, 43–9) and Herrero Carretero, "Tapicería" (133–201), in Bartolomé Arraiza (1999). On embroideries and other weavings in fine cloth, see Martín I Ros, "Tejidos" (9–80), and González Mena, "Bordado y encaje eruditos" (83–130), both in Bartolomé Arraiza (1999). There is some evidence that Garcilaso was a consumer of "tejidos." Aurora Egido (2003, 187) reminds us that in his last will and testament, the poet includes the following: "Debo a Castillo, tejedor de oro tirado, vecino de Toledo, veinte mil maravedís" [I owe Castillo, a resident of Toledo and weaver in gold threads, twenty thousand maravedis]. The citation comes from Morros (1995, 285), who identifies the weaver as Bartolomé Castillo (d. 1550).

5 On Maximilian's staging of images – including books, medals, armour, and a tomb monument – to enhance his authority and spread his imperial ideology, see Silver (2008). On the famous set of commemorative woodcuts commissioned by Maximilian, see Appelbaum (1964).

6 All citations from Garcilaso's poetry come from Morros's edition (1995). Translations are from Dent-Young (2009), unless otherwise indicated.

7 This inventory of the viceroy's possessions records a number of tapestry chambers, including several based on mythological or classical themes (seven tapestries woven in silk and gold of the legend of Paris and Helen, two on Vulcan, ten on Lucretia, and six on Romulus and Remus). Others were listed by genre, millefleurs ("verdura") appearing among other types, such as "ystoria" [history], "figuras" [figures], and many with religious themes (Hernando Sánchez 1993, 51).

8 For a discussion of the relation between weaving and painting in the eclogue within the context of the visual language of ekphrasis and the rhetoric of *enargeia* as conceived by Erasmus, following Quintilian, see Barnard (1992). On artistic dimensions of the eclogue, see also Bergmann (1979), Paterson (1977), and Rivers (1962). See Barnard (1992) on the interrelation between weaving and writing, which I expand upon below. Aurora Egido (2003) makes important observations on this dual enterprise, especially on the double meaning of the word "tinta," purple dye as well as ink (188, n.19).

9 For details on this request, made in a letter dated 1 September 1534, see Lumsden (1952). In a second letter, dated 20 January 1535, Pedro asks the emperor for the postponement of a suit Garcilaso had brought against the powerful Mesta, a request that was denied (Keniston 1922, 131).

10 Mauss extended his observations on gift-giving to ancient Rome, India, and Germany, inviting by implication further inquiry into this cultural practice in other areas and periods. For studies tailoring Mauss to practices in the early modern period, see in particular Davis (2000), Klein (1997), Shephard (2010), and Warwick (1997).

11 Using Mauss as a point of departure, Lisa Klein has examined gift-giving customs at the court of Elizabeth I. Among Klein's examples is the gift presented to the queen by Elizabeth Talbot, Countess of Shrewsbury, whose dynastic ambitions in marrying her daughter to the son of Mary Stuart's mother-in-law, Charles Stuart, made the queen suspect the countess's loyalty. The countess presented a "hand-wrought" gift, an embroidered cloak chosen and designed for Elizabeth to reassure the queen of her "love and fidelity." The gift was memorable, as "the color, trimming, and expense" of the cloak called forth Elizabeth's praise and "promises of continued favor" (1997, 472). Sánchez Cantón (1950, 92–5) comments on gifts of tapestries made by family and friends to Isabella of Castile, which though not "hand-wrought" by the donors were evidently offered to establish personal bonds with the queen, as noted in the formulaic inscription in the royal register: "dado para servicio de su Alteza" [given in service to her Majesty] (92). Among these are the gifts of the Marquesa de Moya, "fidelísima amiga y servidora" [most loyal friend and servant] (92–3) and the small tapestry given by the treasurer, Rui López, "muy rico, con oro e alguna plata" [very rich, with gold and some silver] (94).

12 On models, see Morros's extensive notes (1995, 230–7, 518–26). See also, in particular, Cruz (1988, 106–22) and Lapesa (1985, 158–66), who stress an *ars combinatoria*; Fernández-Morera (1982, 73–100), who focuses especially on the Virgilian sources; and Navarrete (1994, 124–5), who singles out Castiglione's notion of *sprezzatura* as the basis of Garcilaso's "graceful, seemingly artless" lyric.

13 Following Virgil, Sannazaro in his *Arcadia* has nymphs weave tapestries, including one with the story of Orpheus and Eurydice, which Garcilaso uses as a model (1966, 12.136).

14 For various interpretations of the spinners in the foreground, including the old woman as Athena herself, see Jones (1996, 205–6) and Welles (1986, 149–50).

15 In his discussion of the Orphic allusion, Paul Julian Smith suggests that "while Garcilaso appears to appeal to 'voice' as authentic, eternal utterance, he knows that the preservation of that voice is dependent on its duplication by the written word" (1988, 52). Egido offers a similar interpretation (2003, 185), adding that pen and paper are the true protagonists, part of "la poética de una *laudatio* que convierte el acto de escribir en una empresa heroica y, a la par, en un acto de entrega amorosa" [a poetics of celebration that converts the act of writing into a heroic enterprise and, at the same time, into an act of amorous surrender] (185). In Egido's reading, María represents the beloved.

16 Armando Petrucci documents this graphic culture in early modern Italy, which had its antecedents in ancient epigraphic practices (1993, 16–61). Petrucci offers numerous examples of tombstones, including the one erected

by Giovanni Pontano in Naples in memory of his wife, Adriana, with inscriptions imitating classical lettering on its facade and flanks (1993, 22). Garcilaso may have seen it, along with other epigraphic funerary monuments, during his stay in the city.

## WORKS CITED


Appelbaum, Stanley, ed. and trans. 1964. *The Triumph of Maximilian I: 137 Woodcuts by Hans Burgkmair and Others*. New York: Dover.

Balis, Arnout, et al. 1993. *Les Chasses de Maximilien*. Paris: Réunion des Musées Nationaux.

Barnard, Mary E. 1987. "Garcilaso's Poetics of Subversion and the Orpheus Tapestry." *PMLA* 102 (3): 316–25. http://dx.doi.org/10.2307/462479.

Barnard, Mary E. 1992. "Correcting the Classics: Absence and Presence in Garcilaso's Third Eclogue." *Revista de Estudios Hispánicos* 26: 3–20.

Barthes, Roland. 1979. "From Work to Text." In *Textual Strategies: Perspectives in Post-Structuralist Criticism*, edited by Josué V. Harari, 73–81. Ithaca: Cornell University Press.

Bartolomé Arraiza Alberto, ed. 1999. *Artes decorativas II.* In *Summa Artis: Historia general del arte* 45. Madrid: Espasa Calpe.

Bergmann, Emilie. 1979. *Art Inscribed: Essays on Ekphrasis in Spanish Golden Age Poetry*. Harvard Studies in Romance Languages 35. Cambridge, MA: Harvard University Press.

Boscán, Juan, trans. 1994. *El cortesano*. Edited by Mario Pozzi. Madrid: Cátedra.

Bouza, Fernando. 1999. *Communication, Knowledge, and Memory in Early Modern Spain*. Translated by Sonia López and Michael Agnew. Philadelphia: University of Pennsylvania Press.

Bouza, Fernando. 2007. "Letters and Portraits: Economy of Time and Chivalrous Service in Courtly Culture." In *Correspondence and Cultural Exchange in Europe, 1400–1700*, edited by Francisco Bethencourt and Florike Egmond, 145–62. Vol. 3 of *Cultural Exchange in Early Modern Europe*, edited by Robert Muchembled and William Monter. Cambridge: Cambridge University Press.

Brown, Jonathan. 1986. *Velázquez: Painter and Courtier*. New Haven: Yale University Press.

Campbell, Thomas P. 2002. *Tapestry in the Renaissance: Art and Magnificence*. New York: Metropolitan Museum of Art; New Haven: Yale University Press.

Campbell, Thomas P. 2007. *Henry VIII and the Art of Majesty: Tapestries at the Tudor Court*. New Haven: Published for the Paul Mellon Centre for Studies in British Art by Yale University Press.

Castiglione, Baldassare. 1959. *The Book of the Courtier*. Translated by Charles S. Singleton. Garden City, NY: Doubleday.

Catullus. 1988. "The Poems of Gaius Valerius Catullus." In *Catullus, Tibullus, and Pervigilium Veneris*. Translated by F.W. Cornish. Cambridge, MA: Harvard University Press.

Chartier, Roger. 2007. *Inscription and Erasure: Literature and Written Culture from the Eleventh to the Eighteenth Century*. Translated by Arthur Goldhammer. Philadelphia: University of Pennsylvania Press.

Cruz, Anne J. 1988. *Imitación y transformación: El petrarquismo en la poesía de Boscán y Garcilaso de la Vega*. Amsterdam and Philadelphia: John Benjamins.

Davis, Natalie Zemon. 2000. *The Gift in Sixteenth-Century France*. Madison: University of Wisconsin Press.

Delmarcel, Guy. 1999. *Flemish Tapestries*. New York: Harry Abrams.

Delmarcel, Guy. 2000. *Los Honores: Flemish Tapestries for the Emperor Charles V*. Translated by Alastair Weir. [Antwerp]: SDZ / Pandora.

Dent-Young, John, ed. and trans. 2009. *Selected Poems of Garcilaso de la Vega: A Bilingual Edition*. Chicago: University of Chicago Press.

*Diccionario de Autoridades*. 1984. Facsimile edition. Madrid: Gredos.

Egido, Aurora. 2003. "El tejido del texto en la *Égloga III* de Garcilaso." In *Garcilaso y su época: del amor y la guerra*, edited by María Díez Borque José and Luis Ribot García, 179–200. Madrid: Sociedad Estatal de Conmemoraciones Culturales.

Fernández-Morera, Darío. 1982. *The Lyre and the Oaten Flute: Garcilaso and the Pastoral*. London: Tamesis.

Garcilaso de la Vega. 1995. *Garcilaso de la Vega: Obra poética y textos en prosa*. Edited by Bienvenido Morros. Barcelona: Crítica.

González Mena, María Angeles. 1999. "Bordado y encajes eruditos," 83–130. See Bartolomé Arraiza.

Guiffrey, Jules. 1878. *Tapisseries françaises*. Vol. 1, Pt. 1 in *Histoire générale de la tapisserie, 1878–1885*. Edited by Jules Guiffrey, Eugène Müntz, and Alexander Pinchart. 3 vols. Paris: Société Anonyme de Publications Périodiques.

Hernando Sánchez, Carlos José. 1993. "La vida material y el gusto artístico en la Corte de Nápoles durante el renacimiento: El inventario de bienes del Virrey Pedro de Toledo." *Archivo español de arte* 66 (261): 35–55.

Herrero Carretero, Concha. 1999. "Tapicería," 133–201. See Bartolomé Arraiza.

Jones, Ann Rosalind. 1996. "Dematerializations: Textile and Textual Properties in Ovid, Sandys, and Spenser." In *Subject and Object in Renaissance Culture*, edited by Margreta de Grazia, Maureen Quilligan, and Peter Stallybrass, 189–209.

Cambridge Studies in Renaissance Literature and Culture 8. Cambridge: Cambridge University Press.

Jones, Ann Rosalind, and Peter Stallybrass. 2000. *Renaissance Clothing and the Materials of Memory*. Cambridge: Cambridge University Press.

Junquera, Juan José. 1985. *Tapisserie de Tournai en Espagne: La tapisserie bruxelloise en Espagne au XVI^e^ siècle*. Tournai-Brussels-Rijkhoven: Europalia.

Junquera de Vega, Paulina. 1970. "Tapices de los reyes católicos y de su época." *Reales Sitios* 26: 16–26.

Keniston, Hayward. 1922. *Garcilaso de la Vega: A Critical Study of His Life and Works*. New York: Hispanic Society of America.

Kettering, Sharon. 1988. "Gift-Giving and Patronage in Early Modern France." *French History* 2 (2): 131–51. http://dx.doi.org/10.1093/fh/2.2.131.

Klein, Lisa M. 1997. "Your Humble Handmaid: Elizabethan Gifts of Needlework." *Renaissance Quarterly* 50 (2): 459–93. http://dx.doi.org/10.2307/3039187.

Lapesa, Rafael. 1985. *La trayectoria poética de Garcilaso.* 3rd ed. Rev. In *Garcilaso: Estudios completos*. Madrid: Istmo.

Lumsden, Audrey. 1952. "Garcilaso and the Chatelainship of Reggio." *Modern Language Review* 47 (4): 559–60. http://dx.doi.org/10.2307/3719711.

Martín I Ros, Rosa M. 1999. "Tejidos," 9–80. See Bartolomé Arraiza.

Mauss, Marcel. 1990. *The Gift: The Form and Reason for Exchange in Archaic Societies*. Translated by W.D. Halls. New York: Norton.

McLean, Paul D. 2007. *The Art of the Network: Strategic Interaction and Patronage in Renaissance Florence*. Durham and London: Duke University Press.

Morros, Bienvenido. 1995. See Garcilaso de la Vega.

Navarrete, Ignacio. 1994. *Orphans of Petrarch: Poetry and Theory in the Spanish Renaissance*. Berkeley: University of California Press.

Ovid. 1984. *Metamorphoses*. 2 vols. Edited and translated by Frank Justus Miller. Cambridge, MA: Harvard University Press.

Panofsky, Erwin. 1951. "'Nebulae in Pariete': Notes on Erasmus' Eulogy on Dürer." *Journal of the Warburg and Courtauld Institutes* 14 (1/2): 34–41. http://dx.doi.org/10.2307/750351.

Paterson, Alan K.G. 1977. "Ecphrasis in Garcilaso's 'Egloga Tercera.'" *Modern Language Review* 72 (1): 73–92. http://dx.doi.org/10.2307/3726297.

Petrucci, Armando. 1993. *Public Lettering: Script, Power, and Culture*. Translated by Linda Lappin. Chicago: University of Chicago Press.

Rivers, Elias L. 1962. "The Pastoral Paradox of Natural Art." *MLN* 77 (2): 130–44. http://dx.doi.org/10.2307/3042857.

Sánchez Cantón, Francisco Javier. 1950. *Libros, tapices y cuadros que coleccionó Isabel la Católica*. Madrid: Consejo Superior de Investigaciones Científicas.

Sannazaro, Jacopo. 1966. *Arcadia and Piscatorial Eclogues*. Translated by Ralph Nash. Detroit: Wayne State University Press.

Schied, John, and Jesper Svenbro. 1996. *The Craft of Zeus: Myths of Weaving and Fabric*. Translated by Carol Volk. Cambridge, MA: Harvard University Press.

Shephard, Tim. 2010. "Constructing Identities in a Music Manuscript: The Medici Codex as a Gift." *Renaissance Quarterly* 63 (1): 84–127. http://dx.doi .org/10.1086/652534.

Silver, Larry. 2008. *Marketing Maximilian: The Visual Ideology of a Holy Roman Emperor*. Princeton: Princeton University Press.

Smith, Paul Julian. 1988. *Writing in the Margin: Spanish Literature of the Golden Age*. Oxford: Clarendon.

Spitzer, Leo. 1952. "Garcilaso, Third Eclogue, Lines 265–271." *Hispanic Review* 20 (3): 243–8. http://dx.doi.org/10.2307/470708.

Thomson, W.G. 1973. *A History of Tapestry from the Earliest Times until the Present Day*. 3rd ed. Rev. F.P. and E.S. Thomson. East Ardsley, Eng.: EP Publishing.

Vasari, Giorgio. 1996. *Lives of the Painters, Sculptors, and Architects*. Translated by Gaston du C. de Vere. 2 vols. New York: Knopf.

Virgil. 1998. *Eclogues. Georgics. Aeneid. The Minor Poems.* Edited and translated by H. Rushton Fairclough. Rev. G.P. Goold. 2 vols. Cambridge, MA: Harvard University Press.

Warwick, Genevieve. 1997. "Gift Exchange and Art Collecting: Padre Sebastiano Resta's Drawing Albums." *Art Bulletin* 79 (4): 630–46. http://dx.doi.org/ 10.2307/3046279.

Welles, Marcia L. 1986. *Arachne's Tapestry: The Transformations of Myth in Seventeenth-Century Spain*. San Antonio, TX: Trinity University Press.

# 2 Artful Edifices and the Construction of Identity in Montemayor's *Diana* and Lope's *Arcadia*

MARSHA S. COLLINS

In Theocritus's *Idyll* 1, a goatherd promises to award Thyrsis a magnificently fashioned cup if he sings as sweetly as he did in a previous singing contest. The goatherd then launches into a lengthy, ekphrastic passage describing the cup's varied decorations, which include the representation of assorted human dramas. Among the figures depicted on the vessel, one finds a boy so absorbed in weaving a cricket cage that two foxes sneak up on him, one intent on stealing the grapes the youngster neglects to guard, and the other intent on snatching the bread the boy meant to eat. The youth likely represents the poet, or even specifically the pastoral poet, who takes the raw material of nature – in this case, asphodel stalks and rushes – and crafts it into an artful object – the poem or pastoral poem itself that conveys melodious, lyric expression like that of the cricket's song contained by the cage of rustic construction.[1]

Over 1500 years separate the *Idylls* of Theocritus from the bucolic poetry and complex, pastoral romances of sixteenth-century Iberia, yet in the pages of the latter the cricket's song remains as sweet and powerful as ever, and numerous poetic progeny have replaced the absorbed, child artificer in the vineyard. The focus of this essay is not pastoral song, nor even the structure per se of pastoral poetry and narrative in early modern Iberia, but rather the elaborate descendants of that lovingly constructed but ultimately quite simple cage, the artful edifices that often provide in microcosm mirror images of the sometimes labyrinthine, hybrid pastoral romances that contain them. Theocritus's vignette portrays in miniature the humorous, ironic tension between innocent youth and wily fox, between art and nature, and between two different kinds of hunger – one that satisfies the body, the other that satisfies the spirit and the imagination. Frederick A. de Armas has noted similar tensions, albeit on a larger scale, in certain Spanish pastoral romances in which intricate buildings and monuments appear jarringly in the middle of the pastoral landscape, seemingly undermining the traditional juxtaposition between city and countryside identified with bucolic fiction (1985, 332–3).

Essentially these structures, and the episodes in which they figure so prominently, constitute extended examples of ekphrasis. While their *mise-en-abyme* symbolism, and the paradoxically symbiotic relationship they establish between art and nature, render these artful constructions of considerable interest and importance in these works of pastoral fiction, as complex descendants of Theocritus's cricket cage they also embody another tension that lies at the heart of ekphrasis itself. In his classic book *Ekphrasis: The Illusion of the Natural Sign*, Murray Krieger emphasizes the power of ekphrasis to interrupt the temporal flow of discourse, and to create the illusion of freezing the action, and stopping time (1992, 7). Ekphrasis embodies a rhetorical paradox, the deployment of descriptive language, a temporal medium, to fix objects, characters, and the readers' eyes and imagination in space (Krieger 1992, 10). The artful edifices of the Spanish pastoral romances compound this paradox through their function as places and spaces of convergence and transformation that impinge on characterization and plot advancement, and on the construction of the protagonist's identity. So while the scenes that unfold in and around these special buildings may seem to escape narrative time, or stop the narrative flow, in actuality they play a key role in plot and characterization, that is, in moving the narrative forward in terms of time, space, and character development.[2] Two examples will suffice to explore these matters in the pages that follow – Felicia's palace in Jorge de Montemayor's *Diana* (1559) and Dardanio's cave in Lope de Vega's *Arcadia* (1598) – with the understanding that the issues raised should serve as a modest point of departure for further study of the function of ekphrastic structures in these pastoral works and others. More significantly, however, the analysis that follows indicates that the ekphrastic foregrounding of these edifices sets off these constructions and their locales as special, qualitative focal points for readers' attention and imaginative interaction, and marks these edifices and episodes as spaces and times of dynamic transformation, in the type of texts frequently deemed static, stilted, or frozen within literary conventions.

Paul Alpers has observed that Sannazaro's *Arcadia* assimilates the Petrarchan lover to the Virgilian figure of narrative structure in sixteenth-century pastoral. He notes that Montemayor's *Diana* subsequently establishes this transfer and modification as the normative standard for

Renaissance pastoral, as well as the gathering of shepherds associated with classical pastoral metamorphoses, into a convening of lamenting lovers who recognize themselves in others' tuneful complaints, focusing on loss or absence, and pointing the way to pastoral's compensatory offerings (1997, 81, 349–51). In Montemayor's fictional world, an operatic collection of lovers, tales, and poetic exchanges unfolds as a literal gathering up or gathering along the way of virtuous, but frustrated lovers into an aggregate band of pilgrims, set in motion by Felismena's brave defence of the nymphs Polydora, Cinthia, and Dórida – acolytes all of the wise Felicia – when they are attacked by lascivious wild men. The nymphs reward Felismena's valour and virtue, as well as that of the shepherds, with an invitation to accompany them to Felicia's palace in search of remedies for the heterogeneous collection of lovers' ills. Thus, in Book 4, the centre of *Diana*'s seven-book structure, shepherds and nymphs converge on Felicia's palace – a temple, located in dense woods. As Rosilie Hernández-Pecoraro observes, "the magical palace dazzles the reader with its magnificence and opens a space and time where transformation can take place" (2006, 48).

Despite the efforts of some critics to identify this artful edifice with a specific, historical palace, Montemayor actually offers his immediate, target audience – urbane courtiers all, and likely aristocratic women for the most part – with an elaborately designed and decorated building that merges the architecture of literary models – the magical castles of romances of chivalry – with that of Renaissance villas resplendent with formal gardens and the harmonious integration of Graeco-Roman elements.[3] Both architectural models would have been familiar to Montemayor's privileged readers and readily accessible as imaginative visual constructions. Indeed, the single-file approach the pilgrim shepherds must assume along a narrow pathway that opens onto a flat, park-like space flanked symmetrically by two rivers and paved with stones in a checkerboard pattern with an ornate fountain in the middle captures the directed approach to the main entry typical of Italianate villa design at the time, and in a sense, corresponds to an imaginary rendering or animation of perspectival convergence in paintings by artists such as Paolo Uccello or Piero della Francesca, with their foregrounded checkerboard patterns and sharply delineated orthogonals converging on a vanishing point.[4] This path, of course, also signifies the tortuous road the virtuous lover follows, which here leads the entire company through a magical portico that only permits passage to faithful, constant lovers, a supernatural feature reminiscent of similar structures in chivalric romances. The entrance itself resembles a triumphal arch or the grand portal of an intricately wrought Graeco-Roman temple with marble columns set in golden bases and capitals, while the mansion proper is square-shaped – that is, symmetrical, geometric perfection – laden with sculpted figures from classical antiquity:

> Toda la casa parecía hecha de reluciente jaspe con muchas almenas, y en ellas esculpidas algunas figuras de emperadores, matronas romanas y otras antiguallas semejantes. Eran todas las ventanas cada una de dos arcos; las cerraduras y clavazón de plata; todas las puertas, de cedro. La casa era cuadrada y a cada cantón había una muy alta y artificiosa torre.
>
> [The entire house seemed made of glistening, veined marble with many merlons, and in them were sculpted some figures of emperors, Roman matrons, and other, similar antique objects. Each and every one of the windows was double-arched; the locks and nails of silver; all the doors, of cedar. The house was square and at each corner there was a tall and artful tower.] (259)[5]

Precious materials such as marble, silver, and aromatic, biblical cedar, with bas-relief emperors and Roman matrons highlight the characters' crossing of a threshold in the text, a passage they have earned through devotion to pure, constant love, an emotion as rare and refined as the architectural elements described in the narrative. The geometric perfection of the cube-shaped palace mirrors the symmetrical design of the work itself, marking the centre of *Diana*'s seven-book structure, which at the same time correlates with the convergence of the individual cases of unhappy love along with the ascent in the text from the particularities of each pastoral pilgrim's story to a higher level of conceptualization and abstraction about love – an ideological convergence and ascent conveyed in Platonic terms. For if Graeco-Roman design and ornamentation signal entry into the world of the sorceress Felicia, the shepherds' stay with the lady will end with an academy that focuses on love staged in a garden setting, and which reenacts academic gatherings widespread in the urban and court culture of early modern Europe, and reaching back to classical antiquity with particular reference to Plato's *Symposium*.

Once the pilgrims of love enter the interior space of Felicia's palace, a sumptuous, richly detailed series of ekphrastic passages unfolds as the wise lady treats her guests to lavish court entertainment, and Montemayor describes ornate chambers decked in gold, silver, crystal, and precious stones, replete with mosaics, sculpture, and statuary. The crossing of the magic portal threshold, the movement from outside to inside, from natural forest to artful palace rooms also transforms the party of shepherds into spectators who watch and listen with wondering eyes and ears, and in some cases participate in the events carefully planned by their hostess. As Alastair Fowler has pointed out, ekphrasis was a common means of incorporating the viewer in Renaissance literature, although less attention has been paid to the fact that "Renaissance ekphrastic literature may imply subtly differentiated spectator roles" (2003, 77, 81). These subtle distinctions and varied roles come to the fore in Felicia's palace where as non-passive spectators, the shepherds function as *beschouwers*, that is, as representative viewers who direct the gaze of the reader's inner eye and cue an empathic response on the part of the audience, serving as fictional doubles of Montemayor's reading public. Such figures were common in the painting and literature of the time, acting as authorial surrogates, gesturing to significant objects and actions, aiding in the interpretation of scenes, drawing readers / viewers into the work, and the like.[6] In this instance, as a meticulous presenter, the narrator captures and communicates to readers the important elements of the decor, architecture, and performances in Felicia's palace, creating the illusion of freezing the narrative flow and stopping the forward movement of the characters' stories. Although this illusion may be powerful, especially in the wake of the shepherds' pilgrimage through the landscape to achieve this destination, in actuality, Montemayor encourages active intellectual and emotional engagement from his readers as they pause along with the characters to think of the ideas about love staged in debates and conversations, and in performing artefacts that appear in Pygmalian mode to come to life before the eyes of fictional characters and reading public alike.

Consider the first activity staged by Felicia in her palace after a wondrous banquet served at tables set luxuriously, as if for the most refined courtiers. Three nymphs emerge from an adjoining chamber, playing the lute, harp, and psaltery respectively with such lovely harmonies that "los presentes estaban como fuera de sí" [those present were beside themselves] (Montemayor 1999, 261–2). Felicia then coaxes the shepherds to join in the concert with rustic rebecs and a panpipe, which all together create a polyphonic backdrop for the antiphonal exchange of the spontaneously formed choruses of nymphs and shepherds. This salon entertainment constitutes a debate in song form in which the nymphs criticize love harshly as a passion that negates reason and causes intense suffering, while the shepherds defend love as a force that ennobles and gives life despite the torment it may bring. The narrator then informs readers that Felicia and Felismena, cast in the role of representative spectators, "estuvieron muy atentas a la música de las ninfas y pastores, y así mismo a las opiniones que cada uno mostraba tener" [were very attentive to the music of the nymphs and shepherds, as well as to the opinions each one presented] (1999, 265), cuing *Diana*'s public to pay attention as well. When Felicia teasingly asks Felismena if perhaps some of the words may have touched her soul, the young lady responds, "Han sido las palabras tales que el alma a quien no tocaren no debe estar tan tocada de amor como la mía" [The words are such that the soul of the person they cannot touch must not be as touched by love as mine] (1999, 265). In this way the author not only encourages the audience to meditate on both sides of the unresolved debate, emblematic of the conflicted but loyal hearts that characterize the band of pilgrims, but also invites an empathic response from the reading public, suggesting that if they have ever loved, they should identify their own experiences as lovers with the emotional struggles of the shepherds. Through the performance, Montemayor reframes the lovers' troubles of Books 1–3 as universal experiences in which readers see themselves depicted. And while the tuneful singers do not announce a winner of their debate, Felicia afterwards declares that love is virtue and favours those of generous spirit and lively understanding, which she emphasizes has nothing to do with noble blood or distinguished ancestors. This elevation and celebration of virtuous love and lovers endows the characters and their amorous conflicts with an almost heroic stature, a link that Montemayor develops in the subsequent ekphrastic scenes in Book 4, and that foreshadows the successful resolution of the shepherds' respective situations.[7]

The nymphs next lead their visitors on a tour of interior rooms and spaces in which the shepherds marvel at a succession of visual and auditory wonders, encomiastic, "speaking" sculptures, statuary, and monuments that equate the heroic deeds of great men with the virtuous lives of famous women, as Gustavo Correa has stressed.[8] A commemorative column in an interior patio portrays such classical heroes who excelled in arms as Hannibal and Alexander the Great, along with such esteemed Spanish heroes as el Cid and Bernardo del Carpio, eliding the temporal distance and any qualitative distinction between the heroic world of classical antiquity and that of imperial Spain, revealing a nascent nationalistic consciousness apparent elsewhere in Montemayor's text. These sculpted representations lead the characters to another room, in which they find the female counterparts of these glorious male warriors, women of exemplary virtue from antiquity and more recent Spanish history sculpted so skilfully that they seem to reenact their lives before viewers' eyes:

> [E]ntraron en una rica sala, lo alto de la cual era todo de marfil, maravillosamente labrado: las paredes de alabastro y en ellas esculpidas muchas historias antiguas, tan al natural que verdaderamente parecía que Lucrecia acababa allí de darse la muerte [...] Y otras muchas historias y ejemplos de mujeres castísimas y dignas de ser su fama por todo el mundo esparcida ...
>
> [They entered a rich room, the upper part of which was all ivory, marvellously carved: walls of alabaster and in them sculpted many ancient stories, so lifelike that it truly seemed that Lucrecia had just killed herself there [...] And many other stories and examples of chaste women worthy of their fame being spread throughout the world ...] (Montemayor 1999, 274)

The spatial contiguity of the rooms and the symmetry of the artefacts displayed therein generate a metonymic link between exemplary, male martial prowess and remarkable female purity, an association that lends the amorous quests of the pastoral pilgrims an aura of reflected glory.[9]

The viewing of wonders culminates in the square-shaped (again that symbol of symmetrical, geometric perfection) innermost room of the palace, a shrine-like chamber ornamented with golden laurels enamelled in green and featuring a silver fountain in which water pours from the breasts of the statue of a golden nymph, an aquatic artefact resembling those found in Italianate gardens of the time. The *spiritus loci* of this room is the enchanted Orpheus, the arch-poet, arch-musician, and devoted lover par excellence, who magically comes to life as the nymphs and shepherds enter the room. In this space, Montemayor transforms his characters into a tableau vivant, rendering them temporarily immobile and fixing the women visually in the shape of a frieze with Felismena at the centre, while the men sit by the fountain:

> Felismena se sentó en un estrado que en la hermosa cuadra estaba todo cubierto de paños de brocado, y las ninfas y pastoras en torno della; los pastores se arrimaron a la clara fuente. De la misma manera estaban todos oyendo al celebrado Orpheo, que al tiempo que en la tierra de los Ciconios cantaba, cuando Ciparios fue convertido en ciprés, y Atis en pino.
>
> [Felismena sat down on a dais in the beautiful room that was covered with brocade cloths, and the nymphs and shepherdesses around her; the shepherds drew close to the clear fountain. They were listening to the celebrated Orpheus in the same way as in the time when he sang in the land of the

> Ciconians, when Cyparissus was changed into a cypress, and Attis into a pine tree.] (Montemayor 1999, 277)

The world of myth and metamorphosis lives again, blending past and present, even as "el enamorado" [the enamoured Orpheus] turns his gaze to "la hermosa Felismena" [the beautiful Felismena] and sings a 24-stanza laudatory catalogue of virtuous Spanish and Portuguese ladies, primarily members or contemporaries of the aristocratic circle which Montemayor served. Like all of the ekphrastic vignettes in Book 4, this scene undoubtedly has multiple symbolic functions, one of which is to suspend time with wonderment and divert the young lovers from their own suffering during that brief interval: "La canción del celebrado Orpheo fue tan agradable a los oídos de Felismena y de todos los que la oían, que así los tenía suspensos, como si por ninguno de ellos hubiera pasado más de lo que presente tenían" [The song of the celebrated Orpheus was so agreeable to Felismena's ears, and to those of everyone who listened to it, that they were suspended [in time] as if nothing had happened to them except what they had before them] (1999, 293). The spectators' absorption also underscores their empathic response, validating their amorous suffering and placing the shepherdesses, above all Felismena, the lady who presides over this impromptu salon performance, on a par with the objects of Orpheus's praise. Moreover, metonymically the author situates his characters and the exemplary historical figures in contiguous locales, albeit one spatial and visual, and the other in auditory proximity, suggesting that Felismena and her pilgrim companions continue the illustrious tradition and metaphorical lineage of the heroic men and women depicted and celebrated in the rooms and artefacts of Felicia's palace. Since Orpheus faced death and the fearful underworld in an attempt to reclaim his love, fittingly the visitors move from his interior chamber outside to a garden in which they encounter sepulchres of famous women who guarded and carried their virtue to the grave, and who now speak to the living wanderers in the garden through their epitaphs. Finally, the pilgrims walk from the garden cemetery into a garden grove and meadow, back into a more conventional pastoral setting, a place of relaxation for the nymphs, and the ideal space in which to have the academy, in which Felicia makes an eloquent, Platonic defence of pure love: "[T]odo el amor desta manera no tira a otro fin, sino a querer la persona por ella misma, sin esperar otro interese ni galardón de sus amores" [All love of this type has no other objective than to love the person for himself without expecting any reward or profit from that love] (1999, 299).

Throughout Book 4, visual symmetry and musical harmony provide artistic counterparts for the balanced exchanges in debate and dialogue that occur in Felicia's palace, which also serve as an objective correlative for *Diana*'s strong advocacy for controlling destructive, irrational passions as crucial to the attainment of perfect, devoted love. Moreover, these scenes in Felicia's palace, which seem to stop the forward movement of the narrative and retard or undercut the chronological flow of time, linking mythic figures from the distant past with historical figures of Iberia and with the fictional spectators-protagonists of Montemayor's book, constitute an imaginative nucleus of idealized, aggrandized, virtuous love for *Diana*, providing the conceptual impetus and motivation for the successful unravelling and resolution of the multiple, thorny plotlines, that is, for the transformation of the protagonists' unhappy love into amorous joy shared with a partner who reciprocates their love with equal, devoted measure, except for Sireno, who at least appears to regain some of the equanimity suggested by his name (*sereno*) with the timely intervention of Felicia. The promise of pure, devoted love enshrined in the sorceress's temple, and performed before the eyes and ears of the readers' imagination, radiates out from this nucleus, transforming the sorrow and melancholy of the lachrymose Books 1–3 into the happiness and delight of Books 5–7, marred only by the disturbing encounter between Sireno and Diana in Book 6.

Montemayor in fact does present this urbane, sophisticated edifice as a space of transformation, where thanks to Felicia, the worthy, long-suffering pilgrims step on the road to recovery through requited love, although Sireno drinks the much-criticized elixir of forgetfulness. The focus on Felicia's cures and palliative potions, however, which appear in Book 5, has obscured the most interesting transformation that occurs in Book 4, which pertains to Felismena. Indeed, Montemayor does not resolve her case until the end, in Book 7 of the romance, when this female protagonist wanders over the border into Portugal near the author's hometown. There the nymph Dórida fortuitously appears at just the right moment to administer the elixir of remembrance to Don Felis, thus restoring the lovers' *felicidad* (happiness) in the devoted love they share for one another. Felismena, dressed once again like the goddess Diana, saves her beloved from death at the hands of his warrior antagonists with the skilful use of her bow and arrows, while the potion brings his dead, forgotten love for her back to life. In a sense, this heroic beauty succeeds, where the mythic Orpheus failed, in reviving the object of her affection and reclaiming his love, reuniting them as a devoted couple who can now regain their true identities even as they recover each other's love.

From the beginning of this pastoral romance Montemayor has taken great pains to distinguish Felismena from the other pilgrims of love; he accomplishes this in part through the unsubtle linkage of names in the troika Felicia, Felismena, and Felis. Moreover, by blood and experience Felismena is a lady accustomed to the life of city and court (*la gran Soldina*), yet when she first appears she is dressed as a shepherdess bearing the attributes of Diana, a bow and quiver of arrows. Her active defence of the nymphs' chastity from the wild men in Book 2 further emphasizes the mythological connection. Nevertheless, Dórida also identifies her as a child "de la discreta Minerva, que tan gran discreción no puede proceder de otra parte" [of the wise Minerva, for such great wisdom could not originate anywhere else] (Montemayor 1999, 190). Thus, for her, arrival at the palace of the wise woman Felicia is a symbolic homecoming in which the sorceress greets her as a mother might welcome a daughter or certainly a kindred spirit. Felicia separates her almost immediately from the other pilgrims, and sees to it that she is sumptuously dressed in clothing and jewellery corresponding to her elevated social status, and virtually transforms her into a human icon bearing gems that signify passion, chastity, a just spirit, great worth, and so forth, all qualities which arise in the debates and discussions about love that unfold in the palace.[10] Felismena embodies throughout *Diana* the combination of chaste, devoted love and martial prowess commemorated and tied together at Felicia's palace, where a life-size statue of the goddess Diana serves as the reigning spirit of the temple (275) and presides over the room devoted to artwork depicting exemplary women, who are celebrated in the song of Orpheus. Felismena remains in character as the aristocratic lady while she attends the court of Minerva and Diana encapsulated in Felicia and her palace, but assumes the costume of Diana once again when she resumes her active role in quest of Don Felis. Along the way she helps solve the shepherdess Belisa's troubled amorous affair, and so when Felismena finally encounters her own beloved, her bow and arrows must be employed once again to rescue Don Felis and keep their love alive.

Unlike *Diana*, Lope's *Arcadia* presents a retrospective, critical, and subjective anatomy of the author's former love affair with Elena Osorio and of his former self, a project supported by the overall, structural design of the book. In Lope's hands, the pastoral world and the conventions of pastoral fiction become powerful vehicles for self-portraiture and introspective self-analysis. Like Montemayor's romance, Lope's work features a central, pivotal book, in this instance Book 3 of five books, which stages a vignette with a strong ekphrastic focus, here in the shape of Dardanio's cave. As in *Diana*, readers encounter intricate, descriptive detail and an exchange with a male counterpart to Felicia that advances the plot towards the denouement. Yet in contrast to *Diana*'s catalogue of amorous cases, and idealizing, universalizing approach to love, *Arcadia* tells the tale of just one very unflattering type of love – the jealous, possessive kind that blocks upward movement into the higher realm of Platonic purity, and which instead pushes the lover into shattering acts of vindictiveness and self-destruction. Lope's alter ego Anfriso thus moves through madness and recovery, not of his beloved Belisarda, but rather a recovery that is more of a discovery and conversion to the avocation of poet, which unfolds in Book 5 in a series of scenes architecturally framed by Anfriso's admission into the Palacio de Poesía [Palace of Poetry] and the Templo de Desengaño [Temple of Disillusionment or Disenchantment], both described by Lope in rapturous, ekphrastic detail.[11] Ray Keck has characterized *Arcadia* as a "pastoral romance of ascetic pilgrimage," and indeed, rather than *Diana*'s pattern of aggregation of pilgrims of love and their convergence on a magical, beautiful palace that celebrates perfectly harmonious and symmetrical design as a backdrop for discussions that similarly celebrate idealized, Platonic, perfect, heroic love, Lope separates and isolates Anfriso from the rest of the pastoral community, situating him in Book 3 in Dardanio's cave, where events unfold that will further unravel the strained relationship with Belisarda, precipitating her unhappy marriage to another man, and that will propel him into madness, isolating him even more from the shepherd community (1999, 72–3).

While the embodiment of virtuous, exemplary love unites Montemayor's pilgrims on a guided path to Felicia's palace and the happy resolution of their lovers' ills, Anfriso's weakness, his jealous, impetuous nature, leads him astray literally and figuratively. In fact, Lope's very active narrator informs readers that Anfriso leaves Belisarda and the community simply to allow the gossip circulating about them to cool: "[D]espedido y desesperado, salió de la asperísima y agradable sierra sin alma que le guiase ni camino cierto por donde fuese. Y determinado a morir de tristeza … y trocando el hábito de pastor en el de peregrino, por inhabitables montes tomó el camino de la bella Italia" [Dismissed and desperate, he left the harsh and pleasant mountains without a soul to guide him or a sure road to follow. And determined to die of sadness … and changing his shepherd's clothing for that of a pilgrim, he followed the route to beautiful Italy through uninhabitable wilds] (Vega 1975, 221). This change of clothing from shepherd's garb to pilgrim's robes visually signals the initiation of Anfriso's transformation of identity in *Arcadia*. The youth wanders off the path during the night, gets caught in a fearful thunderstorm, and while he laments his fate, the wizard Dardanio discovers him in the wilderness: "Y como sentado sobre una peña suspirase, no de otra suerte que el pájaro solitario en secos árboles, fue oído de un hombre rústico que de aquellas soledades era dueño, y desde sus tiernos años estudiando el arte mágica las habitaba" [And as he sighed while seated on a rock, not unlike a solitary bird in dry trees, he was heard by a rustic man who was the owner of those solitary spaces, and who since his tender years, while studying the magic arts, inhabited them] (1975, 221). Only in retrospect does Anfriso, or the reader, recognize that the protagonist's swerving from his journey to Italy, a trip undertaken as an irrational act of desperation that has only suicide in combat as its destination, and his stumbling into the wizard's domain, provide the axis on which the plot turns and metamorphoses into a pilgrimage towards the embrace of a poet's identity.

Artful rusticity perhaps best describes the cave and milieu of the wizard Dardanio, who wears a curious tunic of leaves and twigs that identifies him with the green world of the forest. Frederick de Armas and Javier Blasco have pointed out that hermetic tradition pervades this episode as well as *Arcadia* as a whole, and de Armas also stresses the association between caves, wisdom, and poetic inspiration, linked to Anfriso's future as a poet.[12] In contrast to the elegant sophistication of Felicia, Dardanio, who is certainly as sympathetic and hospitable as she, resembles an ascetic hermit with his eccentric garb and long locks and beard. While vast expanses and large displays of formal, intricate, precious art and architecture greet the wondering eyes of Montemayor's prilgrims, Dardanio invites Anfriso into the cave to contemplate primarily one artefact that serves as his constant companion: "[E]ntre varias cosas le mostró labrado su sepulcro de blanco mármol, a la cabeza del cual le mostró una pirámide en cuyo hueco, dentro de una caja de acero, pensaba poner sus libros para que después de su muerte se conservasen hasta que en otros siglos fuesen descubiertos" [Among various things he showed him his sepulchre of white marble, at the head of which he showed him a pyramid, inside of which he was planning on putting his books in a steel box so that after his death they would be preserved until in other centuries they were discovered] (Vega 1975, 222). Dardanio and Anfriso slip into the respective roles of presenter and *beschouwer* in this scene, and direct readers not to scan a field of imagery (the indeterminate "varias cosas" [various things]), but rather rivet their gaze on the sorcerer's white marble sepulchre, a perpetual memento mori that silently bespeaks *desengaño* and highlights the wizard's function as *desengañador* (disillusioner or disenchanter), one of Dardanio's multiple functions in the text. The pyramid, an ancient, volumetric, commemorative marker crowns the tomb, and draws the eye to the treasure housed inside in the steel strongbox, which contains Dardanio's books of learning, the legacy he intends to leave future generations. The juxtaposition of the grave, space of fleshly disintegration, with the steel container, which resists decay and protects the thoughts embodied in words, suggests the supremacy of art in general and texts in particular as purveyors of enduring wisdom and lays special claim to art's immortal fame, which extends beyond the death of the books' creator.

These artefacts encapsulate Anfriso's transformation in visual form, too, since that process begins with an experience of profound *desengaño* – the death of his identity as Belisarda's devoted lover – followed by his embrace of the art of poetry as a more worthy object of his enduring passion. The implication, of course, is that poetry will be Anfriso's true legacy and the repository of his eternal fame, as it is that of his creator Lope. This fixing of the audience's contemplative gaze then shifts to a simple repast of wild fruit in this space of retreat and inner reflection, not an extravagant courtly banquet, and this context provides a fitting frame for the intimate, introspective exchange between wizard and shepherd hero, who confesses his intention to die in battle in Italy's wars. Signficantly, Dardanio does not promise him the successful resolution of his love affair, but rather prophesies that Anfriso will triumph over his enemies without specifying what form that victory will take, as long as he can maintain patience: "que como tú tengas paciencia, que las cosas más ásperas quebranta a esa misma envidia pisarás el cuello" [if you have patience, which breaks the harshest thing, you will trample the neck of that very envy] (Vega 1975, 224–5). Yet that patience is precisely the quality that eludes Anfriso at this critical moment in *Arcadia*, and that will subsequently launch him into madness.

No formal entertainment follows the humble dinner or the words of advice that will go unheeded – no singing and dancing, and no philosophical debates that extol the ennobling qualities of idealized love. Yet Dardanio's cave does house a gallery of statues of illustrious heroes past, present, and future from ancient Greece and Italy, and more contemporary Spain, with distiches on the base of the figures that enable them to "speak" silently of their great deeds. This introduces another element of kinship with Montemayor's *Diana*. Significantly, the catalogue of heroic statues begins with Romulus and Remus, identified by Dardanio as "fundadores de la sagrada ciudad cabeza del mundo" [founders of that sacred city, the head of the world] (Vega 1975, 225), which skilfully elides the temporal distance between Roman and Spanish empires, imperial capital and global, religious capital of the Catholic church, tracing continuous lineage from the mythic Roman brothers to the current Habsburg rulers and their pursuit of a global, Catholic empire. Lope freely mixes statues of mythic figures with those of historical heroes, and males and females, and thus Anfriso sees figures of King Arthur and Charlemagne alongside those of Artemisia and Cleopatra. The nascent nationalism apparent in *Diana*'s statuary becomes much more explicit here as Dardanio informs the readers-spectators that "[e]stos de esta parte son algunos españoles dignos de mayor memoria que los antiguos griegos y romanos" [these in this area are some Spaniards worthy of greater memory than the ancient Greeks and Romans] (1975, 227), and predictably begins his list with Bernardo del Carpio and el Cid to end perhaps less predictably with the great Duke of Alba.[13] Lope incorporates gestures into the scene by means of deictic demonstratives such as "este" [this] and "aquel" [that] that emphatically repeated throughout the show-and-tell presentation of Anfriso's magician host serve as a prelude to Dardanio's declamation of the lines written on the base of the sculptures, "porque de tan ilustres varones no te quedes sin oír sus alabanzas" [because you will not stay without hearing the praises of such illustrious men] (1975, 232).[14] The wizard's voice provides a medium through which the illustrious figures speak one by one, encomiastically voicing their own accomplishments in first-person poetry. This performance consolidates the association between poetry, wisdom, heroism, and immortality established in Dardanio's cave and signals the displacement or substitution of *Arcadia*'s previous focus on love, thus marking the beginning of the text's thematic transformation along with the transformation of the protagonist Anfriso. While Montemayor's Felicia appears to rely on pharmacological concoctions linked to time and memory for cures for lovesickness and the happy resolution of the pilgrims' amatory ills, Dardanio employs artwork for therapeutic purposes, setting before Anfriso heroic models for him to emulate, and at the same time distracting him from his own self-pity, self-absorption, and suicidal melancholia. The narrator tells readers that hermit and shepherd while away the night with the statues: "Con estas varias quimeras, que sin estar hechas con el arte transmutatoria le obligaban a creer que formalmente las había, engañaba Dardanio la imaginación del enamorado Anfriso" [With these various chimeras, that without being made by the transmutational art, obliged him to believe they were actually there, Dardanio tricked the imagination of the enamoured Anfriso] (1975, 246).

Lope links Dardanio's cave, then, with veering off the beaten path, swerving from the original goal, substituting poetic ambition for amorous devotion, as Anfriso's love madness metamorphoses at the end of *Arcadia* into the divine frenzy of poetic inspiration, predicated on divergence from the life the protagonist has previously led in the community of shepherds. In this way, Dardanio's modest dwelling plays a crucial part in a structural pattern of displacement and substitution in *Arcadia*, serving as the fulcrum of Anfriso's dramatic change into a poet in the romance, and at the same time functioning as a space of psychological convergence in which the flawed hero's driving passion of jealous love and the opportunity to indulge that weakness fatefully meet. His downward spiral into madness begins when the magician grants Anfriso a wish, like a fairy godfather, and the young man does not choose what readers might expect, such as marriage with Belisarda or even the chance to be with her forever, but rather requests just to see her. And see her he does, but just that alone, thanks to Dardanio's powerful magic that enables them to fly through the air and disguise themselves such that they cannot be recognized. Lope presents a compelling case of "be careful what you wish for" as Anfriso sees Belisarda give Olimpio a ribbon as she attempts to satisfy his irritating, unwelcome wooing with a trinket intended to convince him to leave her alone. The hero has unwisely cast himself in the passive role of a spectator close enough for visual observation, but too distant to hear the exchange of words between his beloved and the rival suitor, leading the unduly jealous, voyeuristic lover to an act of misprision – the erroneous belief that Belisarda has betrayed him – which pushes him beyond the limits of what he can bear and into madness, from which he will eventually emerge a poet.

Lope counterbalances Anfriso's adventure in Dardanio's cave in the second half of Book 3 with a plein-air academy staged by the shepherds that coincides with the protagonist's return. The central section of *Arcadia* thus concludes with a gathering in a pastoral setting that foregrounds the performance of a variety of poetic forms as well as discussions about the arts, featuring such typical topics of debate as the relationship between art and nature and the *paragone* or competition between the sister arts of poetry and painting. This virtuoso display of literary topoi and poetic praxis further emphasizes the dramatic crossover in the text, and signals the marked change in Anfriso's identity from bucolic lover to Orphic poet. At the same time, the academy exalts the calling of the poet, the identity ultimately chosen by Lope-Anfriso, as described by Danteo:

> No sólo ha de saber el poeta todas las ciencias, o a lo menos principios de todas, pero ha de tener grandísima experiencia de las cosas que en tierra y mar suceden, para que, ofreciéndose ocasión de acomodar un ejército o de escribir

> una armada, no hable como ciego, y para que los que lo han visto no le vituperen y tengan por ignorante. Ha de saber ni más ni menos el trato y manera de vivir y costumbres de todo género de gente; y, finalmente, todas aquellas cosas de que se habla, trata y se vive, porque ninguna hay hoy en el mundo tan alta o ínfima de que no se le ofrezca tratar alguna vez, desde el mismo Criador hasta el más vil gusano y monstro de la tierra.
>
> [Not only must the poet know all the sciences, or at least principles of all of them, but he must also have great experience of the things that happen on land and sea, so that, if an occasion to refer to an army or describe a fleet should offer itself, he will not talk blindly, so that those who have seen it will not vituperate him and consider him ignorant. He must know no more and no less than the social discourse, way of life, and customs of all types of people; and, finally, [he must know] all of those things that are said, dealt with, and lived, because there is nothing in the world too high or low that he will not some time have to address, from the Creator himself to the most vile worm or monster on Earth.] (Vega 1975, 268)

As this demiurgic representation of the poet suggests, for the latter part of Book 3, stimulation of the eyes of the mind cedes pride of place to appeal to the readers' powers of understanding.

Yet towards the end of *Arcadia*, as Anfriso approaches the completion of his transformation in the text, Lope makes even greater demands on readers' visualization powers and interpretive abilities. The highlight of Book 4's wedding festivities for Salicio and Belisarda is an aquatic masque and tournament, a combination of a floating procession of allegorical figures and emblems, followed by a festive *naumachia*, an opulent entertainment worthy of a grand, aristocratic court. These activities lead up to Anfriso's conversion to the study of the humanities and the practice of poetry by the wise woman Polinesta in *Arcadia*'s concluding Book 5, which features extensive ekphrastic passages rich in architectural detail and symbolic content, witnessed as readers accompany the protagonist through the Palace of the Seven Liberal Arts, the Palace of Poetry, and finally the Templo de Desengaño. Significantly, when Anfriso first meets Polinesta in Book 4, in a clear, intertextual reference to *Diana* he asks the sorceress for a remedy to make him forget Belisarda, which the wise lady refuses to do in a disdainful manner, stating, "querer un hombre olvidar, y no hacer diligencias para ello, no es dar materia en que pueda imprimirse forma, sino impedir todos los caminos de la humana física" [for a man to want to forget, and not take action to do so, is not to create material in which form can imprint itself, but rather to obstruct all paths of human healing] (Vega 1975, 358). She promises to help him when he is ready by applying a cure of diversion and distraction, that is, through a remedy of displacement and substitution whereby Anfriso will substitute poetry for love, transforming painful memories of lost love into raw material for poetic creativity: "[T]e llevaré al templo del ejercicio y artes liberales, cuya honesta ocupación divierta de manera tu fatigada memoria que no te acuerdes si en tu vida viste a Belisarda" [I will take you to the temple of exercise and liberal arts, whose honest occupation may divert your weary memory so that you will not remember if you saw Belisarda in your life] (1975, 359). Just as Polinesta appears to defeat Felicia in wisdom and healing methods, Lope indirectly asserts through the scenarios and artful edifices at the end of *Arcadia* that he bests Montemayor in ekphrastic practice, and in writing pastoral romances destined for aristocratic audiences, in effect displacing or attempting to displace the bucolic masterpiece of forty years ago.

At first glance, consideration of Felicia's palace and Dardanio's cave as places of convergence and transformation in *Diana* and *Arcadia* respectively elicits a list of fundamental differences. The background of the authors, and the shifts that transpired in Spanish society in between the works' dates of composition, points to a critical perspective based on contrasts rather than similarities. While Montemayor spent most of his life in aristocratic service at peripatetic courts, Lope was a middle-class embroiderer's son, who at the time he composed *Arcadia* sought entrée into the inner circle of the Habsburg court, and unsuccessfully pursued the position of court historian after returning to Madrid from exile.[15] During the years separating the two romances, literary taste shifted and expanded in regards to prose fiction, the reading public grew larger and more diverse, and Madrid became the official capital and centre of the Spanish empire, albeit by 1598 an empire of tarnished lustre and diminished power. Yet clearly Lope and Montemayor continue extant literary conventions of both long-standing and more recent provenance, such as the rhetorical practice of ekphrasis, which originates in classical antiquity; the appearance of carefully described magical caves, temples, and palaces as visual and symbolic anchors for pivotal moments in narrative fiction, which claims ancient antecedents and also more recent models in the romances of chivalry; and extensive, creative passages enacting the oft-cited Horatian dictum *ut pictura poesis*, a simile that plays a leading role in the plot and style of *Diana* and *Arcadia*.

In analysing the artful edifices as transformative spaces in which time stands still, and narrative movement seems to freeze even as the plot actually advances and the protagonists undergo dramatic changes, however, it might prove constructive to add two more traditions to the list above of mutually supportive, nourishing conventions. Fernando Bouza Alvarez has observed that in the "sixteenth and seventeenth centuries there existed a clear awareness that what was oral, visual / iconic, and written (manifested as printed and manuscript texts and as public or silent reading) all fulfilled the same expressive, communicative, and recollective functions" (2004, 11). The scenarios that unfold in Felicia's palace and Dardanio's cave stimulate readers' responsiveness to all three forms of communication, demonstrating the authors' virtuosity in employing written words that evoke and encompass music, poetry, singing, and sonorous phrases, and conjure statues, emblems, monuments, and architecture of great vividness. The deployment of these communicative forms, in ways in which they often overlap or intertwine, distinguishes these scenes from others in the texts and alludes to their significance in the works as a whole. Moreover, the powerful, pleasing appeal to the audience's eyes and ears of the imagination calls to mind the belief at the time in the therapeutic effects of music and painting in balancing the bodily humours, and in providing the mind with alternating moments of engagement and relaxation.[16] This belief implies that these pivotal, ekphrastic scenarios of frozen time actually constitute moments in which readers engage with the text in a qualitatively different manner, and while the music, poetry, and visual imagery divert Montemayor's pilgrims and Lope's alter ego Anfriso and prove therapeutic and transformative to them, they also exercise different aspects of the readers' imagination, entertaining them, inspiring wonder, and also inviting them to rest a moment, and perhaps tune the mind to a quieter, more contemplative key to consider what they hear or see, or maybe just pause simply to enjoy the spectacle staged for them to witness as *beschouwers*. Finally, as a narrative genre, one should not forget that *Diana* and *Arcadia* arise primarily from the melding of pastoral and romance. With characteristic emphasis on combinations and permutations of the themes of love, identity, freedom, and adventure, romance reinforces and alters pastoral's performance of identity through subjective expression, opening up new pathways for the pursuit of other identities and selves, shifting identities that indicate that when the heroes and heroines of pastoral romance execute that final, pendular, homeward return that typifies the plot of these fictional worlds, they return other than when they first left. The magic wielded by the sorceress Felicia and the wizard Dardanio that yields the fulcrum on which the romances turn and the protagonists change, may in fact represent the authors' creative power in the realization of pastoral romance's potential for staging transformative process in the construction of identity.

## NOTES

1 There is a vineyard hung with darkening clusters.
A small boy perches on a dry stone wall to guard them.
Two foxes shadow him. One sneaks along the rows
For plunder; another has fixed her tricky eye
On the quarter-loaf the boy keeps for his breakfast
And will not let him alone till she has snatched it.
Blithely intent, he shapes a cage for a cricket
From asphodel stalks and rushes. The bag with his food
Is forgotten; so are the vines. The toy absorbs him. (Theocritus 1988, 56)

2 On the variety of purposes ekphrasis serves in Golden Age Spanish literature, see de Armas (2005a, 22). For recent studies on ekphrasis in Golden Age Spanish literature, consult the two books edited by de Armas (2004; 2005b). For an interesting point of comparison, see Persin 1997, who focuses on twentieth-century Spanish poetry.

3 On the setting and activities of Felicia's palace as a veiled double for the festivities celebrated in 1549 in honour of then Prince Philip (the future Philip II) at the Binche palace, see Subirats (1968). For more on the aristocratic audience of the *Diana*, see Chevalier (1974). Hernández-Pecoraro notes that Felicia's palace does pay tribute to a number of villas, palaces, and country retreats that actually existed, affirming the class status and hierarchy of Montemayor's audience, and providing a welcoming space for both the readers and fictional shepherds (2006, 49–50). Fernando Bouza Alvarez urges caution, however, in determining the actual audience of such works, citing, for example, the admission by a nun of the Poor Clares that the only non-religious book she had read, and thoroughly enjoyed much to her harm, was *Diana* (1992, 110).

4 On the organization of space in Italian Renaissance gardens, consult MacDougall (1972, 46) and Lazzaro (1990, 70–1, 81). For examples of the relationship between formal garden design and literary works in early modern Europe, see Hunt (1978) and Collins (2002, 171–92).

5 Chevalier (1974, 46–8) is just one of numerous critics who have noted the influence of the chivalric romance on *Diana*, especially in regards to the role of the supernatural. For the longstanding symbolism and magical powers of the

cube and other geometric and volumetric figures, see René Taylor's classic article on magic and architecture in the Escorial (1967). All translations are by the author unless referenced in the appropriate passage.

6 Fowler's chapter 5, "Involved Spectators," addresses the complex, multifaceted roles of spectators incorporated into Renaissance fiction and visual arts (2003, 66–84). Fowler writes of the *beschouwer* (67–8), defining the figure in general terms on p. 210 as "a personage clarifying by mime or gaze the action in a picture."

7 Here for the sake of argument I am overstating the case. It is highly ambiguous whether Sireno's state of indifference to Diana, and his apparent impassiveness, can be viewed as desirable outcomes.

8 In his article on *Diana*, Correa demonstrates that the palace conforms to the structural pattern of the temple of Fame created by Ovid in Book 12 of the *Metamorphoses*, noting: "Lo peculiar en este sistema de configuraciones de la Fama es la fusión de los elementos amorosos (Orfeo) con los heroicos procedentes de la guerra (Marte) en un mismo plano de significación. En virtud de esta fusión el mundo sentimental de la novela adquiere una dimensión heroica en cuanto queda transmutado en sustancia honrosa al par de las acciones ejemplares y guerreras" [The peculiar thing in this system of Fame's configurations is the fusion on the same level of meaning of amorous elements (Orpheus) with heroic ones originating with war (Mars). By virtue of this fusion, the sentimental world of the book acquires a heroic dimension in which it is transmuted into honourable material on a par with exemplary and warlike actions] (1961, 71). The courtiers and ladies who constitute Montemayor's immediate audience likely account in part for this parity of amorous and bellicose fame, while in classical antiquity, of course, one finds the pairing of Venus and Mars. Readers of the wildly popular romances of chivalry also encounter this mixture of matters of love and war, although Montemayor anchors the mixture in historic or legendary Iberian men and ladies.

9 It is important to keep in mind in this regard that as one who worked and travelled among courtiers and royals, Jorge de Montemayor for most of his adult life was part of the circle of several important aristocratic women, including Philip II's first wife, María of Portugal, and Philip's sister the infanta Juana, who married Prince Juan of Portugal.

10 See the article by Márquez Villanueva (1978) on the elaborate symbolism of the gems.

11 See Collins (2004, 887–95) on the author's fictionalization of autobiographical elements and on the symbolic function of the structure of *Arcadia*.

12 See Blasco (1990) and de Armas (1982–3 and 1985).

13 While history certainly supports this organization, note, too, its personal significance for Lope, who was ridiculed for *Arcadia*'s frontispiece, which bears a heraldic shield that asserts his kinship with Bernardo del Carpio, and who also served the young Duke of Alba, Don Antonio Alvarez de Toledo, and was protagonist of a scandalous love affair that in many ways paralleled that of the duke.

14 Susan Stewart notes that deixis implies proximity, and spurs reaction and reciprocity from the receiver: "The word *deixis* connotes the appearance of form in more than its visual dimensions and implies apprehension by touch or motion. Emphasizing the bringing forth of form over notions of imitation and representation per se, deixis yokes rhetoric – that is, an intention to move and a reciprocal receptivity to be moved – to visual and aural appearances. In lyric, painting, sculpture, and other arts, the stored activity of the maker is simultaneous to an implicity and reciprocal capacity for animation in the receiver' (2002, 150).

15 Elizabeth Rhodes stresses that although Montemayor lived and worked in aristocratic circles for most of his life, he was likely of *converso* background, was not from a noble family, and had to work his way into royal favour (1992, 22–5). For more on Lope's ambitions at this moment, see Wright (2001, 13–23). At the risk of oversimplifying, and of stating the obvious, I point out that the baroque aesthetics of *desengaño* and of elaborate, awe-inspiring design and sensory effects predominate in *Arcadia* while Renaissance harmony, symmetry, and balance pervade *Diana.*

16 Brooks (2007) and Gage (2008) are my primary sources here.

## WORKS CITED

Alpers, Paul. 1997. *What Is Pastoral?* Chicago: University of Chicago Press.

Blasco, Javier. 1990. "Entre la 'magia' del amor y la 'magia' de la memoria: Hermetismo y a literatura en *La Arcadia*, de Lope." *Edad de Oro* 9: 19–37.

Bouza Alvarez, Fernando. 1992. *Del escribano a la biblioteca: La civilización escrita europea en la alta edad moderna (siglos XV–XVII).* Madrid: Síntesis.

Bouza Alvarez, Fernando. 2004. *Communication, Knowledge, and Memory in Early Modern Spain.* Translated by Sonia López and Michael Agnew. Philadelphia: University of Pennsylvania Press.

Brooks, Jeanice. 2007. "Music as Erotic Magic in a Renaissance Romance." *Renaissance Quarterly* 60 (4): 1207–56. http://dx.doi.org/10.1353/ren.2007.0367.

Chevalier, Maxime. 1974. "*La Diana* de Montemayor y su público en la España del siglo XVI." In *Creación y público en la literatura española*, edited by Jean-François Borrel and Serge Salaün, 40–55. Madrid: Castalia.

Collins, Marsha S. 2002. *The "Soledades," Góngora's Masque of the Imagination*. Columbia: University of Missouri Press.

Collins, Marsha S. 2004. "Lope's *Arcadia*: A Self-Portrait of the Artist as a Young Man." *Renaissance Quarterly* 57: 882–907.

Correa, Gustavo. 1961. "El templo de Diana en la novela de Jorge de Montemayor." *Thesaurus* 16: 59–76.

de Armas, Frederick A. 1982–3. "Lope de Vega and the Hermetic Tradition: The Case of Dardanio in *La Arcadia*." *Revista Canadiense de Estudios Hispánicos* 7: 345–62.

de Armas, Frederick A. 1985. "Caves of Fame and Wisdom in the Spanish Pastoral Novel." *Studies in Philology* 82: 332–58.

de Armas, Frederick A, ed. 2004. *Writing for the Eyes in the Spanish Golden Age*. Lewisburg, PA: Bucknell University Press.

de Armas, Frederick A. 2005a. "Simple Magic: Ekphrasis from Antiquity to the Age of Cervantes." In *Ekphrasis in the Age of Cervantes*, edited by Frederick A. de Armas, 13–31. Lewisburg, PA: Bucknell University Press.

de Armas, Frederick A, ed. 2005b. *Ekphrasis in the Age of Cervantes*. Lewisburg, PA: Bucknell University Press.

Fowler, Alastair. 2003. *Renaissance Realism: Narrative Images in Literature and Art*. Oxford: Oxford University Press.

Gage, Frances. 2008. "Exercises for Mind and Body: Giulio Mancini, Collecting, and the Beholding of Landscape Painting in the Seventeenth Century." *Renaissance Quarterly* 61 (4): 1167–207. http://dx.doi.org/10.1353/ren.0.0366 .Medline:19235286

Hernández-Pecoraro, Rosilie. 2006. *Bucolic Metaphors: History, Subjectivity, and Gender in the Early Modern Spanish Pastoral*. North Carolina Studies in the Romance Languages and Literatures 287. Chapel Hill: UNC, Department of Romance Languages.

Hunt, John Dixon. 1978. "'Loose Nature' and the 'Garden Square': The Gardenist Background for Marvell's Poetry." In *Approaches to Marvell: The York Tercentenary Lectures*, edited by C.A. Patrides, 331–51. London: Routledge and Kegan Paul.

Keck, Ray M. 1999. *Love's Dialectic: Mimesis and Allegory in the Romances of Lope de Vega*. University, MS: Romance Monographs.

Krieger, Murray. 1992. *Ekphrasis: The Illusion of the Natural Sign*. Baltimore: Johns Hopkins University Press.

Lazzaro, Claudia. 1990. *The Italian Renaissance Garden: From the Conventions of Painting, Design, and Ornament to the Grand Gardens of Sixteenth-Century Central Italy*. New Haven: Yale University Press.

MacDougall, Elisabeth B. 1972. "*Ars Hortulorum*: Sixteenth-Century Garden Iconography and Literary Theory in Italy." In *The Italian Garden*, edited by David R. Coffin, 37–59. Washington, DC: Dumbarton Oaks.

Márquez Villanueva, Francisco. 1978. "Los joyeles de Felismena." *Revue de Littérature Comparée* 52: 267–78.

Montemayor, Jorge de. 1999. *La Diana*. Edited by Asunción Rallo. Madrid: Cátedra.

Persin, Margaret H. 1997. *Getting the Picture: The Ekphrastic Principle in Twentieth-Century Spanish Poetry*. Lewisburg, PA: Bucknell University Press.

Rhodes, Elizabeth. 1992. *The Unrecognized Precursors of Montemayor's "Diana."* Columbia, MO: University of Missouri Press.

Stewart, Susan. 2002. *Poetry and the Fate of the Senses*. Chicago: University of Chicago Press.

Subirats, Jean. 1968. "La *Diane* de Montemayor, roman à clef?" In *Etudes Ibériques et Latino-Américaines: IVe Congrès des Hispanistes Français (Poitiers, 18–20 Mars 1967)*, 105–18. Paris: Presses Universitaires de France.

Taylor, René. 1967. "Architecture and Magic: Considerations on the *Idea* of the Escorial." In *Essays in the History of Architecture Presented to Rudolf Wittkower*, edited by Douglas Fraser, Howard Hibbard, and Milton J. Levine, 81–109. London: Phaidon.

Theocritus. 1988. *The Idylls*. Translated by Robert Wells. Manchester: Carcanet.

Vega, Lope de. 1975. *Arcadia*. Edited by Edwin S. Morby. Madrid: Castalia.

Wright, Elizabeth R. 2001. *Pilgrimage to Patronage: Lope de Vega and the Court of Philip III, 1598–1621*. Lewisburg, PA: Bucknell University Press.

# 3 The Artful Gamblers: Wagering Danaë in Cervantes' *Don Quixote* I. 33–35

FREDERICK A. DE ARMAS

At the very centre of Cervantes' *Don Quixote* an interpolated story is told to those present at an inn entitled *The Novel of the Curious Impertinent* (*El curioso impertinente*). Encompassing three chapters of the novel, it is a misplaced tale, as the author will later acknowledge.[1] Not only is it misplaced, but as Thomas Pavel notes, we cannot place, we cannot understand, the central character's main impetus – his strange and extravagant desires.[2] In this essay I will look anew at this story from the point of view of material culture and theatricality. Within material culture, I include objects that circulate, such as cards and paintings. While the first recalls the emblem, with pictures and letters that can be allegorized, the second points to the presence of the ekphrastic in the tale. Both of these elements exist within the theatricality of the text which serves to point to the representational nature of social appearance in the baroque. Although it might be an exaggeration to state that the object makes the man (or woman), objects do impinge on their subjectivity. In an age as theatrical as the Golden Age, it is by exhibiting one's possessions from clothes, to art, to books, that aspects of a person's subjectivity become visible to others.[3] This was an era of collectionism. As the first collections arose, their curious and diverse nature pointed to the individual's desires. Their sum may not make the persons, but they may approximate their desires.

But let us return to the tale and its placement. Attempting to come to terms with this apparent narrative intrusion, one critic claims that we can look at it from the point of view of rhetoric. In classical rhetoric, the term ekphrasis was used to describe a pause in the narrative to describe an object. Thus, for Françoise Meltzer, the tale itself is such a pause, one that contains a number of objects for viewing.[4] Indeed, the tale is akin to a panting which is framed by the novel itself, much as the shield of Achilles in the Homeric epic is framed by the ocean.[5] Of course, the tale contains many objects, and such a collection might tell us something about the "actors" within it.

While the tale is an ekphrastic pause in the narrative that shows off a number of objects and their subjects, there is a second kind of pause, one that places the "collection" in a most unlikely place – it is a pause in Don Quixote's adventures, for he is not out in the world looking for foes, but resting at the inn. William Hogarth (1697–1764), who did a number of illustrations of *Don Quixote*, uses the stage-coach as a metaphor for life, and the inn as stopping places in our journey.[6] But it is a pause filled with different kinds of activity. Turning to Henry Fielding, an imitator of Cervantes, Hogarth depicts a country inn yard (see fig. 1) where much of the goings on in Cervantes' inns are replicated, such as in the bill that the rotund innkeeper presents to a well-dressed traveller who thinks it immoderate – recalling Don Quixote's refusal to pay his bills to the castle keeper. Hogarth also portrays the amorous farewell of traveller and chambermaid in back of the innkeeper and guest. She is not moved by her mistress's voice or her bell. Again we are reminded of the assignation of Maritornes and the muleteer, disrupted by the amorous Don Quixote, and the chaos that ensues with the arrival of the innkeeper, the law, etc. Indeed, Ronald Paulson defines the inn as one of the "basic metaphors of eighteenth-century fiction" (1984, 200). Cervantes, like Fielding and Hogarth, sees the inn as the gathering place where unfathomable contingencies and coincidences brought about by fortune take place. The wheel in Hogarth's print is certainly no coincidence – being Fortuna's device. One of the guests at the Cervantine inn enjoins others to be ready "acomodándoos a esperar mejor fortuna" [to expect better fortune] (1978, 1.29.360; 1998, 245).[7] And Cervantes, like his English counterparts, also sees the inn as a metaphor for *otium*. Paulson goes on to say, "The inn was also a place where inhibitions could be left behind or stripped away, true or new identities revealed" (1984, 200). Indeed, it is a place for solace and solitude, for storytelling and bragging, for coincidence and anagnorisis, for rowdiness and drinking, for gambling, and sexual license.

The inn is a place of revelry and a meeting place for travellers in the journey of life. It collects people, who themselves bring some of their objects of value. But as a stop in the journey of life, it can also become a moralizing scene, a *vanitas* that shows how all vanishes as the travellers, there for a brief time, soon depart. As such, the tale that is told at the Cervantine inn, with its ekphrastic quality and an ambience of abundance and fleeting pleasures, recalls a number of *vanitas* paintings in the

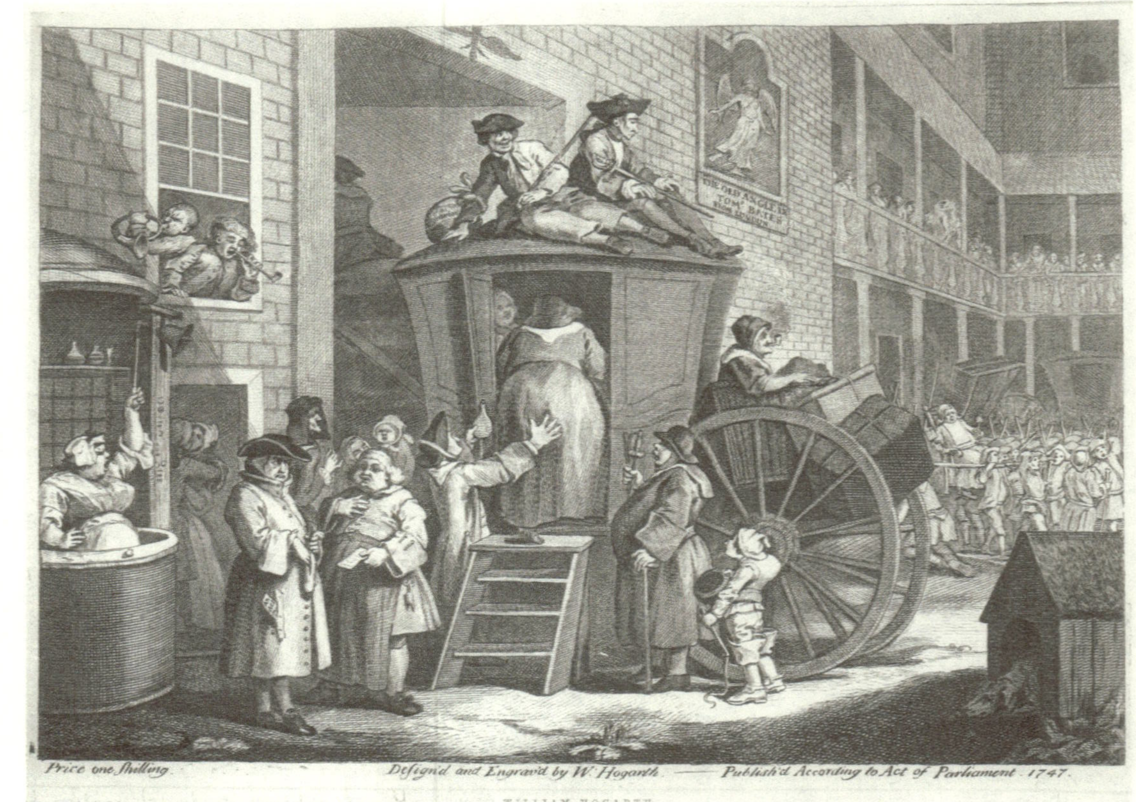


Figure 1 William Hogarth, *Country Inn Yard*, 1747. London. Snark / Art Resource, NY.

Netherlands and Spain. Discussing Antonio Pereda's *Allegory of Vanitas*, Steven Wagschal shows how it is replete with symbolic objects among which are the "flowers, gold coins, and skulls" (Wagschal 2005, 107).[8] (See fig. 2.) Of course, Pereda, in a baroque accumulation, creates a museum of the vanishing that includes not one but seven skulls and adds elements such as "the miniatures of deceased Hapsburg family members as well as a large cameo of Charles V, resting on top of the globe of the world, and a gold medallion of Caesar Augustus [to] attest to the transitory nature of fame and power, and the limits of empire" (Wagschal 2005, 114). One element that Wagschal had no reason to mention, and that has caught my attention, is the use of playing cards. Cards in themselves are a combination of verbal and visual, mixing numbers and letters with designs. As stated above, they can be construed as emblems, each with its own allegorical meaning. Daniel L. Heiple, who has also studied *vanitas* paintings, has used another of Pereda's works, *The Knight's Dream* (Sueño del caballero), in order to better understand certain references in the Spanish picaresque novel.[9] (See fig. 3.) The painting: "shows a sleeping man seated in a chair on the left with an angel behind him, displaying a banner which declares that the arrow of death comes quickly and is fatal. The table is strewn with symbols of transience ... In the front middle lies a deck of playing cards, with several individual cards turned face up" (Heiple 1993, 106). The two of coins, for example, shows a change in fortune for each coin is Fortuna's wheel, one pointing to prosperity and the other to adversity. In Quevedo's picaresque novel *El buscón*, the two of clubs is discarded for the two of coins. In other words, a worthless card is replaced by one of more value. Heiple shows a double meaning here – how the two of clubs (the two fingers of a thief or pick-pocket) is used as a metaphor for the *pícaro* who stealthily extracts a suit of coins from his victims. Benjamin J. Nelson reminds us that in nineteenth-century American literature, the two of clubs can also represent running-out-of-luck and death.[10]

Recalling a number of critics who have used cards or gambling metaphors to discuss *The Novel of the Curious Impertinent*, it seemed to me that the characters in the tale could be portrayed as gamblers: as theatrical gamblers who create new roles to win or accomplish their desires; and as artful gamblers who prize works of Italian Renaissance art concealed within the text and even model themselves after these paintings. Card playing is an apt metaphor for the circulation of objects in society, for merchandise that is bought and sold. As Enrique García Santo-Tomás states: "The cultural resonance of the gambler ... is a fascinating way of re-envisioning early modern urban culture in Spain. It is also a very

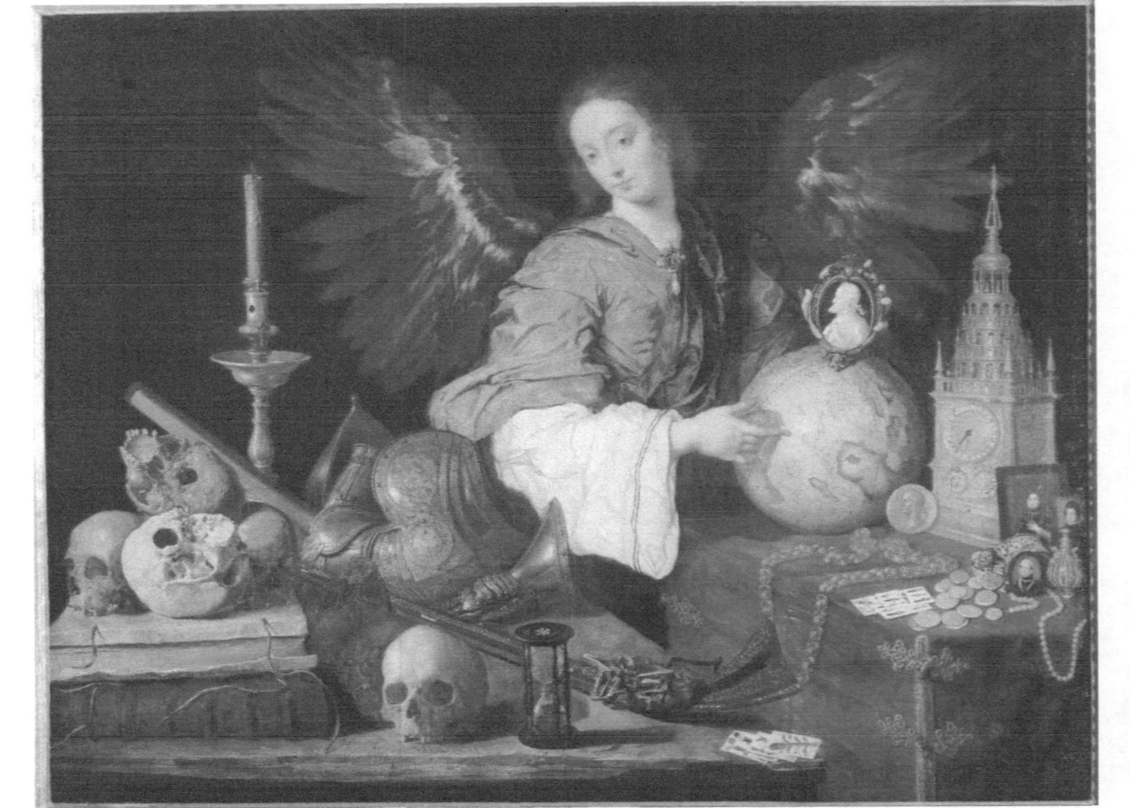

Figure 2 Antonio Pereda, *Allegory of Vanitas* (*Allegory of Fleeting Time*). *The Angel-Genius Holds a Portrait Cameo of Emperor Charles V.* Kunsthistoriches Museum, Vienna, Austria. Erich Lessing/ Art Resource, NY.

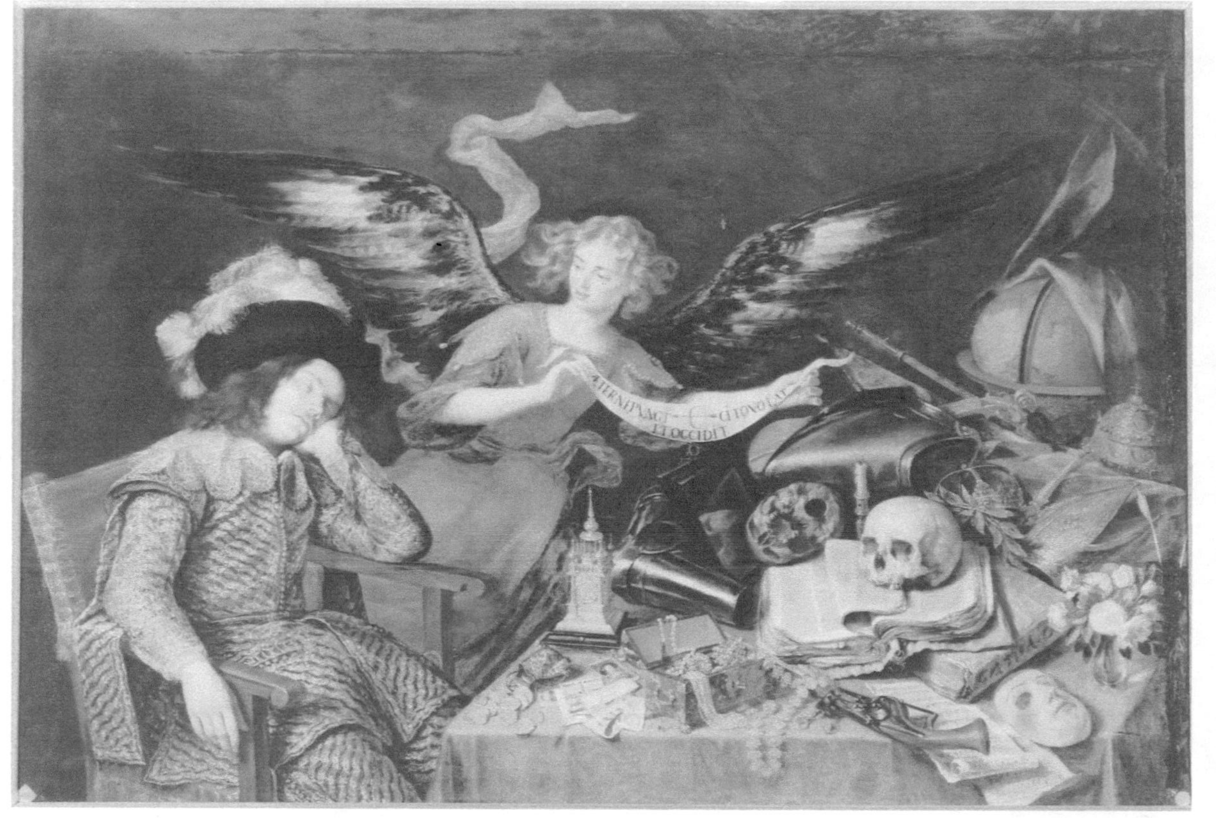

Figure 3 Antonio Pereda, *The Knight's Dream* [*Sueño del Caballero*], 1655. Real Academia de las Bellas Artes de San Fernando, Madrid, Spain. Erich Lessing / Art Resource, NY.

fruitful approach to rethink issues of materiality and visuality in Habsburg Madrid, as this was the time that witnessed the culmination of a long textual genealogy on the topic dating back to Arabic times" (2008, 149).[11] *The Novel of the Curious Impertinent* therefore can be viewed as an interpolated ekphrasis that contains within itself a museum of art. Characters in this museum tragically and playfully wager their life and their possessions in a game of cards – this impetus to gamble helps to explain Anselmo's strange desires and the other characters' willingness to enter his world or game.[12] Indeed, Cervantes is pointing out that this addictive role was the rule of the times: "everyone from the King on down was addicted" (Kennedy 1952, 296). And this is a tale told at an inn, a place for gambling and other such diversions and gratifications, as well as a location that recalls the fleeting nature of such pleasures and the surprises of Fortuna.

Although *Don Quixote* was first published by Juan de la Cuesta, the true editor of the work was Francisco de Robles, who signed the contract with Cervantes, paid for the printing, etc. Robles, who became Cervantes' editor through 1615, was known to have an illegal gambling house in Madrid, and some say it was frequented by Cervantes (Amezúa y Mayo 1951, 347).[13] We do know that Cervantes intersperses throughout his works numerous references to card games as well as the very specialized vocabulary of the gambler.[14] *The Novel of the Curious Impertinent*, as noted, is read at an inn, a location that often offered gambling as a form of entertainment.[15] In Willian Van Herp's seventeenth-century painting *Interior of an Inn with Card Players*, we witness a man winning a game with an ace of spades. While no one is seen playing cards in Cervantes' inn, they do talk about books. While the innkeeper thinks that a number of fictional works are historical, the priest explains that they are written "para entretener nuestros ociosos pensamientos; y así como se consienten en las repúblicas bien concertadas que haya juegos de ajedrez, de pelota y de trucos, para entretener" [for the amusement of our idle thoughts: and as, in well-instituted commonwealths, the games of chess, tennis, and billiards are permitted for entertainment] (1978, 1.32.397; 1998, 277). Thus, we are invited to read or listen to *The Novel of the Curious Impertinent* as a game – and I would add, as a card game. In Cervantes' tale Anselmo seems to shuffle the deck and start the game. David Quint asserts: "Male pride and rivalry have created a *game* of desire in which Camila is more than a pawn" (2003, 42). And yet, I would like to review all three characters (along with a fourth and seemingly less important figure) in this house of cards, and show that although Anselmo may have activated the game, it is Fortuna who holds all the cards – and let us remember that the figure of Fortuna is at the centre of Pereda's *Vanitas*. She is one of the major Arcana in the tarot.

Not only are there three main characters, but Cervantes carefully divides *The Novel of the Curious Impertinent* into three chapters, thus evoking the three acts of a Spanish Golden Age play. Indeed, it is quite clear that he follows the precepts of Lope de Vega's *New Art of Writing Plays* (*Arte nuevo de hacer comedias*). Chapter 33 presents the *caso*, the subject matter; the complications of plot reach their climax in chapter 34; and the action swiftly moves to a conclusion in the following chapter, bringing to a tragic end all the agonists in the love triangle.[16] The theatrical quality of the tale is further enhanced by metadrama, the play within the play, and there are at least three such doublings. The first play is created by Anselmo's curiosity, as he directs Lotario to tempt his wife as he becomes the spectator / voyeur. The second is written, directed, and acted by Camila in order to fully deceive her audience (her husband Anselmo).[17] These doublings are folded into a third play, that of Fortuna. Let us look, then, at some of the main mnemonic images that hold together this three-act play and the three metadramas in which fortune is figured as a deck of cards which she shuffles, assigning each character his or her suit, role, and image.

Anselmo, although seemingly happily married, asks his best friend Lotario to test Camila's virtue. Lotario is averse to testing his best friend's wife and reminds him how Rinaldo, in the *Orlando furioso*, rejected the test of drinking wine from a magical cup (1978, 1.33, 407; 1998, 282), thus bringing us face to face with the first major model and image – the golden goblet, adorned with precious stones.[18] The man asked to test it almost inevitably spills the wine, which shows neither his clumsiness nor his Dionysian debaucheries, but his wife's infidelity. This test, as Diana de Armas Wilson explains, has a long pedigree from the Bible to Arthurian tales.[19] She concludes that "it's best not to test, since women traditionally fail the cup-test – no matter who's drinking. That there is no similar drink to expose the men they have lain with seems to have concerned neither the Lord nor Lotario" (1987, 17).

The golden goblet signals the presentation of the *caso*, the subject matter of the tale.[20] Needless to say, this goblet foregrounds ekphrasis (its description in Ariosto).[21] It is also linked to *vanitas*.[22] As Anselmo metaphorically holds the cup, we envision future spilling, and the entrance of Fortuna into the action. Once Fortuna is activated, she will rule the game. We learn in chapter 33 of "la suerte que las cosas guiaba" [fortune, which directed matters otherwise] (1978, 1.33.415; 1998, 293) and are warned in chapter 34 that "volvió Fortuna su rueda" [fortune turned her wheel]

(1978, 1.34.437; 1998, 313). It is hard to ascertain where Fortuna is looking in Pereda's *Vanitas* painting. She could indeed be glancing at the cards. Anselmo, as the leading male figure holding a cup, may be envisioned as the king of cups in a card game, thus doubling the visual and prophetic impact of the scene with the symbolic tarot and their cartomancy. Ronald Friis posits that Cervantes learned tarot divination while in the service of Cardinal Acquaviva in Rome.[23] Furthermore, there were numerous Spanish works which related card games to divination and allegory.[24] Two Golden Age writers, Luque Fajardo and Francisco de la Torre, through their description of the different cards, allow us to glimpse deeper into Anselmo's actions. Discussing the suit of cups, Torre notes the "conformidad del vino y del amor" [conformity of wine and love] (1654, 85), showing both to be "ardores importunes" [pestering desires] (1654, 85). Thus, the test of the goblet serves to inflame the passions. For Luque Fajardo, cups are "vasos en que se recoge la sangre de los lastimados, y muertos en el juego" [recipients that collect the blood of those wounded and killed in gambling] (1503, 239v). Anselmo will certainly be hurt in his deadly game. Cartomancy predicts passion, blood, and death.[25]

Soon after the goblet is exhibited, Lotario comes up with a number of similes and metaphors to dissuade his friend from this dangerous endeavour. Using the diamond, the ermine, the mirror of crystal, relics, and the beautiful garden, Lotario's speech glitters with visual images as it gathers momentum, turning finally to some verses from a play that he happens to remember. This mnemonic feat confirms that we are approaching our second memory image. The last two lines declaimed by Lotario read as follows: "que si hay Dánaes en el mundo, / hay pluvias de oro también" [Wherever Danaes abound / There Golden Showers will make their way] (1978, 1.33.409; 1998, 288). We are now at the second moment in the text, the pointer to complication in the action. Danaë, locked up in an inaccessible tower by her father, is just another way of viewing the relationship between Anselmo and Camila. The father in the myth and husband in Cervantes' tale keep the woman as precious property, away from others. The world of prophecy and divination is again present: Danaë is supposedly incarcerated because of a prophecy.[26] Anselmo, however, wishes to validate the misogynistic prediction that all women will be unfaithful.

It is curious that these lines alluding to Danaë have remained nearly invisible in readings of the Cervantes' interpolation. The text hints at a possible model by placing them within a play. One of the most famous ekphrastic passages from classical theatre appears in the works of Terence.[27] In his *Eunouchus*, Chaerea after his encounter with Pamphila explains what occurred: "She sits in her room, in the middle of all this bustle inspecting a picture on the wall. A famous subject: Jupiter launching a shower of gold into Danaë's lap. I began to inspect it myself. It repaid attention. Encouraging: here was a god long ago, who'd played almost the same game ... I might be only human, but couldn't I do the same?" (1992, III.3, vv. 584–8, 591). A painting has transformed the lover's intentions; it has impelled him to rape Pamphila as she sleeps. While a god can force a mortal in antique mythology, a citizen can enjoy a slave in antique culture.[28] This would not only be acceptable practice, but a good omen since, according to Michel Foucault: "the word *soma*, which designates the body, also refers to riches and possessions; whence the possible equivalence between the 'possession' of a body and the possession of wealth" (1986, 3:27). Chaerea's action, albeit not a dream, turns out to be a good omen. At the play's denouement, Pamphila is revealed as the long-lost daughter of a citizen of Athens, and thus Chaerea can court her and eventually enjoy her body and her family's wealth.

Cervantes transforms and problematizes the hierarchical and gender relations found in the classical text. Although Lotario has no right to Camila as a married woman, he still presents her in terms of Danaë and of Pamphila. Although Lotario denies it, he wishes to be Jupiter and Chaerea. These two characters arrive at their enjoyment in opposing ways. While the god's metamorphosis is based on power, Chaerea's transformation feigns weakness – he is disguised as an enslaved eunuch. Although Lotario may wish to be Jupiter, he acts as a Chaerea. Anselmo, however, impels him to be Jupiter. The shower of gold is transformed into all the golden coins given to Lotario by Anselmo in order to seduce Camila (1978, 1.33.414–15; 1998, 292). Thus, Lotario, as the bearer of coins can be viewed as the knight of coins in the playing cards, as someone subservient to the king of cups. Indeed the way Anselmo asks his friend to shower these coins upon Camila / Danaë recalls how rich merchants scatter their coins in card games. The image of the gambler as a Jupiter is found, for example, in a poem by Bartolomé Leonardo de Argensola. Here, Spanish players so press a Genoese that "en la lluvia de Dánae lo convierte" [in Danaë's shower he is transformed] (1975, 101; v. 234).[29] Lotario as a doubling of Jupiter appears subservient to Anselmo, the provider of coins, while Camila / Danaë is the recipient. But as events unfold, Anselmo will lose his position of power, becoming the dupe in this love triangle. Like Chaerea, Lotario seems to triumph following the example of Terence.

Needless to say, this ekphrastic example, became, for Christian writers, an *exemplum* of pagan immorality. Augustine often cited the passage from

Terence "to demonstrate the evil effects of lascivious pictures" (Ginzburg 1989, 77).[30] During the Spanish Golden Age, Juan de Mariana, for example, provides us with a long moralizing discussion of Terence's play and how modern plays which exhibit such "paintings" can have a deleterious effect on the morality of the audience. He dutifully refers the reader to Augustine (1854, 434). But, by railing against this image, theologians and moralists imbued it with a certain allure and talismanic quality.

In Spain, it was Titian's *Danaë* that became controversial.[31] The Italian canvas (see fig. 4) was presented to Philip II while he was still crown prince, and is usually dated 1552–3; this was the first of two *Danaës* painted by the Venetian artist.[32] One may wonder at the artist's choice – giving the prince the most tantalizing female image from the pagan world.[33] During his reign (in 1589), Juan de Pineda would recall the Danaë in Terence and place her painting among Tiberius's lustful contemplations.[34] Pineda would warn of "tan gran pecado de pintores desalmados, y el descuido de los príncipes que no castigan cosa tan prejudicial en el reino" [such a great sin in painters without a soul and the neglect of princes who do not punish a thing so prejudicial to their kingdom] (1964, 66). Was Philip II's erotic *camerino* replete with Titian's mythologies to be equated with that of one of the most detested Roman emperors? It is true that in later years Philip asked for more religious figures. But the fact remains that he, like emperors of old, could view the forbidden.[35]

Of course, such exhibits can always be rationalized in terms of Platonic allegories or political mandates. Titian's painting could represent Philip as a new Jupiter, endowing him with a talisman to conquer all – in this sense, woman and empire are but one. After all, Jupiter was often used by the Habsburgs as an image of imperial might. But the political implications certainly recede at the pagan violence unleashed here. Titian easily outdoes his competitors with a "partly open space" that "denies the basis of the story" (incarceration in a tower) and thus, according to Leonard Barkan, "dramatizes the intrusion via metamorphosis of pagan nature into familiar domesticity" (1986, 190). Barkan also emphasizes sexual longing: "The bulk of the golden shower directs itself toward Danaë's sexual organs" (1986, 190). In many ways, Barkan's interpretation coincides with Terence's representation. And it is through Terence's eunuch that Lotario can appear harmless to Camila. But, instead of the erotic violence of Terence and Titian, Cervantes presents us with a consensual act.[36]

While Titian has foregrounded the *raptus* of paganism, he has also provided a Renaissance viewer with a certain demystification since the golden shower can be viewed as "literal wealth for which the hag can compete

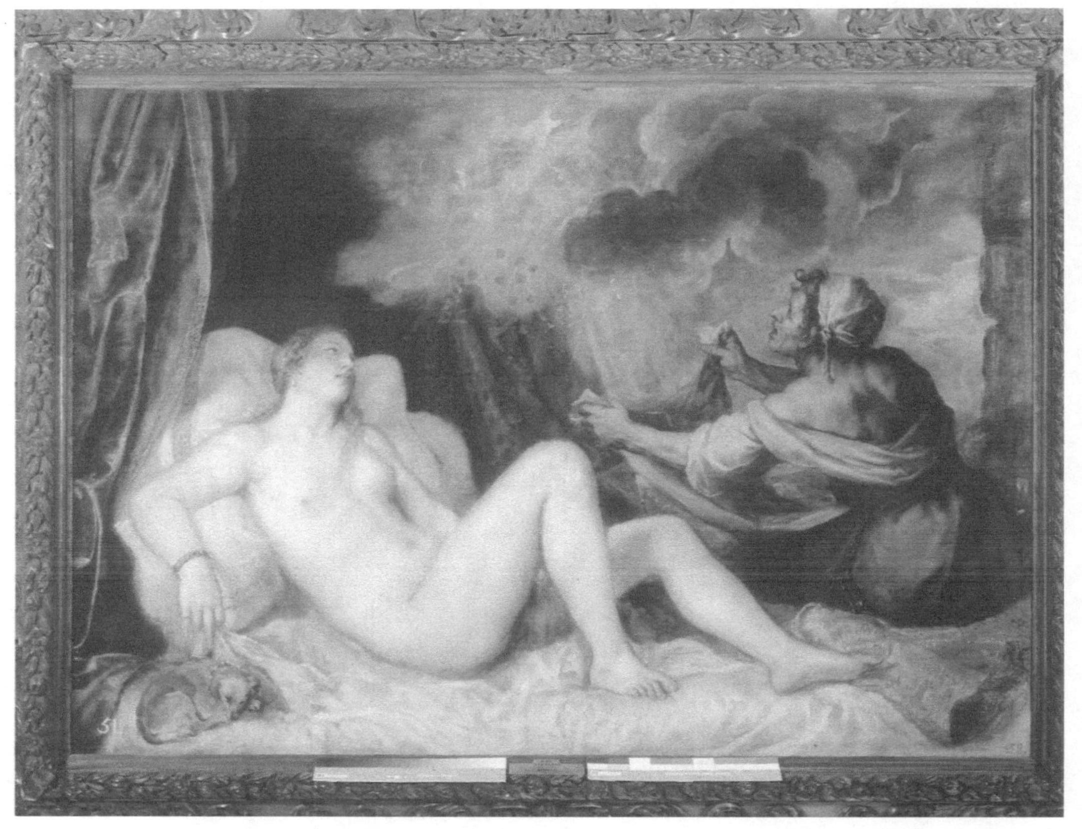

Figure 4 Titian, *Danaë*, 1553–4. Museo del Prado, Madrid, Spain. Scala / Art Resource, NY.

with Danaë" (Barkan 1986, 193). In this sense, Philip could view his painting as admonition against the lure of new riches and new lands. In Cervantes' tale, the political undertones are also muted since the hag is transformed into Leonela, who does not seek golden coins but the sexual treasures of a lover she introduces into Camila's home. It would seem, then, that this second image, in spite of political and moral allegories, enjoins pagan enjoyment in its talismanic and alluring presence.[37] If Anselmo is the king of cups, then Camila must be the queen, whose sexual goblet receives the riches of her two lovers. And yet, Fortuna's wheel, forever present in the tarot, will turn even as the lovers delight in amorous mendacity. After all, Titian's painting is not all delight. For some, the shower of gold is menacing and the servant's greed points to unrestrained passions that must be held in check. Long before Barkan, Erwin Panofsky had viewed Titian's golden shower with "dark foreboding" (1969, 150).

Jealousy menaces with unravelling the game and Camila must intervene to preserve the status quo. Together with Lotario and Leonela, she composes a play that will deceive her husband. As Anselmo, the audience, hides behind a tapestry, she receives Lotario, rejecting his past and present advances and his coins: "Cuando tus muchas promesas y mayores dádivas fueron de mi creídas ni admitidas?" [When were your many promises and greater presents believed or accepted?] (1978, 1.34.433; 1998, 310). Holding a dagger, she seems to want to kill him, but when she feigns and fails, she wounds herself. The play is nothing more than an imitation of the ancient story. As Camila herself admits, it derives from "Lucrecia de quien dicen que se mató sin haber cometido error alguno" [Lucretia of whom it is said that she killed herself without committing any fault] (1978, 1.34.430; 1998, 307).

Her image became commonplace in early modern Europe, as Marcantonio Raimondi disseminated a print of Raphael's drawing *The Death of Lucretia* (ca. 1510–11) (see fig. 5). It was imitated by many other artists, including Guido Reni. The popularity of these prints and paintings, according to Richard Spear, had to do with "the iniquitous excitement derived from watching women suffer in extremis" (Spear 1997, 86). But, of course, Camila only pretends to follow Lucretia's example. Hers is truly a fiction that is meant to deceive her husband as she manages the dagger: "y guiando su punta por parte que pudiese herir no profundamente, se la entró y escondió por más arriba de la islilla del lado izquierdo, junto al hombro, y luego se dejó caer en el suelo, como desmayada" [and directing the point to a part where it might give but a slight wound, she stabbed herself above the breast, near the left shoulder, and presently fell to the ground as in a swoon] (1978, 1.33.434; 1998, 311).

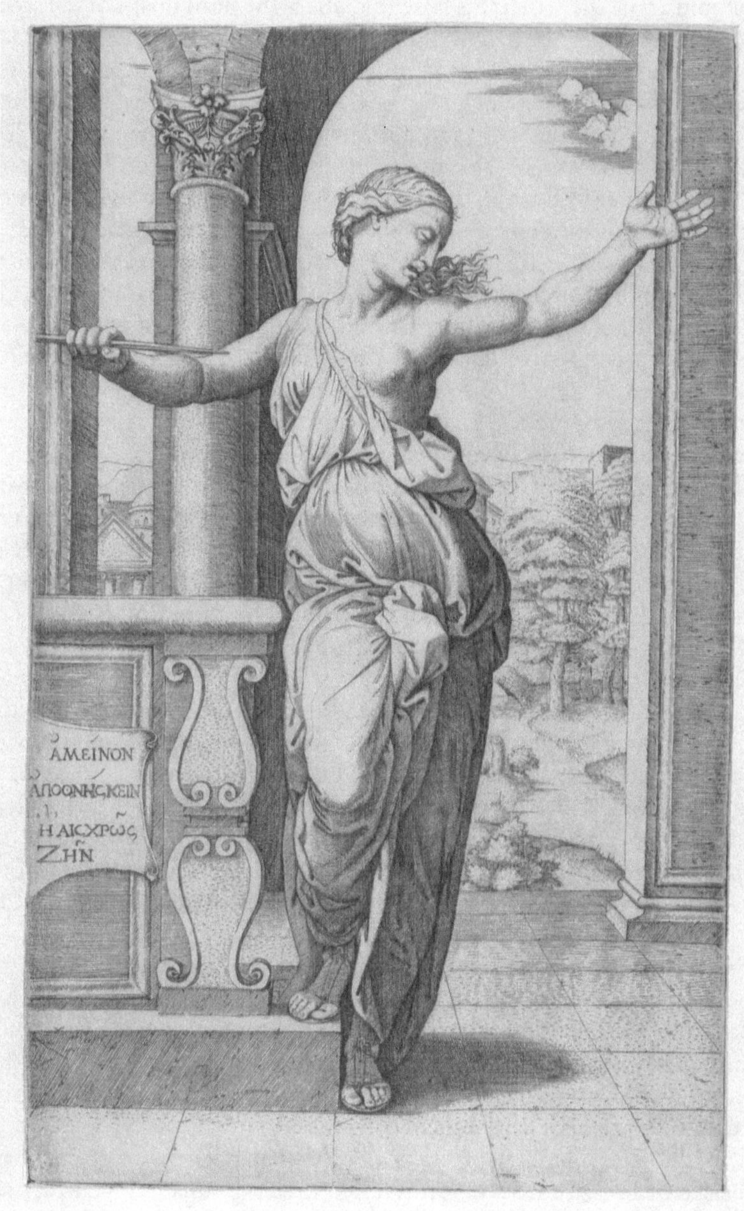


Figure 5 Marcantonio Raimondi, *Death of Lucretia*. Kupferstichkabinett, Staatliche Museen, Berlin, Germany / Art Resource, NY.

I would argue then, that this false Lucretia is the third image of the work, the one that reaches the height of complication in the third act. Camila, as a Raphaelesque Lucretia, is not the queen of cups, but the queen of swords. Three problems present themselves with this identification. The first is that Camila is carrying a dagger, not a sword. But, let us reconsider. The four suits of cards were Arabic in origin (coins, cups, swords, and batons), and as they entered Europe they acquired new shapes and even different identifications in different regions.[38] Spain and Italy remained closest to the Arabic cards. The Italian swords had curved blades like the scimitars used in Egypt by the Mameluks. In Spain, they turned into smaller blades that seemed like daggers. Thus, Camila's dagger fits very well with the queen of swords. Newer decks, however, have changed daggers back to swords. When Gustave Doré, in the nineteenth century, drew the scene where Camila stabs herself, he included a sword instead of a dagger. Could he have been influenced by the playing cards of his period?

The second problem, as previously stated, is that the Spanish deck did not have queens. But this is not to say that Spanish writers and players were not keenly aware of this lack, and the possibility of using foreign cards that would include this figure. Lope de Vega, for example, speaks of "Una reina de oros, / carta nueva en la baraja" [A queen of coins / a new card in the game] (cited in Étienvre 1990, 305).

The third would be to ascertain the meaning of this card, which is not explained in Spanish treatises against gambling or other manuals. Asserting that "cartonomancy flourished in the Renaissance and Baroque periods," Heiple finds that modern readings accord with early ones (1993, 112).[39] Thus, the queen of swords is commonly believed to represent the capacity to solve a problem. This is indeed what Camila does in the work, rejecting the patriarchal tower in favour of a freedom that lets her enjoy the favours of her chosen god. And yet, the game will fail and the comic play will turn into tragedy. After all, as a woman, Camila cannot change the Spanish cards or her fortune since woman (the suit of queens) is absent from the game. Second, she uses the sword or dagger in the only way she can, as a trick or lie. Thus, if the card were to exist in Spain, it would be reversed, negating the possibility of solving the problem.

We are still missing the card that signals the denouement, the fall from fortune.[40] This fourth card should belong to the one suit we have yet to find in the tale. The suit of clubs is often considered lowly and base. Francisco de la Torre y Sevil, for example, dividing suits into genres, finds clubs to represent the comic or burlesque style. And it should be recalled that it is also associated with *pícaros* and thieves. Even when an exalted figure is depicted, such as the king of clubs, it tends to acquire a negative connotation.[41] In Cervantes' text, Leonela, the maid, belongs to the lower classes in a hierarchical society, and thus can be equated with clubs. As in countless *comedias*, she mirrors in a comic key her mistress's actions. She thinks that she can act with impunity and bring her lover home, imitating Camila. But she does not have Camila's wits in this case. She thus becomes key to the *peripeteia* that leads to the fateful end, since she escapes from Camila's home believing that she will be punished, having been caught by Anselmo in an assignation. Her bad luck brings about the demise of the other characters, and she thus becomes the ominous two of clubs, pointer to ill-luck and death. Once the king of cups (Anselmo) starts the game and provides the initial prophecy, none seem able to change it. Lotario accepts his role as the bearer of coins, Camila as queen of swords cannot reverse the terms of fortune, and Leonela reveals her hand, and exposes her bluff and her malefic card, the two of clubs.

Barry Ife describes the approaching end metaphorically: "The house of cards will come down, blown apart by social pressures beyond the control of the protagonists" (2005, 680). For me, it is more than a metaphor since cards in the tale (the king of cups, the knight of coins, the queen of swords, and the two of clubs) are representations of characters who have become extreme gamblers, who have bet everything they have, even their life, in a losing game. It may be no coincidence that the simulated play of daggers ends in the tragic play of swords, as Lotario dies battling those responsible for the sack of Rome in 1527.[42] During the sack, the imperial troops of Charles V and their cohorts raped and pillaged, and stole many of the artistic monuments of the city.[43] They then moved to Naples where the army faced the French, headed by Lautrec. Lotario would then have died in a losing battle against Charles V's forces, but a battle that held the high moral ground, if there was such a thing in the Italian wars.

As for the king of cups, Anselmo, he perishes while he writes of his poisonous draught, having long ago prepared the conclusion of his story. His admonitions vie with the play of fortune, attempting to grasp for authorship and also a moral high ground as legacy. The invisible queen of swords (she does not belong in the Spanish deck) remains just that, cloistered and dying of melancholy – but this humour belongs to the visionary and we might view her invisibility as a vision of future deliverance for her gender. This tragic museum, then, is filled with objects that are desired, admired, used, misused, circulated, and discarded. These objects belong to those who would defend art, who would write in search of fame, and who would gamble with their very existence. *The Novel of the Curious*

*Impertinent* is a game ruled by art and fortune where we discover the false eunuch, the enraptured Danaë, the theatrical Lucretia, the metamorphic Jupiter, the king as voyeur, the bluffing maid, and Fortuna with her roulette or wheel. The power of these images beckons readers to view, play, and gamble at deciphering them again and again.

## NOTES

1 In part 2, Sansón Carrasco claims that readers criticize it "por no ser de aquel lugar" [for having no relation to that place] (1978, 2.3.63; 1998, 488). I use the Jarvis translation of *Don Quixote*. Translations of other texts are my own.

2 Thomas Pavel emphasizes that Anselmo's desires are vague and useless. They go against his own interests and he does not understand them (2003, 123). Thus, Pavel compares them to the strange desires of the Princess of Cleves in Madame de La Fayette's novel (2003, 129).

3 On baroque theatricality, see Orozco Díaz.

4 Françoise Meltzer has argued that "ecphrasis may be seen as an earlier version of the intercalated story' (1987, 22).

5 I have labelled this specific device as an interpolated ekphrasis (2005b, 22).

6 The poet's adage, All the world's a stage,
Has stood the test of each revolving age;
Another simile perhaps will bear,
'Tis a Stage Coach, where all must pay the fare;
Where each his entrance and his exit makes,
And o'er life's rugged road his journey takes.' (83)

From *Times of the Day*. In *The Works of William Hogarth in a Series of Engravings: With Descriptions, and a Comment on their Moral Tendency by the Rev. John Trusler*. See The Gutenberg Project at www.gutenberg.org/files/22500/22500-h/22500-h.htm.

7 It is Cardenio who makes this statement. After all, he has emerged from the verge of madness in Sierra Morena and is now closer to seeing his wishes fulfilled.

8 Wagschal foregrounds the study of Norbert Schneider in the analysis of *vanitas* (2005, 76–87).

9 Heiple describes the painting thus: "It shows a sleeping man seated in a chair on the left with an angel behind him, displaying a banner which declares that the arrow of death comes quickly and is fatal. The table is strewn with symbols of transience: books, a skull, flowers, a carnival mask, jewels, coins, and a

small clock. In the front middle lies a deck of playing cards, with several individual cards turned face up, showing the two of coins on top" (1993, 112).

10 See, for example, Bret Harte's *The Outcasts of Poker Flat.*

11 In another essay published the following year, Enrique García Santo-Tomás has pointed out that card games have not received the attention they should: "No se ha llevado a cabo tampoco una reflexión a fondo sobre el efecto que pudo tener la representación de los juegos de naipes en la percepción de lo geográfico ... o lo genérico" [There has not been a thoughtful and in-depth consideration of the effect of the representation of card games in the perception of geography and gender] (2009, 13).

12 As García Santo-Tomás reminds us, the gambling houses of the times "were frequently associated with violence and death" (2008, 150).

13 This and other factors have led Jean-Pierre Étienvre to ask the question: "¿Era él tahúr de vocablos ... jugador de naipes continuo y desenfrenado?' [Was the master at wordplay ... a constant and unrestrainable gambler?] (1990, 34). Robles was born in Madrid around 1564 and died in 1623. He bought the rights of *Las novelas ejemplares* and *Don Quixote*.

14 Cervantes' bookseller, Francisco de Robles, who printed the *Quixote* and the *Novelas ejemplares*, had a gaming house in Madrid. Cervantes lists a number of card games in *Rinconete y Cortadillo* and in *Pedro de Urdemalas*. There are also numerous of references to cards in *El coloquio de los perros* and *El rufián dichoso*. Étienvre also notes their presence in the *Viaje del Parnaso* and in *Persiles y Sigismunda* "aunque a nivel estrictamente metafórico" [even though only at a metaphorical level] (1990, 37). There are a number of references to cards in *Don Quixote*, but mainly in Part Two. For example Altisidora curses the knight as he departs the palace of the duke and the duchess, wishing him bad luck in cards:

Si jugares al reinado,
Los cientos, o la primera,
Los reyes huyan de ti;
Ases ni sietes no veas (1978, 2.57.468)

Jarvis's translation deviates somewhat from the original, but preserves an allusion to a card game:

If, brisk and gay,
Thu sitt'st to play
At Ombre or at Chess,
May ne'er Spadill
Attend thy will,
Nor luck thy movements bless (1998, 837)

15 Within the *Curioso* we have a number of games, including the four "s" of lovers as well as the alphabet of love as told by Leonela (1978, 1.34.424–5, 1998, 302).

16 Lope conceives of the third act as having two parts – the extreme complication represented in the first half and a rapid denouement in the second.

17 On Cervantes' theatricality, see Jill Syverson-Stork. David Quint asserts: "Camila playacts before the hidden Anselmo, but she is also an unwitting actress in a play that is not of her devising and whose author remains hidden from her to the very end" (2003, 40).

18 Thomas Greene has explained that the myths of origins provided by authors for their texts represent but one obvious reading, while the "unconfessed genealogical line may prove to be as nourishing as the visible" (1982, 19). Greene is slightly uncomfortable with this insight, arguing that "this proliferation does not obscure the special status of that root work the work privileges by its self-constructed myth of origins" (1982, 19). Perhaps because it is too visible, the first image or model is often set aside.

19 "The father of all these secular cup-tests, as it turns out, is Moses. As spokesman for the Lord in the Old Testament, Moses articulates the so-called law of jealousies in Numbers 5:11–31" (de Armas Wilson 1987, 17).

20 Comparing Ariosto's text with Cervantes', Barry W. Ife asserts that "the overall impression is one of difference" (2005, 674). On the other hand, see the very thoughtful analysis of Cervantes and Ariosto in Marina Scordilis Brownlee (1985, 220–37).

21 This is a metadescriptive ekphrasis, "based on a textual description of a work of art which may or may not exist" (de Armas 2006, 22).

22 In Ariosto, the sorceress Melissa tries to tempt her host with the cup. When this fails, she has him disguise himself and court his own wife. He now offers Melissa's magic cup to Rinaldo.

23 "The first instance is in 1569 during his visits to the Vatican as envoy to Cardinal Acquaviva; ironically, during this time, the Vatican's libraries, frescoes, and vaults represented the world's premiere forum for Hermeneutic texts. One account mentions a strong resemblance between tarot images and frescoes in palaces such as Schifanoia in Ferrara" (Friis 1998, 47).

24 In the fifteenth century Fernando de la Torre creates a poem with 48 stanzas which correspond to the 48 cards in the Spanish deck. Each tells its allegorical significance: "El poeta imagina unas rigurosas correspondencias entre los amores, los colores, y los palos de la baraja" [The poet imagines a rigorous correspondence between love, colours and the suits in the deck of cards] (Étienvre 1990, 17). This work may have appealed to Cervantes since it portrays a crazed gambler who runs away from learning, but imagines books

everywhere he attempts to escape, even in the water and in the air. His castles in the air are not far removed from Don Quixote's (or Anselmo's) imagination. In Francisco de la Torre y Sevil's *Entretenimiento de las musas en esta baraja nueva de versos* (1654), the four suits are related to genres: "A los oros corresponden los asuntos sacros; a las espadas, los asuntos heroicos; a las copas, los asuntos líricos; a los bastos, los asuntos burlescos" [Coins corresponds to sacred matters; swords to heroic subjects; cups to lyric topics; and wands to the comic] (Étienvre 1990, 17). Each section contains poems on the subject. We discover Charles V under swords (Torre 1654, 49) and Celestina under wands (Torre 1654, 123). A moral reading is found in Diego del Castillo's *Tratado muy útil en reprobación de los juegos* (1528) (Étienvre 1990, 320). To these, Heiple adds numerous references to foretelling in works by Marcelino da Forli and Matteo Boiardo (Heiple 1993, 108–9).

25 In Lope de Vega's *La desdichada Estefanía* the "rey de copas' [king of cups] is mentioned in Act 3, in a conversation between Mudarra and Isabel, but it serves only as a pun on drinking, and does not seem to have allegorical / prophetic significance (1975, vv. 2372–6).

26 The oracle foretells that Acrisius would be killed by his grandson. To prevent this from happening (and from having a grandson), Acrisius incarcerates his only daughter. However, when she has a son, Perseus, Acrisius sets them adrift upon the waters.

27 While this writer of comedies survived the Middle Ages through textbooks for learning Latin, during the Renaissance he became a worthy subject of imitation by playwrights. His popularity continued during the Spanish Golden Age, where he again was used as a manual for learning Latin and as a writer worthy of imitation. The 1577 translation into Spanish by Simón Abril "is printed in double face with the Latin original … to serve as an aid to learning Latin" (Beardsley 1970, 54, #96). Lope de Vega, Cervantes' rival, at times spoke against him. Together with Plautus, he places him under lock and key in his *Arte nuevo de hacer comedias*, and in *Lo fingido verdadero*, he has the emperor Diocletian reject both Plautus and Terence as being too old and worn. This may be an ironic passage since the text cited by the Roman emperor, the *Andria*, was the first ever produced during the Renaissance, in Florence in 1476. It was so prized by Italian playwrights that it was also translated by both Ariosto and Machiavelli.

28 In his *History of Sexuality*, Michel Foucault explains how even in dreams the sexual actor must play his role as social actor. Thus, a favourable dream would show, for example, a citizen sexually penetrating a slave (1986, 3.32–3).

29 On the image of Danaë in Argensola, see de Armas (2000, 190–2).

30 "Hence the young profligate in Terence … accepts this as authoritative precedent for his own licentiousness, and boasts that he is an imitator of God"

(Augustine 1950, 46). The example continued to be used in the Renaissance, from the Dominican Catarino Politi to Johannes Molanus. Ginzburg explains how Molanus used the example in 1570 to warn against images that incite lust, while Politi in 1542 was more interested in the efficacy of images – they could arouse religious fervour or erotic desire (1989, 77).

31 Before Titian, Correggio executed a *Danaë* in Rome (1530–2). There were copies made of Titian's *Danaë*. In the *Casos prodigiosos y cueva encantada* by Juan de Piña, there is a description of Don Antonio de Sotomayor's house in El Espinar. There one finds "una galería tan rica y adornadas de pinturas del Tiziano y de los más excelentes pinceles" [a rich and adorned gallery of paintings by Titian and by the most excellent of painters] (cited in Vosters 1990, 154). Piña describes Titian's *Tarquin and Lucretia* and the *Danaë*. Vosters surmises: "Quizá poseyese copias de dichas pinturas" [Perhaps he owned copies of said paintings] (1990, 154).

32 For the date of the first *Danaë*, see Pedrocco (2000, 222). The second was painted in Rome for Cardinal Alessandro Farnese (1545–6), where the model for Danaë is the cardinal's mistress (Talvacchia 1999, 46). Some critics claim that the mistress was named Angela and is "a relative of Signora Camilla" (Robertson 1992, 72); others claim it was Camilla Pisana, a brothel keeper and famed courtesan (Santore 1991, 415). If the latter is true and Cervantes was aware of it, then the link Camilla / Camila may be quite significant.

33 Phillip also inherited Titian's *Tantalus* – but this was not initially given to him.

34 "tenía su aposento lleno de pinturas carnalísimas para con su vista y contemplación se provocar a lujurias" [he had his chamber filled with highly erotic paintings for him to see and contemplate which causes lust] (1964, 65).

35 "But it seems that Philip's 'camerino,' the reconstruction of which has been much discussed … was never realized, since when they arrived in Spain the canvases were placed in different locations, to be brought together only early in the seventeenth century" (Pedrocco 2000, 222).

36 Indeed, Camila's newly awakened desire may derive in part from Terence, where Pamphila looks with longing at the painting of Jupiter and Danaë.

37 Even Giulio Camillo, in his magical *L'Idea del theatro* at least twice points to Jupiter's golden shower as "buona fortuna" [good fortune] (1991, 29, 80).

38 The French, for example, developed diamonds (coins), clubs (batons), hearts (cups), and spades (swords).

39 Heiple shows that "the meanings of the cards must have been somewhat common, for there are two seventeenth-century paintings that feature a pack of cards as an element of their iconology" (1993, 112). As noted, he discusses Antonio de Pereda's *El sueño del caballero* (1640) "with several individual cards turned face up, showing the two of coins on top" (1993, 112). He also

points to Juan Valdés de Leal's *Allegory of Vanity* (1660) with another two of coins on top of a deck of cards. This card always represents change. Pereda also shows the ace of wands, which also appears in Velázquez's *Riña ante la embajada de España*. Heiple does not mention the earlier Pereda painting.

40 Before drawing the card, the tale is suddenly interrupted at the beginning of chapter 35 when Sancho bursts in claiming that Don Quixote is battling with the giant Pandafilando (1978, 1.35.437; 1998, 313). It turns out that the knight has mistaken some wineskins for giants. Their blood is nothing but wine, something that the innkeeper is not too happy about. What we have here is a comic interlude (*entremés*). Indeed Cervantes was the author of a number of such short comic works performed in the theatres between acts. Although they often have nothing to do with the play, at times they parallel its subject matter. The spilling of the wine here recalls Ariosto's test which becomes in the story the testing of Camila's faithfulness. It is an anticipatory spill, coming shortly before Anselmo will find out that he has failed the test, that he has indeed spilled the wine from the cup before drinking it. The interlude also parallels the main action in that Don Quixote now assumes the role of a playing card; fighting with his sword he can be seen as the knight of swords. The spilling of wine may save Princess Micomicona, but it serves as prelude to the fall of the queen of swords, Camila.

41 See Moreto's play, *El lindo don Diego*. Here, the maid Beatriz consults the cards to learn the future and discovers "o mentirá el rey de bastos / o no ha de querer casarse" [the king of clubs will eitheir lie / or will not want to get married] (vv. 2581–2). The mock-hero, Don Diego thus becomes a king of clubs.

42 "en una batalla que en aquel tiempo dio monsieur de Lautrec al Gran Capitán Gonzalo Fernández de Córdoba en el reino" [in a battle fought about that time between Monsieur de Lautrec, and the Great Captain Goncalo Hernandez of Cordova, in the Kingdom of Naples] (1978, 1.35.446; 1998, 321). For some critics the battle mentioned in Cervantes' tale is that of Ceriñola in 1503, when Lautrec was just beginning his career. However, Diego Clemencín believed that Cervantes is referring to 1527 when Lautrec became the French commander at the time that the Prince of Orange led Charles V's forces (Cervantes 1833, 2:89). In February of 1528, the force, "laden with gold and loot, descended on Naples" (Chastel 1983, 35). Even though Lotario died in battle, the imperial army prevailed and the French were defeated. If the historical circumstance of Lotario's death is correct, then the mention of the Gran Capitán is an anachronism, which points once again to the mutability of fortune, since he came to be shunned by Charles V, who feared his fame. Given the historical references, the tale takes place either around 1502 or around 1527. In either case, there are inconsistencies. If the

*Danaë* painting points to Titian, then there is anachronism since it was done in 1552–3; and, if the tale refers to Pineda's attack on Philip's erotic *camerino*, then the tale must be placed in the 1580s.

43 "The most astonishing piece of fraudulence was the theft of the papal tapestries. Woven ten years before from Raphael's cartoons, they were intended to be used on state occasions in the Sistine Chapel" (Chastel 1983, 97).

## WORKS CITED

Amezúa y Mayo, Agustín G. de. 1951. "Cómo se hacía un libro en nuestro Siglo de Oro." In *Opúsculos histórico-literarios*, 1:331–73. Madrid: Consejo Superior de Investigaciones Científicas.

Argensola, Bartolomé Leonardo de. 1975. *Rimas*. Edited by José Manuel Blecua. Vol. 1. Madrid: Espasa-Calpe.

Ariosto, Ludovico. 1983. *Orlando furioso*. Translated by Guido Waltman. Oxford: Oxford University Press.

Augustine, Saint. 1950. *The City of God*. Translated by Marcus Dods. Introduction by Thomas Merton. New York: The Modern Library.

Barkan, Leonard. 1986. *The Gods Made Flesh: Metamorphosis and the Pursuit of Paganism*. New Haven and London: Yale University Press.

Beardsley, Theodore S. 1970. *Hispano-Classical Translations Printed between 1482 and 1699*. Pittsburg: Duquesne University Press.

Brownlee, Marina Scordilis. 1985. "Cervantes as Reader of Ariosto." In *Romance: Generic Transformation from Chrétien de Troyes to Cervantes*, edited by Kevin Brownlee and Marina Scordilis Brownlee, 220–37. Hanover and London: University Press of New England.

Camillo, Giulio. 1991. *L'Idea del teatro*. Parlemo: Sellerio.

Cervantes, Miguel de. 1833. *Don Quijote de la Mancha*. Edited and introduction by Diego Clemencin. 3 vols. Madrid: E. Aguado.

Cervantes, Miguel de. 1978. *El ingenioso hidalgo don Quijote de la Mancha*. 2 vols. Edited by Luis Murillo. Madrid: Castalia.

Cervantes, Miguel de. 1998. *Don Quixote*. Translated by Charles Jarvis. Introduction by E.C. Riley. Oxford: Oxford University Press.

Civil, Pierre. 1990. "Erotismo y pintura mitológica en la España del Siglo de Oro." *Edad de Oro* 9: 39–49.

Chastel, André. 1983. *The Sack of Rome, 1527*. Translated by Beth Archer. Princeton: Princeton University Press.

de Armas, Frederick A. 1992. "Interpolation and Invisibility: From Herodotus to Cervantes's *Don Quixote*." *Journal of the Fantastic in the Arts* 4: 8–28.

de Armas, Frederick A. 2000. "Painting Danae, Diana, Europa and Venus: Titian and Argensola's *A Nuño de Mendoza.*" *Calíope* 6: 181–97.

de Armas, Frederick A. 2005a. "Cervantes and Della Porta: The Art of Memory in *La Numancia, El retablo de las maravillas, El licenciado Vidriera* and *Don Quijote.*" *Bulletin of Hispanic Studies* 82 (5): 633–48. http://dx.doi.org/10.3828/bhs.82.5.6.

de Armas, Frederick A. 2005b. "Simple Magic: Ekphrasis from Antiquity to the Age of Cervantes." In *Ekphrasis in the Age of Cervantes*, edited by Frederick A. de Armas, 13–31. Lewisburg: Bucknell University Press.

de Armas, Frederick A. 2006. *Quixotic Frescoes: Cervantes and Italian Renaissance Art.* Toronto: University of Toronto Press.

de Armas Wilson, Diana. 1987. "'Passing the Love of Women': The Intertextuality of *El curioso impertinente.*" *Cervantes* 7: 9–28.

Étienvre, Jean Pierre. 1990. *Márgenes literarios del juego: Una poética del naipe siglos XVI–XVII.* London: Tamesis.

Foucault, Michel. 1970. *The Order of Things: An Archeology of the Human Sciences.* New York: Random House.

Foucault, Michel. 1986. *The History of Sexuality.* 3 vols. Translated by Robert Hurley. New York: Random House.

Friis, Ronald. 1998. "The Devil, the Tower and the Hanged Man: The Hermetic Tarot of the *Numancia.*" In *A Star-Crossed Golden Age: Myth and the Spanish Comedia*, edited by Frederick A. de Armas, 46–61. Lewisburg: Bucknell University Press.

García Santo-Tomás, Enrique. 2008. "Outside Bets: Disciplining Gamblers in Early Modern Spain." *Hispanic Review* 77 (1): 147–64. http://dx.doi.org/10.1353/hir.0.0039.

García Santo-Tomás, Enrique. 2009. "Barroco material / material barroco." In *Materia crítica: formas de ocio y de consumo el la cultura áurea*, edited by Enrique García Santo-Tomás, 11–31. Madrid: Iberoamericana.

Ginsburg, Carlo. 1989. *Clues, Myths and the Historical Method.* Johns Hopkins University Press.

Greene, Thomas M. 1982. *The Light in Troy: Imitation and Discovery in Renaissance Poetry.* New Haven and London: Yale University Press.

Hahn, Juergen. 1972. "*El curioso impertinente* and Don Quijote's Symbolic Struggle against *Curiositas.*" *Bulletin of Hispanic Studies* 49 (2): 128–40. http://dx.doi.org/10.1080/1475382722000349128.

Hart, Bret. 1996. *The Outcasts of Poker Flat.* Woodstock, IL: Dramatic Publishing.

Heiple, Daniel L. 1993. "The Two of Coins: An Unheeded Omen in *El buscón.*" *Crítica hispánica* 15 (1): 105–15.

Ife, B.W. 2005. "Cervantes, Herodotus and the Eternal Triangle: Another Look at the Sources of *El curioso impertinente.*" *Bulletin of Hispanic Studies* 82 (5): 671–82. http://dx.doi.org/10.3828/bhs.82.5.8.

Kennedy, Ruth Lee. 1952. "The Madrid of 1617–1625: Certain Aspects of Social, Moral, and Educational Reform." In *Estudios hispánicos: homenaje a Archer M. Huntington*, 275–309. Wellesley, MA: Department of Spanish, Wellesley College.

Lope de Vega Carpio, Félix. 1975. *La desdichada Estefanía*. Edited by Hugh W. Kennedy. University, MS: Romance Monographs.

Luque Fajardo, Francisco. 1503. *Desengaño contra la ociosidad, y los juegos, utilísimo a los confesores, y penitentes, justicias, y los demas, a cuyo cargo está limpiar de vagabundos, tahures, y fulleros la Republica Cristiana*. Madrid: Miguel Serrano de Vargas.

Mariana, Juan de. 1854. *Tratado contra los juegos públicos: Obras del padre Juan de Mariana.* Biblioteca de autores españoles 31. Madrid: Rivadeneyra.

Meltzer, Francois. 1987. *Salome and the Dance of Writing*. Chicago: University of Chicago Press.

Moreto, Augustín. 1987. *El lindo don Diego*. Edited by Frank P. Casa and Breislav Promorac. Madrid: Cátedra.

Orozco Díaz, Emilio. 1969. *El teatro y la teatralidad del barroco*. Barcelona: Planeta.

Panofsky, Erwin. 1969. *Problems in Titian: Mostly Iconographic*. New York: New York University Press.

Paulson, Ronald. 1984. "Hogarth's Country Inn Yard at Election Time: A Problem in Interpretation." In *English Satire and the Satiric Tradition*, edited by C.J. Rawson, 196–208. Oxford: Blackwell. http://dx.doi.org/10.2307/3508310.

Pavel, Thomas. 2003. *La pensée du roman*. Paris: Gallimard.

Pedrocco, Filippo. 2000. *Titian*. New York: Rizzoli.

Pineda, Juan de. 1964. *Diálogos familiares de la agricultura cristiana.* Biblioteca de autores españoles 169. Madrid: Atlas.

Quint, David. 2003. *Cervantes's Novel of Modern Times*. Princeton: Princeton University Press.

Robertson, Clare. 1992. *"Il gran Cardinale." Alessandro Farnese, Patron of the Arts*. New Haven and London: Yale University Press.

Santore, Cathy. 1991. "Danae: The Renaissance Courtesan's Alter Ego." *Zeitschrift fur Kunstgeschichte* 54 (3): 412–27. http://dx.doi.org/10.2307/1482582.

Schneider, Norbert. 1994. *The Art of Still Life: Still Life Painting in the Early Modern Period*. Cologne: Taschen.

Spear, Richard E. 1997. *The "Divine" Guido: Religion, Sex, Money and Art in the World of Guido Reni*. New Haven and London: Yale University Press.

Suida Manning, Bertina Suida, and William Suida. 1958. *Luca Cambiaso: La vita e le opere*. Milan: Casa Editrice Ceschina.

Syverson-Stork, Jill. 1986. *Theatrical Aspects of the Novel: A Study of Don Quixote*. Valencia: Albatross.

Talvacchia, Bette. 1999. *Taking Positions: On the Erotic in Renaissance Culture*. Princeton: Princeton University Press.

Terence. 1992. *The Comedies*. Edited by Palmer Bovie. Translated by Palmer Bovie, Constance Carrier, and Douglass Parker. Baltimore and London: Johns Hopkins University Press.

Torre, Feniso de la. [Francisco de la Torre y Sevil] 1654. *Entretenimiento de las Musas en esta baraxa nueva de versos dividida en cuatro manjares de asuntos sacros, heroicos, líricos y burlescos*. Zaragoza: Juan de Ybar.

Vosters, Simon A. 1990. *Rubens y España. Estudio artístico-literario sobre la estética del Barroco*. Madrid: Cátedra.

Wagschal, Steven. 2005. "From Parmigianino to Pereda: Luis de Góngora's Beautiful Women and *Vanitas*." In *Ekphrasis in the Age of Cervantes*, edited by Frederick A. de Armas, 102–23. Lewisburg: Bucknell University Press.

Yates, Frances A. 1966. *The Art of Memory*. Chicago: The University of Chicago Press.

# 4 The Things They Carried: Sovereign Objects in Calderón de la Barca's *La gran Cenobia*

MARÍA CRISTINA QUINTERO

The stage of early modern Spain is cluttered with things: objects that designate identity, social status, wealth, and often, political authority. Objects are central, even indispensable, in communicating the *comedia's* multiplicity of meanings – the *alcalde*'s [mayor's] staff used by Pedro Crespo that establishes his authority; the sword hilt in which Gutierre, "el médico de su honra" [the physician of his honour],[1] identifies the threat to his honour; Rosaura's sword in *La vida es sueño*, which carries within it the history of her mother's seduction and a clue to her own identity; the misdirected letters or dropped handkerchiefs that compromise lovers in countless *comedias de enredo* [comedies of intrigue]; and, of course, the portraits that – as Laura Bass has superbly demonstrated – often play a crucial role in the plots. These props go well beyond the status of mere decoration and are all part of the material fabric of a play in performance, contributing to the construction of meaning in the imagination and experience of the spectator.

The incorporation of objects on the stage was also a factor in the history and development of the *comedia* as practice. In the bare *tablas* [stage] of the *corrales* in sixteenth-century Spain, objects complemented and supplemented the minimalist scenery and lack of theatrical devices. Even as the theatre became more elaborate, carefully selected objects metonymically imparted crucial information to the audience. Candles, torches, and blindfolds, for example, created the illusion of nighttime in outdoor performances that had to take advantage of the light of day. Jose María Ruano de la Haza has seen parallels between the sometimes stark seventeenth-century public stage and the modern theatre:

> la técnica de representar en los teatros comerciales del siglo XVII tiene mucho en común con la de un teatro moderno experimental, en el que unos cuantos

> objetos, más o menos realistas, pueden dar al público una idea bastante exacta del lugar donde se desarrolla la acción …
>
> [the staging technique in the commercial theatres of the seventeenth century has a great deal in common with that of modern experimental theatre, in which a few more or less realistic objects give the public a fairly exact idea of where the action takes place …] (2000, 31–2)

As the *comedia nueva* developed and visual elements became more and more prevalent, objects acquired an importance far beyond the suggestion of specific settings for the dramatic plot. Some years ago, there was a debate among critics on whether the *comedia* was primarily meant to be heard or to be seen and whether the use of decor and stage properties had any real importance in the performance of the plays. Alicia Amadei-Pulice, for example, argued that the relative starkness of the early *corral* stage was an indication that these plays were "para oír" [to be heard], and that it was not until the development of the *teatro palaciego* [courtly theatre] that the *comedia* acquired a true spectacular visual dimension:

> El corral era un estrado pobre, con escasísimos elementos, decorado con la palabra poética, el verso, la imagen descriptiva, la alusión simbólica, la cadencia de la rima, algún que otro gesto del recitante.
>
> [The *corral* was a modest platform, with very scarce devices, decorated only with poetic words, verse, descriptive images, symbolic allusions, the cadences of rhyme, the occasional gesture of the performer.] (1990, 36)

In his analysis of Lope de Vega's play *Los comendadores de Córdoba,* Manuel Abad Gómez goes so far as to assert that the play is "un claro ejemplo de un teatro dirigido a un público […] que acude a los corrales para oír, no para ver […] Teatro que parece exigir oyentes, no espectadores" [a clear example of a drama meant for an audience […] that goes to the *corrales* to hear, not to see […] This theatre seems to demand hearers, not viewers] (1984, 12). Other critics, prominently Ruano de la Haza and Victor Dixon, have rightly restored the importance of the visual dimension of the *comedia* even in the outdoor *corrales*: "Es absurdo afirmar que la dimensión visual está ausente de la Comedia, o que la comedia es un género meramente auditivo, o que la parte espectacular del teatro, todo lo que percibía la vista, casi no contaba" [It is absurd to affirm that the visual dimension is absent from the *comedia,* or that the *comedia* is solely an auditory genre, or that the spectacular dimension of the theatre, everything that was visually perceived, did not count for much] (Ruano 2000, 13). At the same time, it is true that the appearance of theatrical spaces such as the Coliseo del Buen Retiro and the Salón Dorado in the Alcázar promoted a dazzling evolution in stagecraft. The *teatro palaciego* would become a complex exercise in materiality with its multiple use of extralinguistic devices, the sophisticated *tramoyería* [stage machinery], elaborate costumes, and illusionist scenery all requiring the participation of talented men such as Cosimo Lotti and Baccio del Bianco, the special effects technicians of their day. As Amadei Pulice states, in the palace theatre: "el decorado es tan espectacular que habla de por sí, emite signos significativos de un lenguaje plástico" [the decor is so spectacular that it almost speaks on its own; it emits the important signs of a plastic language]; and it is not surprising that in his treatise on drama, *Nueva idea de la tragedia antigua*, Jusepe Antonio González de Salas deemed it necessary to emend Aristotle's theories of tragedy by adding two new components: *música* [music] and *aparato* [apparatus] (Amadei Pulice 1990, 73). Stage properties, or *utilería*, were an important component of that *aparato.*

A consideration of the use of stage properties in individual plays, whether in the palace or the *corrales*, continues to provide insights into the polyphonic aesthetic of the *comedia*. In this study, I am concerned specifically with those devices that designate and simultaneously problematize monarchical authority in an early play by Calderón de la Barca, *La gran Cenobia* (1625). It is recognized that the theatre of seventeenth-century Spain was obsessively concerned with dramatizing kingship;[2] in the hands of playwrights such as Lope, Calderón, Tirso de Molina, and Bances Candamo, among others, theatre became a particular manifestation of the *speculum principis* tradition. That is, the *comedia* provided a singularly suggestive space for dramatizing lessons in kingship, lessons that often echoed the criticism and advice that appeared in political treatises written by *arbitristas* and respected political theorists such as Diego de Saavedra Fajardo and Juan de Mariana. Within the theatrical representation and exploration of monarchical power, stage properties played an important role. In this study, I will limit myself to analysing three events in *La gran Cenobia* where objects are used in such a way that they transform the action on the stage and even seem to compete with the characters for the attention of the spectator. Although, for the most part, the modern reader experiences these *comedia* objects as embedded textual events, I am interested in exploring how they might have functioned as part of an actual performance on stage, and how they might have been experienced by an audience in the seventeenth century.[3] I have chosen

*La gran Cenobia* as an example because the play offers a double performance of power where positive and negative exemplars of monarchy are simultaneously presented. What makes the play particularly appealing to modern sensibilities is that, in the almost Manichean opposition between enlightened and disastrous models of authority, the positive exemplar is a woman. What is more, in the gendered struggle for power that this play enacts, stage objects become essential components in establishing and simultaneously commenting on monarchical authority.

The first event that I will examine occurs at the very beginning of *La gran Cenobia* when Aureliano, a ruthless and ambitious Roman general, appears "en pieles" [in furs]. His attire is an early indication that he will embody an uncivilized and dangerous force. Juan de Mariana, among other theorists of the monarchy, ascribed animalistic attributes to ambitious and cruel princes, as a warning against the dangers of tyranny. In his *Del rey y de la institución real*, for example, Mariana explicitly exclaims, "el tirano es una bestia fiera y cruel" [the tyrant is a fierce and cruel beast] (1854, v. 482]. The association is an ancient one; Plato in the *Republic* and the *Gorgias* called the tyrant a "natural" man, nearer in character to an animal because he seeks only to satisfy his own ambition.[4] The *pieles* worn by Aureliano would have immediately communicated his unsuitability as a prince. Equally as important as Aureliano's costume, however, is the presence in this first scene of two objects charged with dramatic and ideological significance. They emerge first not as concrete objects, but rather as references in a soliloquy in which Aureliano relates a dream that he has just had. In this oneiric vision, the dead emperor Quintilio had addressed him and said: "Ves aquí mi laurel, mi cetro toma, que tu serás emperador de Roma" [Look at my laurel crown and take my sceptre, for you shall be the emperor of Rome] (1974, vv. 21–2).[5] Shortly afterwards, according to the stage direction, "*Descúbrese sobre un peñasco la corona y el cetro en una rama*" [*On a crag, the crown and sceptre are revealed on a branch*] (1974, 4). Aureliano's words have materialized into actual objects on the stage, experienced in three dimensions by the audience.[6] Here, the playwright seems to be enacting what Andrew Soffer in *The Stage Life of Props* calls the "uneasy position between text and performance" (2003, vi) that stage props occupy. That is, the crown and the sceptre manifest themselves first as embedded textual events through Aureliano's speech; but then, these textual signifiers are translated into concrete objects upon the stage. This dynamic replicates the status of props in drama in general in that they "appear" first as textual signifiers but are invisible to the *reader* who may or may not capture their importance. It is only in the actual performance that these objects become "materialized" and are perceived by a spectator as important dramatic signifiers.

Returning to Calderón's play, it is worth considering what sort of objects the crown and sceptre represent, and what might confer upon them the category of true dramatic prop rather than merely a decoration. The laurel crown and the sceptre, as universally recognized emblems of monarchy, bring with them overly determined historical, cultural, and ideological baggage. And yet, here, they appear first only as static objects, hanging on a branch, in a kind of suspended animation. Despite the familiarity of these objects, simply by virtue of appearing on a stage they "acquire an invisible set of quotation marks," a process Umberto Eco calls "phenomenon ostension" (Soffer 2003, 7). The effect of this ostension is to make the audience take in not only the actual object but an entire series of connotations – in this case royalty, power, and authority. At the same time, the placement of these objects upon a branch would also provide an iconic representation of disembodied or perhaps absent monarchy. When Aureliano takes the items down from the branch and puts them on, however, they abandon their condition as motionless emblems and become concretized and activated on the stage, literally put into play by the actor playing the Roman general. And it is this motion through the space of the stage and the time of the performance that distinguishes a prop from other stage objects. That is, the three-dimensionality of the object on stage is not enough. According to Soffer, "motion is the prop's defining feature" and "a prop demands actual embodiment and motion on the stage in order to spring to imaginative life" (2003, vi). Aureliano himself recognizes the galvanizing power of these objects when he exclaims as he reaches out for them: "un aliento Nuevo / un espíritu altivo que me inflama el coraçon, / a tanto honor me llama" [a new force, a new arrogant spirit that inflames my heart, beckons me towards such high honour] (1974, vv. 56–8). David Hildner in his discussion of reason and the passions in *La gran Cenobia* highlights the importance of the crown and sceptre: "It is the crown and the scepter which exert the influence suggested by the active verbs *inflamar* and *llamar,* while the speaker becomes the direct object of their action" (1982, 52).

The objects in question are acted upon, put into motion, by the figure of Aureliano, and, interestingly, they in turn transform him. When Aureliano as bearer and motivator of these two props proceeds to admire himself in a pool of water – "En este lisongero / espejo fugitivo mirar quiero / cómo el resplandeciente / laurel asienta en mi dichosa frente" [In this flattering and fugitive mirror I want to see how this resplendent laurel sits on my fortunate forehead] (1974, vv. 67–70) – the objects placed on his body confer upon him a new identity and authority. As he stares, newly adorned with these props, at his reflection he sees himself drastically changed: he is no longer a mere man but an actual representation of the world itself:

> Pequeño mundo soy, y en esto fundo
> Que en ser señor de mí, lo soy del mundo.
>
> [I am a microcosm, a small world, and based on this, I believe that by mastering myself, I will become master of the world] (1974, vv. 65–6)

As Frederick de Armas has pointed out, "Here Aureliano is applying the Renaissance theory of man as a microcosm. Since he can rule himself, he claims, he can also rule the world, which is part of the macrocosm" (1986, 73). In addition, Aureliano himself has become an image, an almost inanimate object. Indeed, he goes on to consecrate that image of himself reflected in the pool of water by describing it as a painting, an icon that demands reverence and adoration:

> ¡O sagrada figura!,
> haga el original a la pintura
> debida reverencia,
> quando llevado en mis discursos hallo
> que yo doy y recibo la obediencia,
> siendo mi Emperador y mi vasallo.
>
> [Oh sacred figure! Let the original give due reverence to the painting, when in the midst of my eloquence I find that I both demand and receive obedience, since I am both my emperor and my vassal] (1974, vv. 70–5)

In this (perhaps ironic) internal rendering of the *speculum principis* topos, Aureliano becomes at once viewer and image, *original* and *pintura* [painting], both subject and object. The sequence of events involving Aureliano and his interaction with these props on the stage could have communicated a series of simultaneous messages to the audience. We have already said that when the disembodied objects are revealed hanging on a tree branch, the suggestion may be of an abandoned, discarded monarchy. They also suggest parts of a theatrical costume that can be taken on and off, with the monarch being merely a player who can don this particular disguise as easily as any other. Indeed, the movement from branch to the body of Aureliano might also suggest the mutability and the arbitrariness of power. More important, the incongruous juxtaposition on the same body of animal skins with objects that carry with them a long cultural history designating authority would have provided a rather bizarre visual tableau. Aureliano becomes an ambulatory oxymoron, a beast that is transformed into a prince and an uncivilized presence claiming to be a sacred image. Familiar signifiers become thus de-familiarized, allowing the audience to interpret them anew and, indeed, to question and confront the received meaning of these symbols. The play was most likely staged first in a *corral* but we do know that it was also performed in the royal palace in 1625,[7] when Philip IV was twenty years old and had been on the throne for only four years. Given that this was a time of considerable social and political turmoil presided over by an inexperienced and somewhat irresponsible king, *comedias* took advantage of the stage to impart lessons on monarchy. The presence and manipulation of these objects in the initial scene in *La gran Cenobia* suggest a critique of the current state of affairs, particularly the instability of the monarchy and a warning to the pleasure-loving king against allowing his "instinctual" nature to distort his duties as a monarch. These props, therefore, also illustrate the potential ideological dimension in Calderón's handling of stage properties.

Queen Cenobia, the eponymous character of the play, will provide a distinct contrast to the unsettling figure of Aureliano. She is a strong military leader (in fact, when the play begins, she has just defeated the Roman forces led by the Roman general Decio) and she is also a wise and generous ruler – a philosopher queen. Her dramatic subjectivity, like Aureliano's, will be defined in great part by the things she carries and manipulates on stage. For one thing, her presence on stage repeatedly provides a positive alternative to the incongruous tableau presented by Aureliano at the beginning of the play. In the second act, for example, Cenobia enters "*con armas negras, vestida de luto, leyendo en un libro*" [*with black armour, dressed in mourning, reading a book*] (1974, 34). The austere costume and the armour will communicate immediately to the audience her strength and gravitas, in sharp contrast to her Roman foe. Cenobia's armour will serve as a reminder to the audience that she has recently triumphed militarily over Rome, and her mourning attire supplements the news that her husband Abdenato has died and she is now sole ruler. The book she carries acquires particular significance as well. While it is not clear who the author is, the book is an account or chronicle of, as she puts it, "qué se dize por aí de Cenobia" [what people are saying about Cenobia] (1974, vv. 1146–7). She reads from it aloud to Libio and Irene:

CENOBIA: Oye ...
(*Lee*) "Que, viendo a Decio vencido,
vino al Oriente Aureliano
con todo el poder Romano
de su poder ofendido;
y que, habiéndole cercado
enemiga, la asaltó
tres veces, y tres bolvió
rompido y desbaratado
...
También se dize que hoy es
cuando la batalla quiere
dar; y lo que sucediere
della se dirá después."

[CENOBIA: Listen ... (*she reads*) "Since he saw a vanquished Decio, Aureliano came to the East with all the Roman might offended by her power; and having besieged the enemy, he attacked three times, and three times, he returned broken and defeated ... It is also said that today is when he will fight again, and what happens then will be recounted later." (1974, vv. 1156–64, 1179–82)

What is remarkable about this account is that the textual prop that she carries summarizes the action of the play right up to that very moment ("hoy es ...") when she finds herself reading out loud. In addition, the book also anticipates Libio's treason which will take place later in the second act:

CENOBIA: Buelvo, Libio, a proseguir:
(*Lee*) "En este tiempo embiudó;
y, atreviéndose por ver
en el Reino una muger,
no faltó quien procuró
de secreto conjurar
la gente y, dándole mano
al exército Romano
y tributo, conspirar
a la Corona ..."

[CENOBIA: I shall continue reading, Libio: [*she reads*] "It was around this time that she became a widow; and emboldened at seeing a woman on the

> throne, there were some who tried in secret to rouse the populace and, collaborating with the Roman army, to conspire against the Crown ..."] (1974, vv. 1186–95)

The document that Cenobia is reading, therefore, conflates three different "historical" and dramatic moments: the recent past of her victory against Rome; the present moment of reading that is also the day when Aureliano will attack again; and the future, in that it alludes to a betrayal that has not yet taken place.

Cenobia will handle yet another "book" in a later scene of the second act. The stage directions state: "*Dexan un bufete con aderezo de escrivir y Cenobia se sienta a escrivir*" [*They leave a small desk and writing materials and Cenobia sits and starts writing*] (1974, 53). In addition to her military triumphs, the queen reveals herself as the author of a "historical" narrative (perhaps it is one and the same, but this is never made quite clear):

> Por no dejar que olvide
> el tiempo mi alabanza,
> papel que siempre finge
> a la verdad grandezas
> y a la envidia imposibles,
> la mujer que pelea
> es la misma que escribe,
> que a un mismo tiempo iguales
> espada y pluma rige.
> Historia del Oriente
> la llamo; así prosigue: *Escrive.*
>
> [So as not to permit the passage of time to forget my accomplishments, the paper that always simulates great deeds from the truth and impossible exploits to inspire envy, [for] the woman who fights is also the one who writes, and she wields equally a sword and a pen at the same time. I call it *The History of the Orient* and I proceed thus: (*she starts writing*).] (1974, vv. 1800–10)

The volume *Historia oriental* chronicles the history of Cenobia's people and includes descriptions of her recent triumphs as a military and political leader. The audience then observes her in the very act of composing a history that is also *her*-story, a verbal iteration to some of the actions that the spectators have already witnessed or heard about:

Retirose a este tiempo
Aureliano y, humilde,
socorros poderosos
a Egipto y Persia pide.

[At that time, Aureliano retreated and, humbled, he asks for powerful help from Egypt and Persia.] (1974, vv. 1811–14)

Cenobia's connection to this *Historia oriental* is simultaneously as author, reader, and subject. Moreover, in this dramatization of the act of writing, there ensues a remarkable moment in which the notion that props can acquire a life of their own on the stage becomes quite literal. As the queen writes in the memoir a description of Libio, her unscrupulous nephew, the paper – an inert prop – becomes animated:

"... en este tiempo Libio ..."
El *Libio,* ¡ay de mí, triste!,
escrito está con sangre
y, al ir a repetirle,
sangre brotó la herida
y mesa y papel tiñen
deshojados claveles
o líquidos rubíes.

["... at that point in time, Libio..." Woe is me! The "Libio" is written in blood; and, when I tried to repeat it, the wound blossomed anew with blood, and both table and paper are stained with petal-less carnations or liquid rubies.] (1974, vv. 1815–22)

We are again reminded of Soffer's notion that a prop demands actual embodiment and motion on the stage in order to spring to imaginative life. Calderón brilliantly illustrates this dynamism of objects through what we might call the transubstantiation of the paper into a body that bleeds. Yolanda Novo explains that this effect might have been accomplished in performance through the use of "una tintura roja que la actriz llevase debajo de la manga de su vestido o el papel previamente teñido de color rojo" [a red tincture that the actress could have carried under her sleeve or a paper previously dyed in red] (2003, 377). The paper covered with blood is evidence of the crime that Libio has already committed – he has murdered Cenobia's husband Abdenato; in fact, the "ghost" of Abdenato, appears simultaneously as the paper bleeds. It is also a premonition of future crimes – the blood that will be shed when Aureliano attacks Palmyra after Libio betrays the queen.

Incidentally, although not as spectacular as this "living prop," there are other written texts in the play that are important to the development of plot and character. We have, for example, the *memoriales* carried by the soldiers to an audience with Cenobia in the first act. These petitions, objects presented to the queen, contribute to her characterization as a wise and compassionate ruler, as the soldiers make clear: "¡Qué govierno!" "¡Qué muger!"/"¡Qué valor!" and "¡qué prudencia!" [What authority! What a woman! What valour! What prudence!] (1974, vv. 648–9). In the third act, there will be a parallel scene where other soldiers also present *memoriales* to Aureliano, only to have him arrogantly dismiss their petitions – "!Qué cansados pretendientes!/¿Qué más premio han de tener/los soldados? ¿El servirme/no basta para interés?" [What dreary claimants! What more reward do these soldiers want? Isn't the honour of serving me enough?] (1974, vv. 2613–16) – and even go so far as to destroy the written requests: "No me digas más;/romper puedes ese memorial,/que ya premiado se ve:/ya tiene más que merece/donde me vio" [Don't say another word; you can tear up that petition; he has already been rewarded. Indeed, what else could he want after gazing upon me?] (1974, vv. 2634–8). The manner in which these two characters interact with the same objects vividly illustrates the differences in their natures and their suitability (or lack thereof) to govern judiciously. Other documents that will play a significant role in the play are the falsified papers that the cowardly servant Persio steals from the body of the dead soldier, Adriano:

> Un soldado venial
> soy, que nunca mortalmente
> reñí. Un soldado valiente
> muerto hallé en un arenal
> y estos papeles, que son
> de sus hechos testimonio,
> quité. Llamábase Andronio
> y, gozando la ocasión
> a pretender he venido
> mudando el Persio en su nombre.

[I am but a venial soldier, for I've never fought to the death. I found the body of a dead valiant soldier in a sandy terrain and I took these papers, testimony of his deeds. His name was Andronio and, taking advantage of this opportunity, I have come seeking favours substituting "Persio" for his name.] (1974, vv. 741–50)

Although they appear but briefly, Persio /Andrenio's papers become a subtle metadramatic device, a witty allusion to the ease with which actors take up new roles or "papeles." This being a typical Calderonian play, Persio will not be the only character who will self-consciously assume different roles and identities through items of clothing: the Roman general Decio, more than once, will hide his face behind a "banda" [sash] so as not to be recognized; and Libio and Irene will don the disguise of "villanos" [peasants] in the third act.

The last event I want to examine occurs in the last act as well. Cenobia's military prowess will lead to a second defeat of the Roman forces led by the brutal general. This stunning humiliation at the hands of a woman will inspire in Aureliano a blinding and obsessive desire to avenge himself and he vows to vanquish Cenobia and place her "humilde a mis pies postrada" [humbled and prostrate at my feet] (1974, v. 503). He makes good on his promise and this will generate another remarkable activation of the *utilería* of the play. We learn that, through Libio's treachery, Aureliano has been able to capture Cenobia and is about to enter the city in triumph manufacturing an ostentatious pageant of victory. The stage directions are as follows: "*Suena la música, y entran Soldados delante, y detrás un carro triunfal, en el cual viene Aureliano Emperador, y a sus pies Cenobia, muy bizarra, atadas las manos, y tirando del carro cautivos y detrás gente*" [*Music is heard and soldiers enter first; behind them, there appears a triumphal carriage on which stands the emperor Aureliano; and, at his feet, Cenobia, elaborately attired, her hands tied; with slaves pulling the cart; and behind, more people*] (1974, 64). Numerous objects are simultaneously presented on stage: a *carro triunfal*, a throne; and Aureliano calls special attention to the gold crown he is wearing, which he contrasts to the laurel he had donned in the first act:

No de laurel coronado
llego a verte, porque fuera
a tanta ocasión pequeño
señor; inmortal diadema

de oro corona mi frente,
que ya quiero que esta sea
insignia de emperadores,
ciñendo yo la primera.

[No longer crowned in mere laurel do I appear before you, because that would make me a lesser lord in an occasion as grand as this; instead, an immortal diadem of gold crowns my brow and it is my wish that by being the first to wear it, it may henceforth become the insignia of emperors.] (1974, vv. 2103–10)

All these attributes of power pale in comparison to the real prize: Cenobia's abject and objectified body. Decio, who is in love with Cenobia, is a witness and provides a verbal description to accompany this spectacle of humiliation:

En un triunfal carro, a quien
en vez de rústicas fieras
racionales brutos tiran,
atados cautivos llevan;
él en lo más eminente
del triunfal carro se asienta
en un trono, a imitación
hermosa de algún Planeta.
Luego va Cenobia … ¡Ay triste!
¿Tendrá espíritu la lengua
para decirte que va
Cenobia a sus plantas puesta,
ricamente aderezada,
hermosamente compuesta,
donde, como en centro viven
piedras, oro, plata y perlas?
Atadas las blancas manos
con riquísimas cadenas
de oro (prisiones, en fin,
¿qué importa que ricas sean?),
va a sus pies, y él, profanando
el respeto y la belleza,
el sagrado bulto pisa,
la imagen rica atropella.

> [In a triumphal chariot, drawn by shackled slaves and not rustic beasts, there he sits upon a throne in the most prominent position of the triumphal car, a beautiful imitation of some Planet.[8] Then comes Cenobia ... ¡oh, woe is me! Can my tongue be strong enough to tell you that Cenobia – richly dressed, beautifully composed, in the centre where there are precious stones, gold, silver, and pearls – lies at his feet? The white hands are tied with rich chains of gold (they are prisons so what does it matter how rich they are?), she lies at his feet and he, profaning both respect and beauty, treads on her sacred body, abusing her rich image.] (1974, vv. 2051–74)

Cenobia is laden with objects: "oro," "piedras," "plata," "perlas," and "riquísimas cadenas de oro." Furthermore, according to Decio's account, the chariot is being pulled by "brutos racionales" that is, slaves, human beasts of burden, men and women who have been transformed into chattel and are themselves moving stage properties in Aureliano's pageant. Cenobia herself is in chains, also hardly more than a prop, a "santo bulto," an "imagen rica." Wearing her most ostentatious and dazzling garb, she has become part of Aureliano's booty, a "trofeo infelice / de un traidor y un tirano" [unhappy trophy of a traitor and tyrant] (1974, vv. 1780–1). As the tyrant tramples her almost inanimate "bulto," Cenobia becomes an object that literally bolsters or *props* up his authority. The semioticians Shoshana Avigal and Shlomith Rimmon-Kenan have stated that for an item to be an effective theatrical prop, certain basic requirements must be fulfilled: first it must be either already inanimate or capable of becoming inanimate; second, it must be capable of being transported by another character; third, it must be deprived of intentionality; that is, the object is manipulated but cannot itself initiate discourse (1981, 13). These three conditions apply to greater or lesser degrees to the character of Cenobia in this triumphant entrance where, as she is being displayed and transported in the *carro triunfal*, the queen is rendered almost inanimate and momentarily silent. In the previous scenes considered here, objects like the sceptre, the crown, and the paper seem to acquire a life of their own by being moved through space or by being animated by the subjects that manipulate them. Here, a moving, breathing subject is reified, virtually made into an object through a cruel performance of enslavement and humiliation. There is, what is more, a gendered component to this spectacle. Earlier in the play, when Aureliano wanted to punish Decio, he did so by depriving him of his sword – thus symbolically unmanning him. This humiliation is effected through the removal of an overly determined prop from his body, but there is no question that Decio remains a free agent able to move about and escape Aureliano's ire. In Cenobia's case, nothing but subjugation and reification will do, as precious objects are piled on her body and she becomes little more than yet another static signifier of Aureliano's power. It is worth noting at this point that in Calderonian plays that dramatize women who assume political authority, we often witness singularly harsh spectacles of punishment for these queens. Semiramis in *La hija del aire* is crushed and broken after being thrown into a precipice, her body riddled with arrows. In the last scene of *La cisma de Inglaterra*, Ana Bolena's headless body lies at the base of the throne wrapped in a silken cloth. *La gran Cenobia*, a play that ostensibly presents a woman as a capable and wise leader, nevertheless also stages a singularly ostentatious way of putting a powerful woman in her place through the activation of a whole assortment of stage properties. Interestingly, after this point in the play, Cenobia will never again recapture her majesty; when she does regain the throne, it will be only as Decio's consort.[9]

The anthropologist Arjun Appadurai tells us that objects possess "life histories or careers of exchange that invest them with social significance and cultural value" (1986, 34). In the *comedia*, objects on stage acquire significance, not only through their symbolic associations, but also through their repeated theatrical use. In Calderonian plays dealing with monarchy and the negotiation of power, many of the same props tend to appear over and over again. A brilliant manipulator of theatrical codes, Calderón deliberately appropriates the symbolic life of an object and puts it into play. Stage properties, according to theatre semiotician Marvin Carlson, "are retrospective, they are 'ghosted' by their previous stage incarnations, and hence by a theatrical past they both embody and critique" (1994, 12). I would suggest that Calderón, in employing certain superannuated props is not just invoking theatrical tradition but also infusing these symbols of power with new meaning. Through their frequent use on the stage, objects like sceptres, crowns, thrones, and books all acquire an accumulated cultural significance and resonance, readily accessible to spectators. However, these devices truly achieve their performative potential when their cultural value and social significance are made strange before an audience. A man in animal skins wearing a crown and a sceptre, a paper that bleeds, a bejewelled woman reduced to an immobile *bulto* to be trampled are all testaments to the potential ideological power implicit in Calderón's creative manipulation of props. Familiar signifiers become defamiliarized, allowing the audience to interpret them anew and question and confront the received meaning born by these objects. At a time of dire social and political circumstances presided over by kings who were increasingly viewed as ineffectual, the *comedia* often served as a way of simultaneously preserving symbols of monarchy and, at the same time, critiquing their debasement. The manipulation of certain objects in plays like *La gran Cenobia* contributed to the continuing construction, negotiation, and interrogation of power. If we remember that the actual monarch himself was often the privileged intended spectator of these plays, we might be tempted to claim that it is the play's things that catch the conscience of the king and that of the *comedia* audience of early modern Spain.

## NOTES

1 All translations from Spanish to English are by the author unless otherwise referenced in the appropriate passage.

2 See, for example, Fox, *Kings in Calderón*, Hampton, *Writing from History*, and McKendrick's magisterial *Playing the King*.

3 This approach is necessarily conjectural. I am here attempting what theatre historians Judith Milhous and Robert D. Hume have called "production analysis," the "interpretation of the text specifically aimed at understanding it as a performance vehicle" (1985, 10). In this type of reading, the excellent reconstruction work of critics such as N.D. Shergold, John Varey, and Ruano de la Haza is indispensable. For *La gran Cenobia* specifically, Yolanda Novo provides a helpful reconstruction of the staging of the play in "Rasgos escenográficos" [scenographic features] but she does not deal with props in any detailed manner. Although the play was written in 1625, Novo bases her reconstruction on the "escritura didascálica de la primera edición de 1636" [stage directions of the first edition of 1636] (2003, 364) on the assumption that it corresponds to the play's debut in the *corrales* and its prompt transfer to the palace.

4 In his study of the play, Frederick de Armas establishes an association between Aureliano's bestial nature and an imbalance of the humours: "His fiery temperament and his frustrated ambitions, nurtured in the wilderness, have caused an imbalance in his humoral constitution (*discrasia*)" (1986, 72–3). See also Hollmann, "El retrato del tirano Aurelio en *La gran Cenobia*," for a discussion of Aureliano's character.

5 All quotes are taken from Valbuena Briones's edition of the play in *Primera parte de comedias de don Pedro Calderón de la Barca*. When quoting the

dialogue, I will indicate verse numbers; for the stage directions, I will use page numbers.

6 Yolanda Novo suggests that the objects were there from the beginning and are "discovered" when the character of Aureliano moves across the stage towards where they are located (2003, 369).

7 For the dates of the play, see the articles by Shergold and Varey, "Some Early Calderón Dates" and "Some Place Performances of Seventeenth-Century Plays." The play was restaged in the palace as late as the 1680s, after Calderón's death.

8 It is worth remembering at this point that Philip IV, one of the spectators of this performance in the palace, would become known as "el Rey Planeta" [the Planet King].

9 Perhaps the most studied aspect of the play is the shifting fortunes of the characters. The play, frequently emphasizing the rise and fall of the wheel of Fortune and the allegorical figure of Fortuna, has been associated with the character of Astrea and with Cenobia herself. See Frederick de Armas, A. Valbuena Briones, and Rina Walthaus.

## WORKS CITED

Abad Gómez, Manuel. 1984. "Un romance cordobés en el teatro de horror de Lope de Vega." In *El barroco en Andalucía*, edited by Manuel Peláez del Rosal et al, 11–22. Córdoba: Ediciones El Almendro.

Amadei-Pulice, María Alicia. 1990. *Calderón y el barroco: Exaltación y engaño de los sentidos*. Amsterdam and Philadelphia: John Benjamins.

Appadurai, Arjun. 1986. *The Social Life of Things: Commodities in Cultural Perspective*. Cambridge: Cambridge University Press.

Avigal, Shoshana, and Shlomith Rimmon-Kenan. 1981. "What Do Brook's Bricks Mean? Toward a Theory of the 'Mobility' of Objects in Theatrical Discourse." *Poetics Today* 2 (3): 11–34. http://dx.doi.org/10.2307/1772462.

Bass, Laura. 2008. *The Drama of the Portrait: Theater and Visual Culture in Early Modern Spain*. University Park, PA: Penn State University Press.

Calderón de la Barca, Pedro. 1974. *La gran Cenobia.* In *Primera parte de comedias de don Pedro Calderón de la Barca*, edited by A. Valbuena Briones, 1: 1–85. Madrid: Clásicos Hispánicos.

Carlson, Marvin. 1994. "The Haunted Stage: Recycling and Reception in the Theatre." *Theatre Survey* 35 (1): 5–18. http://dx.doi.org/10.1017/S0040557400002520.

de Armas, Frederick A. 1986. *The Return of Astraea: An Astral-Imperial Myth in Calderón*. Lexington: University Press of Kentucky.

Dixon, Victor. 1986. "La comedia de corral de Lope como género visual.' *Edad de oro* 5: 35–58.

Fox, Dian. 1986. *Kings in Calderón: A Study in Characterization and Political Theory*. London: Tamesis.

Hampton, Timothy. 1990. *Writing from History: The Rhetoric of Exemplarity in Renaissance Literature*. Ithaca: Cornell University Press.

Hildner, David. 1982. *Reason and the Passions in the* comedias *of Calderón*. Amsterdam, Philadelphia: Johns Benjamins.

Hollmann, Hildegard. 1979. "El retrato del tirano Aurelio en *La gran Cenobia*." In *Hacia Calderón: cuarto coloquio Anglogermano*, edited by Hans Flasche, Kart-Hermann Korner, and Hans Mattauch, 47–55. Berlin: Walter de Gruyter.

McKendrick, Melveena. 2000. *Playing the King: Lope de Vega and the Limits of Conformity*. London: Tamesis.

Milhous, Judith, and Robert D. Hume. 1985. *Producible Interpretation: Eight English Plays, 1675–1707*. Carbondale: Southern Illinois University Press.

Mariana, Juan de. 1854. *Del rey y de la institución real.* In *Obras del Padre Juan de Mariana*, 2:463–576. Biblioteca de autores españoles. Madrid: M. Rivadeneyra.

Novo, Yolanda. 2003. "Rasgos escenográficos y reconstrucción escénica de *La gran Cenobia* (1636), una tragedia histórica de la *Primera Parte*." In *Teatro calderoniano sobre el tablado: Calderón y su puesta en escena a través de los siglos: XIII Coloquio Anglogermano sobre Calderón*, edited by Manfred Tietz, 359–90. Stuttgart: Franz Steiner Verlag.

Ruano de la Haza, José María. 2000. *La puesta en escena en los teatros comerciales del Siglo de Oro*. Madrid: Editorial Castalia.

Shergold, N.D., and John E. Varey. 1961. "Some Early Calderón Dates." *Bulletin of Hispanic Studies* 38 (4): 274–86. http://dx.doi.org/10.1080/1475382612000338274.

Shergold, N.D., and John E. Varey. 1963. "Some Palace Performances of Seventeenth-Century Plays." *Bulletin of Hispanic Studies* 40 (4): 212–44. http://dx.doi.org/10.1080/1475382632000340212.

Soffer, Andrew. 2003. *The Stage Life of Props*. Ann Arbor: University of Michigan Press.

Valbuena Briones, A. 1975. "El tema de la fortuna en *La gran Cenobia.*" *Quaderni Ibero Americani* 45–6: 217–23.

Walthaus, Rina. 2000. "La fortaleza de Cenobia y la mutabilidad de Fortuna: dos emblemas femeninos en *La gran Cenobia* de Calderón." In *Que toda la vida es sueño, y los sueños, sueños son: Homenaje a don Pedro Calderón de la Barca*, edited by Ysla Campbell, 109–28. Ciudad Juárez, México: Universidad Autónoma de Ciudad Juárez.

Walthaus, Rina. 2002. "'Representar tragedias así la Fortuna sabe': La representación de Fortuna en dos comedias tempranas de Calderón (*Saber del mal y del bien* y *La gran Cenobia*." In *Calderón 2000: Actas del Congreso Internacional IV Centenario del nacimiento de Calderón (Universidad de Navarra, 2000)*, edited by Ignacio Arellano, 2: 397–409. Kassel: Reichenberger.

# 5 Beyond Canvas and Paint: Falling Portraits in the Spanish *Comedia*

CHRISTOPHER B. WEIMER

Among the material objects most frequently present on sixteenth- and seventeenth-century Spanish playhouse stages, few evince the semiotic and discursive complexities of painted portraits. Many onstage paintings, of course, are nothing more than inert objects, such as the miniatures which lovers and suitors exchange, bestow, cherish, steal, and discard in numerous romantic comedies. Other *comedia* paintings possess the power to captivate and enamour their beholders. Even Neoplatonic ideas of a visual representation suffused with its subject's soul, however, are insufficient to explain the phenomenon of portraits that play more active roles in a small number of *comedias*: at critical moments these paintings unexpectedly function as surrogates for their absent subjects, falling from the walls on which they hang over open doorways and thereby blocking would-be murderers' and rapists' access to their intended victims. By virtue of the apparent agency thus displayed, these portraits at least briefly become more than mere inanimate objects. The present essay will examine how such likenesses transcend their material nature in four *comedias*, beginning with Damián Salucio del Poyo's use of this device in *La próspera fortuna de Ruy López de Ávalos* [The Prosperous Fortunes of Ruy López de Ávalos] and then turning to two playwrights who included similar episodes in subsequent works: Luis Vélez de Guevara in *El lucero de Castilla y Luna de Aragón* [The Shining Star of Castile and the Moon of Aragon] and Tirso de Molina in both *La prudencia en la mujer* [Prudence in Woman] and *La firmeza en la hermosura* [Constancy in Beauty].[1]

As Laura R. Bass notes, "It is no accident that Spain's so-called Golden Age of literature during the seventeenth century was also its Golden Age of painting" (2008, 3). Spain during this era was a culture entranced by the idea of representation, a fascination revealed by the simultaneous proliferations of portraiture and playwriting in an age when the visual and literary arts were often paralleled, following Horace's dictum *ut pictura poesis* [as is painting so is poetry].[2] This correspondence was specifically applicable to dramaturgy in the eyes of many playwrights, among them Tirso de Molina: in his *Cigarrales de Toledo* [Country Houses of Toledo], Tirso notes that "no en vano se llamó la poesía *pintura viva*" [not in vain was poetry called living painting] and argues that a playwright should construct and organize a *comedia* using illusionistic techniques analogous to those used by a painter, such as perspective (1996, 226). Moreover, this parallel between the two modes of artistic mimesis was visually as well as theoretically apt. *Comedias* were at least initially intended for performances in which the characters, not unlike figures in paintings, would be given bodily form and often luxurious garb for the pleasure of the spectators' gaze.[3] Actors playing roles oscillated between the two-dimensional and the three-dimensional onstage; in the theatres, static paintings seemed to come to life even as performers seemed to transform themselves into simulacra of portraits, creating a perceptual and conceptual liminal space between *lo vivo* and *lo pintado*, between living reality and artistic representations of it.

It is thus significant though hardly surprising that Lope de Vega could write one *comedia*, *El Brasil restituido* (Brazil Restored), in which an absent king's portrait is treated as if it were the monarch himself, and another, *El servir con mala estrella* (Serving under an Evil Star), in which a present king is treated as though he were merely an inert portrait of himself. In the latter play, King Alfonso VIII comes illicitly to the home of Don Tello to woo the latter's sister, only to be surprised there by Tello's unexpected return. Regally scorning the ignominy of concealment or self-defence, Alfonso chooses instead to remain motionless where he stands, in effect assuming the guise of his own image. Rather than confront his sovereign directly, Tello accepts this pretence so that he can criticize Alfonso, taking advantage of a painting's inability to hear or retort: "¿Quién trajo á casa el retrato, / hermana, del señor Rey? / ¿Véndese esta figura? / Cierto que es muy parecida, / Y que no he visto en mi vida / Tan extremada pintura" [Who brought this portrait of the king here, sister? Is this figure for sale? It is certainly an excellent likeness, and never in my life have I seen such consummate painting] (1952, 50). It is unfortunate, Tello continues in "an exquisitely tactful but barbed rebuke" (McKendrick 2000, 59), that the artist chose to depict the king as a furtive lover rather than as a noble warrior, thus diminishing his subject's majesty with an image which is neither a flattering nor a worthy one.[4] In contrast, at the conclusion of *El Brasil restituido* Don Fadrique de Toledo unveils a uniquely exemplary portrait of Philip IV when the Spaniards' vanquished foes seek reconciliation and forgiveness. Fadrique instructs them to kneel before the painting while he speaks to it as though it were the king: "Magno Felipe, esta gente / pide perdón de sus yerros. / ¿Quiere Vuestra Majestad / que esta vez les perdonemos? / Parece que dijo sí" [Great Philip, these people beg pardon for their errors. Does Your Majesty want us to pardon them this time? It appears that he said "yes"] (1970, 294). The rebels receive the mercy they seek ostensibly from Philip's portrait, the quality of which transcends mere visual likeness, since it is somehow imbued with the full force of Philip's majesty as well as the capacity for clemency lauded by Lope. That Lope deemed both these devices theatrically valid reveals just how ambiguous and liminal a representational space the Spanish stage – as well as the Spanish portraitist's canvas – could be.

*La próspera fortuna de Ruy López de Ávalos* (1604) is the first half of Damián Salucio del Poyo's theatrical diptych devoted to its eponymous protagonist, the royal favourite and Constable of Castile under Enrique III and then Juan II until Álvaro de Luna's ascension.[5] It is also this play in which Salucio del Poyo utilizes the falling portrait device in an episode that Luis Vélez de Guevara and Tirso de Molina, among other playwrights, will imitate (Peale 2004, 138–40).[6] The portrait in question is that of the infanta Catalina de Inglaterra – Catherine of Lancaster, granddaughter of Pedro I of Castile and her cousin Enrique III's future queen. Though Catalina, with the support of her family and political allies, covets the Castilian throne Enrique already occupies, her true feelings for Enrique are soon revealed to be more amorous than rivalrous.[7] While conferring privately with the Spanish commander Gonzalo de Estremera, Catalina's assurances of her peaceful nature quickly give way to transparent questions about her cousin: "¿Cómo Enrique no se casa? / ¿Ha puesto en una dama / su pensamiento, á quien ama? / ¿Quiere á alguna bien?" [Why has Enrique not yet married? Has he set his heart on a woman whom he loves? Does he adore anyone?] (1857, 443c). When told that Enrique in fact does love a count's very beautiful daughter, Catalina immediately calls for her own portrait to be sent to Enrique, a likeness which will be no mere miniature: "Hola, dadme aquel retrato / Que está colgado en mi tienda, / Para que tu rey entienda / Que como a deudo le trato" [Bring me that portrait hanging in my tent, so that your king will understand that I treat him as a kinsman] (1857, 443a). Once the *retrato grande* [large portrait] is brought forth onstage, Catalina demands that Gonzalo tell her which is more beautiful, Enrique's young countess or her own painted image. The perceptive

Spaniard assures her that Enrique would immediately forget her rival were he to see the portrait, to which the infanta replies: "Si este retrato ha de ser / Bastante para quitalle / El amor, quiero envialle / Adonde le pueda ver" [If this portrait will be enough to purge him of his love, I want to send it to where he can see it] (1857, 443a).

Despite the political context of *La próspera fortuna*, Catalina's portrait is nevertheless introduced in this scene within the recognizable Neoplatonic discourse of enamouring likenesses. Melveena McKendrick notes that "the connection between beauty, desire, and eye is crucial" to the dramatic treatment of love inspired by images:

> The belief that love was stirred most readily through the eye – the noblest of senses for the neoplatonists, for whom beauty led most effectively to the contemplation of the divine – pervaded Early Modern thinking and sensibilities. There are numerous plays where the picture of an unknown person gives access to love. (1996, 11)

Likenesses could awaken love, the Neoplatonists further argued, because painting could both convey external beauty and lay bare a subject's inner nature – the mind, character, and even the soul – to the viewer's gaze. Calderón himself, in his deposition defending painting as an aristocratic calling, argued that in a portraitist's rendering of a man's features, "llegó su destreza aun a copiarle el alma" [his skill even succeeded in copying his soul] (2007, 11).[8] As Frederick de Armas explains of this tradition, "The work of art, the *retrato* can move the soul since it partakes of soul" (1998, 6). This is the philosophy underpinning Catalina's impulsive decision to send her portrait to Enrique: in Catalina's mind, it is entirely plausible that Enrique might fall in love with her likeness and reciprocate her feelings prior even to meeting her in person.

This is, of course, one practical reason why Catalina asks Gonzalo to compare her unseen rival's beauty to that of the portrait rather than Catalina's own: it is the painted image which she hopes will ignite Enrique's passion for her. At the same time, however, the question serves to foreground the simultaneous presence onstage of Catalina and her likeness – which, like all the paintings included here, must be of substantial size if the portrait will prove large enough to block a doorway later in the play. This scene confronts Gonzalo and the audience with two Catalinas, one *viva* and one *pintada*, who are separate yet also the same, sharing both physiognomy and character. It would be difficult to imagine staging a more effective illustration of representation's ambiguities than this tableau: it is the painted Catalina whose beauty is discussed in the third person by her original, as if she were a separate entity, but who is also intended to charm and beguile Enrique, as if she were the "authentic" Catalina.

Following her instructions, in the second act Gonzalo hangs Catalina's portrait over the doorway leading to Enrique's bedchamber, where the king himself sees it for the first time. He initially calls for its removal but quickly changes his mind, reasoning that its subject's virtuous character makes her a trustworthy guardian for his slumbers. He then addresses the likeness directly, as though it were Catalina herself:

> ENRIQUE: Retrato, quedáos ahí
> En guarda deste lugar,
> Y mirad que habéis de dar
> Mañana cuenta de mí;
> Que aunque sois figura muerta,
> En vuestra fe me aventuro,
> Y me entro á dormir seguro
> Con mi enemiga á la puerta.

> [ENRIQUE: Portrait, remain there to stand guard over this place, and remember that tomorrow you will be held accountable for me; although you are a dead image, I trust myself to your good faith, and I retire to sleep securely with my rival at my door.] (1857, 451a)

Again the difference between original and likeness is problematized, since Enrique is asking the inert two-dimensional painting to act with the perceptions and agency of its subject, despite his admission that it is a dead image. More important, however, in this speech Salucio del Poyo begins to extend the powers discursively associated with Catalina's portrait beyond the conventionally amatory with Enrique's command that the image exercise a protective responsibility as well. By introducing this new textual element, which Schack significantly described as "la idea de convertir á un retrato en ángel protector de una vida amenazada" [the idea of transforming a portrait into an endangered life's guardian angel] (1887, 313), the playwright destabilizes the painting's prior implicit categorization as a secular likeness: active beneficent powers were most often associated with religious paintings and icons in medieval and early modern Western cultures. The Council of Trent, refuting Protestant charges of Catholic iconolatry, had insisted that "it was not the images themselves that were to be worshiped, but rather the sacred figures they represented" (Bass 2008,

80).[9] That distinction notwithstanding, however, the saints, the Virgin Mary, and Jesus Christ were believed to be in some way present in their material representations – and even more important, they were believed to work through those representations on behalf of the faithful. As Hans Belting notes, "Authentic images seemed capable of action, seemed to possess *dynamis*, or supernatural power" (1994, 6). Indeed, in early modern Spain the crafting of "extremely lifelike, evocative" polychrome sculptures of Christ and Mary in order to "move the viewer to devotion" during religious processions relied on precisely this sense of inherent dynamism (Webster 1998, 110).[10]

There exist innumerable accounts of miracles accomplished by religious likenesses, to which were often attributed apotropaic powers. According to grateful believers, for example, the seventeenth-century Italian image known as the Madonna of the Oak not only saved women in childbirth, as might be expected from an icon of the Virgin, but also cured the dangerously ill and protected its believers from a breathtaking catalogue of dangers: "it saved people from possession by the devil, from attacks by seven kinds of animals, from attacks by robbers and brigands, from a host of watery accidents, from fire, from falls from trees and ladders, from military disasters, from imprisonment and vehicular accidents" (Freedberg 1989, 141). Even more significantly for our purposes, there also existed any number of accounts of religious images themselves transcending their inert material nature to take action in the physical dimension. Caesarius of Heisterbach's thirteenth-century *Dialogue on Miracles* relates stories of portraits turning towards or away from people and even of statues administering corporal punishment to sinners.[11] Another well-known trope was that of the statue of Christ on the Cross suddenly coming to life and reaching out to embrace a faithful worshipper; paintings by Spanish artists depicting these visions or miracles, such as Ribalta's *Christ Embracing Saint Bernard of Clairvaux* and Murillo's *Saint Francis Embracing Christ on the Cross*, were produced well into the seventeenth century, suggesting that such tales would have been a part of the cultural currency shared by Salucio del Poyo's audiences (Freedberg 1989, 287–9, 294–6).

Salucio del Poyo can thus be seen to have carefully prepared his own seventeenth-century spectators for Catalina's portrait to take visible action in Enrique's defence. After the king retires to his chambers, the Jewish physician Don Mair appears "*con un vaso en la mano, como que lleva dentro veneno*" [*with a glass in his hand, like he is carrying poison within it*] (1857, 451b). He announces his regicidal intentions to the audience, only to be thwarted by the image which the king had only moments before commanded to protect him: "*Va á entrar y cáese el retrato, tápale la puerta, y queda espantado.*" [*He goes to enter and the portrait falls, blocking the door, and he stands frightened*] (1857, 451b). Mair's initial fearful response is a superstitious one, regarding this unexpected event as a "mal agüero" [bad omen] (1857, 451b), but he soon focuses on the portrait as a representation of its subject rather than as a large, heavy object: "Animo, no hay que hacer caso, / Que esta es una tabla muda; / Parece que se demuda / Y me amenaza si paso" [Courage! There is no need to pay any attention, since this is a mute panel; it seems to be changing, growing upset, and threatening me if I pass] (1857, 451b). Mair's effort to reassure himself that Catalina's likeness is only a *tabla muda* gives way to his sense that it knows what crime he has come to commit and looks menacingly at him, thus strengthening the suggestion that the portrait, somehow possessing both perceptions and agency, functions as the absent Catalina's surrogate and deliberately fell to block his path. This impression is only enhanced, of course, by the visual image presented by the fallen portrait no longer looking down on the stage floor from above, but rather standing now on the same level as the actors, in effect confronting the physician face-to-face. Enrique and Ruy López, startled by the noise, arrive and uncover Don Mair's plot, and then the young king praises the painting with rhetoric that reinforces the likeness's supra-material representation in this text, now calling it a "retrato vivo" [living portrait] instead of a "figura muerta" [dead image] and declaring it "de mis ojos el postrer milagro" [in my eyes the ultimate miracle] (1857, 452a).

Vélez de Guevara similarly incorporated a portrait's protective fall into another *privanza* drama, *El lucero de Castilla y Luna de Aragón* (1613–14).[12] In this *comedia* the subject of the portrait is the play's long-suffering protagonist Fadrique de Trastámara, the Duque de Arjona, who is betrayed by the Conde de Santorcaz, his one-time protégé at court and unsuccessful rival for the hand of his wife Aldonza. By the third act, Santorcaz has succeeded in discrediting Fadrique in the eyes of the king and bringing about his imprisonment on false charges, in part so that he can force his attentions on the presumably defenceless Aldonza in her husband's absence. It is this assault from which Fadrique's painted image will protect her.

Unlike Salucio del Poyo, Vélez does not incorporate the portrait into the action prior to the scene in which it falls: while the earlier play needed to explain the presence of Catalina's likeness in her political rival's chambers, it is natural that Fadrique's image would hang in his own apartments. The audience first notices its presence when the distressed Aldonza commands her maid Elvira to draw back the drapery covering the portrait: "Esté descubierto siempre / porque mis ojos le miren" [Let it always be visible so that my eyes can behold it] (forthcoming, 2615–16). As in *La próspera fortuna*, the text foregrounds a connection between love and a painted image, but in this *comedia* the *retrato* has the intended purpose of reinforcing conjugal love rather than awakening a new passion; Aldonza gazes upon the portrait to feel closer to her incarcerated husband. In Fadrique's absence, his likeness will serve as his surrogate, as Aldonza makes clear when she dismisses Elvira: "dejadme sola, que quiero / con el Duque divertirme" [leave me alone, for I want to distract myself with the duke] (forthcoming, 2627–8). And once Elvira has left, Aldonza addresses the portrait in a long monologue in which she consciously seeks to blur the distinction between *lo vivo* and *lo pintado*: "Ya que hemos quedado solos, / quiero, señor, persuadirme / que sois vuestro original" [Now that we are alone, my lord, I want to persuade myself that you are your own true self] (forthcoming, 2633–5).

Most significantly, Aldonza confesses the jealousy she cannot help feeling at the false reports that Fadrique sexually abused women under his authority, and then imagines his furious reaction:

> ALDONZA: Parece, señor, que airado
> de ver que esta ofensa hice
> a la fe de vuestro amor,
> y al dolor que contradice
> en vos culpas tan enormes
> y delitos tan civiles,
> me repondéis por los ojos
> con rayos, y que pusistes
> la'mano en la espada agora.
> ¡Tened, escuchadme, oídme,
> Duque, señor, dueño, esposo!
>
> [It seems, my lord, that in anger at my offence against the good faith of your love, and against the pain that belies in you any such enormous offences and heinous crimes, you respond to me with lightning in your eyes and you are now putting your hand on your sword. Wait, listen to me, hear me, duke, my lord, my master, my husband!] (forthcoming, 2665–75)

As in *La próspera fortuna*, an anxious character attributes human reactions to a portrait and fears the image's capacity for retribution; her emphasis on its gaze also associates it with religious discourses, recalling Nicholas of Cusa's explanation of how a painted icon's eyes will be seen to gaze continuously and unchangeably at each and every monk in its presence (1962, 134–7). Aldonza's attribution of emotion to the portrait serves in part to foreshadow its fall soon thereafter, once she has retired for the night and the Conde de Santorcaz arrives, intending to overcome her resistance to his advances. The painting crashes to the floor just as he approaches Aldonza's door:

> CONDE: Pero ¿qué es esto? Señor
> Duque, vuecelencia mire
> que yo ... que ... cuando ... que el Rey ...
> después que ... nunca ... Terrible
> susto el retrato me ha dado,
> que es de suerte lo que vive
> de su original, que pudo
> sobresaltarme, y temíle
> como a marido [...]
>
> [CONDE: But what's this? My lord Duke, your Excellency, look, I ... that ...when ...since the king ... after ... never ... The portrait has given me a terrible fright, since it looks so much like its subject come to life that it startled me, and I feared it as I would a husband [...] (forthcoming, 2723–31)

Santorcaz's perturbation here is noteworthy: for a few moments he seems genuinely confused and responds to the painting with real fear, as though Fadrique himself stood in the doorway rather than his likeness. This portrait is indeed presented as more than inert matter, given the visceral reactions it can elicit from both Fadrique's wife and his rival as well as its apparent ability to protect the former's chastity from the latter's concupiscence: the sound of its fall brings the young Álvaro de Luna to the scene in time to defend Aldonza's honour.

To the best of my knowledge, Tirso de Molina is the only playwright to have incorporated falling portraits into more than one *comedia*.[13] Ever since Hartzenbusch's identification of the source in his 1848 edition of *Prudencia en la mujer* (ca. 1622–3), there has been a critical consensus that Tirso borrowed Salucio del Poyo's device for perhaps the most famous scene of this historical play, in which the widowed and politically beleaguered Queen María de Molina's portrait bars another regicidal, poison-brewing Jewish physician from entering her sleeping son's chambers.[14]

Despite the obvious similarities, however, the Mercedarian substantially reworked his source material. Like Vélez, Tirso has no need to introduce the queen's portrait before the scene in which it falls: it is logical that María de Molina's likeness would hang in the royal palace. Furthermore, if Catalina sends Enrique a portrait representing her primarily as a desirable woman and if Fadrique's *retrato* captures him primarily as a husband concerned for his honour, then María de Molina's depicts her in her public capacity as a ruler. Like Philip IV's portrait in *El Brasil restituido* and like all such images of sovereigns (Bass 2008, 79–82), the queen's likeness is fundamentally iconic, created and displayed as a representation of the power and authority she both wields and embodies as a monarch.[15] Tirso relies on precisely this aspect of a royal portrait to create an effective tableau even prior to the painting's fall in *Prudencia*, when the treacherous and ambitious infante Don Juan and the physician Ismael plot the young king's murder in the latter's own apartments under the silent gaze of his mother's likeness. This stage image visually conveys the arrogant would-be usurper's contempt for the queen, whom Don Juan considers negligible and unfit to rule by virtue of her gender (1968b, 919b).[16]

After Don Juan departs, Ismael conquers his misgivings in a soliloquy and then prepares to enter the sleeping king's bedchamber. Unlike in Salucio del Poyo's original scene, however, the portrait over the doorway gives the would-be assassin pause even before it falls. The stage directions state: "*Al querer entrar en el aposento del Rey, repara en el retrato de la REINA, que está sobre la puerta*" [*When he starts to enter the king's room, he catches sight of the queen's portrait, which is over the door*] (1968b, 920a). Ismael expresses his agitation in words that immediately foreground the liminality of the painting, which he clearly cannot dismiss as nothing more than pigments on canvas:

> ISMAEL: Mas, ¡cielos!, ¿no es el retrato
> este de su madre? Sí.
> No sin causa me acobarda
> la traición que juzgo incierta,
> pues puso el rey a su puerta
> su misma madre por guarda.
> ¡Vive Dios, que estoy temblando
> de miralla, aunque pintada!

[But heavens, is this not his mother's portrait? Yes. Not without cause do I fear the treason which I judge to be uncertain to succeed, since the king placed his mother herself to guard his door. I swear to God that I tremble to look at her, even painted!] (1968b, 920a)

For Ismael, María de Molina cannot easily be considered utterly distinct from her framed image, which he guiltily regards as a watchful sentinel conscious of his intentions:

ISMAEL: ¿No parece que enojada
muda me está amenazando?
¿No parece que en los ojos
forja rayos enemigos,
que amenazan mis castigos
y autorizan sus enojos?
No me miréis, reina, airada.

[Does it not look like she is threatening me furiously and mutely? Does it not look like she is forging hostile lightning bolts in her eyes, threatening me with punishments and affirming her grievances? Do not gaze angrily at me, queen.] (1968b, 920a–b)

As in *El lucero de Castilla*, the portrait's viewer focuses on the subject's eyes, imagining menacing *rayos* radiating out of the painting which provoke pleas for clemency. Ismael, however, will receive no mercy from María de Molina, who will ultimately force him to drink his own poison after he confesses his guilt.

The queen's portrait falls to block the doorway just as Ismael summons the resolve to commit the regicide which will enable Don Juan's claim to the throne. As Serge Maurel's description of the scene indicates, this is the moment when the painting most obviously transcends its material nature: Ismael "l'interpelle, essaie d'apaiser sa colère; l'image s'anime et, en manière de réponse, tombe à ses pieds, lui interdisant le passage alors qu'il allait entrer" [speaks to it, tries to appease its anger; the image comes to life and in response falls at his feet, barring him from the passageway he was going to enter] (1971, 365). This fortuitous fall also strengthens in *Prudencia* the religious elements less directly present in *La próspera fortuna* and *El lucero de Castilla*: in those plays, the portraits' falls were rendered at least more poetically credible by their apotropaic functions, which evoked the abilities popularly attributed to miraculous images, but there was no suggestion that the images possessed power because Catalina and Fadrique themselves were candidates for sainthood, despite their virtuous characters. As various critics of *Prudencia* have observed, however, in this work the queen's moral exemplarity cannot help but bring to mind her namesake, the Virgin Mary, for whom María is in fact "credibly an analogue" (Wilson and Moir 1971, 96). Margaret Wilson points out that María de Molina "is the mother of an infant son who is poor and persecuted, yet a king" (1977, 94), while de Armas has further enumerated the many parallels between the text's presentation of the *niño rey* Fernando and the Christ Child (1978). Thus María's portrait can even more plausibly exert its "miraculous powers" (Wilson and Moir 1971, 93) precisely because of its subject's obvious associations with the Virgin.

When María de Molina herself arrives a few moments later, her entrance creates another striking tableau which offers perhaps the most imaginative exploitation of the visual potential inherent in such falling portrait scenes devised by any playwright; as we shall see, Tirso likewise employs it in *La firmeza en la hermosura*.[17] Spanish playhouse stages in this era featured two doorways facing the audience through which characters entered and exited; *Prudencia*'s stage directions indicate that once the queen's portrait has blocked his access to one of these doors, Ismael attempts to flee through the other – only to encounter the actual queen making her entrance through that same doorway, coming to her son's aid and obstructing Ismael's path in a fashion identical to that of her painted image only moments before. There must even occur at least a brief moment during which María de Molina is framed by one doorway even as her framed likeness stands in front of the other. Tirso thus achieves onstage a remarkable doubling effect which carries the erosion of distinctions between *lo vivo* and *lo pintado* to new heights. What, this tableau seems to ask the spectator, separates the "true" María de Molina from her image?

Finally, Tirso de Molina's *La firmeza en la hermosura* (ca. 1632–3) combines a scenario reminiscent of *El lucero de Castilla* with the discourses and representations of portraiture used by Tirso himself in *Prudencia*; like the latter play, *Firmeza* foregrounds a woman's exemplary virtue and it announces that theme with a similar title.[18] In *Firmeza* Don Juan de Urrea is forced to feign his own death, leaving his betrothed, Doña Elena Coronel, to remember and mourn him with the life-size *retrato* which hangs in the humble apartments to which she is reduced after his alleged demise. This likeness's fall to block a doorway follows what by now emerges as the predictable pattern, beginning with the arrival of the Conde de Urgel, this play's villain. Like the Conde de Santorcaz's passion for Aldonza in *El lucero*, Urgel's obsession with the chaste heroine drives him to attempt a nocturnal assault on her virtue. And like Ismael in *Prudencia*, the Conde de Urgel delivers a soliloquy in which he contemplates and justifies to himself the dishonourable action he is about to take before moving towards Elena's door, at which point he "*detiénese viendo sobre la puerta el retrato de DON JUAN*" [*stops when he sees the portrait of Don Juan over the door*] and exclaims, "La imagen de don Juan miro / valientemente copiada" [I see the likeness of Don Juan boldly copied] (1968a, 1441b). Again Tirso undermines the difference between reality and representation, for Urgel immediately speaks to the portrait as though it were his rival present in the flesh. Calling him "joven inadvertido" [imprudent boy], the count reproves Juan for his arrogance in daring to compete for Elena's favours and for his naive trust in her virtue, and then dismisses the *retrato* as he approaches the door, "No estorbarás más mi intento" [You will hinder my plans no more] (1968a, 1441b–2a).

It is at this moment, of course, that Juan's portrait crashes to the floor in an exercise of its protective function on the real Juan's behalf, blocking the doorway and frightening Urgel towards a re-awakening of his suppressed honour: "Por Dios, que le estoy temblando: / cobarde su copia miro" [I'm trembling, by God: I look at his likeness with dread] (1968a, 1442a). He even goes so far as to doff his hat in a demonstration of respect that recalls Santorcaz's belated acknowledgment of the deference he owed Fadrique: "Respetemos su presencia, / deseos inadvertidos, / porque un esposo, aunque en sombra, / de veneración es digno" [Let us respect his presence, imprudent desires, because even the image of a (betrothed) husband is worthy of veneration] (1968a, 1442a). The portrait's fall, as in the other three plays, brings the life-sized painted image literally face-to-face with the villain, heightening the illusion that Juan's essence or soul somehow animates the likeness. Even this, however, does not prepare Urgel for the real Juan de Urrea's appearance in the unobstructed doorway: "*En la puerta del otro lado aparece DON JUAN con la espada desnuda, la punta al suelo, en cuerpo y sin moverse*" [*In the door on the other side appears Don Juan with his sword drawn, its point on the floor, in the flesh and motionless*] (1968a, 1442a). Again the audience sees the doubling effect devised by Tirso for *Prudencia*, here made even more explicit by Juan's motionless pose framed in the second doorway and by the words with which Urgel declares his astonishment: "¡Allí don Juan retratado! / ¡Aquí, cielos, don Juan vivo! / ¿Dos esposos en dos puertas / y en entrambas dos el mismo?" [There stands Don Juan painted and here, good heavens, stands the living Don Juan! Two husbands in two doorways and in both of them the same man?] (1968a, 1442a). In this tableau dictated by the stage directions, the immobile Juan seems, like King Alfonso in *El servir con mala estrella*, to be imitating his own portrait even as it shares the stage with him; the resultant symmetrical stage picture draws *lo vivo* and *lo pintado* so closely together that the distinctions between them essentially collapse.

Lastly, just as he did in *Prudencia*, Tirso also overtly links the *retrato* to religious discourses of miraculous images. Prior to its fall, the grieving Elena addressed a lengthy monologue of love to the portrait, vowing fidelity to Juan's memory and eagerly anticipating the reunion of their souls in the hereafter. Not only does this passage declare Elena's Penelope-like loyalty, but her language here is also evocative of another, non-theatrical Golden Age literary tradition:

> ELENA: Mi amor, malogrado mío,
> como accidente forzoso
> del alma, que tras vos vuela,
> os sigue a los dulces ocios
> de la quietud que os asista;
> que bien puede, aunque no en rotos
> lazos del cuerpo, buscaros
> en éxtasis y en arrobos.
>
> [My untimely-dead beloved, my love – like an inescapable accident of the soul which flies after you – follows you to the sweet freedom of the serenity where you dwell; well may my love, although not in the broken bonds of the body, seek you in ecstasy and raptures.] (1968a, 1436a)

This talk of souls winging their way to otherworldly repose and ecstasy partakes of the language of mysticism, immediately recalling the poetry of San Juan de la Cruz. In such mystical verse, of course, the soul yearns for and sometimes achieves union with *el Amado*, the Loved One, who is none other than Christ himself. As a result, Elena's desire for just such a future rapture with Juan by extension rhetorically associates him with Christ, a connection that the text will reinforce when the Conde de Urgel, terrified at the appearance of the rival he thought dead and buried, considers Juan's return a resurrection and cries out: "hasta los sepúlcros se abren" [even the graves are opening up] (1968a, 1442b). And if Juan is associated with Jesus Christ, even by allusion, then his portrait can be regarded as sharing its protective capacity with the paintings and statues of Jesus credited with saving and comforting the weak, the innocent, and the devout.

In conclusion, this essay has aimed at delineating some of the ways in which a select number of painted portraits in the *comedia* transcend their materiality and function as much more than inanimate objects. In the four plays examined here, it is not enough for likenesses to serve as objects of exchange or even as Neoplatonic images capable of awakening love: instead, previously inert paintings of absent characters unexpectedly exercise agency, saving embattled kings and vulnerable noblewomen from death or dishonour. Not only do these scenes capitalize on an effective stage device, but more important, they also foreground the ambiguities and contradictions already present in early modern Spanish discourses of both theatrical and pictorial representation. In these four works by Salucio del Poyo, Vélez de Guevara, and Tirso de Molina, there is much more to some portraits than initially meets the eye.

## NOTES

1 Students of the *comedia* will likely already be familiar with the episode in Calderón's *El mayor monstruo del mundo* (The Greatest Monster in the World) in which Mariadnes's portrait falls between Herodes and Octaviano as the former attempts to kill the latter; Herodes plunges his dagger into the painting, just as he will later murder Mariadnes herself. Unlike in the four plays examined here, Calderón uses a portrait's protective fall primarily to foreshadow violence to come. The substantial scholarly commentary on this episode includes Bass (2008, 84–99); Blue (1978); Gómez (1997, 281–5); and McKim-Smith and Welles (1996). Following Klaus Toll's notes to his 1937 edition of Salucio del Poyo's *El rey perseguido*, Caparrós Esperante also cites instances of falling portraits in Claramonte's *De lo vivo a lo pintado*, Jiménez de Enciso's *La mayor hazaña de Carlos V*, and Rojas Zorilla's third act of *La Baltasara* (1987, 137 n159). Space does not permit consideration of these plays here.

2 See also Calvo Serraller (1991), Lacourt (1990), and Morán Turina (2001). All translations are mine unless otherwise referenced.

3 See Bass (2008, 45–6) on painting and theatre as "sites of sartorial display."

4 See McKendrick (2000, 57–63) for an analysis of portraits in this play.

5 See Cauvin (1957), MacCurdy (1978), and Peale (2004) on the *comedia de privanza*. For commentary on Salucio del Poyo, see Caparrós Esperante (1987) and Hernández Valcárcel's edition of several of the *comedias* (1985).

6 McClelland takes a dim view of Salucio del Poyo's use of the falling portrait device, which she considers "cheap enough from the standpoint of absolute values," but argues that Tirso makes it more persuasive in *Prudencia en la mujer* with stronger characterization (1948, 53).

7 This is pure fiction. The actual Catherine and Enrique were married in a political alliance negotiated by their families in 1388 – when she was fifteen years old and he was only nine.

8 See also Curtius (1990, 559–70), Damiani (1989), and ter Horst (1982).

9 See also Saint-Saëns (1995) on Tridentine Spanish art.

10 See Webster (1998, especially 57–110 and 164–88) for an analysis of such processions.

11 See, for example, 1:501–2 and 2:23–4, 26, 77–8. See also Loomis (1948) for a compendium of miracles, and Belting (1994) and Trexler (2004) on religious images.

12 I am greatly indebted to C. George Peale for sharing with me the newly edited text of *El lucero de Castilla* from the forthcoming critical edition in Manson and Peale's ongoing series of Vélez de Guevara's complete plays. For a brief discussion of the play, see Cauvin (1957, 108–13).

13 See Weimer (2003) for my preliminary considerations of the falling portraits in *Prudencia* and *Firmeza*.

14 See de Armas (1987, 183–5), de los Ríos, editor of Tirso de Molina's *Obras completas* (1968, 902–3), Fucilla (1961, 3), Gregg (1977, 302–3), Kennedy (1948, 1136 n12); Lida de Malkiel (1973, 79 n6), and Morel Fatio (1900, 102–7) for critical agreement concerning this relationship as well as varying perspectives on possible historical counterparts to the Jewish physicians in the two plays.

15 See also Belsey and Belsey's essay on portraits of Elizabeth I (1990).

16 See Blue (1998, 454) for a summary of the play's conflicting perspectives on María.

17 As Agheana (1972, 48–50) and Sullivan (1981, 111–12 n12) observe, Tirso repeatedly exploits visually striking, often emblematic tableaux in *Prudencia* as well as in other plays. See also Hughes (1984) for instances of such scenic devices and visual images in Tirso's religious theatre and Restrepo-Gautier (2001) on Tirso's use of emblems.

18 *Firmeza* was performed in 1633 under the title *Sin peligros no hay fineza*, while a 1635 manuscript of the text also calls it *Amor no teme peligros*. See Jones and Williamsen (1981) for details of the play's textual history and attribution.

## WORKS CITED

Agheana, Ion Tudor. 1972. *The Situational Drama of Tirso de Molina*. New York: Plaza Mayor.

Bass, Laura R. 2008. *The Drama of the Portrait: Theater and Visual Culture in Early Modern Spain*. University Park: Pennsylvania State University Press.

Belsey, Andrew, and Catherine Belsey. 1990. "Icons of Divinity: Portraits of Elizabeth I." In *Renaissance Bodies: The Human Figure in English Culture c. 1540–1660*, edited by Lucy Gent and Nigel Llewellyn, 11–35. London: Reaktion.

Belting, Hans. 1994. *Likeness and Presence: A History of the Image before the Era of Art*. Chicago: University of Chicago Press.

Blue, William R. 1978. "Las imágenes en *El mayor monstruo del mundo* de Calderón de la Barca." *Hispania* 61 (4): 888–97. http://dx.doi.org/10.2307/340936.

Blue, William R. 1998. "Portraying Queens in Painting and in Three Plays by Tirso de Molina." *Romance Languages Annual* 10: 453–6.

Calderón de la Barca, Pedro. 2007. *Memorial dado a los profesores de pintura*. Barcelona: Linkgua.

Calvo Serraller, Francisco. 1991. "El pincel y la palabra: Una hermandad singular en el barroco español." In *El Siglo de Oro de la pintura española*, edited by Alfonso E. Pérez Sánchez, 187–203. Madrid: Mondadori.

Caparrós Esperante, Luis. 1987. *Entre validos y letrados: La obra dramática de Damián Salucio del Poyo*. Valladolid: Universidad de Valladolid.

Cauvin, Mary Austin. 1957. "The *Comedia de privanza* in the Seventeenth Century." Unpublished PhD dissertation, University of Pennsylvania.

Curtius, Ernst Robert. 1990. *European Literature and the Latin Middle Ages*. Translated by Willard R. Trask. Princeton: Princeton University Press.

Cusa, Nicholas of. 1962. *Unity and Reform: Selected Writings of Nicholas of Cusa*. Edited by John Patrick Dolan. South Bend, IN: University of Notre Dame Press.

Damiani, Bruno M. 1989. "Los dramaturgos del Siglo de Oro frente a las artes visuales: prólogo para un estudio comparativo." In *El mundo del teatro español en su siglo de oro: ensayos dedicados a John E. Varey*, edited by J.M. Ruano de la Haza, 137–149. Ottawa: Dovehouse.

de Armas, Frederick A. 1978. "La figura del niño rey en *La prudencia en la mujer*." *Bulletin Hispanique* 80 (3): 175–89. http://dx.doi.org/10.3406/hispa.1978.4257.

de Armas, Frederick A. 1998. "Poison in a Golden Cup: A Senecan Image in Claramonte's *Comedias*." *Crítica Hispánica* 10: 3–19.

Freedberg, David. 1989. *The Power of Images: Studies in the History and Theory of Response*. Chicago: University of Chicago Press.

Fucilla, Joseph G. 1961. "The Ismael Episode in Tirso's *La prudencia en la mujer*." *Bulletin of the Comediantes* 13: 3–5.

Gregg, Karl C. 1977. "The Probable Source for Tirso's Jewish Doctor." *Romance Notes* 17: 302–4.

Gómez, María Asunción. 1997. "Mirando de cerca 'mujer, comedia, y pintura' en las obras dramáticas de Lope de Vega y Calderón de la Barca." *Bulletin of the Comediantes* 49 (2): 273–93.

Hartzenbusch, Juan Eugenio, ed. 1848. *Teatro escogido de Fray Gabriel Téllez: Biblioteca de autores españoles*. Vol. 5. Madrid: Rivadeneyra.

Heisterbach, Caesarius of. 1929. *The Dialogue on Miracles*. Translated by H. von E. Scott and C.C. Swinton Bland. Introduction by G.G. Coulton. 2 vols. London: George Rutledge and Sons.

Hughes, Ann Nickerson. 1984. *Religious Imagery in the Theater of Tirso de Molina*. Macon, GA: Mercer University Press.

Jones, Harold G., and Vern G. Williamsen. 1981. "Dos refundiciones tirsianas: *Amor no teme peligros* y *Los balcones de Madrid*." In *Homenaje a Tirso*, 133–55. Madrid: Revista Estudios.

Kennedy, Ruth Lee. 1948. "*La prudencia en la mujer* and the Ambient That Brought It Forth." *PMLA* 63 (4): 1131–90. http://dx.doi.org/10.2307/459610.

Lacourt, Christiane Faliu. 1990. "Espejos, reflejos y retratos en la comedia (1600–1660)." In *Teatro del siglo de oro: Homenaje a Alberto Navarro González*, edited by Víctor García de la Concha, et al., 141–57. Kassel: Reichenberger.

Lida de Malkiel, María Rosa. 1973. "Lope de Vega y los judíos." *Bulletin Hispanique* 75 (1): 73–112. http://dx.doi.org/10.3406/hispa.1973.4097.

Loomis, C. Grant. 1948. *White Magic: An Introduction to the Folklore of Christian Legend*. Cambridge, MA: Medieval Academy of America.

MacCurdy, Raymond R. 1978. *The Tragic Fall: Don Álvaro de Luna and Other Favorites in Spanish Golden Age Drama*. Chapel Hill: University of North Carolina, Department of Romance Languages.

Maurel, Serge. 1971. *L'univers dramatique de Tirso de Molina*. Poitiers: Université de Poitiers.

McClelland, I.L. 1948. *Tirso de Molina: Studies in Dramatic Realism*. Liverpool: Institute of Hispanic Studies.

McKendrick, Melveena. 1996. *The Revealing Image: Stage Portraits in the Theatre of the Golden Age. Papers in Spanish Theatre History* 2. London: Department of Hispanic Studies, Queen Mary and Westfield College.

McKendrick, Melveena. 2000. *Playing the King: Lope de Vega and the Limits of Conformity*. London: Tamesis.

McKim-Smith, Gridley, and Marcia L. Welles. 1996. "Portrait of a Lady: The Violence of Vision." In *Brave New Words: Studies in Spanish Golden Age*

*Literature*, edited by Edward H. Friedman and Catherine Larson, 221–46. New Orleans: University Press of the South.

Molina, Tirso de. 1968a. "La firmeza en la hermosura." In *Obras dramáticas completas*, edited by Blanca de los Ríos, 3: 1407–43. Madrid: Aguilar.

Molina, Tirso de. 1968b. "Prudencia en la mujer." In *Obras dramáticas completas*, edited by Blanca de los Ríos, 3: 893–951. Madrid: Aguilar.

Molina, Tirso de. 1996. *Cigarrales de Toledo*. Edited by Luis Vázquez Fernández. Madrid: Castalia.

Morán Turina, Miguel. 2001. "Velázquez, la pintura y el teatro del Siglo de Oro." *Boletín del Museo del Prado* 19: 47–71.

Morel-Fatio, Alfred. 1900. "Études sur le théatre de Tirso de Molina: *La prudencia en la muger.*" *Bulletin Hispanique* 2 (2): 85–109, 178–203. http://dx.doi.org/10.3406/hispa.1900.1217.

Peale, C. George. 2004. "Comienzos, enfoques y constitución de la comedia de privanza en la *Tercera parte de las comedias de Lope de Vega y de otros autores.*" *Hispanic Review* 72 (1): 125–56.

Restrepo-Gautier, Pablo. 2001. *La imaginación emblemática en el drama de Tirso de Molina*. Newark: Juan de la Cuesta.

Saint-Saëns, Alain. 1995. *Art and Faith in Tridentine Spain (1545–1690)*. New York: Peter Lang.

Salucio del Poyo, Damián. 1857. *La próspera fortuna del famoso Ruy López de Ávalos*. In *Biblioteca de Autores Españoles*, vol. 43, *Dramaturgos contemporáneos a Lope de Vega*, edited by Ramón de Mesonero Romanos, 437–63. Madrid: Rivadeneyra.

Salucio del Poyo, Damián. 1985. *Comedias*. Edited by María del Carmen Hernández Valcárcel. Murcia: Academia Alfonso X el Sabio.

Schack, Adolf Friedrich von. 1887. *Historia de la literatura y del arte dramático en España*. Vol. 3. Translated by Eduardo de Mier. Madrid: M. Tello.

Sullivan, Henry W. 1981. *Tirso de Molina and the Drama of the Counter Reformation*. Amsterdam: Rodopi.

ter Horst, Robert. 1982. "The Second Self: Painting and Sculpture in the Plays of Calderón." In *Calderón de la Barca at the Tercentenary: Comparative Views*, edited by Wendell M. Aycock and Sidney P. Cravens, 175–92. Lubbock: Texas Tech Press.

Toll, Klaus, ed. 1937. Damián Salucio del Poyo, *El rey perseguido y Corona pretendida (Comedia). Mit einer Bibliographisch-kritischen Einführung*. Leipzig: R. Noske.

Trexler, Richard C. 2004. "Being and Non-Being: Parameters of the Miraculous in the Traditional Religious Image." In *The Miraculous Image in the Late*

*Middle Ages and Renaissance*, edited by Erik Thunø and Gernhard Wolf, 15–27. Rome: L'Erma di Bretschneider.

Vega, Lope de. 1952. *El servir con mala estrella*. In *Biblioteca de autores españoles*. Vol. 52. Edited by Juan Eugenio Hartzenbusch, 47–67. Madrid: Atlas.

Vega, Lope de. 1970. *El Brasil Restituido*. In *Biblioteca de autores españoles*. Vol. 233. Edited by Juan Eugenio Hartzenbusch, 257–96. Madrid: Atlas.

Vélez de Guevara, Luis. (Forthcoming). *El lucero de Castilla y Luna de Aragón*. Edited by William R. Manson and C. George Peale. Introduction by Gareth Davies. Newark, DE: Juan de la Cuesta.

Webster, Susan Verdi. 1998. *Art and Ritual in Golden-Age Spain: Sevillian Confraternities and the Processional Sculpture of Holy Week*. Princeton: Princeton University Press.

Weimer, Christopher B. 2003. "Los retratos salvadores en dos comedias de Tirso de Molina (*La prudencia en la mujer* y *La firmeza en la hermosura*)." In *El sustento de los discretos: La dramaturgia áulica de Tirso de Molina*, edited by Eva Galar and Blanca Oteiza, 149–58. Madrid: Instituto de Estudios Tirsianos.

Wilson, Edward M., and Duncan Moir. 1971. *A Literary History of Spain: The Golden Age: Drama 1492–1700*. London: Benn.

Wilson, Margaret. 1977. *Tirso de Molina*. Boston: Twayne.

# PART TWO

# The Matter of Words

# 6 Book Marks: Jerónimo de Aguilar and the Book of Hours

HEATHER ALLEN

In 1511 Juan de Valdivia's expedition from Panama to Santo Domingo was shipwrecked on the Yucatan peninsula. As many histories of the conquest of Mexico relate, the few men who escaped drowning reached shore only to be captured, enslaved, or sacrificed and eaten by the Maya inhabiting the land. Jerónimo de Aguilar, a Spaniard and ordained Franciscan priest, was one such survivor who was enslaved rather than killed or sacrificed. Living as a slave for eight years, he eventually became almost indistinguishable from his captors, wearing not much more than a threadbare loincloth and cloak, his hair grown long and matted. The only characteristics that set him apart from the Maya were his full beard and – depending on which history one reads – a tattered book of hours he carried in a sack slung over his shoulder. Indeed, in 1519 when Aguilar was rescued by Cortés, who was looking for a translator to facilitate his expedition, the Spanish troops only recognized him after he uttered several words in Castilian and brandished his book of hours like a talisman proving his Christianity (Gómara 1932, 117–18; Díaz del Castillo 1960, 102–3). Yet in histories where the book of hours is absent, performative acts usually replace the devotional text, chosen to emphasize equally well Aguilar's cultural difference from the Amerindians, and his firm Christian faith in spite of the bodily and spiritual temptations he faced as a captive among infidels.

Whether featured prominently or mentioned briefly, Jerónimo de Aguilar appears in numerous histories of the conquest of Mexico. Colonial-era historiographers wrote and rewrote his narrative, minimizing or emphasizing the role of the book of hours in his rescue according to what best supported their own agendas.[1] Through a close analysis of the intertextual relationships between several versions of this episode, I argue that this text becomes an ambivalent signifier, paradoxically marking both

Aguilar's religious and literate superiority over the Amerindians, and his liminality to both Spanish and Mayan societies after eight years of captivity. To this end, I discuss how the authors deploy (or decline to deploy) the book of hours within their histories, and the slippage that occurs in such employment. The result of this slippage may come to embody the displacement and distortion of the book's meaning caused by the colonial encounter (Bhabha 1994, 105),[2] and thus take on meanings that undermine the authors' ideological frameworks.

I will begin my investigation by considering two Spanish historians who note the presence of the book of hours among Aguilar's belongings: Francisco López de Gómara, a historian and priest who never travelled to the New World and yet was able to write his history based on what he learned as Cortés's chaplain (Jiménez 2001, 15); and Bernal Díaz del Castillo, a conquistador who participated in three expeditions to New Spain, including that of Hernán Cortés (Díaz del Castillo 1960, 39–80). It is neither surprising nor unusual that both of these authors include a book of hours in their histories, since this small, illustrated, yet relatively inexpensive religious text was a medieval and early modern best-seller (Reinburg 1993, 20). In placing it on Aguilar's person, they describe a common, almost quotidian sight in Europe during the fifteenth and sixteenth centuries that would have been quite familiar to their readers. Books of hours first appeared in the late thirteenth century as an adaptation of the psalter portion of the breviary (Calkins 1983, 243), and were meant to provide the laity with a text they could use to follow along with Mass or read at home as part of a daily religious practice. By the late fifteenth century, cheaply printed editions became widely available and formed part of the Catholic Church's attempt to develop and improve lay catechization and even clerical education (Nalle 1999, 133–5).

Like the breviary, the book of hours was divided into eight canonical hours, but was usually organized thematically rather than temporally. However, while individual books of hours tended to have similar components, their exact contents differed according to each book owner and the religious preferences popular within a given geographical region (Calkins 1983, 243). Common elements present in most editions included psalms; the Offices of the Virgin, the Passion, the Trinity and the Dead; the Hours of the Cross and Holy Spirit; a calendar marking saints' feast days; and a rubric. The calendar – the section which Aguilar uses, as I discuss later, to help him keep track of time during his captivity – showed the reader which day to recite the corresponding Offices, while the rubric included instructions on how to correctly use the text (Calkins 1983, 245; Saenger 1989,

147–8). Books of hours were available both in Latin and the vernacular; however, the rubric, calendar, and liturgical responses were usually in the vernacular[3] so that the reader could understand them completely and thus use the text correctly (Saenger 1989, 147–8). Laity and clergy with little education tended to own vernacular editions, while educated laity and clergy tended to own Latin editions (Reinburg 1988, 40); yet even illiterate owners were able to grasp much of the content based on the illustrations contained within, which visually hinted at the meaning of the printed words (Boureau 1989, 16). In addition to the sections found in most books of hours, owners often added religious pamphlets, *pliegos* (loose sheets of paper), and other devotional materials, turning their books into individualized works in progress (Reinburg 1988, 40).

Of the several historians under investigation, Gómara and Díaz del Castillo are the only two who mention the devotional text. Yet this correspondence is hardly unexpected when we consider that, in addition to the best-seller status of books of hours, Gómara was widely used as a source by later conquest historiographers. In fact, Díaz del Castillo is recognized for both criticizing his predecessor – denouncing him by name and identifying specific inaccuracies in a chapter devoted exclusively to the topic – and using him extensively as a source (Chicote 2003, 270; Díaz del Castillo 1960, 79–80).[4] In both authors' histories, the book of hours functions primarily as a symbol of difference between Aguilar and the indigenous people who accompany him to Cortés's camp. The text's presence sets him apart from the natives in three essential ways: intellectually, because it suggests he knows how to read alphabetic script, while the indigenous are illiterate in the strict Western sense of the word; in terms of religious belief, because the book's subject matter reinforces a Christian faith that is perhaps in doubt due to his long captivity among a group the Spaniards considered to be heathens (Rico 2000, 96; Romero 1992, 355); and physically, because without the book it would be difficult to tell him apart from the Mayans based solely on exterior appearance.

Gómara comments on Aguilar's physical appearance in the *Historia general de las Indias*. Cortés's troops watch as a mysterious canoe lands on the coast and from it disembark "cuatro hombres desnudos en carnes, sino era sus vergüenzas, los cabellos trenzados y enroscados sobre la frente" [four men, naked except for their parts of shame, with hair braided and coiled around their foreheads] (1932, 72).[5] It is not until Aguilar asks in Castilian, "Señores, ¿sois cristianos?" [Sirs, are you Christians?], that they are finally able to distinguish him from his companions and respond to his question in the affirmative (1932, 72). Upon hearing their answer, Aguilar

> [a]legróse tanto con tal respuesta, que lloró de placer. Preguntó si era miércoles, porque tenía unas horas en que rezaba cada día. Rogóles que diesen gracias a Dios; y él hincóse de rodillas en el suelo, alzó las manos y ojos al cielo, y con muchas lágrimas hizo oración a Dios, dándole gracias infinitas por la merced que le hacía en sacarlo de entre infieles y hombres infernales, y ponerle entre cristianos y hombres de su nación.
>
> [became so happy at this response that he cried with joy. He asked if it were Wednesday, because he had a book of hours with which he prayed every day. He begged them to give thanks to God; and he knelt on the ground, lifted his hands and eyes to the heavens, and with many tears prayed to God, giving infinite thanks for the mercy he showed in removing him from among infidels and devilish men, and placing him among Christians and his countrymen.] (1932, 72)

Díaz del Castillo likewise notes the physical similarity between Aguilar and the Amerindians in his *Historia verdadera de la conquista de la Nueva España*, explaining that the Spaniards

> le tenían por indio propio, porque de suyo era moreno y tresquilado a manera de indio esclavo, y traía un remo al hombro, una cotara vieja calzada y la otra atada en la cintura, y una manta vieja muy ruin, y un braguero peor, con que cubría sus vergüenzas, y traía atada en la manta un bulto que eran Horas muy viejas. Pues desde que Cortés los vió de aquella manera también picó, como los demás soldados, que preguntó a Tapia que qué era del español, y el español, como le entendió, se puso en cuclillas, como hacen los indios, y dijo: "Yo soy."
>
> [they thought he was an Indian because he was dark-skinned and his hair was shorn like an Indian slave's, and he carried a paddle on his shoulder, was wearing one old sandal and had the other tied at his waist, an old ragged cloak, and a worse loin cloth, with which he covered his shame, and carried, tied up in the cape, a bundle that was a very old book of hours. When Cortés saw him like this, he was deceived like the other soldiers, and asked Tapia where the Spaniard was, and the Spaniard, because he understood, crouched down like an Indian, and said, "I am."] (1960, 102–3)

These two passages narrate first-hand accounts of Aguilar's anti-anagnorisis – the Spaniards' failure to recognize him as a compatriot due to his unfamiliar physical appearance – a recurring theme in the captive's return

(Voigt 2009, 120). Rather than physical difference, it is speech that sets Aguilar apart from the natives and leads to his being recognized (2009, 92). Gómara's troops and Díaz del Castillo's Cortés are only able to identify Aguilar as a fellow Spaniard and Christian after exchanging words in Castilian with this apparent *indio*. The book of hours supports his oral language, physically signalling Aguilar's mother tongue and *patria* with its briefly mentioned presence.

Yet although the religious text points to Aguilar's cultural origin in both histories, there are subtle differences in the work it does for each author: in Gómara's *Historia de la conquista* it is much more active, while in Díaz del Castillo's *Historia verdadera* it plays a more latent role. In the former, both the historical characters and the author himself make the book of hours more prominent. When Aguilar arrives at the Spanish encampment, he asks the troops "si era miércoles, porque tenía unas horas en que rezaba cada día" [if it were Wednesday, because he had a book of hours with which he prayed each day] (1932, 72). Demonstrating his active stance – it is he who initiates contact and conversation with the Spanish troops – the rescued slave announces his attempts to mark the passing of Christian time during his captivity by praying each day with his book of hours. In fact, he is so sure of the accuracy of his count and by extension of his own faith that he does not wait for an answer to his question about the day of the week, but instead assumes that he is correct. The readers know he is not, for Gómara states several paragraphs earlier that it is the first Sunday of Lent, but the soldiers do not disabuse Aguilar of this notion. His confidence that he successfully maintained liturgical time among pagans, as well as his physically and verbally expressed relief at being rescued – demonstrated by falling to his knees and offering a prayer of gratitude – accentuates his firm religious faith (Castillo Sandoval 1992, 186).

In contrast to Gómara's work, in Díaz del Castillo's account the book does not explicitly aid in Cortés's recognition of the captive, nor does Aguilar give it a vital role in revealing himself to his countrymen or confirming his purity of faith. The conquistador historian's more quietly reserved captive responds only when he is implicated in the conversation (Gaylord 2000, 75) and refrains from ostentatious displays of piety such as falling to his knees and praying, or verifying that he has been correctly following the Christian calendar in captivity. The fact that Aguilar himself does not bring up the book of hours is surprising, given that Díaz del Castillo goes to the trouble of declaring its presence, and that Gómara, whom the conquistador historian uses as a source, does have Aguilar explicitly refer to the object. Instead, the book remains untouched, seemingly forgotten, in the *bulto* on Aguilar's back. Nevertheless, by including it in his detailed description of the captive, the conquistador historian hints at his own preoccupation with the importance of the written word in creating authority and legitimacy. As he explains in the prologue to his *Historia verdadera*,

> lo que yo vi y me hallé en ello [la conquista] peleando, como buen testigo de vista yo lo escribiré, con la ayuda de Dios, muy llanamente, sin torcer a una parte ni a otra, y porque soy viejo de más de ochenta y cuatro años y he perdido la vista y el oír, y por mi ventura no tengo otra riqueza que dejar a mis hijos y descendientes, salvo esta mi verdadera y notable relación
>
> [what I saw and found fighting in it [the conquest], I will write as a good eyewitness, with the help of God, very clearly, without twisting from one part to another, and because I am an old man of more than eighty-four years and have lost my sight and hearing, and because of my bad fortune I have no other riches to leave to my sons and descendants except for this, my true and notable history] (1960, 38)

Thus he presents his eyewitness version of events as the authoritative history, creating at the same time a physical legacy for his descendants and solid, tangible evidence in support of his account. The book of hours takes on a similar significance within the *Historia verdadera* itself, serving for Díaz del Castillo and the reader – if not for Cortés or the shipwrecked captive – as physical proof of Aguilar's oral assertion that he is Spanish and Christian.

When Gómara depicts Aguilar falling to his knees, raising his hands to the sky, and thanking God for delivering him from the infidels, the historian is actually describing an image of the Annunciation commonly found in books of hours. During the fifteenth and sixteenth centuries, two Annunciation illustrations were in fact widespread. One shows Mary kneeling with her hands raised towards the angel Gabriel in prayerful supplication; in the other, she is quietly reading a book of hours with her hands near her heart in prayer position when the divine messenger interrupts her study. Early modern readers of Gómara's history would have immediately recognized such familiar images, also found in religious art from stained glass windows, paintings, and pamphlets (Saenger 1989, 152). In his narration of Aguilar's return to Spanish society, Gómara fuses the two styles – Mary praying and Mary reading – by describing Aguilar's oral and outward display of faith, and his use of the book of hours for silent daily prayer according to the canonical hours. In this way, Gómara doubly affirms the captive's faith.

In spite of the variations in the authors' representations of Aguilar and how he treats his book of hours during the anagnorisis scene, both utilize the devotional text to underscore the importance of the written word in certifying the captive's Christian and Spanish identity (Roa-de-la-Carrera 2005, 172). During the protracted history of religious wars and skirmishes between Christian and Muslim Iberia and North Africa, kidnapping and ransoming captives had become a common established practice with well-known procedures (Voigt 2009, 8–9). Upon returning to Spain, the ransomed captive was expected to write an *información*, a document on "his life and habits during his captivity not only on his personal services, but also as a proper justification vis-à-vis the civil authorities and the Inquisition of having sustained his Catholic faith and not having renounced it among the infidels" (Garcés 2005, 99). Although this was not an established practice for Spaniards returning from the New World because the Amerindians were not considered as big a threat to Catholicism as the Muslim infidels, Gómara and Díaz del Castillo, as well as the captive himself, would have been aware that upon returning to Spain, Aguilar may have been asked to file just such a written report in order to reaffirm his Catholic faith and loyalty to the Spanish Crown and its projects in the New World. The book of hours, a Catholic devotional text, is another written document whose very possession bolsters such a claim.[6]

Indeed, outwardly visible manifestations of piety were an important component of medieval faith because they demonstrated to the rest of the world interior beliefs that were otherwise invisible. In order to outwardly and ostentatiously display their own Christian piety, noblemen and other members of the upper class often commissioned beautifully bound and illuminated books of hours to flaunt in their homes, while members of the lower classes who could not afford such volumes were still able to show their devotion by bringing their cheaper editions with them to Mass and following along with the sermon (Poos 1988, 34). However, although it was important to prove one's faith via outer signs, clerics were aware of and troubled by the fact that such displays could be deceiving. Friars involved in the New World evangelization project such as Bernardino de Sahagún often expressed concern that newly converted Amerindians, although they correctly practised the visible aspects of Catholicism, in fact hid idolatrous beliefs in their hearts (Sahagún 1999, 1).[7]

As I have argued, in depicting Aguilar with a book of hours Gómara and Díaz del Castillo take advantage of its recognizability and obvious religious function as a way to materially declare Aguilar's faith, which his ambiguous outer appearance and time in captivity undermine. A closer look at the talismanic properties of this devotional text will help shed light on other possible reasons why Gómara and Díaz del Castillo use this narrative strategy. Constant daily use, along with the cheap paper and materials used to print and construct editions marketed to the middle and lower classes, means that few books of hours of this type survive today (Peña Díaz 1996, 539). This fact, along with their eclectic, individualized composition, makes it difficult to reconstruct the exact contents of Aguilar's personal volume. However, considering that it survived shipwreck followed by eight years of captivity in the wilds of the Yucatán peninsula, it was probably damaged, possibly to the point of being illegible. This may explain why Díaz del Castillo's Aguilar leaves it untouched in his pack, although Gómara affirms that he was able to read the calendar and the associated daily prayers, common sections in most books of hours.

Yet even if Aguilar could no longer read his book of hours, it could still fulfil an important function for him. In addition to physically manifesting his faith, which his long captivity puts into question, the devotional text's presence helps explain his apparently miraculous survival. When he recounts the story of his captivity to Cortés in both authors' histories, Aguilar reports that all but two of the shipwreck survivors from Valdivia's expedition have perished (Gómara 1932, 72–3; Díaz del Castillo 1960, 103).[8] Gómara and Díaz del Castillo may have believed that Aguilar survived such brutal conditions due to the nature of his treasured possession. Because the book of hours contains excerpts from scripture and other holy texts supposedly written by Jesus himself, as well as apostles and saints, in the medieval and early modern periods the physical object itself was considered to have sacred properties (Boureau 1989, 16–17). Even if the owner could not read the book in the sense of obtaining complete comprehension of the written contents, leafing through it or merely carrying it on one's person could protect the bearer from physical and moral harm, and even miraculously heal illnesses and injuries (Saenger 1989, 156). Thus, for Gómara and Díaz del Castillo, Aguilar's book is a talisman of protection that keeps him from bodily harm and reaffirms the providential nature of the conquest: just as God watches over Cortés's expedition and ensures its success, he keeps Aguilar alive so that he can subsequently save the Amerindians' souls.

Indeed, both authors report that Aguilar works to evangelize the natives once he has reunited with Cortés's troops. Gómara describes a sermon that Aguilar gives to the indigenous of Cozumel before leaving for the mainland with the Spanish expedition. His sermon, given in their native Chontal Maya, the language of his former captors, immediately convinces the Amerindians of the island to convert to Catholicism (Gómara 1932, 75); Díaz del Castillo relates a conversation with the local caciques in which he advises them to have "reverencia a la santa imagen de Nuestra Señora y a la cruz" [reverence for the holy image of Our Lady and the cross] and teach this reverence to their subjects (1960, 104).

However, narrative traces indicate that the book of hours, rather than acting as a constant reminder of and guide for his faith, may not necessarily have signified the same for Aguilar as captive. As an ordained Franciscan priest and practising Catholic, Aguilar would have used the book of hours to guide his daily devotions and observances of holidays, feast and saints' days (Reinburg 1993, 21) because closely following the liturgical calendar was an important component of medieval and early modern Catholicism (Nalle 1992, 141). Yet living with a Mayan tribe he had no external social or calendrical structure to help him accurately monitor the passing of Catholic time. Indeed, the Mayans had their own holy days and celebrations with which they order their existence.

Both Gómara and Díaz del Castillo let slip this evidence of Aguilar's possible lack of synchronicity with Catholic time, although in different ways. In Gómara's history, a more proactive Aguilar declares his continuing use of the book of hours according to its intended purpose, and yet he is also unable to maintain and exercise the order and authority contained within its structure.[9] That is, although he attempts to monitor the date using the liturgical calendar, he ultimately fails in this venture. As Gómara tells us, when Aguilar first approaches the Spanish troops, he "[p]reguntó si era miércoles, porque tenía unas horas en que rezaba cada día" [he asked if it were Wednesday, because he had a book of hours with which he prayed each day] (1932, 72). Although Aguilar is allowed to continue on oblivious to his error – none of the Spanish soldiers corrects him – Gómara has already informed the reader several paragraphs earlier that it is not Wednesday, but the first Sunday of Lent (1932, 71). That is, he has been praying the wrong prayers and celebrating feast days on the wrong dates, putting himself out of sync with the Catholic world.

In Díaz del Castillo's *Historia verdadera*, the book's possibly differentiating significance is expressed in another way: the book of hours is mentioned only once, and in that instance by the narrator, not the captive. This lapse could be due to the eight years Aguilar has spent in a foreign culture that lacks the structures necessary for the volume to signify as "book" in the Spanish sense of the object, and even less in the sense of a religious artefact (Mignolo 2003, 81; 118). As Walter Mignolo describes in *The Darker Side of the Renaissance*, the materiality, social role, and conceptualization of things such as "book," "reading," and "writing" vary among cultures (2003, 76). In this situation, therefore, Aguilar perhaps does not mention his book to his countrymen because it may remind him of his isolation in a culture where it does not signify. By not referring to the book of hours again, even though it plays a more prominent role in one of Díaz del Castillo's source texts, Aguilar's obliviousness to the book slung in a sack over his shoulder hints that it is no longer useful to him, which marks his difference from his original position in the literate European culture he seeks to rejoin.

Alternatively, Díaz del Castillo may have chosen to leave out the reference to the calendar in the book of hours in order to obscure the alienating or transformative effects that a prolonged New World experience can have on Christians. As a soldier with extensive New World experience – unlike Gómara, who has none – he would have a better sense of what Aguilar's daily life was like. He reports in detail the difficulty of existence in the New World during the various expeditions in which he participated, facing violent and often fatal skirmishes with the Amerindians while attempting to gather the water and food necessary to maintain shipboard life (Díaz del Castillo 1960, 42–60). If he referenced Christian time, like Gómara does, he would draw attention to the fact that Aguilar was unable to keep track of it due to the arduous process of survival. This in turn reveals to the Spaniards that he no longer practises a chronologically regulated Catholicism, an indication of his difference from his countrymen as a result of his captivity (Voigt 2009, 12).

Thus both historians, perhaps inadvertently, reveal that during his captivity Aguilar has lived – although without intending to – according to indigenous time, which has idolatrous resonances due to its religious calendar regulating sacrifices to pagan gods. Moreover, he is out of step with the Western world, suggesting partial integration – whether voluntary or involuntary – into a pagan culture. In this way, the book of hours reveals itself as a double and ambivalent symbol, and highlights the rupture caused by the colonial encounter. As Spaniards and members of the colonizing society, Gómara and Díaz del Castillo situate the text as a sign marking Aguilar's intellectual, cultural, and religious difference from his indigenous captors (Roa-de-la-Carrera 2005, 172). However, the book is no longer within its original context in the Yucatán peninsula and therefore lacks the social supports necessary to maintain its significance outside of Aguilar's individual perception. It is at the same time, accordingly, a sign of the captive's displacement and of the turmoil colonization causes. It serves as a reminder of his origins while simultaneously emphasizing his solitude and isolation from them. Although it may be situated as a sign of European alphabetical superiority (Roa-de-la-Carrera 2005, 172), therefore, the book of hours is also a sign of difference and displacement. The colonizers' authoritative position, expressed in these triumphalist historical narratives, is much less consolidated or unequivocal than previously assumed.

The concern Gómara and Díaz del Castillo express for marking Aguilar's firm faith and Spanish origin in spite of his native-like physical appearance is mirrored in one history in which the book of hours is omitted, the *Historia de la nación chichimeca* by Fernando de Alva Ixtlilxóchitl, a *mestizo letrado* [learned *mestizo*] from the Anáhuac region of Mexico.[10] Although Gómara and Díaz del Castillo are two of the few authors who include the book of hours, Ixtlilxóchitl's omission is striking in its turn because of the apparent extent to which he uses Gómara as a source for his version of Aguilar's rescue. It is not uncommon to see Gómara cited as a reference in colonial histories; in fact, his work is lauded – and criticized – by many of his contemporaries, especially Díaz del Castillo. Ixtlilxóchitl himself explicitly cites Gómara in numerous chapters (1985, 223, 224, 233, 266), as well as in the one recounting Aguilar's appearance. Indeed, he praises Gómara's in-depth elaboration of Cortés's life and conquest of Mexico, referring the reader several times to the *Historia general de las Indias* for a more complete version of the account than the one Ixtlilxóchitl himself offers (1985, 223, 233).

Ixtlilxóchitl thus clearly respected Gómara enough, in spite of some veiled criticisms,[11] to consult him as an authority.[12] In fact, in his section describing Aguilar's anagnorisis several concordances strongly indicate that the mestizo author used Gómara as a direct and exclusive source. These striking similarities become evident when we compare a passage quoted above from Gómara and its equivalent from Ixtlilxóchitl :

> [Aguilar] dijo luego en castellano: "Señores, ¿sois cristianos?" Respondieron que sí y que eran españoles. Alegróse tanto con tal respuesta, que lloró de placer. Preguntó si era miércoles, porque tenía unas horas en que rezaba cada día. Rogóles que diesen gracias a Dios; y él hincóse de rodillas en el suelo, alzó las manos y ojos al cielo, y con muchas lágrimas hizo oración a Dios, dándole gracias infinitas por la merced que le hacía en sacarlo de entre infieles y hombres infernales, y ponerle entre cristianos y hombres de su nación.
>
> [[Aguilar] said then in Castilian: "Sirs, are you Christians?" They responded yes and that they were Spaniards. He became so happy at this response that he cried for joy. He asked if it were Wednesday, because he had a book of

hours with which he prayed every day. He begged them to give thanks to God; and he knelt on the ground, lifted his hands and eyes to the heavens, and with many tears prayed to God, giving infinite thanks for the mercy he showed in removing him from among infidels and devilish men, and placing him among Christians and his countrymen.] (Gómara 1932, 72)

[Aguilar] comenzó a hablar en español y dijo: "señores, ¿sois cristianos?" de que se maravillaron los nuestros y respondieron: "sí somos y españoles." Entonces se puso de rodillas y dijo llorando de placer: "infinitas gracias doy a Dios que me ha sacado de entre infieles y bárbaros. ¿Qué día es hoy señores?, que yo pienso que es miércoles." Respondiéronle que no era sino domingo.

[[Aguilar] began to speak in Spanish and he said: "Sirs, are you Christians?" at which our men marvelled and responded, "Yes we are, and Spaniards." Then he knelt and said crying with joy: "Infinite thanks I give to God, who has taken me from among infidels and barbarians. What day is today sirs? I think it is Wednesday." They responded to him that it was not Wednesday, but Sunday.] (Ixtlilxóchitl 1985, 225–6)

The several correlations between these histories include use of analogous vocabulary; parallel syntax; and identical events in almost the same order, including the conversational exchange between Aguilar and the Spaniards; Aguilar crying for joy; kneeling and praising God for delivering him from the infidels; and his question regarding the day of the week. This last detail is so striking, not because both authors include it, but because they are the only two historians to locate it within Aguilar's speech, and because Ixtlilxóchitl's Aguilar makes no follow-up explanatory reference to the book of hours. What is more, Gómara's Aguilar is not directly told that his day count is incorrect; as I mentioned above, the reader is only aware of the miscalculation because Gómara mentions several paragraphs earlier that it is the first Sunday of Lent (1932, 71). Ixtlilxóchitl's Aguilar, on the other hand, is immediately informed of his error and told the correct day: when he asks if it is Wednesday, they "[r]espondiéronle que no era sino domingo" [responded to him that it was not Wednesday, but Sunday] (1985, 226). And finally, although the mestizo author closely follows Gómara's order of events, he moves the question about the date to the end of the anagnorisis sequence, rather than placing it towards the beginning as the Spanish historian does.

Given the close resemblance between the two versions, it seems that Ixtlilxóchitl purposely chose to make these alterations, which in turn have several consequences. In Gómara's history, the book of hours accounts for Aguilar's question because it offers a concrete way to count his days in captivity. It also creates a clear connection between Aguilar's relief at being rescued from idolatrous natives and his own unwavering faith, particularly because he begins to pray immediately after bringing up his book. Yet Gómara does not portray the Spanish troops as informing Aguilar of the correct date, suggesting that he does not want to overly emphasize the fact that the captive could not maintain proper daily religious observances. Ixtlilxóchitl, on the other hand, relocates the question, disrupting what had been until now his close parity with Gómara, and drawing even more attention to the gap he leaves by omitting the book of hours. Nor does Ixtlilxóchitl hesitate to reveal that Aguilar has lost count of the days and been living according to indigenous time; to the contrary, he explicitly reveals this fact when the troops correct Aguilar's error. What is more, when he deletes the book of hours, the question about the date becomes a non sequitur. Unlike in Gómara, the inquiry, "¿Qué día es hoy señores?" follows, rather than precedes, his prayer of thanks for being reunited with his countrymen. The question itself is not followed by any reference to the connection between religious faith and calendrical time; a connection the presence of the book of hours implicitly puts forward. Instead, the scene changes and Aguilar is taken to Cortés, whom he informs about the circumstances leading up to his shipwreck (Ixtlilxóchitl 1985, 226). Ixtlilxóchitl's omission thus disconnects Aguilar's question from any explanatory context, and creates a question for us. Why did the mestizo author omit the book of hours when he so closely follows Gómara as a source?

One possible answer is that by eliminating the book, he avoids the ambiguity that may arise due to its nature as a symbol of both colonial power and the displacement of this power. Instead of indicating the captive's unwavering Christian beliefs and cultural superiority with a devotional text, he relies more heavily on oral and performative signs of Aguilar's religious dedication during his eight years with the Maya.[13] An oral sign of his Christianity appears in the words exchanged during his reunion with the Spanish troops, when the captive asks his countrymen, "¿sois cristianos?" [are you Christians?] (1985, 225). To further cement his dedication to the colonial evangelization project, the mestizo author, like Gómara, has Aguilar give a sermon to the indigenous people at Cozumel before the troops depart for the mainland. His homily, spoken in the Amerindians' language, unsurprisingly leads to the rapid conversion of all (Ixtlilxóchitl 1985, 226). Thus, unlike the two Spanish historiographers, Ixtlilxóchitl does not accentuate the role of European literacy in the conquest via the book of hours; instead, he focuses on Aguilar's evangelical and translating functions. However, both narrative strategies, the use of the book and his speech acts, serve a similar purpose: to eliminate any doubt in the reader's mind that Aguilar's eight-year captivity weakened or corrupted the strength and purity of his faith.

It may also be that Ixtlilxóchitl wishes to deemphasize the book of hours, an object of European alphabetical culture that Gómara uses as a sign of European alphabetical superiority over the Amerindians (Roa-de-la-Carrera 2005, 172), in order to implicitly valorize indigenous record-keeping methods and sources that he himself uses to compose his history. Indeed, Walter Mignolo and Jorge Cañizares-Esguerra argue that Ixtlilxóchitl positions indigenous and graphic systems as equal in value to European texts, in the sense that they, too, are capable of accurately recording and preserving the past (Mignolo 2003, 93; Cañizares-Esguerra 2001, 65). One could counterargue that when Ixtlilxóchitl writes his account, albeit from an indigenous point of view, he is using the very forms – the codex and the roman alphabet – whose dominance he seeks to mitigate. However, rather than completely rejecting the colonizing culture, Salvador Velazco contends that Ixtlilxóchitl seeks a new transcultural space in which both cultures can become integrated.[14] One such transcultural space is his history itself, which he wrote using early modern Western organizational format and topical conventions for writing history, yet incorporating indigenous sources such as pictorial manuscripts and oral reports that Europeans did not always accept as valid, trustworthy, historiographical sources (Mignolo 2003, 127).

Another possible reason for the book's omission can be found in Ixtlilxóchitl's purpose in writing the *Historia de la nación chichimeca*. As Edmundo O'Gorman and Velazco demonstrate, in his book Ixtlilxóchitl offers a providential indigenous history in which Anáhuac is implicitly compared to an Old Testament pre-Christian settlement open to receiving the word of God (Velazco 2003, 44). In an effort to portray the Texcocans as ready for conversion, he minimizes indigenous cultural elements that could suggest perplexing differences, one of which is their alternate method of record-keeping, which included a rich oral tradition and complex pictorial manuscripts but lacked a phonetic alphabet capable of representing human speech (Mignolo 2003, 127). As I have mentioned, books of hours were an important component of medieval and early modern Catholicism because they outwardly manifested the bearer's inner piety. Texcocan culture, however, does not have an equivalent object which could replace the book of hours in making public the Amerindians' acceptance of

Catholicism. If Ixtlilxóchitl were to give Aguilar a book of hours, he would draw attention to a cultural difference he attempts to minimize in order to portray the Texcocans as easily brought into the Christian fold.

The historiographers discussed in this article, Francisco López de Gómara, Bernal Díaz del Castillo, and Fernando de Alva Ixtlilxóchitl, utilize a part of early modern material culture – the book of hours, or the striking gap its absence creates – as a narrative strategy designed to further their historiographical projects. Although all three underscore Jerónimo de Aguilar's purity and strength of faith in order to portray his role as communication facilitator and priest as essential to the colonial evangelization mission, only the two Spanish authors take advantage of the book of hours to do so. For them, the book additionally serves to differentiate the captive from his indigenous captors, because the effects of eight years of captivity have left his skin tanned, his hair matted, and his clothes ragged to such a degree that he is no longer physically distinguishable from them. The religious text, then, whether mentioned by Aguilar himself or only by the narrator, is an alternate sign of Aguilar's cultural difference, marking his Christianity, ability to read Roman text, and therefore his intellectual superiority.

In addition to being positioned as a sign of religious faith and cultural difference, the book of hours also indicates the importance of literacy in the conquest for the two Spanish authors. On one level it differentiates and marks as alphabetically superior the colonizers from the colonized, while on another level, it legitimates and confers importance on the historians' own record-keeping efforts. As historians writing new versions of the conquest of Mexico, which several other authors had already published, Gómara and Díaz del Castillo believed they, too, had something valuable to contribute to the written archive, and indeed that the archive itself was a vital contribution to imperial expansion. In this way, Aguilar's book of hours becomes a synecdoche for the historiographers' own texts.

However, in spite of Gómara's and Díaz del Castillo's efforts, the book of hours also carries alternate meanings that actually detract from their representation of Aguilar as a pious Catholic and one of the first evangelists in the New World. Because the text lacks the social supports necessary for it to sustain an exclusively Western significance in the Yucatán peninsula among the Maya, it takes on distinct implications beyond the authors' control. As a result, it also implies the rupture caused by Aguilar's captivity and isolation from European culture. Indeed, both Gómara and Díaz del Castillo reveal (albeit in different ways) that the book of hours has failed to fulfil its intended liturgical calendrical function. In placing the question about the day of the week in Aguilar's mouth, Gómara divulges that he has lived according to indigenous time. Díaz del Castillo may have chosen to reference the book of hours only once and to leave out any date references that would reveal Aguilar's error, in order to disguise the fact that life in the New World hinders Catholic observances. But he, too, is still unable to obscure the possibility that Aguilar may have been in misstep with Catholic time. Thus, on another level the book of hours emphasizes his difference from his countrymen as well as his difference from the Mayans, even though the authors present it as a sign of his maintenance of Christianity and a European identity.

When Ixtlilxóchitl so closely follows Gómara in his version of Aguilar's anagnorisis yet erases all trace of the book from the pious captive's hands, he further supports his own goals in writing a Texcocan history of the conquest. Like Gómara and Díaz del Castillo, he is still concerned with showing Aguilar's firm faith, but rather than using the book of hours to do so, he relies more on the captive's performative role as evangelizer and cultural translator. In this way, Aguilar implicitly becomes a synecdoche for Ixtlilxóchitl himself. Like the captive, he retrospectively "evangelizes" the pre-Cortesian Texcocans in his own historical narrative; as a mestizo historian eager to incorporate his own people's history into the European conception of world history and create a transcultural space within his own work, he, too, is a cultural translator. Moreover, rather than accepting the book as a sign of European alphabetic superiority, as Gómara utilizes it, Ixtlilxóchitl's omission leaves space for his indigenous sources to be given more equal footing as legitimate historical sources alongside European alphabetical works such as Gómara's.

Investigated in a comparative framework, we therefore see how these three historians exemplify literacy's varying uses in supporting Catholicism and its diffusion in a foreign setting, as well as how it can serve as an aid in constructing a new, transcultural environment. We also see how Díaz del Castillo and especially Ixtlilxóchitl read, critique, and build upon Gómara's more popular and influential history, gaining insight into how they use this intertextual relationship in order to construct their own arguments and put forward their own, in their opinion more accurate, versions of the conquest.

## NOTES

1 Sabine MacCormack and Patricia Seed have investigated the role of the European religious text in the Peruvian colonial situation, focusing specifically

on the Inca ruler Atahualpa's reaction to Fray Valverde's Bible during Francisco Pizarro's expedition (MacCormack 1989; Seed 1991).

2 Concepts of the distortion and displacement of the colonizer's power structures and cultural beliefs, including the socially constructed meaning of texts and reading, have been developed by postcolonial theorist Homi Bhabha. In his study, *The Location of Culture*, he explores the role of the book and literacy within the colonial British context, identifying text as an ambivalent hybrid symbol. Through an example of native appropriation of a Bible in Hindi, Bhabha explains that the book is a double and therefore equivocal sign: the colonizers believe it to be an accurate and exact representation of their power and superiority over the colonized; but at the same time it is a displacement, distortion, and repetition of this representation, since it now operates within a different culture and therefore context (1994, 103, 107). Although he focuses specifically on the British colonial situation, it shares clear parallels with the Spanish American context, where literacy also played a role in the conquest and colonization of the continent.

3 Castilian, in the case of Aguilar.

4 See Nora Edith Jiménez for a discussion of Díaz del Castillo's attitude towards and treatment of Gómara.

5 All translations are by the author unless cited in passage.

6 In 1573, fifty years after Aguilar was rescued with his book of hours, the Inquisition banned many editions, hoping to reassert control over personal scriptural interpretation and private, individualized religious practices that had become uncomfortably opaque and heterodox (Nalle 1999, 136–7). Just fifty years later, then, Aguilar's book of hours would have labelled him as a dissident rather than affirming his orthodox belief. Gómara and Díaz del Castillo, however, wrote before these major reforms began to take effect.

7 The problem of being unable to trust visible manifestations of faith arose in Iberia with the issue of *conversos*, or Jews who were forced by Isabel and Ferdinand in 1492 to convert to Catholicism or leave the country. Many *conversos* continued to practise Judaism secretly, in spite of outwardly displaying adherence to the Christian faith (Coleman 2003, 45).

8 Aside from Aguilar himself, the other survivor is the (in)famous Gonzalo Guerrero, a Spaniard who "goes native" and refuses to return to Spanish society because he has pierced and tattooed his body, married an indigenous woman, and has several children (Gómara 1932, 73; Díaz del Castillo 1960, 103–4).

9 Bhabha explains that for the colonizers, the European book functions to maintain civil order within a foreign social order, which can seem chaotic to Europeans. He offers the example of Marlow in Joseph Conrad's *Heart of*

*Darkness* in order to illustrate this idea. Marlow is travelling to the heart of the African jungle, and the journey is slowly pushing him towards madness because he perceives the jungle as an uncontrollable, chaotic, and therefore threatening force. But when he discovers an English book about navigation, reading it gives him an ordered refuge according to the Western social norms to which he is accustomed (Bhabha 1994, 106). The book of hours fulfils a similar function for Aguilar during his captivity among the indigenous people. But it is not enough to impose Christian order upon the outside world, for Aguilar still loses count of the days.

10 Ixtlilxóchitl was the son of a Spaniard and a mestizo Texcocan Amerindian who was descended directly from Moctezuma II, the last *tlahtoani* (ruler) of Tenochtitlán. He wrote several *relaciones*, or histories, of pre-Cortesian Mexico and the conquest and relied heavily on Amerindian oral and material sources to do so (Vázquez 1985, 19, 28).

11 Although Ixtlilxóchitl praises the Spanish historians' thoroughness, he gives two reasons for either refusing to write his own or providing an alternate version: "Y porque los autores que han escrito las conquistas que estos señores tuvieron, especificadamente nos las cuentan por extenso, porque las hallaron en sus historias [...] sólo refiero lo que me pareció convenía tratar de ellas, según las pinturas y anales que tengo citados" [and because the authors who have written about the conquests of these gentlemen, specifically they recount them [the conquests] extensively to us, because these conquests are found in their histories [...] I only relate what seems to me convenient to treat, according to the paintings and annals that I have cited] (1985, 215). Through his praise of such comprehensiveness, Ixtlilxóchitl implicitly criticizes these same historians for being long-winded while simultaneously omitting the indigenous historical perspective that his own sources relate. Instead of rewriting histories that he considers praiseworthy – albeit to a limited degree – his purpose is to write an indigenous history of the conquest (Vázquez 1985, 36). In doing so, he aims not only to preserve this history for posterity, but also to incorporate an indigenous past into the European conception of world history (Velazco 2003, 54).

12 Domingo Francisco de San Antón Muñón Chimalpahin Quauhtlehuanitzin, an Amerindian historian and copyist who, like Ixtlilxóchitl, hailed from a region near Tenochtitlán, also wrote an alternate conquest history based on Gómara's work and indigenous sources (Voigt 2006, 14–15, 21).

13 Some of these oral and physical signs (oral confirmation of cultural origin and religious affiliation, a sermon for the local Amerindians, change of clothes) are also present in the histories of Díaz del Castillo and Gómara.

14 Ixtlilxóchitl further promotes cultural mestizaje when he (erroneously) claims that Aguilar married Marina, or La Malinche, an Amerindian woman with whom he formed a translating team on Cortés's expedition (Ixtlilxóchitl 1985, 229).

## WORKS CITED

Bhabha, Homi. 1994. *The Location of Culture*. New York: Routledge.

Boureau, Alain. 1989. "Franciscan Piety and Voracity: Uses and Stratagems in the Hagiographic Pamphlet." In *The Culture of Print*, edited by Roger Chartier, and translated by Lydia G. Cochrane, 15–58. Princeton: Princeton University Press.

Calkins, Robert G. 1983. *Illuminated Books of the Middle Ages*. Ithaca: Cornell University Press.

Cañizares-Esguerra, Jorge. 2001. *How to Write the History of the New World*. Stanford: Stanford University Press.

Castillo Sandoval. Roberto. 1992. *Cautelosas simulaciones: Pineda y Bascuñán y su* Cautiverio feliz. Dissertation, Harvard University.

Chicote, Gloria B. 2003. "La lexicalización de la experiencia: el romancero en la prosa historiográfica de Bernal Díaz del Castillo." *Romance Quarterly* 50 (4): 269–79. http://dx.doi.org/10.1080/08831150309600438.

Coleman, David. 2003. *Creating Christian Granada*. Ithaca: Cornell University Press.

Díaz del Castillo, Bernal. 1960. *Historia verdadera de la conquista de la Nueva España*. 2 vols. México: Porrúa.

Garcés, María Antonia. 2005. *Cervantes in Algiers*. Nashville, TN: Vanderbilt University Press.

Gaylord, Mary Malcolm. 2000. "Jerónimo de Aguilar y la alteración de la lengua (la *Mexicana* de Gabriel Lobo Lasso de la Vega)." In *Agencias criollas: la ambigüedad "colonial" en las letras hispánicas*, edited by José Antonio Mazzotti, 73–9. Pittsburgh: Instituto Internacional de Literatura hispánica.

Gómara, Francisco López de. 1932. *Historia general de las Indias*. 2 vols. Madrid: Espasa-Calpe.

Ixtlilxóchitl, Fernando de Alva. 1985. *Historia de la nación chichimeca*. Edited by Germán Vázquez. Madrid: Historia 16.

Jiménez, Nora Edith. 2001. *Francisco López de Gómara: Escribir historias en tiempos de Carlos V*. Michoacan: El Colegio de Michoacan.

MacCormack, Sabine. 1989. "Atahualpa and the Book." *Dispositio* 14 (34): 141–68.

Mignolo, Walter. 2003. *The Darker Side of the Renaissance*. Ann Arbor: University of Michigan Press.

Nalle, Sara T. 1992. *God in La Mancha*. Baltimore: Johns Hopkins University Press.

Nalle, Sara T. 1999. "Printing and Reading Popular Religious Texts in 16th Century Spain." In *Culture and the State in Spain, 1550–1850*, edited by Tom Lewis and Francisco J. Sánchez, 125–48. New York: Garland.

Peña Díaz, Manuel. 1996. "Religiosidad y libros 'populares' en el siglo XVI." In *Política, religión e inquisición en la España moderna*, edited by Pablo Fernández Albaladejo, José Martínez Millán, and Virgilio Pinto Crespo, 529–47. Madrid: Ediciones de la Universidad Autónoma de Madrid.

Poos, Lawrence R. 1988. "Social History and the Book of Hours." In *Time Sanctified*, edited by Roger S. Wieck, 33–8. New York: George Braziller.

Reinburg, Virginia. 1988. "Prayer and the Book of Hours." In *Time Sanctified*, edited by Roger S. Wieck, 39–44. New York: George Braziller, Inc.

Reinburg, Virginia. 1993. "Hearing Lay People's Prayer." In *Culture and Identity in Early Modern Europe, 1500–1800*, edited by Barbara B. Diefendorf and Carla Hesse, 19–39. Ann Arbor: University of Michigan Press.

Rico, José. 2000. "Gonzalo Guerrero: La frontera del imaginario español." *Latin American Literary Review* 28 (55): 87–109.

Roa-de-la-Carrera, Cristián. 2005. *Histories of Infamy: Francisco López de Gómara and the Ethics of Spanish Imperialism*. Translated by Scott Sessions. Boulder: University Press of Colorado.

Romero, Rolando J. 1992. "Texts, Pre-Texts, Con-Texts: Gonzalo Guerrero in the Chronicles of the Indies." *Revista de estudios hispánicos* 23 (5): 345–67.

Saenger, Paul. 1989. "Books of Hours and the Reading Habits of the Later Middle Ages." In *The Culture of Print*, edited by Roger Chartier, and translated by Lydia G. Cochrane, 141–73. Princeton: Princeton University Press.

Sahagún, Bernardino de. 1999. *Historia general de las cosas de la Nueva España*. México: Porrúa.

Seed, Patricia. 1991. "'Failing to Marvel': Atahualpa's Encounter with the Word." *Latin American Research Review* 26 (1): 7–32.

Vázquez, German. 1985. "Introducción." In *Historia de la nación chichimeca*, edited by Germán Vázquez, 7–41. Madrid: Historia 16.

Velazco, Salvador. 2003. *Visiones de Anáhuac*. Guadalajara: Universidad de Guadalajara.

Voigt, Lisa. 2006. "Peregrine Peregrinations: Rewriting Travel and Discovery in Mestizo Chronicles of New Spain." *Revista de Estudios Hispánicos* 40: 3–24.

Voigt, Lisa. 2009. *Writing Captivity in the Early Modern Atlantic*. Chapel Hill: University of North Carolina Press.

# 7 Embodying the Visual, Visualizing Sound in Sor Juana Inés de la Cruz's *Primero sueño*

EMILIE L. BERGMANN

> Óyeme con los ojos,
> ya que están tan distantes los oídos
>
> [Hear me with eyes alone,
> since ears are out of hearing's farthest reach.]
> Sor Juana Inés de la Cruz, *Lira* (1951, 211; 1988, 71)[1]

In the metaphorical framework of Sor Juana's *Primero sueño* [First Dream], as in the baroque in general, visual perception is the central vehicle. The spaces envisioned in the mind's epistemological quest, however, resonate with sounds: voices haunting the microcosm of the body and birdcalls in a terrestrial landscape. The baroque poetics of *Primero sueño* transform figurations of the visual into metaphors of sound, beginning with the description of nightfall in lines 1–96 and the gallery of somnolent creatures in lines 97–150. Night signals the temporary release of the dreaming mind from the sleeping body, freeing "Alma," the protagonist of the epistemological narrative, to explore earthly and celestial phenomena.

In these opening passages, darkness and silence are made visible and audible through contrasts with distant light or fading sounds. Night is represented as a shadow reaching towards the ever-changing moon and the scintillations of stars in the opening lines, "Piramidal, funesta, de la tierra/sombra" [Pyramidal, lugubrious,/a shadow born of earth] (1951, 1.335, line 1; 1988, 171), while the imposition of silence on the creatures of earth calls attention to the continuing, albeit diminishing, presence of "Este, pues, triste són intercadente" [This dismal intermittent dirge] (1951, 1.337, line 65; 1988, 173) which "menos a la atención solicitaba/que al sueño persuadía;/antes, sí, lentamente,/su obtusa consonancia espaciosa/al sosiego inducía" [insisted on attention less/than it coaxed a listener asleep./Indeed, with all deliberation/its dull and drawn-out harmony/invited all to rest] (1951, 1.337, lines 68–71; 1988, 173). I approach *Primero sueño* through the interplay of the sounds of words, read aloud or imagined as they are read silently, with the visual and auditory sensations that are their referents, and the metaliterary references to systems of signs and discourses of knowledge. These symbolic systems are exemplified by the astronomical diagrams suggested in the opening lines and musical notation that doubles the textual supplement within the description of birdcalls. This essay explores the ways in which the poem brings visual models of knowing into dialogue with the poem's inscription of sound. I address the interlinking phenomena of sights and sounds, architecture and music, beginning with the architecture of the macrocosm, and concluding with the codifications of music and the resonance of fantasized voices in the microcosm of the body. Within this context, I focus on some of the ways in which this long lyric poem simultaneously stages and challenges discourses of power.[2]

At stake in early modern philosophies of both visual perception and music theory was a powerful, totalizing cosmology that lent its authority to religious and political institutions. In the field of optics, "linear perspective came to symbolize a harmony between the mathematical regularities in optics and God's will" (Jay 1988, 5–6). While the hierarchical social and political order derived its authority from the concept of a divinely ordained natural order, this correspondence was threatened by astronomical discoveries made possible through new optical technologies. These developments challenged the geometrical symmetry of the solar system and the mathematical proportions among the perfectly spherical orbits of planets, imagined as generating the "music of the spheres." Catherine Bryan perceives a challenge to the scientific model of Cartesian optics in Sor Juana's poetry (Bryan 2007, 107).[3] In positing a "situated knowledge" in Sor Juana's work, she draws upon Donna Haraway's proposal of an objectivity grounded in "particular and specific embodiment" as opposed to the illusion of "infinite vision" produced by optical technologies, "the god-trick of seeing everything from nowhere" (Haraway 1998, 192).

*Primero sueño* exemplifies both the ocularcentrism of early modern epistemology and the doubts and anxieties that arose from the study of optics. In his 2009 article "Fortunes of the *Occhiali Politici* in Early Modern Spain" Enrique García Santo-Tomás examines the figurative use of mirrors, magnifying lenses, and telescopes in seventeenth-century

Spanish satirical narratives as "an indicator of the tensions in Spain between artistic experimentation and religious constraints" (García Santo-Tomás 2009, 60).[4] He draws upon Martin Jay's concept of "the overloading of the visual apparatus with a surplus of images in a plurality of spatial planes" (Jay 1994, 48) to study the seventeenth-century Spanish critiques of baroque "spectacle, fantasy, and a continuous collapse of the traditional frame ... In this new scopic regime, the perspectival arrangement is as fluid as it is spatially limitless" (68). Pertinent to the metaphors of optics in *Primero sueño* is his discussion of "the increasing tensions between astronomy and religion stemming from the use of lenses as stargazing tools" (60). Tellingly, the mind, or Alma in Sor Juana's poem, is not aided by spectacles as she attempts to scale the mountain of knowledge: "la vista perspicaz, libre de anteojos, / de sus intelectuales bellos ojos" [the probing gaze, by lenses unencumbered, / of her beautiful intellectual eyes] (1951, 1.346, lines 440–1; 1988, 182). Cognitive processes connecting external objects and mental concepts are figured in terms of the concave mirror in the lighthouse at Alexandria that collected distant images in lines 258–91, and the projection of images in the eye as a "magic lantern" in lines 873–86. Notwithstanding the comparisons with ancient and modern technologies, the failure of the epistemological quest is metaphorically attributed to the inadequacies of the human sense of sight.

In addition to the pyramidal form described by the opening lines of *Primero sueño*, the syllables form a phonetic pattern in two groups of four syllables flanking a three-syllable central word: "Piramidal, funesta, de la tierra." Each term in the sequence of three elements makes a distinct visual and spatial reference: first shape, then darkness, and finally a link between the shadow and its cause, endowing the abstract form and the darkness with astronomical dimensions. Phonetically, these eleven syllables also present a reverse of the pyramidal shape of the aspiring shadow reaching towards the stars: the deep "u" of "funesta" is surrounded by high, sharp "i" sounds, which convey the spatial effect of an inverted triangle. Thus, the first line produces, semantically and phonetically, the conceptual figure, apparently drawn from Athanasius Kircher's *Oedipus Aegyptiacus* (1653), of two intersecting pyramids that form the central figure in the long passage beginning in line 340. One is the "cuerpo opaco" [opaque body] with its base on the earth, aspiring towards spiritual perfection; the other, luminous, corresponding to the soul, with a celestial base and a single point of contact with the earth.[5] This initial condensation of the poem's conceptual and narrative structures in one line signals the multiple kinds of signification in poetic language that will be brought into play throughout *Primero sueño*. The phonetic and rhythmic patterns of the poem and the convolutions produced by baroque hyperbaton create virtual temporal and spatial dimensions, capable of enhancing or contradicting the semantic significance of the sounds and visual objects the poem describes.

From the first words of *Primero sueño* and the images they evoke, the paradox of the natural world and the verbal structures of the poem, are at odds with the narrative of knowledge as system and control. In this lyric gateway, the materiality of language is, paradoxically, represented through darkness and silence. In a literal sense, it is impossible to represent silence through words, but Josefina Ludmer's discussion of the *Respuesta a sor Filotea* [Answer to Sister Filotea] shows how Sor Juana invests the signifier "silence" with multiple meanings as it is aligned against knowing and saying. Knowing and not saying, referring to knowing what must not be said without saying it, create the fantasmal voice of a subject who has been silenced, or threatened with being silenced. The adjectival phrase describing the pyramidal shadow "born" of the earth is interrupted emphatically by two caesuras, indicated by commas. The sentence flows on after the staccato enunciation of these three elements, in convoluted syntax that pits the imagined sound of a series of words and phrases against the necessary rearrangement of the sequence in order to decipher its rational meaning.

Thus, the poem exploits at least three registers of signification. First, the sounds – pronounced aloud or imagined in the process of silent reading – create a visual illusion, conveying effects of light and dark through vowels and consonants. In the affective register, the dark "u" sound of "funesta" matches semantically the words evoking doom, some with long "o" sounds ("sombra," "vanos," "tenebrosa guerra," "pavorosa sombra fugitiva") [shadow, vacuous, shadowy war, dreadful moving shade] (1951, 1.335, lines 2, 3, 7, 9; 1988, 171). The sonorous effect of these lines is enhanced by its resonance with Luis de Góngora's ominous "infame turba de nocturnas aves" [infamous mob of nocturnal fowls] (Rivers 1988, 165) of *Polifemo* line 39. While the meaning of words and phrases is modified by words and phrases that follow them, the word order necessitates a pause and a reversal of the temporal flow of the lines, in order to unravel the hyperbaton. In addition, words and phrases are recollected in webs of repetition and allusion, thereby transforming verbal linearity into a multidimensional process. Mary M. Gaylord observes that Góngora uses "*syntax* to disrupt absolutely the regular march of meter, at the same time that he uses *meter* to confound the ordering power of syntax" (1993, 244; italics in original). In *Primero sueño*, the rhythm of the words has another effect. If the geometrical diagram of the pyramidal shadow in the macrocosm imposes order and creates an illusion of control, the irregular rhyme and combination of seven and eleven-syllable lines in the *silva* is appropriate to Alma's epistemological flight and the ultimate failure of reason to systematize the cosmos. The attempt to impose orderly, rational limits on nature is suggested by the clear-cut geometrical shape of the pyramid while the pauses indicated by commas between the powerful words "piramidal" and "funesta," and the rolling "de la tierra sombra" obstruct the rhythmic flow of the first line before giving way to the meandering sentences that follow.

The sonorities of the opening lines of *Primero sueño* constitute a verbal gateway, phonetically and semantically. A brief consideration of the architectural project of the triumphal arch outlined in Sor Juana's *Neptuno alegórico* [Allegorical Neptune] can illuminate the baroque architecture of the portal to *Primero sueño.*[6] The ephemeral structure of wood, plaster, papier-mâché, and pigment was designed to celebrate the arrival of the new viceroy, Tomás de la Cerda, Marquis of la Laguna, and his wife María Luisa Manrique de Lara y Gonzaga, Countess of Paredes in 1680. The complexities of the arch's symbolism are described in detail in the text of *Neptuno*, which ends with a series of poems briefly summarizing the conceptual configurations of each of eight allegorical paintings and six emblematic "hieroglyphs." The sonnet that concludes the explication of the arch's symbolism posits another, "immaterial" structure consisting of form rather than matter, whose potentially infinite dimensions are more appropriate to the viceroy's grandeur (2009, 202). The metaphysical double of the ephemeral arch, which was constructed for a single event, has survived in textual form. As words shape the visual image and then displace it, Sor Juana's metaphor, "voces de colores" [voices consisting of colours] (2009, 190), folds back on itself. The doubling, mirroring, and echoing in the *Neptuno alegórico* as well as in *Primero sueño* exemplify twentieth-century views of baroque and neobaroque. Sor Juana's aesthetic seems to anticipate Gilles Deleuze's discussion of dynamic models of perception in *The Fold: Leibniz and the Baroque*. Although Cuban writer Severo Sarduy did not address Sor Juana's poetry directly, her poetry adds a cognitive dimension to his characterization of the baroque figurative language of Góngora's *Soledades* as "metáfora al cuadrado" [metaphor squared]. He frames this aesthetic in mathematical terms, but also describes it as "cambio perpetuo, como substitución siempre inestable y nacimiento precario de signos, allí donde tiene lugar esa pulsación entre lo externo y la verdad: allí en la frontera oscilante de la página" [as perpetual change, as ever-unstable substitution and precarious birth of signs, there at the place of pulsation between the external and truth: there on the oscillating frontier of the page] (1969, 60).

With the eventual dismantling of the arch in the Zócalo of Mexico City, what remains is the baroque text, the explication of the decorative program, an "immaterial" structure, an always-unstable substitution for wood, plaster, and paint. In contrast to the baroque design and purpose of the arch constructed in 1680 to honour the Spanish monarchy's political and ideological power in New Spain, the opening lines of *Primero sueño* set the stage for the drama of questioning rather than control. They constitute a formal entrance into an uncertain realm, the parallel temporal dimension of dream. Staging the reader's access, these lines present an auditory counterpart to the symmetrical arrangement of structural elements and spaces occupied by images in the architectural design of the *Neptuno*.

The initial visual element in the verbal gateway to the *Sueño*, the pyramid, suggests at least two intellectual contexts: the arcane knowledge of ancient Egyptian civilization (and implicitly of pre-conquest Mexican culture) and the diagram of a geometrical solid composed of static points, angles, and lines on paper, inscribing in a quantifiable system of human knowledge the astronomical phenomenon of light and dark created by sun, moon, earth, and stars in space and time. The epistemological quest that structures the *Sueño* invokes a network of graphic images: geometric figures, emblematic woodcuts, musical notation, and printed texts superimposed upon macrocosm and microcosm in time and space. The second word of the poem charges the initial shape with emotion. "Funesta" is the affective shadow of the astronomical "sombra de la tierra," casting its melancholy foreshadowing of failure upon Alma's (soul's / mind's) vain attempts to scale the heavens: "de vanos obeliscos punta altiva, / escalar pretendiendo las Estrellas" [towering tips / like vacuous obelisks bent on scaling stars] (1951, 1.335, lines 3–4; 1988, 171). The first four lines can be read as a preview of the next 971; Verónica Grossi sees them as a *mise-en-abîme* of the poem as a whole (2007, 42). Throughout the poem, metaphorical relationships stage the baroque drama of ambition and failure, creating a series of condensed versions of the searching mind pitting itself against unattainable knowledge.

The cosmic pyramid that extends into galactic space in the first lines of the poem magnifies a human-scale counterpart: the optical pyramid, a model of visual perception in which light reflected from objects outside the eye converges on the retina. In Sor Juana's poem, the striving of earth's shadow to reach the moon prefigures Alma's doomed quest.[7] In the

Cartesian optical model of perception and cognition, however, the pyramid's apex reaches its goal, the retina of the eye, a point of connection between the interior of the human body with objects exterior to it. Martin Jay gives a rough definition of Cartesian perspectivalism as positing a monocular view of space and the objects in that space in terms of Euclidean geometry (1988, 5–6).[8] A comparison of Sor Juana's figuration of the physical process of visual perception with Cartesian perspectivalism shows some expected similarities but also reveals significant divergences; Ruth Hill argues that the passages on optics, visual perception, and mental processes show a greater affinity with Gassendi (2000, 64–5). In lines 267–79, Sor Juana describes the activities of memory and the mental faculty she terms "fantasía" [imagination]. She refers to the retina-like convex mirror at the ancient port of Alexandria as "tersa superficie" [polished surface] (1951, 1. 342, line 268), shimmering like an "azogada luna" [quicksilver moon] (line 274)[9] with the activity of processing "imágenes diversas" [diverse images], gathering information about "el número, el tamaño y la fortuna / que en la instable campaña transparente / arresgadas tenían" [their number, size, and fortune, / and the risk they ran / in the transparent / unsteady country of the deep] (1951, 1. 342, lines 275–7; 1988, 178) on the turbulent surface of the Mediterranean.

While mirrors and lenses were key to seventeenth-century scientific exploration, Jay and Crary both explain the centrality of another technological model of human perception in the early modern period, the camera obscura, in which images are projected onto the wall of a dark room through a small opening in the opposite wall. In Descartes's and Leibniz's models, the light that enters the camera obscura through the single peephole provides "a vantage point onto the world analogous to the eye of God" (Crary 1990, 48). A natural version of the camera obscura can be perceived in Góngora's description of the dense vegetation that hardly allows any light to penetrate the mouth of the cyclops's horrifying cavern where nightbirds circle ominously in *Polifemo*, lines 33–40.[10] In contrast to the widespread scientific acceptance of a monocular model of visual perception, the singularity of Polyphemus's vision is monstrous. A cave, similarly dark at midday, inhabited by the "king of beasts," a creature both feared and admired, is described in lines 97–102 in *Primero sueño*. However, in an ingenious inversion of space, Sor Juana first turns the camera obscura inside out in lines 25–38. In addition to the moon and stars of the opening lines, this passage reveals another source of illumination amid the darkness of night: the lamplit interior of a temple. Through the windows and the interstices of the doors the owl breaches the boundaries of sacred space to drink the consecrated oil: "la avergonzada Nictimene acecha / de las sagradas puertas los resquicios ... y sacrílega llega a los lucientes / faroles sacros de perenne llama / que extingue, si no infama, / en licor claro la materia crasa / consumiendo" [shamefaced Nictimene keeps watch / by chinks in sacred portals ... / to desecrate the brightly shining / holy lamps perpetually lit, / extinguishing, even defiling them] (1951, 1.336, lines 27–36; 1988, 172). In this spatial transformation, interior and exterior, sacred and profane, change places. The perceptive model for the female intellectual is not the camera obscura, surrounded by light; rather, the ambivalently transgressive nightbird must seek out the luminous temple whose imperfectly sealed doors and windows allow some of its light to escape.

Towards the end of the poem, lines 873–86 refer to another optical device, as morning light interrupts the dream and the body awakens. Within the eye, light-images of external objects are projected, at first blurred, then clearer as the eyes become accustomed to light. The eye is imagined as a "magic lantern," a device described in the Jesuit polymath Athansius Kircher's *Ars Magna Lucis et Umbrae* (1646; second, revised edition 1671). It is a device whose basic principles are far older, while its basic design anticipates that of the modern slide projector, with a convex mirror behind the transparent image rather than a lens in front of it to magnify the images cast on a flat surface in a dark room. Sor Juana's choice of model is significant. Kircher emphasizes both the importance of the emotional effect of the images and the ethical necessity of demystifying its images by explaining the technology to viewers. He describes the exhibition of objects made to move by using threads or magnets, or a series of slides with which "whole satiric plays, theatrical tragedies and the like can be shown in a lifelike way" (Musser 1994, 19–21 citing Kircher 1671, 768–70). Motion and sequential displays of images are key to Kircher's presentation of the device in *Ars Magna*, while Sor Juana imagines visual perception in dynamic rather than static terms. Sor Juana presents both devices in narrative contexts: the ancient lighthouse with its mirror that displays the fate of distant ships, and the "magic lantern" whose images can accompany a recitation or words printed on the slides.

As the epigraph from Sor Juana's poem affirms, eyes can become ears. Words on a page function symbolically as visual and aural signs, whether voiced aloud or in imagination, while their sounds are commonly described phonetically in terms of spatial relationships and visual imagery – "high" and "low" pitch, "bright" and "somber" tone quality. The *Sueño* exploits the full range of resources, in the sounds of words (obvious and subtle onomatopoeia, alliteration, emphasis, hyperbaton, enjambment, and caesura), discursive registers (authoritative third-person description, direct address in first person), and the vocabularies and syntax of legal and political authority including argumentation and punishment. And yet, there is a paradox of sound in the *Sueño* that corresponds to that of the poem's visual paradox: the dream quest takes place in the darkness and silence of night. The voices of birds fade in the description of nightfall in the opening lines, creating the illusion of a silence that is interrupted by nine first-person interjections, eight of these consisting of the single word "digo" in lines 47, 226, 328, 399, 460, 690, 795, and 947 of the 975-line poem (translated by Trueblood as "I mean," "as I was saying," and "I speak of"). In addition, clarifications and elaborations set off by parentheses or dashes are more subtle techniques of creating the illusion of a speaking voice interrupting itself in mid-sentence. My approach to the poem focuses on the interplay of the sounds of words, the visual and auditory sensations they evoke, and the metaliterary references to systems of signs: words, diagrams, and musical notes. These symbols encode sounds into visually apprehensible form and displace the sensory and emotional with a quantitative version of the sonorities of the world that the questing subject in the poem seeks to know.

While vision provides the predominant mode of access to knowledge in *Primero sueño,* in the first ninety-two lines nightfall shifts the poem's mode of perception from sight to sound. These lines foreground the sense of hearing and the sounds of words while describing silence at nightfall, an "overture," as Stephanie Merrim describes it, to the revelation of dream vision (Merrim 1999, 191). Ruth Hill's commentary on this passage finds in it evidence of a "highly sophisticated knowledge of then-modern theories of sound and its movement through space," knowledge she attributes to Sor Juana's familiarity with Gassendi's writings on auditory phenomena and music (2000, 56–7).

Electa Arenal observes the poet's "overriding interest in the reorchestration of sounds and silences" (1991, 125–6) in a feminine key, and discusses the central role of "Música" in staging a display of the perfect structure of Nature in Sor Juana's *Loa a los años del Reverendísimo Padre Maestro Fray Diego Velázquez de la Cadena* [*Loa* in honour of the birthday of Father Diego Velázquez de la Cadena], dating from 1687/8 (1951, 3.483–502). Mario A. Ortiz explains the use of the notes of the scale as allegorical characters in another brief dramatic work, *Loa* 384, "Encomiástico poema a los años de la Excma. Sra. Condesa de Galve" [Encomiastic Poem on the Birthday of Her Excellency, the Countess of Galve] (1951, 3.462–82), a condensed treatise on music theory (Ortiz 2007b, 242).

While Sor Juana's *Loas* stage a geometrical model of music theory, the intervals of the Western scale were in the process of modernization. The baroque disruption of the correspondence of the order of nature with a mathematical ideal was not limited to models of visual perception and representation. While seventeenth-century theories of perception revealed the geometrical principles of optics as well as the ways in which the eye could be deceived by appearances, musicians and composers were struggling to develop practical solutions to the problems of notation and instrumental tuning resulting from discrepancies between the ideal of geometrical perfection on one hand, and on the other, human acoustical production and perception of pitch and duration. Although R.O. Jones wrote that "[m]usic and references to it in poetry were a shorthand sign for the harmony of the universe," a system of "overtones that held the universe in a shimmering web of harmony" (1966, 30–1), John Hollander finds that English literature of the period from 1500 to 1700 reflects "a gradual process of disconnection between abstract musical mythology and concrete practical considerations of actual vocal and instrumental music" (1961, 19). A shift in musical style towards greater expressive range through chromatic and rhythmic contrasts revealed the limits of the medieval scale and notation.

The traditional Pythagorean or "speculative" theory was based on simple whole-number ratios – the octave, the fifth, and the third – as manifestations of the ideal harmony of the cosmos. The practical application of this celestial system, "just intonation," worked well enough with plainsong, but with the increase in compositions for instrumental accompaniment and ensemble playing, this traditional approach produced anomalies of pitch and limited the possibilities for key modulation. The system of equal temperament was a practical compromise, celebrated in Bach's *Well-Tempered Clavier*, which allowed a player to shift among all the possible major and minor keys without retuning. Pamela Long and Mario A. Ortiz explain how Sor Juana addresses these conflicting musical theories in *Romance* 21 (1951, 1.61–5), written to her learned patron the Countess of Paredes, "excusándose de enviar un Libro de Música" [excusing herself from sending a Book of Music] (Long 2009, 28–41; Ortiz 2007a, 250–60). Line 127 of this romance mentions an apparently lost theoretical treatise which the poet refers to as *Caracol* (Spiral Shell). Lines 23–4 refer to proportions, qualities, and intervals, aspects of music that differed according to the basis of each system: Pythagorean or practical, that is, by ear.[11]

Long, Ortiz, and other musicologists agree that Pietro Cerone's synthesis of sixteenth-century musical theory, *El Melopeo y maestro* [The Musicmaker and Master] (Naples, 1613) was the major influence on Sor Juana's theory of music, as well as on the *Maestros de Capilla* [music masters] of seventeenth-century New Spain who composed music for the sets of carols or *villancicos* she wrote for religious occasions at the cathedrals of Mexico City and Oaxaca (Long 2009, 7; Ortiz 2007a, 248). Ortiz, however, observes that in *Romance* 21, Sor Juana questions, adapts, and revises Cerone's theories (2007a, 244).[12] His interpretation of the poem proposes that the spiral envisioned in the title *Caracol* is not the "circle of fifths" of equal temperament, in which the intervals between semitones are uniform rather than those determined by geometrical intervals based on the octave. The figure of the spiral, he argues, preserves the anomalies of just intonation. For Sor Juana, he argues, mathematical purity, rather than sensory perception, is the basis for aesthetic judgment (2007a, 255).

The cosmic and optical diagrams of the first line can be approached through their reference to writing and print culture. The references to musical notes, however, dramatically foreground the abstract and arbitrary nature of the sign. Nictimene, the daughters of Minyas, and Ascalaphus, transformed into owls and bats, form a fearsome, discordant choir,

máximas, negras, longas entonando,
y pausas más que voces, esperando
a la torpe mensura perezosa
de mayor proporción tal vez, que el viento
con flemático echaba movimiento,
de tan tardo compás, tan detenido,
que en medio se quedó tal vez dormido.

[droning long and longer lengthened notes,
and pausing more than singing,
to hang on the torpid, lazy measure,
more dragged out still at times, kept by the wind
to a phlegmatic beat,
so slow in tempo, so sustained,
that sometimes the wind would doze between two notes]
(1951, 1.336, lines 56–62; 1988, 173)

The notes floating in crepuscular space designate indeterminate pitch and duration of sound. Although lyric poetry is closely linked to music, it is important to note the significant differences between the two kinds of visual sign. References to sight throughout the poem use visible symbols on the page to call attention to the subject of perception. Verbal references to musical notation, however, defer the imagined sound through one more level of signification, textualizing the materiality of human and animal voices while creating a textured backdrop for the attenuated narrative line with the rhythm and timbre of birdcalls. In addition, lines 57–68 are all endecasyllabic, imposing upon the process of reading the very lethargy they describe. A few lines after the birds' voices are envisioned as musical notes, the ancient personification of silence places a finger to both lips to signal the cessation of sound: "uno y otro sellando labio obscuro/con indicante dedo,/Harpócrates, la noche, silencioso;/a cuyo, aunque no duro,/si bien imperïoso/precepto, todos fueron obedientes" [Night, an index finger/sealing her two dark lips–/silent Harpocrates – enjoined/ silence on all things living,/a summons, however peremptory, complied with easily and promptly obeyed by all] (1951, 1.337 lines 76–82; 1988, 173). Significantly, this imposing figure cannot restrain the continuing voice of the poem.

The voices of birds in these lines are transformed into visual sign, silent in itself. There are no fixed, preexisting objects signified by the sonorous and semantic aspects of the "overture" or by their metaliterary references to texts, diagrams, and, in the lines quoted above, musical notes; rather, their meaning is contingent, conveyed only in relationship to others in the same system. In *Primero sueño*, letters, phonemes, words, and lines of poetry are in spectacularly complex dialogue with those around them, and with other texts, ancient and modern. The preceding and subsequent words and phrases also establish the material qualities of objects mentioned in the poem. For example, the geometrical figure of the pyramid named in the first word of the poem has, initially, the potential for astronomical expansion or contraction to terrestrial, human dimensions. Its relative size, however, is roughly indicated by the textual references to sun, moon, and earth in lines that follow. In lines 20–64, references to musical notation call attention to the contingent value of all textual signs; however, unlike the phonemes signified by linguistic signs, pitch and duration can only be imagined, played, or sung within frameworks of key and tempo.

Phonetically and visually, the description of the "capilla pavorosa" [fearsome choir] (1951, 1.25 line 57) of winged denizens of Sor Juana's philosophical night resonates with the description of Polyphemus's cave, mentioned above. It also transposes into a minor key the "polyphony" of birdsong and youths in procession towards a wedding, which is "sustained by the natural figured bass" of a brook in lines 540–2 of *Soledad primera* (Collins 2002, 104–5). While Góngora compares the music of nature to courtly and rustic instruments, Sor Juana inscribes the nightbirds' calls as musical notation. The textuality of music in Sor Juana invokes the self-referentiality of *Soledad primera*, exemplified in a much-commented passage:

Pasaron todos pues, y regulados
cual en los equinocios surcar vemos
los piélagos en el aire libre algunas
  volantes no galeras,
  sino grullas veleras,
tal vez creciendo, tal menguando lunas
  sus distantes extremos,
caracteres tal vez formando alados
en el papel diáfano del cielo
  las plumas de su vuelo.

[Onwards they went with undiminished pace,
Such as we see in autumn or in spring
Ploughing the boundless ocean of the air,
  Which are not ships that fly,
  But cranes that sail the sky,
Like moons that wax and wane, their outmost pair
  Closing and opening,
While letters with their flying quills they trace,
And on the sky's transparent parchment write
  The record of their flight] (Góngora 1972, 649–50, lines 602–11; 1972, 45)

However ancient the connection between the V-formation of migrating birds and the origin of the alphabet, this brilliantly self-reflexive passage is quintessentially baroque. Its "incorporation of the act of writing into the text" has been illuminated by Chemris (2007, 74), Ruiz Pérez (1996, 244), and Sánchez Robayna (1983, 40–53). *Soledad primera* transforms landscape and birds into writing; Sor Juana adds musical notation to the web of textualities. By referring to the calls of the nightbirds not as human instruments, as Góngora does in *Soledad primera*, but as written notes, Sor Juana introduces another deferral of signification to her representation of sound.

Despite the importance of the diminishing sounds of birds in the opening lines of the *Sueño*, vision is the privileged sense and words the privileged form of signification throughout the poem, with one other notable exception. As the body falls asleep and the soul is freed, the heart and lungs continue their action, "uno y otro fiel testigo" [these two witnesses, then, reliable, unimpeachable, in fact] (1951, 1.341, line 227; 1998, 177). Meanwhile, the tongue becomes mute, thus disavowing the evidence of the heart and lungs in a miniature courtroom drama: "mientras con mudas voces impugnaban / la información, callados, los sentidos /–con no poder replicar solo defendidos–, / y la lengua que, torpe, enmudecía, / con no poder hablar los desmentía" [while the silent senses, vocal silently, / impugned their testimony, / citing their very silence, / and the torpid tongue by silence of its own / disputed them as well] (1951, 1.341, lines 229–33; 1988, 177). These verses create the illusion of an intimate theatre of the body in which silence resonates as if it were sound. Although the bodily tongue is silent, the poetic speaker's is not: scattered throughout the poem are first-person interjections ("digo") and parenthetical comments that abruptly call attention to the voice that the poem represents through the text on the page. This voice objectifies the body, speaking externally, as an observer of interior mechanisms of production and theatrical space. The imagery of the visual in the long passage regarding the body is located not in the eye but in the mind, the "fantasía" that is compared to the mirror in the lighthouse at Alexandria, with the difference that it can reveal not only what is near and far away, but also what does not have visible form. Thus the imagination, the faculty that processes the information of the senses and the mind, is the link between interior and exterior, microcosm and macrocosm. However, as the body awakens in the last hundred lines of the poem, the "magic lantern" of the eye resumes its role as bridge between body and mind, and between mind and cosmos, the world surrounding the body.

While the speaker's gender is not made evident until the last, feminine, word of the poem, "despierta," the opening lines present a series of mythological women whose transgressions can be interpreted as analogous to the nun's daring narrative of her intellectual voyage: the incestuous Nictimene, transformed into an owl; the Minyades, transformed into bats as punishment for preferring domestic labours to the celebration of Bacchus; and Ascalaphus, also transformed into an owl as punishment for telling the gods that Persephone had eaten the seeds of a pomegranate in Hades. Rather than ascribe to these transgressive figures a stable feminine subjectivity, Merrim locates them within "the fluid nightworld" where binaries are blurred and "order loses its sway" (Merrim 1999, 240). From the outset, this mythological drama has the effect of destabilizing the connotations of light and dark. Nightfall brings intellectual freedom, while sunlight, associated with order, signals failure.

The references to pagan gods, goddesses, and the human victims who were turned into the nightbirds in the opening lines superimpose onto the everyday phenomenon of nightfall the ancient narratives of divine retribution for defying the incest taboo in the case of Nictimene and the daughters of Minyas's refusal to render proper homage to Bacchus. In multiple registers, the opening lines of the poem enact challenges to laws that seem immutable; however, the narrative thread of the poem, the sound of vowels and consonants, the syntax (particularly hyperbaton), and the form of the *silva* – that is, the words themselves – defy Alma's quest for an orderly, rational method of knowledge. Their excess and convolutions present a verbal counterpart to the vastness and complexity of the natural world, the intended object of knowledge. The first hundred lines of *Primero sueño* are a preview of the extended drama of restless nature against rational form, the central trope of the poem. While they foretell the failure of the project, they also present an embodied, voiced epistemological subject. In the opening lines of *Primero sueño*, the signifying mouth is Harpocrates's, symbolically blocked by a finger that signals the prohibition of language; in the closing lines it is vision rather than the voice that represents the return to consciousness, but it is an embodied rather than a transcendent vision.

## NOTES

1 All translations of Sor Juana's poetry are Trueblood's unless otherwise indicated. All other translations are mine. Citations from Sor Juana's *Obras completas* are indicated with volume, page number, and line.

2 For a detailed study of Sor Juana's major works in their sociopolitical and ideological context, see Grossi.

3 Bryan addresses Sor Juana's treatment of colour in two sonnets, "Este que ves, engaño colorido" [These lying pigments facing you] (1951, 1.277; 1988, 95) and "Verde embeleso de la vida humana" [Green allurement of our human life] (1951, 1.280–1; 1988, 101).

4 García Santo-Tomás analyses Luis Vélez de Guevara's use of "mirrors, lenses, telescopes, spectacles, and even the eye's retina" in *El diablo cojuelo* [1641] as "doubly fascinating, for it revels in the eternal follies of spectacles while cautiously inquiring about the new mysteries of the skies above" (67).

5 In his note to lines 400–7, Méndez Plancarte cites Vossler's interpretation based on the explication of an engraving of intersecting triangles in Kircher's treatise (1951, 1.594).

6 Grossi reads *Primero sueño* in architectural terms, perceiving the images of the pyramid, the mountain, the Tower of Babel, and the magic lantern as "retratos" [portraits] of the structure of the poem as a whole (2007, 42). Patricia Saldarriaga compares geometrical and architectural references in the poem to Juan Bautista Villalpando's 1596 treatise on sacred architecture.

7 Although he acknowledges some scholars' claims that the opening lines describe a lunar eclipse in which the earth's shadow covers the moon, Alberto Pérez Amador Adam explains how the image of earth projecting its shadow without reaching its goal is a figure for the failed attempts at ascent in the poem, anticipating the ultimate defeat of the project of comprehending the universe through human intellect (1996, 114).

8 The relationship between the epistemological endeavour of Sor Juana's long poem and Descartes's scientific methodology continues to be a matter of debate (Merrim 1999, 241; McKenna 2000, 241–3).

9 "Luna," literally "moon," is a lexicalized metaphor for "mirror" in Spanish; however, the moon as feminine symbol is also important in *Primero sueño*.

10 Other references to optical phenomena in *Soledad primera* are addressed by Collins (2002, 94–5).

11 Although the practicality of equal temperament has rendered it the default tuning, and most listeners are not aware of the musical "compromise," some twentieth-century composers, among them John Adams, Lou Harrison, György Ligeti, and Pauline Oliveros, specify the use of just intonation for a particular quality of sound in some of their compositions.

12 In his notes to *Romance* 21, Méndez Plancarte refers to Sor Juana's handwritten notes in the convent's copy of Cerone's treatise (1951, 1.386–7). Ortiz also observes that in addition to her critical approach to the *Melopeo*, Sor Juana commented ironically on Cerone's emphatic opposition to women's study and performance of music in a marginal note, "su discípula, Sor Juana Inés de la Cruz" (2007a, 248).

## WORKS CITED

Arenal, Electa. 1991. "Where Woman Is Creator of the Wor(l)d, or, Sor Juana's Discourses on Method." In *Feminist Perspectives on Sor Juana Inés de la Cruz*, edited by Stephanie Merrim, 124–41. Detroit: Wayne State University Press.

Bryan, Catherine. 2007. "Gendered Ways of Seeing with Sor Juana: 'Situating Knowledge' in New Spain." In *Approaches to Teaching the Works of Sor Juana Inés de la Cruz*, edited by Emilie L. Bergmann and Stacey Schlau, 103–11. New York: Modern Language Association.

Chemris, Crystal. 2007. *Góngora and the Problem of Modernity*. London: Támesis.

Collins, Marcia. 2002. *The Soledades, Góngora's Masque of the Imagination*. Columbia: University of Missouri Press.

Crary, Jonathan. 1990. *Techniques of the Observer: On Vision and Modernity in the Nineteenth Century*. Boston: Massachusetts Institute of Technology Press.

García Santo-Tomás, Enrique. 2009. "Fortunes of the *Occhiali Politici* in Early Modern Spain: Optics, Vision, Points of View." *PMLA* 124 (1): 59–75. http://dx.doi.org/10.1632/pmla.2009.124.1.59.

Gaylord, Mary M. 1993. "Góngora and the Footprints of the Voice." *MLN* 108 (2): 230–53. http://dx.doi.org/10.2307/2904634.

Góngora y Argote, Luis de. 1968. *The Solitudes of Luis de Góngora*. Translated by Gilbert F. Cunningham. Baltimore: Johns Hopkins University Press.

Góngora y Argote, Luis de. 1972. *Obras completas*. Edited by Juan and Isabel Millé y Giménez. Madrid: Aguilar.

Grossi, Verónica. 2007. *Sigilosos v(u)elos epistemológicos en Sor Juana Inés de la Cruz*. Madrid: Iberoamericana.

Haraway, Donna. 1998. "The Persistence of Vision." In *The Visual Culture Reader*, edited by Nicholas Mirzoeff, 191–8. New York: Routledge.

Hill, Ruth. 2000. *Sceptres and Sciences in the Spains: Four Humanists and the New Philosophy (ca. 1680–1740)*. Liverpool: Liverpool University Press.

Hollander, John. 1961. *The Untuning of the Sky: Ideas of Music in English Poetry 1500–1700*. Princeton: Princeton University Press.

Jay, Martin. 1988. "Scopic Regimes of Modernity." In *Vision and Visuality*, edited by Hal Foster, 3–23. Seattle: Bay Press.

Jay, Martin. 1994. *Downcast Eyes: The Denigration of Vision in Twentieth-Century French Thought*. Berkeley: University of California Press.

Jones, R.O. 1966. *The Poems of Góngora*. Cambridge: Cambridge University Press.

Juana Inés de la Cruz, Sor. 1951. *Obras completas*. Vol. 1. *Lírica personal.* Edited by Alfonso Méndez Plancarte. México: Fondo de Cultura Económica.

Juana Inés de la Cruz, Sor. 2009. *Neptuno alegórico*. Edited by Vincent Martin and Electa Arenal. Madrid: Cátedra.

Kircher, Athanasius. 1671. *Ars Magna Lucis et Umbrae*. 2nd ed. Rome.

Long, Pamela. 2009. *Sor Juana / Música: How the Décima Musa Composed, Practiced, and Imagined Music*. New York: Peter Lang.

Ludmer, Josefina. 1984. "Tretas del débil." In *La sartén por el mango: encuentro de escritoras latinoamericanas*, edited by Patricia Elena González and Eliana Ortega, 47–54. Río Piedras, PR: Ediciones Huracán.

McKenna, Susan. 2000. "Rational Thought and Female Poetics in Sor Juana's *Primero sueño*: The Circumvention of Two Traditions." *Hispanic Review* 68 (1): 37–52. http://dx.doi.org/10.2307/474355.

Merrim, Stephanie. 1999. *Early Modern Women's Writing and Sor Juana Inés de la Cruz*. Nashville, TN: Vanderbilt University Press.

Musser, Charles. 1994. *The Emergence of Cinema: The American Screen to 1907*. Berkeley: University of California Press.

Ortiz, Mario A. 2007a. "La musa y el Melopeo: los diálogos transatlánticos entre Sor Juana Inés de la Cruz y Pietro Cerone." *Hispanic Review* 75 (3): 243–64. http://dx.doi.org/10.1353/hir.2007.0023.

Ortiz, Mario A. 2007b. "Musical Settings of Sor Juana's Works and Music in Works of Sor Juana." In *Approaches to Teaching the Works of Sor Juana Inés de la Cruz*, edited by Emilie L. Bergmann and Stacey Schlau, 239–46. New York: Modern Languages Association.

Pérez-Amador Adam, Alberto. 1996. *El precipicio de Faetón: Nueva edición, estudio filológico y comento de Primero sueño* de Sor *Juana Inés de la Cruz*. Frankfurt am Main: Vervuert; Madrid: Iberoamericana.

Rivers, Elias L. (Original work published 1966) 1988. *Renaissance and Baroque Poetry of Spain*. Prospect Heights, IL: Waveland Press.

Ruiz Pérez, Pedro. 1996. *El espacio de la escritura: en torno a una poética del espacio del texto barroco*. Bern: Peter Lang.

Saldarriaga, Patricia. 2006. *Los espacios del Primero sueño de Sor Juana Inés de la Cruz: Arquitectura y cuerpo femenino*. Madrid: Iberoamericana.

Sánchez Robayna, Andrés. 1983. *Tres estudios sobre Góngora*. Barcelona: Ediciones del Mall.

Sarduy, Severo. 1969. *Escrito sobre un cuerpo*. Buenos Aires: Editorial Sudamericana.

Trueblood, Alan S. 1988. *A Sor Juana Anthology*. Cambridge, MA: Harvard University Press.

# 8 Picaresque Partitions: Spanish Antiheroes and the Material World

EDWARD H. FRIEDMAN

> The warning message we sent the Russians was a calculated ambiguity that would be clearly understood.
>
> Alexander Haig

> I'm not Jack Nicholson. I'm not Brando. But I do mumble.
>
> Benicio Del Toro

Material objects are indispensable to picaresque narratives, which deploy variations on the theme of acquisition and its antonyms. The *pícaros*, after all, are have-nots who want to attain and obtain, and their stories record their generally unsuccessful quests. Lázaro de Tormes starts a process that culminates, in many ways, in the account of Pablos the *buscón*. Objects become psychological, even subconscious, tools of personal histories and social skirmishes. A key feature of Francisco de Quevedo's *La vida del buscón*, first published in 1626, is its baroque language, which attests to the inscription of the author in his narrative, and specifically to his conceptual and rhetorical skills. At the same time, Quevedo gives the Segovian narrator/protagonist Pablos a psyche and a set of circumstances that distinguish him from his creator. The *Buscón* combines artistry and anxiety, aesthetic flourishes and an emotional self-portrait by the *pícaro* as outsider. Perhaps unwittingly, Quevedo cedes space to a character that he would hardly have respected or valued in any way. The "materiality" of words in the *Buscón* – the concrete objects that appear in the text and the verbal signs themselves – makes them symbols of social reality and analogues of the world outside. This essay puts forth the argument that the perspectives implicit in the dialectics of author and narrator are based on particular semiotic presuppositions. Quevedo puts words on display, while Pablos hides behind words, and the resulting discourse reflects dazzlingly, if at times inadvertently, the conflictive age in which the novel was composed.

It has become a commonplace of criticism of the *Buscón* to debate the primary feature of Quevedo's text: its conspicuous exhibition of verbal wit – its *conceptismo* – or its intensification of the conventions of picaresque narrative. Which is the dominant element? Which is at the service of the other?[1] The polemics parallel the case of Mateo Alemán's *Guzmán de Alfarache* (1599, 1604), which has been deemed both a set of sermons bolstered by picaresque episodes to maintain reader interest and a picaresque tale with appended sermons to pay homage to the Tridentine emphasis on didacticism.[2] There is in the *Buscón* technically only one voice, the first-person voice of Pablos, but it would by no means be a stretch to recognize a voice-over, the mark of a literary ventriloquist at work. Pablos is definitely a presence in the novel. He is the acknowledged storyteller, and the story is his. Moreover, the construct of the "implied author," as outlined by Wayne Booth in *The Rhetoric of Fiction* and refined in subsequent decades,[3] applies most heartily to the elitist and bigoted Quevedo's intervention in the *Buscón*, as architect of a brand of determinism that mirrors the sensibility of the hierarchical society in which he thrived and suffered. One set of words, then, can do double, triple, or quadruple duty. Pablos self-consciously narrates his story, and Quevedo refashions or recontextualizes it according to his own plan, a plan laden with derision, irony, and, gloriously, an openness that likely would not have been intended or desired by the consummate satirist. It may be worthwhile to recall that the aspiration for upward mobility would not have been an admirable social trait in early modern Spain.[4]

Pablos is an antisocial figure on a number of levels. He is not only a New Christian, but the offspring of despicable parents and the member of a clan of outcasts. He is, arguably, the lowest of the low, but he does have an education of sorts, elementary and middle schooling and a time at the University of Alcalá de Henares, thanks to his colleague and master Don Diego Coronel. The question of whether his academic background can justify the height of ingenuity that he reveals is a significant factor in assessing the place of Pablos in the narrative. Much depends on the reader's inclination to enter the world and mindset of the narrator or to envision a puppeteer behind the mask of an autobiographical chronicler. The vying for space helps to define the structure of the *Buscón* and to establish the links between the shape of the story and the shape of things far beyond the pages of the book. The degree of sympathy that a reader might have for

Pablos is conditioned by one's attitude towards the social rebel or underdog, itself conditioned by the mores of a given period and locus. A majority of readers in the new millennium probably would be more inclined to favour the antihero than the rigid and prescriptive (and proscriptive) protocols of Habsburg Spain.

It is possible that Quevedo wrote the *Buscón* well before its publication date and that the manuscript circulated as early as 1603 or 1604.[5] In any event, he would have been familiar with *Lazarillo de Tormes* and *Guzmán de Alfarache*, each of which hurls its narrator into a mine field of irony. Discourse can be incriminating, even when the narrator seems to wish to defend himself. Lázaro de Tormes initiates a paradigm of breaking a protective silence. He is, in every sense, a town crier, publicizing wines and his private business as the gossipmongers hang onto every word. In setting out his defence, his explanation of "the case," Lázaro aims at fabricating a rhetoric that will glorify and historicize his rise from life's nadir, and yet his untenable position shows through. He wants readers to see him as indifferent to the code of honour – and some readers and critics most certainly do – but he is not fully convincing.[6] He ultimately is trapped by his confessions, plotted and unpremeditated. His masters are specialists at verbal deception; they use language to abuse their charge and to profit from trickery, and their lessons in "how to do things with words" instruct Lázaro on the nature of signs and on the multiple faces of reality.[7] The narrative ends on a wonderfully ambiguous allusion to prosperity, which follows an account of a thorny marital situation and what has to have been a traumatic public scandal. As a precocious spin doctor, Lázaro allows the incipient picaresque genre to rely on and to relish its polysemous base and its rich and mutable subtexts.[8]

Although the author of *Guzmán de Alfarache* is not anonymous, he is a controversial and puzzling figure, whose public persona had an air of mystery. Mateo Alemán was likely a New Christian attempting to pass as an Old Christian.[9] In the narrative, he constantly attempts to distance himself from his protagonist, but his palpable exasperation with life's daily struggles and his incorporation of social critique tend to cloud the distinction between the fictional speaker and his real-life progenitor. Guzmán and Alemán fail, to an extent, at extricating themselves from an objectionable other, a father and a rogue, respectively. The wish to deny one's bloodlines operates in a dualistic and ironic manner. Alemán foregrounds an overcompensating narrator/protagonist while inserting himself into the scheme, protesting a bit too much, and suggesting throughout the narrative process that people cannot escape the hand that fate has dealt them.

When a pseudonymous author publishes a false continuation of the novel in 1602, Alemán exerts considerable effort in his own second part to allegorize the theft, to expose the imposter (the author and an alter ego who makes his way into the legitimate sequel), and to stress the superiority of his brainchild, text and *pícaro*. He does not seem to comprehend that his defence of Guzmán goes against the condemnation of his character's actions and thoughts in Part 1. The very act of taking Guzmán's side runs counter to the air of morality that lies at the core of the narrative, however convolutedly. Guzmán is to be despised, and then judged as somehow better than his surrogate. *Guzmán de Alfarache* connects the literary form known as the miscellany with the novel-in-the-making, as it anticipates *Don Quijote*. Alemán lacks the control and the dispassionate authority of his contemporary Miguel de Cervantes, who sustains balance within his narrative while denouncing an intrusive continuation. The notable shift in focus in the second part of Alemán's novel blurs the boundaries between the historical writer and the implied author, but Guzmán's vita is complex and fascinating. The imprecise design of the narrative does not detract from the trials and tribulations of the title character, who, despite his baseness, despondency, and alterity, manages to serve the cause of exemplarity. The reader's response to *Guzmán de Alfarache* is, finally, a function of accepting or rejecting the professed conversion of the narrator, who alleges to have repented his sins and to have been delivered from evil. Engagingly, the only manifestation of that conversion is encoded in the discourse itself, since the recounted events themselves are pre-conversional.

Quevedo has a model for the picaresque and a strong perception of the social order. The protagonist of the *La vida del buscón* is doomed from the start, persistently endeavouring to be a gentleman at any cost, and Pablos, in fact, pays dearly for his ruses. He is a pawn of fortune and of the man who casts him in plots – and in a plot – that fail him. His brashness and the risks that he takes become greater as his story progresses, as does his punishment. One of the most unsettling aspects of the *Buscón* is a baroque excess within linguistic and referential frames. Violence, cruelty, and the infliction of pain seem omnipresent and inevitable, and language adapts itself to the milieu. Quevedo is unsparing in his recourse to the extremes, and Pablos, deprived of free will, can only rush headlong into a chain of calamities, disappointments, thwarted plans, and humiliations. He offers a moral and closing words of self-deprecation to his story. Nonetheless, the reader may discover a surprising and paradoxical twist to Quevedo's rendering of the *pícaro*, whose figurative imprisonment within the first-person discourse carries a symbolism of its own. The anonymity of *Lazarillo de*

*Tormes* allows the reader to configure the author as an abstraction, as invisible strings, so to speak. Mateo Alemán in *Guzmán de Alfarache* becomes increasingly involved in the narrative that he is, at once, inventing and forsaking. He tries to detach himself from his protagonist, while his interests and his stake in the well-being of Guzmán make separation difficult. Within the expanse of his manuscript, Alemán seems less committed to a unified vision or to psychological consistency than to the projection of a society fraught with stumbling blocks and ill will. His grievances are mixed with those of Guzmán, pariah and soulmate. The reader may be able to disentangle Alemán from Guzmán, and vice versa, and, on occasion, may find that their paths and their voices cross, enigmatically but also as part of a strange internal logic of mutual dependency.

What could be classified as a love-hate relationship in Alemán's novel loses the love in Quevedo's *Buscón*. Pablos is an untouchable, with negligible redeeming qualities. His goal of success is stated and restated only to underscore the fruitlessness of his labours. He is the antithesis of a responsible citizen, for he refuses to conform to the rules of decorum, rules that would have him adhere to a standard of subservience. Further, he is the antithesis of the proud and arrogant nobleman Quevedo, who obviously would not condone an egalitarian spirit or a social climber from the lower depths. The more one knows about Quevedo, the greater the chasm between creator and creation. Lázaro de Tormes provides a theory of relativity as rationalization for his conduct and for his dubious triumphs, which he hopes to qualify for Vuestra Merced. This rather modest proposal is daring for mid-sixteenth-century Spain. Lázaro does not bear the slings and arrows of mockery alone, for *Lazarillo de Tormes* brilliantly fuses, and confuses, the subjects and objects of satire. The mistreated and cuckolded protagonist cannot remove himself from harm's way or eradicate his complicity in the marital woes, but he is persuasive enough to implicate those around him. Goodness in the world of *Lazarillo de Tormes* is like the food in the early chapters: neither prevalent nor painless to obtain. Lázaro's point that he has come a long way and that he and his wife are no worse than their neighbours is well taken. They are not innocent, but they are not more guilty than their fellow men and women. Perspective in *Lazarillo* is crucial to the innovative format, because the marginal voice expands the frame of the narrative and thus the scope of the social analogue. With an irony of its own, the picaresque challenges the culture of exclusion by opening doors as the narratives depict the closing of doors. The genre captures the restrictive atmosphere and the sites of power through unique and special agents, who previously had been elided from narrative discourse.

Guzmán de Alfarache's conversion extends the ambitions of the *pícaro*, who now asks the reader to believe his claims and his sincerity. Alemán intensifies the delinquency of the protagonist and the hardships that he must endure.[10] Guzmán has been lost, but he declares himself saved, and his narrative becomes a testament to his liberation. The rhetoric of *Lazarillo de Tormes* is aligned with self-preservation; Lázaro is writing on command and is mounting a defence. He prepares his reader to expect a calculated strategy, that is, to expect some type of overstatement. Guzmán, in contrast, does not confirm the complete parameters of his thesis – his spiritual transformation – until he reaches the conclusion, and books have been written by scholars sceptical of the change of heart.[11] The rhetorical formula of *Guzmán de Alfarache* is far more intricate than the plan of *Lazarillo*, due not only to the massive text but also to the mental meanderings of the narrator and the insistence on his disenchantment, his disillusionment. He demonstrates over and over again that he can trust no one. He intimates that God has forsaken him, but religion gives him comfort in the end. That is, without a doubt, a good decision, but not an easily verifiable one. The test requires a reliable narrator, and the anguished, downtrodden, and much-maligned Guzmán is not necessarily the ideal candidate. On the other hand, if *Lazarillo* maps a new direction – and a new aesthetic and social domain – for the outsider, *Guzmán* amplifies the narrative space exponentially. The extraordinarily pessimistic view of society comes from the man who communicates the events of his life story after he has gone through a climactic conversion. The resulting tension is a reigning trope of the lengthy and detailed narrative. From a theological standpoint, Alemán may be expressing faith in redemption for even the lowest of the low, but the cynicism that underlies the story and the discourse of *Guzmán* competes with any positive outlook that one may posit. This dualism may shape a reading of the novel, yet the desperation behind Guzmán's voice – affecting his idiolect and the laying bare of his psyche – would seem to break the balance. In the many pages of the narrative, the agony, abjection, and misery of Guzmán's existence never cease. The distance that should accompany the dedication to higher thoughts, and that should affect the narrator's persona (as opposed to that of the protagonist), does not make its way into the discourse. Alemán must contend, as well, with an earthly problem: the spurious sequel and his own literary reputation.

In 1605 and in 1615, Cervantes devises in *Don Quijote* a special place for the reader and a special place for irony. He has seen both, I would submit, in the picaresque, which was a recent phenomenon, but one of which we know he was cognizant.[12] The reader as arbiter is a sine qua non of *Lazarillo de Tormes* and of *Guzmán de Alfarache*, which demand an understanding of the markers of irony. The complexity of baroque art builds upon this base by pushing the limits of the act of deciphering. Lázaro de Tormes's self-fashioning, a fictionalization of the autobiographical mode, gives added meaning to the authority of words. The character represents – re-presents – himself to a narratee who must, in one way or another, read between the lines. Words become form and substance, and Guzmán de Alfarache's contribution in this regard could not be more substantial. The presumed judgment of Vuestra Merced inaugurates a narrative practice that isolates and empowers the consumer of literature; in short, it is a figurative contractual agreement to analyse and interpret the words of the narrator and, by extension, to uncover the rhetorical technique of the author. The *pícaro* as narrator evokes an environment through words, and, in the archetypal texts, that environment is closely allied to material objects. First, words replace events themselves; historiography replaces history, and words become the partners of revisionism. Second, words are stand-ins for things; one set of signs replaces another, or others. Third, the picaresque often concerns itself with lack, and words, as presence, have to convey absence. Ironically, the medium for producing that message is frequently hyperbole. The neglect that Lazarillo de Tormes suffers at the hands of the blind man, the cleric, and the squire, for example, is rendered in a language that exaggerates scarcity that plays against insufficiency. Hunger is the signified, but the signifiers are replete with materiality. The images of the narrative have a circular feel to them, and Lázaro's possessions – most notably, the clothing that he purchases at the end of chapter 6, reminiscent of the squire's attire – summon the spectres of the past. His words, as *pregonero* and as a wronged husband, resonate to publicize his wretched state.

The discourse of Guzmán de Alfarache may be said to constitute a mannerist middle ground between his predecessor and successor.[13] Guzmán is about as insignificant as one could be in the social structure of his day. He is a whipping-boy, an exemplar of the negative, a stain on all he touches, the bad that allows light to shine on the good. His attainments are regularly devalued, denied, or overruled. In the allegory of Part 2, even Guzmán's name is in jeopardy. The book that begins by using his own words to ridicule him mercilessly later embarks, ironically, on a campaign to redeem him, by exorcising a sequel, a phantom namesake, and an insidious author, and by a last-minute conversion. Throughout his life, Guzmán has had many exploits and encounters, but he has little to show from his travails. The exception is his book, with copious testimony, not merely of incidents but of thoughts and feelings, past and present. Guzmán, one could note, lives in a vacuum. He is a cipher, a nonentity, or, worse, a scapegoat. The narrative object that belittles him and questions his conversion – in spite of his nominal position of control – ends by immortalizing him, by preserving his words and freeze-framing his social interaction, as caught in the blind alley in which he exists. The space allotted to the picaresque narrator / protagonist is enormous. Guzmán writes about his blood relations and about those who have raised him, about his education and training, about love and hate, about justice and injustice, about topics inspired by his experiences or that simply occur to him. The "real" and the anecdotal come together, and so, it seems, do the interests of Guzmán de Alfarache and Mateo Alemán. Whereas for Lázaro de Tormes brevity is the soul of wit, for Guzmán verbosity takes over. Rarely before or since has an underdog been given such an opportunity to vent his frustrations or to put forth, emulating Lázaro, his case. The vast panorama of *Guzmán de Alfarache* encompasses the social spectrum as Spain entered a new century, a century of turmoil and strife on numerous fronts, and of rapidly changing subjectivities.

The dynamism and the vitality imparted by words in the earlier narratives continue in *La vida del buscón*, in which Quevedo and Pablos seem to spar for dominance. Simultaneously, the two could be seen to join forces to surpass the achievements of the picaresque novels (and novelists) that come before them. Baroque intensity drives the story, the discourse, and the overall composition of the *Buscón*, whose deep structure is predicated on rivalry and competition. Like *Lazarillo*, and unlike the adroitly meandering *Guzmán*, the *Buscón* is a manageable text, with a few digressions but by no means a miscellany. There is a clear pattern to Pablos's life, from lowly lineage to maturity, along with a clear message, which the narrator himself imparts as a moral when he brings his autobiographical document to a close. Quevedo charts a distinctive course by pairing language and psychology as perhaps the most striking dialectical elements of the narrative. I want to address and to affirm the statement that, in the *Buscón*, Pablos has a mind of his own. I consider the statement to be both absurd and valid, while some will see it as solely absurd. I agree with Edwin Williamson that Pablos steps out of Quevedo's "coercive grasp,"[14] which helps to explain how words – in current parlance – multitask *and* obscure meaning in the narrative. Giving the word to Pablos replicates the narrative transfer of the preceding texts, but the effect is different. Quevedo goes beyond baroque artistry to advance the growth of the novel, and he has not typically been given accolades for doing so. This could be because he and his protagonist, while compelling, are prodigiously disagreeable.

Through Pablos, Quevedo immediately attaches *conceptismo* to picaresque convention. The humble genealogy of the opening chapter is mired in wordplay, but this is excess in reverse, a surfeit of bad blood and a mockery of Christian ideals. Quevedo enjoys not only artistic detachment as he showcases his verbal gifts, but he takes advantage of the first-person narration to spotlight Pablos, willing to share details and unaware of the snares of irony into which he is falling. Pablos unmasks his parents, who try to conceal their true selves through euphemism, apparently without realizing that he is doing the same thing. The rhetorical artifice – and edifice – is set up at the beginning: Pablos is clever and artful, but his words betray him. His assertions and conclusions, such as the gratitude that he pays to (indisputably wayward) parents so mindful of his welfare, are, more often than not, empty, misguided, and untrue. The Renaissance self-refashioning[15] of *Lazarillo de Tormes* acquires a baroque thrust. By pumping up the rhetoric, Pablos may give an unaccustomed materiality to words, but the very language that is being exalted threatens to overshadow its subject. Pablos has no status in society. He is a hollow man, and yet he is perforce the centre of the narrative. An implied author would seem to want to dislodge him by decentring his speaker. A way to do that would be to discredit him, or to have Pablos discredit himself by showing one thing and telling another; the narrator would be misrepresenting the truth and therefore could not be trusted. In addition, the more elaborate and sophisticated the discourse, the greater the odds that the reader would contemplate the work of the artist over the rationale of the character.

Pablos's various progenitors and parental figures are prominent from the beginning, and the instruction is that those disfavoured by destiny cannot overcome the obstacles on their passage through life. The father is a thief, the mother a prostitute and a witch who has not raised him. Quevedo is not inclined to defend his literary issue. As a man of letters, Pablos can make a silk purse out of a sow's ear – can adjust the data, rename, and reappraise – but the separate reality has a temporary quality, an air of make-believe. The words of the *Buscón* generate a conundrum that forms the crux of the narrative. Words are the source of Pablos's centrality and, it could be argued, the source of his undoing. They are, in theory, his entrée to decent society, but, in practice, testimony to his ill-founded pretensions. Quevedo, Tantalus-like in his burlesque of paternity, situates Pablos in a propitious site, a site of authority, of authorial strength, and then envelops

– or, appropriately, swaddles – his discourse in irony. Quevedo abuses Pablos as society abuses its objectionable denizens, by strategizing to place him in the periphery of his own narrative. This is a magisterial example of ironic distance. It is Quevedo's admonition against civil disobedience that may seek to overwhelm the disobedient civilian. Quevedo permits Pablos to represent himself in the court of public opinion, with every confidence that the *pícaro* has a fool for a client. The urge to be a gentleman motivates Pablos, and the prospect of foiling the notion – repeatedly and resoundingly – animates Quevedo. While Lázaro de Tormes and Guzmán de Alfarache yearn for respectability, Pablos – who first makes the wish as a child – wants, instead, the accoutrements of success, not goodness, precisely, but goods, not self-improvement but improved surroundings. He can never afford to be sensitive, nor can he rechannel the negative energy with which heredity and environment have endowed him. His masters and his neighbours will not waste a moment to ponder his innermost reflections or the depths of his soul. Pablos is innately unworthy of deferential treatment and of integration into mainstream society, no matter how uncompromising or unwavering his commitment may be. His condition is, alas, chronic, unremitting, and irreparable.

In one plotting of *La vida del buscón*, Quevedo occupies the centre and Pablos the margins. The author has on his side the inquisitorial and hierarchical order, and the *pícaro* only the indicators of disorder. Eventually, a new order – modern, and with a broad range of inflections – and a modified plotting can identify the inequity of the social system, find some compassion for the persecuted, and "read" Pablos, and the antihero in general, more sympathetically. Modernity likewise brings a new scientific imperative and, irony upon irony, an improbable team of advocates: Sigmund Freud and succeeding psychoanalysts. The picaresque, in *Lazarillo de Tormes* (and maybe even before, in Francisco Delicado's *La lozana andaluza*, of 1528), precociously puts forward a cumulative approach to characterization. The mature protagonist is the product of a process enacted in the text. Control is proven to be a misnomer, an illusion. Lázaro scorns the squire's fixation on honour, for example, but his purchase of clothing and his reaction to the gossipmongers of Toledo may divulge his own latent preoccupation. Guzmán de Alfarache fights to free himself of his father, and his discourse has much to do with free association. *Guzmán de Alfarache* brings the conflict with the father to bear on an author who becomes ever more decisively a supplement of the narrator / protagonist and a subconscious subject. The dissolute Pablos may be the most transparent product of discrimination to be found in picaresque fiction.

From childhood, Pablos grapples with the burden of his family's unsavoury reputation. No memory seems to be devoid of trauma. He is reviled, attacked, called names, and, he thinks, confused with his parents. He admits that he seethed with rage, but hid his feelings, and it is this bottled-up anger that manifests itself in his offensive behaviour. His descriptions disclose the trait of overcompensation, as he does his utmost to win approval, to little avail. He is who he is, and, in a frightfully harrowing moment for the young boy, his mother refuses to deny the accusations that have been made against her. He cannot liberate himself from his familial ties or from his name and the depravity that it connotes. Throughout his life, he will concoct names and identities as a means of obliterating the past, a past that cannot be erased from his mind and that finds ways of catching up with him. Even before he joins a theatre company, Pablos pursues the performance arts, as a prankster who moves up (or down) the ladder to felon. He flaunts these skills as a writer, when he lets words suppress and disguise emotions. His parents mark him as inferior, and his peers do battle with him. A schoolmaster, the licentiate Cabra, nearly starves him, and Pablos's commentary on the ordeal is a masterpiece in miniature of baroque conceits. Here, as elsewhere, abundance trumps lack, and evasion trumps acknowledgment, which would denote weakness and vulnerability. When Pablos writes of the shortage of food, he reduces himself to skin and bones, to a disappearing body that must be metaphorically resurrected with words. He seems to be preparing the reader for the torment and torture that await him in Alcalá de Henares, where he goes in service to Don Diego Coronel. This may be the quintessential section of the narrative. On the road to the university, Pablos and Don Diego are equals – and equally naive – but, on their arrival, everything changes. Don Diego is received with warmth and enthusiasm, and Pablos is insulted, trampled upon, and disgraced. It is at this point that Pablos realizes that he can succumb to social pressure and accept his station in life, or he can opt for notoriety. Needless to say, he chooses the latter.

Pablos insists that he is content with life on the wrong side of the law. He brags that he has never felt better. Outwardly, he is fearless and adamant in his defiance of the rules by which the virtuous abide. His discourse is, however, patently contradictory in its representation of the highs and lows of his stay in Alcalá. The best of times and the worst of times become intermingled. Pablos seems to forget the devastating welcome that he received – and inscribes into the text – as he boasts of his fame and satisfaction as a full-fledged criminal. He contrasts himself with the studious and upright Don Diego, and his encomiums seem somewhat forced, as well as generous, given that the privileged Don Diego did not balk at the tricks played against Pablos and that he would return as Pablos's nemesis some years later. Pablos credits Don Diego with enjoining him always to be on the alert, to watch out for himself since he alone would do so, and this becomes his maxim. At the end of Book 1 (chapter 7), Don Diego, under orders from his father, cannot continue to employ Pablos, but he is willing to find him a position as servant. Pablos informs Don Diego that he is now "another" man, who feels that he has a higher calling. He has received word of his father's death, and he returns to Segovia in order to collect his inheritance and to take his leave for good. As a petty thief, miscreant, and carouser, Pablos is uninterested in possessions. He does not steal food to survive or filch items that he needs or wants. He cannot attain renown, but bad repute will suffice. He has hit upon an outlet for his pent-up aggression, and he has a name, if not a proper one. The exhilaration that comes from this social victory is multilayered, alternately sincere and heartfelt, grandstanding and self-deceptive. There is, nevertheless, an unmistakable facet of the narrative that rises above the flair and ostentation of the *pícaro*'s hoaxes: Pablos confesses to the reader the shame, the horror, and the indignity that he has felt. He may not see the connections between his background and his actions in the present, but we do.

Never at home in Segovia, Pablos once more finds himself guilty by proxy – or, at least, mortified – when he sees his father "quartered" on the road, and when his uncle Alonso greets him and introduces him to a rogues' gallery of acquaintances. Pablos grabs his "legacy" and sneaks away in the night. The birthright becomes money alone. Quevedo shrewdly follows the break from the father and the family with Pablos's meeting of Don Toribio on the journey to Madrid. Pablos now has a father figure and a ready-made family in the band of rascals over whom Don Toribio presides. In this realm, the tangible and the material – and material, literally – carry ample weight. Life for Don Toribio and his henchmen is tromp l'oeil, a game of deception in which the visible is misleading and the real is less than promised. Don Toribio's wardrobe, for example, seems elegant and complete, but the cloth is in tatters. The magicians of the eye dupe the unsuspecting and try to stay one step ahead of the law. Pablos feels at home in this brotherhood, and he learns to take liberally from others, as the episode of the free lunch at the home of the licentiate Flechilla in Book 3, chapter 2, illustrates. In a month, Pablos acquires a solid education in this school of hard knocks. His adventures become gradually more complicated and more dangerous, and he begins to use aliases. The group is rounded up and jailed by officers of justice. Pablos intuits that money speaks, and he bribes his way out of prison. He helps his cause by befriending a warden and his wife and daughters, objectionable and unattractive New Christians with horrendous credentials. Even though they serve his selfish intentions, they are an ironic replacement family for Pablos, who sets out from his detention in search of new blood, as it were.

The *pícaro* then pursues a series of women, culminating in the courtship of a nun. He goes after the daughter of his landlord and remarks that people grant him more respect when he has lured them into thinking that he is wealthy. Although his plan fails, he acts more boldly in his betrothal to a young lady, Doña Ana, who believes that he is Don Felipe Tristán, a well-to-do aristocrat. He is all but wallowing in the lap of luxury when Don Diego Coronel, Ana's cousin, appears unexpectedly and corners Pablos, who must relive the past as he listens to a recitation of his family history and burns from within while camouflageing his feelings. The past again haunts him shortly thereafter, when a horse that he has "borrowed" dumps him into the mud in yet another emblematic fall. From this episode, Pablos is left wounded, unguarded, immobile, and penniless, beaten physically and emotionally, and plagued by reminders of a past from which he cannot extract himself. He has nothing to show for his social battles but scars, external and internal. He has come close to conquering an adversarial order; marriage to Doña Ana would have brought him into the Coronel family, but the cycle that awaits him is grimmer and more deterministic, a cycle of inescapability and of failure. Because of his injuries, Pablos cannot flee from Madrid. Because of his transgressions, he cannot remain in the city. The impasse epitomizes the motif of wasted efforts that moves the plot of *El buscón*. Quevedo apportions Pablos the room to test his talent and to execute his gentlemanly proposition. He continually gives Pablos a false sense of security. There is no harm in this, because failure is certain, preordained by an author who knows that the falls are more stunning when they are unexpected by the protagonist. The destitute Pablos finds another father figure in a beggar named Valcázar, who teaches him the mendicant craft. As he starts the trek towards Toledo, Pablos must remake himself from scratch.

Pablos gains fame and a good income as an actor and writer, performing under the name of Alonsete. He goes so far as to picture himself with his own troupe, but when the manager of his company is jailed, he changes his mind. He writes that he has no real love of theatre, but that he is grateful to have had the diversion and full pockets on his departure from the profession. He next assumes a bizarre role, though one not new to Spanish literature or ecclesiastical history: a suitor of nuns, which he relates to the

Antichrist.[16] Pablos not only courts his chosen religious lady, but he defrauds her, relieving her of property and abandoning her. He travels from Toledo to Seville, where he joins the criminal underworld, the antisocial elite and the last of his substitute families. In this setting, mayhem and murder are the bread and butter of the would-be gentleman. After having taken sanctuary in the Iglesia Mayor while fleeing agents of the law, Pablos undergoes something akin to a spiritual transformation, vowing to lead a righteous life by settling in the New World with La Grajales, one of the women ("ninfas") he met in the church.[17] He does not detail his adventures in America, but alludes to a second part, which does not materialize and which does not have to, for he supplies the ending. Pablos had hoped that the change of locale would change his luck, but, in his final words, "fueme peor, como v. m. verá en la segunda parte, pues nunca mejora su estado quien muda solamente de lugar, y no de vida y costumbres" [I was worse off, as your Honour will see in the second part, since no one has ever improved his status by just moving and not changing his life or habits] (Quevedo 1998, 308). There is, according to Pablos himself, a character trait that prohibits him from taking an exemplary path, an ingrained resistance to goodness that may be an upshot of his heritage, a response to social stimuli, a personal idiosyncrasy, or a combination of one or more of these elements. The answer is hard to ascertain, but what is straightforward is the coming together of Pablos and Quevedo – ideological enemies working at cross-purposes – in the explicit statement of a theme. In the end, Pablos reads himself much as Quevedo will have read him. This convergence bestows a neatness on the resolution, but is not altogether credible within the dialectical structure of the narrative.

The picaresque begins with things, namely food: grapes, wine, sausages, turnips, pieces of bread, and so forth, in *Lazarillo de Tormes*.[18] A rhetoric of hunger leads to exaggerated descriptions of what is not there. The emphasis on food switches to social gestures related to honour, respectability, and the sanctity of marriage, and language once again is employed to indicate lack. Metaphor, metonymy, and allegory become more discernible as the narrative progresses. Biblical and folkloric diction serve new and ironic contexts, and a new kind of narrator / protagonist utters the words that evoke and, more audaciously, critique the norms and codes of society. At the conclusion of his story, Lázaro has the creature comforts that were denied him as a child, but, ironically, symbolism has become important to him, and the opinion of his neighbours matters to him. Material possessions may not be enough to promote tranquility. Guzmán de Alfarache, in turn, is a reflective man; thoughts weigh heavily on him. His creator Mateo

Alemán shares his intellectual sharpness, his loquaciousness, his opinionated nature, and his tendency to veer off on tangents. As with Lázaro, Guzmán's story has a vertical force, but a negative destiny uniformly blocks success. Guzmán may want prosperity – things – but he is more driven towards recognition for his achievements. The road is filled with obstacles, and the hurdles are never-ending. Finally, he asks the reader to take his conversion on faith, but one can judge him on the basis of discourse analysis, on the way in which he writes about his life after he professes to have changed. *Lazarillo de Tormes* has a visual and aural style; we can visualize Lazarillo growing into Lázaro, amid the images that punctuate his experiences, and we can hear his voice in what Claudio Guillén refers to as an "epístola hablada" [spoken epistle] (1957, 268).

*Guzmán de Alfarache* has a more abstract structure, and it foreshadows stream-of-consciousness and free association. Picaresque narrative is commonly cited as bringing psychological development to the fore.[19] *Lazarillo* does this beautifully and economically; this little book can never be exhausted. *Guzmán*, in contrast, is exhausting, and that is a fundamental part of its appeal. The psychological vehicle becomes a psychological roller coaster. The reader enters Guzmán's mind, with a corresponding glance at Mateo Alemán's mental processes as a bonus. Consistency's loss can be seen as profundity's (and perspectivism's) gain. The dominant possession in the novel is the book itself, united with the emblematic theft and false protagonist within the text of Part 2. Guzmán himself has goals that are abstract – cerebral, social, and judicial – and outwardly viable, signs of acceptability and tolerance. Society sees him as an outcast and a troublemaker, without looking for the causes of his delinquency and the reasons for his displeasure with the status quo. The eye of the storm in the picaresque is the questionable birthright. This is the opposite of the biblical Jacob and Esau, who vie for Isaac's approval. The *pícaro* struggles for independence from the father and from the burden of names. Lázaro faces a "case," whereas Guzmán contends against the world at large and, with Alemán, against ghosts of the past and present. If *Don Quijote* – with everything else, of course, including a master class in baroque technique and ideology – displays the height of optimism and appreciation of art, *Guzmán de Alfarache* is the epic of pessimism, the saga of man's race against time and malevolence.

The amorphousness of *Guzmán de Alfarache* places the narrative at a stage in which the novel was finding itself, inventing itself. *Don Quijote*, published shortly afterwards, reaches near perfection by focusing on its status as a work in progress. Cervantes is playful, calm, and in control, infuriated but not defeated (or deferred) by the Avellaneda sequel. Alemán is far more somber, far more incensed, and far more distracted by the Juan Martí continuation,[20] and he does some shifting of gears that, with some frequency, upsets the narrative rhythm. The fact that the reader sees two minds at work, in isolation and in tandem, investigates and broadens characterization, discourse, and, last but not least, the very human issue of authorial control. Standing between *Lazarillo de Tormes* and *Don Quijote*, and between *Lazarillo* and *La vida del buscón*, *Guzmán de Alfarache* seems to have a less formal concept of structure, but Alemán lets the vagaries of life and the muddled curriculum vitae of his narrator / protagonist steer the movement of the text. *Lazarillo* is an early but superlatively orchestrated novel, impressive in its concision, in which things fall into place. In *Guzmán* (to reference William Butler Yeats and Chinua Achebe), things fall apart,[21] but life – and *the* life – goes on. Autobiography and the precedent of *Lazarillo* give the narrative its design, which is complemented in Part 2 by the response to the sequel and by the lead-up to the conversion. The assortment of literary forms – literary *materials* – fills to overflowing the field of signifiers. Guzmán is disreputable. His voice is mediated from the outset by regulators inside and outside the narrative. He has to concede authority, and this restricts him, yet, paradoxically, frees him from restrictions that those above him must obey. He can be a sounding board for Alemán and for others who can be denounced for their words and even for their silences. *Guzmán de Alfarache* functions as a symbol of lettered culture, wherein language and rhetoric have the ability to reify – to conceive a space for – the unrepresented and the underrepresented. The graft transposes centre and margin, and the transposition presages, among other things, postmodern ideological shifts.

*La vida del buscón* is a well-wrought novel. Its pieces fit together, and its protagonist sticks to a program of social climbing, overreaching, and descent into criminality. Memories of childhood traumas reverberate in his head, and traces of the past *materialize* within the narrative trajectory. The war between morality and immorality is an uneven clash, whose results are predetermined. The *Buscón* is not fueled by suspense but by ironic distance, which noticeably places story and discourse under the aegis, respectively, of an author's sensibility and a voice-over. Quevedo is not a subtle figure here, hiding behind his words. For him, emplotment becomes entrapment. He shines as a star of conceptist invention and as a self-imposed social watchdog and avenging angel. In short, he exerts himself in order to keep Pablos in his place. Quevedo may have surprised himself, and the reader, by delving deeper into Pablos's psyche than he may have wished and, through what can only be tagged as a special precognitive intuition, by coordinating his character's thoughts and actions with psychoanalytical theory. The adult Pablos is exactly what one would expect him to be, having endured a lifetime of abuse. His resistance, his resentment, and his aggressive behaviour are the logical consequences of his contact with a hostile world. His subordination in the narrative – despite his subject position – is an analogue of his subordination in society. Nevertheless, exposure works both ways. Pablos is loathsome, but the disposition is not entirely of his making. This subtext of the *Buscón* is no less powerful because it is, it would seem, accidental, as irony begets irony. The display of ingenuity becomes a social artefact. A common denominator is identity. The protean Pablos seeks to inflate his worth, and intransigent Quevedo encroaches on his plans. The first adapts new identities in search of a *vita nuova*, and the second guards against change. The spoken word evaporates into the air as it is enunciated. The written word survives. Pablos's loss is memorialized in his – in Quevedo's – book, which readers can interpret and reinterpret over time.

Pablos is not an obvious candidate for sympathy, but his hurt may strike the reader as profoundly as his sins against society. His misdeeds and his attitude are comprehensible, if not easy to condone. There is a persona (albeit *non grata*) behind the barrage of conceits and behind the braggadocio, that is, a soul behind the mechanisms of deferral and the survival mechanisms. Lázaro de Tormes and Guzmán de Alfarache rewrite their histories, as a means of excusing their conduct and rationalizing their flaws, which remain ironically on display. Pablos articulates the suppression of his feelings of pain and anger, but the information is presented without a cry for pity and without recasting his negative traits. In the picaresque order, Pablos should be the least verisimilar of the archetypal protagonists, but I would list him as the most "real," the most lifelike. In appraising Quevedo's take on materiality, I would prioritize the artistry and the concreteness of verbal constructs. Quevedo expands one's perception of the universe through language, in much the way that Pedro Salinas describes the poetry of his contemporary (and bitter enemy) Luis de Góngora. In remaking reality, the author of the *Buscón* turns nature into the microcosm and literary expression into the macrocosm, from what Salinas terms "the simple level of material reality" to a higher aesthetic or poetic reality (1966, 141).[22] We have seen, as well, a psychological reality that adds to Quevedo's appropriation of the models of the picaresque and the baroque. That a hardened criminal assumes centre stage in this production is ironic, but perhaps not as unpleasant as it may seem. Pablos is forthright and elusive, a puppet who often undermines the puppeteer, and, for me, a fictional character who stays with the reader even when the most ingenious of puns may begin to fade.

## NOTES

1 For a summary of the arguments on both sides, see the opening of Williamson's essay, Friedman (1987, 238–9 n36), and Dunn (1993, 72–87).
2 See Friedman (1987, 236–7 n26) and Dunn (1993, 46–72) on approaches to *Guzmán de Alfarache*. Seminal in this regard is the work of Enrique Moreno Báez. See also, as starting points, the general studies of Alemán and the *Guzmán* by Donald McGrady and Ángel San Miguel.
3 On the "implied author" and related topics, see Booth, Chatman (1978, 146–95; and 1990, 74–108), Lanser (1981, 49–52, and 130–7), Rimmon-Kenan (1983, 86–9, and 100–5), Genette (1998, 135–54), Currie (1998, 19–29), and Lothe (2000, 11–27), and, for general considerations, Keen and the essays in van Peer and Chatman. In his study of lacunae in the picaresque, Parrack relates silence to the intervention of the implied author.
4 In important studies, Amelang gives nuanced readings of the social structure of Spain and of Europe in general.
5 On the dating of the *Buscón*, see, for example, Díaz-Migoyo (1980).
6 Frank Casa reads Lázaro as detached from the obsession with honour. For a different slant in the same journal, in a special number dedicated to *Lazarillo de Tormes* and guest-edited by Robert Fiore, see Friedman (1997).
7 The reference is to J.L. Austin's book and to speech-act theory (1975).
8 The question of *polisemia*, especially as it relates to *Lazarillo de Tormes*, is a major concern of Francisco Rico in *La novela picaresca y el punto de vista.*
9 See Yovel for commentary on Alemán (2009, esp. 270–5) and for a comprehensive consideration of New Christian identity.
10 Parker (1967) uses the criterion of degree of delinquency to classify narratives as picaresque. *Lazarillo de Tormes* is, for Parker, a "precursor," so his dating starts at 1599, with the publication of *Guzmán de Alfarache*. For a sense of current directions in picaresque studies, see Cruz (2008).
11 See Arias (1977), Brancaforte (1980), Whitenack (1985), and Rodríguez Matos (1985), who share the view that Guzmán is an unreliable narrator whose conversion is suspect. See also Shipley (1982), for an ingenious reading of Lázaro's rhetorical strategies.
12 Ginés de Pasamonte famously alludes to *Lazarillo de Tormes* in Part 1, ch. 22, of his own version of *Don Quijote*.

13 Domínguez Castellano (2003) reads the *Guzmán* from this perspective.
14 Pablos's metatheatrical feat – a form of independence from his author – is the thesis of Williamson's essay (1977, 59).
15 The phrase forms the title, and topic, of a study of early modern English literature by Stephen Greenblatt (1980).
16 In his edition of the Quevedo's *Buscón*, Domingo Ynduráin explains that it was said that the Antichrist would be born of a priest and a nun (1998, 289 n372).
17 Pablos writes, "Pasábamoslo en la iglesia notablemente, porque, al olor de los retraídos, vinieron ninfas, desnudándose para vestirnos" [We spent our time at church because, remarkably, at the smell of poverty, nymphs came over and undressed themselves in order to clothe us] (1998, 306).
18 Among a number of examples, see the studies of Javier Herrero on the imagery of *Lazarillo de Tormes* (1978).
19 A complete (and complex) psychoanalytical reading of picaresque narrative – Freudian, in this case – is Johnson's *Inside Guzmán de Alfarache* (1975). See also Iffland (1979) on Pablos's ownership of the discourse in the *Buscón*, also Freudian in orientation. Johnson (1996) explores Guzmán's subject position, as does Bandera (2002) with respect to Pablos in the *Buscón*.
20 In Part 2, Alemán identifies the pseudonymous author as Mateo Luján de Sayavedra. On the responses by Alemán and Cervantes to the spurious sequels, see Friedman (2000).
21 Yeats writes in "The Second Coming": "Things fall apart; the center cannot hold" (1997, 68). Achebe uses the first part of the verse in the title of his now-classic novel of Nigeria.
22 In "Subjects and Objects in the *Guzmán*" (2005, 108–29) and in *Writers on the Market* in general, Donald Gilbert-Santamaría offers an engaging view of "literary consumerism." In "The Destabilized Sign," William H. Clamurro (1980) relates language (and material considerations) in the *Buscón* to the concept of *cosificación*, which he borrows from the work of José Corrales Egea. I cannot reflect on the *Buscón* without thinking of the analysis of Arnold Weinstein in *Fictions of the Self* (1981), which I first read many years ago. Weinstein writes that Quevedo's novel "is a filthy book. It takes the materialist premise of *Lazarillo de Tormes* to its logical conclusion; spirit and transcendence not only yield to matter, but they are reduced to the lowest animal common denominator: excrement" (1981, 31). Given that this is the work of a devoted poet, Weinstein acknowledges that "even the most repugnant scenes are doing double duty" (1981, 31). The commentary has inspired me, over time and in different ways, to look at the dualistic nature of the text. For examples, see Friedman (1996 and 2006, 33–106).

## WORKS CITED

Achebe, Chinua. 1959. *Things Fall Apart*. New York: Anchor Books.

Alemán, Mateo. 1997. *Guzmán de Alfarache*. 2 vols. Edited by José María Micó. Madrid: Cátedra.

Amelang, James S. 1986. *Honored Citizens of Barcelona: Patrician Culture and Class Relations, 1490–1714*. Princeton: Princeton University Press.

Amelang, James S. 1998. *The Flight of Icarus: Artisan Autobiography in Early Modern Europe*. Stanford: Stanford University Press.

Arias, Joan. 1977. *Guzmán de Alfarache: The Unrepentant Narrator*. London: Tamesis.

Austin, J.L. 1975. *How to Do Things with Words*. 2nd ed. Edited by J.O. Urmson and Marina Sbisà. Cambridge, MA: Harvard University Press.

Bandera, Cesáreo. 2002. "Satan Expelling Satan: Reflections on Quevedo's *Buscón*." In *Never-Ending Adventure: Studies in Medieval and Early Modern Spanish Literature in Honor of Peter N. Dunn*, edited by Edward H. Friedman and Harlan Sturm, 155–74. Newark, DE: Juan de la Cuesta.

Booth, Wayne C. 1961. *The Rhetoric of Fiction*. Chicago: University of Chicago Press.

Brancaforte, Benito. 1980. *Guzmán de Alfarache: ¿Conversión o proceso de degradación?* Madison, WI: Hispanic Seminary of Medieval Studies.

Casa, Frank P. 1997. "In Defense of Lázaro de Tormes." *Crítica Hispánica* 19 (1–2): 87–98.

Cervantes, Miguel de. 1998. *Don Quijote de la Mancha*. Edited by Francisco Rico. Barcelona: Crítica.

Chatman, Seymour. 1978. *Story and Discourse*. Ithaca, NY: Cornell University Press.

Chatman, Seymour. 1990. *Coming to Terms: The Rhetoric of Narrative in Fiction and Film*. Ithaca, NY: Cornell University Press.

Clamurro, William H. 1980. "The Destabilized Sign: Word and Form in Quevedo's *Buscón*." *MLN* 95 (2): 295–311. http://dx.doi.org/10.2307/2906617.

Cruz, Anne J., ed. 2008. *Approaches to Teaching* Lazarillo de Tormes *and the Picaresque Tradition*. New York: Modern Language Association of America.

Currie, Mark. 1998. *Postmodern Narrative Theory*. New York: Palgrave.

Delicado, Francisco. 1969. *La lozana andaluza*. Edited by Bruno Damiani. Madrid: Castalia.

Díaz-Migoyo, Gonzalo. 1980. "Las fechas en y de *El Buscón* de Quevedo." *Hispanic Review* 48 (2): 171–93.

Domínguez Castellano, Julia. 2003. "La estética manierista en el *Guzmán de Alfarache*." In *Proceedings of the 23rd Louisiana Conference on Hispanic

*Languages and Literatures*, edited by Alejandro Cortazar and Christian Fernández, 57–65. Baton Rouge: Department of Foreign Languages and Literatures, Louisiana State University.

Dunn, Peter N. 1993. *Spanish Picaresque Fiction: A New Literary History*. Ithaca, NY: Cornell University Press.

Fernández de Avellaneda, Alonso [pseud.]. 1987. *El ingenioso hidalgo don Quijote de la Mancha, que contiene su tercera salida y es la quinta parte de sus aventuras*. Edited by Fernando García Salinero. Madrid: Castalia.

Friedman, Edward H. 1987. *The Antiheroine's Voice: Narrative Discourse and Transformations of the Picaresque*. Columbia: University of Missouri Press.

Friedman, Edward H. 1996. "Trials of Discourse: Narrative Space in Quevedo's *Buscón*." In *The Picaresque: Tradition and Displacement*, edited by Giancarlo Maiorino, 183–225. Minneapolis: University of Minnesota Press.

Friedman, Edward H. 1997. "Coming to Terms with Lázaro's Prosperity: Framing Success in *Lazarillo de Tormes*." *Crítica Hispánica* 19 (1–2): 41–56.

Friedman, Edward H. 2000. "*Guzmán de Alfarache, Don Quijote*, and the Subject of the Novel." In *Studies in Honor of Edward Dudley*, edited by Francisco La Rubia Prado, 61–78. Newark, DE: Juan de la Cuesta.

Friedman, Edward H. 2006. *Cervantes in the Middle: Realism and Reality in the Spanish Novel from* Lazarillo de Tormes *to Niebla*. Newark, DE: Juan de la Cuesta.

Genette, Gérard. 1988. *Narrative Discourse Revisited*. Translated by Jane E. Lewin. Ithaca, NY: Cornell University Press.

Gilbert-Santamaría, Donald. 2005. *Writers on the Market: Consuming Literature in Early Seventeenth-Century Spain*. Lewisburg. Bucknell University Press.

Greenblatt, Stephen. 1980. *Renaissance Self-Fashioning: From More to Shakespeare*. Chicago: University of Chicago Press.

Guillén, Claudio. 1957. "La disposición temporal del *Lazarillo de Tormes*." *Hispanic Review* 25 (4): 264–79. http://dx.doi.org/10.2307/470736.

Herrero, Javier. 1978. "The Great Icons of the *Lazarillo*: The Bull, the Wine, the Sausage, and the Turnip." *Ideologies and Literature* 1 (5): 3–18.

Iffland, James. 1979. "'Pablos' Voice: His Master's? A Freudian Approach to Wit in *El Buscón*." *Romanische Forschungen* 91: 215–43.

Johnson, Carroll B. 1975. *Inside Guzmán de Alfarache*. Berkeley: University of California Press.

Johnson, Carroll B. 1996. "Defining the Picaresque: Authority and the Subject in *Guzmán de Alfarache*." In *The Picaresque: Tradition and Displacement*, edited by Giancarlo Maiorino, 159–82. Minneapolis: University of Minnesota Press.

Keen, Suzanne. 2003. *Narrative Form*. New York: Palgrave. http://dx.doi.org/10.1057/9780230503489.

Lanser, Susan Sniader. 1981. *The Narrative Act: Point of View in Prose Fiction.* Princeton: Princeton University Press.

*Lazarillo de Tormes.* 1997. Edited by Francisco Rico. Madrid: Cátedra.

Lothe, Jakob. 2000. *Narrative in Fiction and Film.* Oxford: Oxford University Press.

Martí, Juan [Mateo Luján de Sayavedra]. 2007. *Segunda parte de la vida del pícaro Guzmán de Alfarache.* Edited by David Mañero Lozano. Madrid: Cátedra.

McGrady, Donald. 1968. *Mateo Alemán.* New York: Twayne.

Moreno Báez, Enrique. 1948. *Lección y sentido del* Guzmán de Alfarache. Madrid: *Revista de Filología*, Anejo 40.

Parker, Alexander A. 1967. *Literature and the Delinquent: The Picaresque Novel in Spain and Europe, 1599–1753.* Edinburgh: Edinburgh University Press.

Parrack, John C. 2008. "Reading the Silence: The Picaresque Game of Lacunae and Contradiction." *Revista Canadiense de Estudios Hispánicos* 32 (2): 291–314.

Quevedo, Francisco de. 1998. *La vida del Buscón llamado Don Pablos.* Edited by Domingo Ynduráin. Madrid: Cátedra.

Rico, Francisco. 1970. *La novela picaresca y el punto de vista.* Barcelona: Seix Barral.

Rimmon-Kenan, Shlomith. 1983. *Narrative Fiction: Contemporary Poetics.* New York and London: Methuen. http://dx.doi.org/10.4324/9780203426111

Rodríguez Matos, Carlos Antonio. 1985. *El narrador pícaro: Guzmán de Alfarache.* Madison, WI: Hispanic Seminary of Medieval Studies.

Salinas, Pedro. 1966. *Reality and the Poet in Spanish Poetry.* Translated by Edith Fishtine Helman. Baltimore: Johns Hopkins University Press.

San Miguel, Ángel. 1971. *Sentido y estructura del* Guzmán de Alfarache *de Mateo Alemán.* Madrid: Gredos.

Shipley, George A. 1982. "The Critic as Witness for the Prosecution: Making the Case against Lázaro de Tormes." *PMLA* 97 (2): 179–94. http://dx.doi.org/10.2307/462186.

van Peer, Willie, and Seymour Chatman, eds. 2001. *New Perspectives on Narrative Perspective.* Albany: State University of New York Press.

Weinstein, Arnold. 1981. *Fictions of the Self: 1550–1800.* Princeton: Princeton University Press.

Whitenack, Judith A. 1985. *The Impenitent Confession of Guzmán de Alfarache.* Madison, WI: Hispanic Seminary of Medieval Studies.

Williamson, Edwin. 1977. "The Conflict between Author and Narrator in Quevedo's *Buscón.*" *Journal of Hispanic Philology* 2: 45–60.

Yeats, William Butler. 1997. "The Second Coming." In *The Yeats Reader*, edited by Richard J. Finneran, 68–9. New York: Scribner.

Yovel, Yirmiyahu. 2009. *The Other Within. The Marranos: Split Identity and Emerging Modernity.* Princeton: Princeton University Press.

# 9 Francisco de Quevedo and the Poetic Matter of Patronage

ROBERT TER HORST

Professors of the literature of the past in the United States work among and by means of the books that preserve writing in an architectural environment that houses the memories which books contain and provides the spaces for them to be read, analysed, discussed, and perpetuated. At the same time, nearly all buildings on an academic campus are named (as they likewise are everywhere else), and one finds such names, those of donors, savants, artists, and even professors, incised onto the façades, pediments, lintels, and doors of the edifices that recall the achievements of the rich, the famous, and the relatively obscure. A campus is thus the repository of the unforgotten, whose memory lives on both in immaterial words and in quite palpable stuff such as stone.

A major feature of civilization is its striving not to fall into oblivion. To ward off their erasure, cultures have devised two main agencies, one a material monument and the other the non-material structure provided by words as they form a fabric of discourse in poetry, poetry rather than prose because poetry is primordial, and stubbornly endures by virtue of its being mnemonic. Indeed, memory is for the Spanish Golden Age the supreme faculty of mind. In Cervantes' *El licenciado Vidriera*, the *novela* begins with its protagonist's awakening to a quest for fame through learning, a pursuit for which Tomás Rodaja is prodigiously well-qualified as in Salamanca he wins renown for his excellence in law and secular literature, *letras humanas*: "Su principal estudio fue de leyes; pero en lo que más se mostraba era en letras humanas; y tenía tan felice memoria, que era cosa de espanto; e ilustrábala tanto con su buen entrendimiento que no era menos famoso por él que por ella" [His major was law but literature (i.e., classics) was where he really shone and he had such gifts of memory, which he richly illuminated with his fine intelligence, that he was no less renowned for the one than the other] (Cervantes 1981, 44).[1]

Likewise, memory and remembrance provide a major motif in the classicizing verse of Francisco de Quevedo, whose superb command of the Latin and Greek languages and literatures engages him in a dialogue with antiquity of an intensity more characteristic of the Renaissance pursuit of the past than of the baroque, in which recovery of lost greatness gives rise to a conflicted and complex meditation on the meaning of Graeco-Latin culture in the context of a modern Christian world. Thus, Quevedo combines an earlier devotion to the farther past with a proud and knowing comprehension of actuality. Rodrigo Cacho Casal brilliantly expounds these "creative tensions" in "The Memory of Ruins: Quevedo's *Silva* to 'Roma antigua y moderna.'" Here, in briefer and much more modest compass, I follow a different path from that of Cacho Casal's admirable essay. My analysis discovers a theme, one might almost call it a topos, although it is not to be found in Curtius, one that recurs in the course of literary expression from very ancient times. This is the rivalry between architecture and poetry as to which of them is the better preserver of memory. A late expression of this tension occurs in John Ruskin's pronouncement in prose in *The Seven Lamps of Architecture* as to the superiority of architecture to poetry as the agent of recall. Historically, this faculty moves from Egypt to Greece and to Rome. Poets in Greece were paid professionals but their Roman counterparts often had to have recourse to potentates for support and fame. This need drew them into the ancient political economy of patronage, a system of veiled interaction by means of largesse rather than the modern method of overt exchange. Accordingly, the recipients of largesse joined, nolens volens, the structure that sustained political hegemony, a situation most marked in the case of the great poets of the late Republic and the early Empire. Their condition offers a model for Quevedo, whose prose sought to influence policy and whose poetry is inherently political as it would supersede, in commemoration of the mighty, perishable material monuments with deathless words, whose fame constitutes rich remuneration. Further, Quevedo expands the classical notion of the poet, disengaged and at lyrical ease in pastoral or agricultural *otium*, to project him into the world of *negotium*, war and politics, where repose is not only an alternative to the pursuit of power but also the experience of withdrawal into meditation in the very midst of strife, this *otium* a truce rather than a lasting peace. Naturally, those who war mainly with words judge them to be more effective memorials than stone monuments. But we have a nineteenth-century redress of the balance between memory that functions in words as against memory that expresses itself in matter with John Ruskin's somewhat perfervid weighing of the merits of each in "The Lamp of Memory" segment of *The Seven Lamps of Architecture*:

> There are but two strong conquerors of the forgetfulness of men, Poetry and Architecture; and the latter in some sort includes the former, and is mightier in its reality: it is well to have, not only what men have thought and felt, but what their hands have handled, and their strength wrought, and their eyes beheld, all the days of their life. (Ruskin 1980, 203)[2]

Ruskin's binary is not altogether unsubtle; "the latter in some sort includes the former." His is as well a most ancient opposition found, surprisingly perhaps, in a poem on papyrus celebrating the greater claim to perpetuity that scribes have over the privileged people who resort to sumptuous tombs for their burial:

> Man decays, his corpse is dust,
> All his kin have perished,
> But a book makes him remembered
> Through the mouth of its reciter.
> Better is a book than a well-built house
> Than Tomb-chapels in the west;
> Better than a solid mansion,
> Than a stela in the temple. (Lichtheim 1976, 177)

After this Egyptian expression of the rivalry between poetry and architecture, their opposition comes to be symbolic in the Greek practice of the epitaph, as of course it also was in Egyptian funerary culture, with much writing on buildings and tombs. In Greece, however, the epitaph becomes a genre when it takes the poetic form of the epigram which, according to Moses Hadas, is "a verse inscription on hard material, gravestones or offerings, usually composed for pay by a professional poet. The conciseness and finish of the lapidary style then came to be used for expressions of similar sentiment where there was no thought of an actual inscription" (Hadas 1950, 217). Thus the epigram became detachable from the hard surface on which it originally had been designed to be inscribed, while yet retaining the memory of the tomb, so that one might with reason reverse Ruskin's dictum and declare that poetry "in some sort includes" architecture.

The great collection of sepulchral inscriptions, actual and imagined, in Greek is *The Greek Anthology*, published most comprehensively in five volumes of the Loeb Classical Library edition by W.R. Paton. The thousands of brief poems it contains extend from 700 BCE to 900 CE and are immensely various even as epigram and the lapidary style conjoin them. A proem of Agathicis Scholasticus to a collection of new epigrams composed in imperial Byzantium iterates, pace John Ruskin, the idea of the greater staying power of the written record:

> Columns and pictures and inscribed tablets are a source of great delight to those who possess them, but only during their life; for the empty glory of man does not much benefit the spirits of the dead. But virtue and the grace of wisdom both accompany us there and survive here [,] attracting memory. So neither Plato nor Homer takes pride in pictures or monuments, but in wisdom alone. Blessed are they whose memory is enshrined in wise volumes and not in empty images. (Ruskin 1980, 4.4)

In a cluster of poems celebrating Sappho, Tellius Laureas composes an invented epitaph for her tomb, probably one from a group of competing eulogies of the poet:

> When thou passest, O Stranger, by the Aeolian tomb, say not that I, the Lesbian poetess, am dead. This tomb was built by the hands of men and such works of mortals are lost in swift oblivion. But if thou enquirest about me for the sake of the Muses, from each of whom I took a flower to lay beside my nine flowers of song, thou shalt find that I escaped the darkness of death, and that no sun shall dawn and set without memory of lyric Sappho. (1980, 6.17)

Among the imagined inscriptions, Evenus of Ascalon rather fancifully personifies the city of Troy, speaking from its ruin:

> Strangers, the ash of ages has devoured me, holy Ilion, the famous city once renowned for my towered walls, but in Homer I still exist, defended by brazen gates. The spears of the destroying Achaeans shall not again dig me up, but I shall be on the lips of all Greece. (1980, 9.62)

Quite naturally, the poets are wont to proclaim the superior staying power of their verse over all the materials that commemorate. These are necessarily included in it, or implied, in the role, as above, of a ruined rival. But I am aware of the incorporation of the rival into the fabric of the poem as first occurring only in a great, celebrated, and vainglorious Latin ode of Horace, the thirtieth in the *Third Book of Odes*. This is, as editors

Shorey and Laing observe, Horace's "Epilogue to the three books of the Odes..."(411) and as such a quite immodest but not inaccurate summary of his achievement in them as a poet:

Exegi monumentum aere perennius
Regalique situ pyramidum altius,
Quod non imber edax, non Aquilo impotens
Possit diruere aut innumerabilis
Annorum series et fuga temporum.
Non omnis moriar, multaque pars mei
Vitabit Libitinam: usque ego postera
Crescam laude recens, dum Capitolium
Scandet cum tacita virgine pontifex.
Dicar, qua violens obstrepit Aufidus
Et qua pauper aquae Daunus agrestium
Regnavit populorum, ex humili potens
Princeps Aeolium carmen ad Italos
Deduxisse modos. Sume superbiam
Quaesitam meritis et mihi Delphica
Lauro cinge volens, Melpomene, comam.

I have completed a monument more durable than bronze and loftier than the pyramids' regal mass, one that neither the onslaughts of wind and rain nor the endless flight of time down through the years can bring down. I shall not altogether die, for a significant portion of myself will thwart the rites of burial. As I, constantly renewed by the praise of posterity, shall grow in stature for as long as the high priest ascends with a voiceless Vestal the Capitolium, I, a potentate though humbly born where the rushing river Aufidus resounds and where trickling Daunus [river as well as king] once ruled over his rude subjects, I shall be proclaimed the first to have brought Aeolian strains to Italic measures. Gladly accept, Melpomene, high distinction achieved through merit and gird my brow [hair] with Delphic laurel. (1960, 3.30)

For this ode to be fully Napoleonic, it wants only the act of Horace crowning himself instead of Melpomene graciously acceding to the poet's command (*sume*). And it constructs Horace's rise to artistic immortality on the architectonics of *monumentum*, the very matter of remembrance in the shape of the pyramids and the form of the Capitolium.

Indeed, the pyramidical is the encompassing concept of the poem. It bases its movement to that structure by a first reference to the matter of durability, with "aere," verse will outlast *aes*, money as coin, and *aes* also as the bronze on which laws are published and promulgated and *aes* as the bronze from which statues are cast. The form of the pyramid also has biographical resonance, for in having risen "ex humili" to supreme mastery of his art, Horace's career rests upon an extremely broad base among the semi-savage folk of his native Apulia from which this son of an ex-slave has mounted by degrees, each one less gross, to a poetic pinnacle where, free of matter, Melpomene, the muse of lyric, crowns him in the inaugural act of a reign (he is after all "princeps") that will outlast the structures that the political potentates have commissioned to perpetuate their pharaonic and Augustan images. Melpomene reminds one of Maecenas, the minister and favourite of Octavian who so discerningly extended his grace and favour to a poet who had no social standing. In consequence, Horace's artistic origins in Greek lyric take on an Italic, a very Roman, style, as he makes his way up to Parnassus on the hundred steps of the Capitolium. It was the essential edifice of the city and its empire (*urbs et orbis*). Lemprière asserts that the earliest form of it was "finished by Tarquinius Superbus, and consecrated by the consul Horatius after the expulsion of theTarquins from Rome" (1984, 139). The negative epithet applied to Rome's last king, *superbus* = proud, haughty, chimes curiously with Horace's term for the high honour of his achievement, *superbia*, but the name of the consecrator of the temple puts the poet on home ground.

A citadel as well as a shrine, the Capitolium was triadic, for it had three *cellae*, or chapels, housing respectively the images of Jupiter, Juno, and Minerva, the main Roman deities. The verb that Horace uses to characterize his ascent, "scandet," suggests that he climbs up to eminence not only by rising physically, but also metrically, poetically, through the force of his "numbers." The noun form of *scandere*, to climb, ascend, is *scansio*, the act of ascending, but also it signifies the quantitative metre of both Greek and Latin verse, *scansion*. The two senses don't seem at all related except perhaps by association of the human with the metrical foot. As for the actual temple, it was disturbingly vulnerable. First destroyed in the civil wars of the Republic, it was rebuilt by Sulla, then destroyed again under Vitellius, partly restored then ruined under Vespasian, and then rebuilt for the last time under Domitian. Almost nothing of it remains. It would seem strange for the poet to equate the durability of his verse with the survival of a building so subject to ruin, even in Horace's own lifetime, but it is the persistence of the Capitolium that would justify the analogy, even though the poem has far outlived the temple, which continues in word alone, and not in stone, to the putative dismay of John Ruskin. In any case, Horace's prodigious ode 3.30 contains two additional constructs in its enveloping pyramidicality, those of both the Capitolium, a mount, a citadel, a temple, and a Greek Parnassus. Accordingly, one could rightly say of it that its poetry embodies architecture, lastingly.

Only potentates can erect structures such as those which enable Horace to rise. The "exegi monumentum" ode draws great strength from its maker's intimacy, one might almost say cohabitation, with political and military power. He himself had a brief engagement with advancement through arms when "early in 43 [B.C.E.] ... he joined M. Brutus' republican army, receiving the rank of Military Tribune which was usually held by young men of family and position. Brutus' defeat and death at Philippi in the following year at the hands of Mark Antony and Caesar Octavian ended Horace's military career" (Bailey 1982, 9). Returning to Italy, he earned through his verse an invitation to join the circle of Gaius Maecenas, Augustus's powerful *valido*. Maecenas became and remained Horace's patron for almost all of the rest of their respective lives. Augustus himself once invited Horace to become his private secretary but the poet, wisely one would think, demurred.

Artists do well to keep their distance from the mighty who engage them. Surely Velázquez would have painted more if Philip IV had not named him his *aposentador mayor.* But the patronage system causes the dependent to draw closer to the source of his sustenance, often with remarkable results, as when much of the power of *Las meninas* derives from the domesticity of the painter in the household of the king, an association that permits the equation of the mastery of the artist with that of the monarch. In the first twenty-five years of his voluminous *Mémoires* the duc de Saint-Simon grapples constantly with the sovereign might of Louis XIV as it gradually levels the aristocracy down to an equality common to all the subjects of despotism and autocracy, lamenting the *déclassement* of the *grands seigneurs* while vainly aspiring to a favour with the king that would make him powerful and influential, a status he achieves dubiously only during the regency of the duc d'Orléans. Power repels and attracts, is both feared and loved. This paradox, with its conflicting centrifugal and centripetal tendencies, confronts the greatest poets, Virgil and Horace, of the late republican and early imperial age, in the persons of Maecenas and Caesar Octavian Augustus. Their considerable largesse to each man further complicates the matter, for the talented artist finds a personal autonomy in her creative ability of which the material cognate is the possession of land. For the poet, the original expression of the myth of artistic independence occurs in pastoral, bucolic verse. Shepherds would seem freer than farmers, tied to chores and to the seasons. But the same family farm still persists today as a related myth of relative immunity from oppression. In the lives of Horace and Virgil, farmland plays a major role, for both men, of quite humble stock, saw their paternal acres expropriated so that these could be bestowed upon military veterans of the protracted civil wars that began in full with the assassination of Julius Caesar in 44 BCE and which ended with the victories of Philippi, and of Actium (31 BCE), by Caesar's great-nephew, Octavian. Yet both men recovered their modest patrimony as gifts, as benefactions proffered by Maecenas or Augustus himself, in addition to the sporadic gifts of actual money that the emperor may have made (Bowditch 2001, 57).

In the first,[3] but not chronologically so, of his ten eclogues Virgil places himself at the greatest Theocritan remove from the seat of power, with a conversation between the two shepherds Tityrus and Melioboeus. One would expect these elegantly styled countrymen to treat mostly of love, unrequited or requited. And indeed Tityrus is enamoured of one Amaryllis, but she is not the subject of their song. It is rather the military and political realities of Rome in strife reaching to the confines of the known world which have occasioned Meliboeus to be dispossessed of his land when in bitter contrast Tityrus retains his peaceful abode, and so commits himself to reverence for the "deus nobis haec otia fecit," the *divus*, perhaps first Antony and then the triumphant Octavian becoming Augustus who "won for us this peace." *Otia*, here peace, is wonderfully polysemous. It is the antonym of *negotium* < *nec otium*, or non-repose in the form of the concerns of government, warfare, business, freedom from which permits the literary pursuit of higher culture, especially in the form of poetry, above all pastoral, which may be said to live and thrive in that privileged parenthesis provided by *otium*.[4] However, the surcease that Tityrus enjoys is not an evocation of an uncontaminated atmosphere such as that which Theocritus conjures, a separate, autonomous world.[5] It is rather a *gift* from the almighty mighty, and as such places the recipient in a posture of gratitude and dependence.[6] Virgil's *First Eclogue* owes much to a *princeps*, *in bello et in pace*. War despoils Meliboeus, while peace protects Tityrus. Moses Hadas observes that "the *Eclogues* are so closely copied from Theocritus that it is possible to charge Virgil with misunderstanding his original in one or two passages" (Hadas 1952, 143). Yet, the *First Eclogue* notably occludes the Theocritan idyll by introducing into it a Meliboeus forced into exile and a Tityrus beholden to an urban majesty that he had not even been capable of imagining before he visited Rome. Traditionally the pastoral poem occupies the daylight hours from dawn to dusk. But the *First Eclogue* omits sunrise and midday so as to place its colloquy at the end of the diurnal span, towards dusk and the onset of night. Virgil's vision here is thus in a darkening perspective.

Similarly, Horace evokes an Edenic rural landscape made poetically possible by *otium*, as well as made physically possible by Maecenas's gift to him of the Sabine farm, and so replacing but not identical to his own lost "Paterna rura," in the celebrated "Beatus ille" Epode 2.[7] This dream of agricultural plenty and independence would place the poet at the farthest remove from his patron intent in Rome on all manner of business. The farmer is blessed to be "procul negotiis," and so making Maecenas the antonymic figure to the happy possessor of *otium*. Debt is the genus of servitude that the countryman avoids by being entirely free of it: "Solutus omni faenore" (Putnam 1982, 4). At the same time he renounces the careers of fearsome ambition: the life of the soldier on land, of the merchant at sea, of the politician currying favour with the powerful. In their stead, he proposes a series of delicious images of self-sufficiency, so compelling that the reader is shocked to discover that these are the fantasy of Alfius the usurer, whose withdrawal from commerce to rural retirement is notably short-lived, since only a few weeks after he liquidated his holdings, he is back in the market.

But the poem's abrupt return to debt and credit is more than a sardonic twist. It is structural, anticipated in the "solutus omni faenore," for Horace's "rura" are unhappily not "paterna"; they constitute the largesse of a magnate to a deprived poet who, though not precisely the client required to pay his respects every morning, in person, to his benefactor, as *salutatio*, is nonetheless obligated to express his gratitude and thanks, not once but continually. The benefaction is a principal sum that cannot be repaid and that charges interest in the form of verse. In this manner the poet is indentured to his patron, indefinitely. What mitigates the pattern is the "gifted" artist's pursuit of parity with the benefactors through a mastery of his art that is tantamount to their supremacy. Here, Horace anticipates Titian in his relationship with his exalted patron the emperor Charles V who "treated him as an equal in spirit, if not in rank ... their correspondence occasionally reads like that between two great and equal powers" (Panofsky 1969, 8). This progress to parity begins when the bond between artist and patron loses some of its imbalance to a feeling of what might be called friendship, *amicitia*, in which the two participants, joined together like spouses in a long, solid, successful marriage, take on some of the traits of their opposite number, so that poet in some measure impersonates patron and patron poet. This assumption of a degree of the coloration of the other infuses Velázquez's great pictorial claim to parity with Philip IV in *Las meninas*, as the painter quietly dominates the scene with the magisterial brush that will fill the huge foregrounded canvas, whereas the monarch and his consort, though central, look rather dimly on, from the background. They are peripheral. The painter is in command.[8]

In Horace's Ode 30.3, it is likewise the poet who takes command, polysemously, for from the earth, "ex humili," humble, yes, but also conveying the sense of the soil, the closeness to it, that nurtures the *sermo humilis* of pastoral song, from which springs the "potens" Princeps. His rise "ex humili" is an ascent to mastery; "potens," the technique of that mastery, is his induction of Greek forms into Italic matter, a method in which he may not be first, *primus*, but of which he is a leader, a master, *princeps*. Horace himself also applies the noun to the great-nephew of Julius Caesar in the middle phase of his ascent to supremacy. Caesar Octavian Augustus is the poet's ultimate patron. Horace identifies his art with his ruler's power (he, as poet, is "potens") and on the strength of it claims parity with his sovereign, like him anointed, crowned, exalted, and deified. The distance from Virgil's recumbent Tityrus (he is "recubans," lying flat on his back, thus a most true *humilis*) to the Augustan pinnacle on the Capitoline is immense, socially as well as artistically. Yet both he and Horace negotiate it, not without the help of Alfius, as well as, of course, that of Maecenas, himself a "faenerator" in the poetry market.

Many of the fundamental factors conditioning the development of Graeco-Latin poetry as in the works of Horace and Virgil created under the management of their patrons, the *duces* Maecenas and Caesar Octavian Augustus, re-assert themselves in a great and representative sonnet of Francisco de Quevedo:

Con mas vergüenza viven Euro y Noto,
Licas, que en nuestra edad los usureros;
sosiéganse tal vez los vientos fieros
y, ocioso, el mar no gime su alboroto.
No siempre el Ponto en sus orillas roto
ejercita los roncos marineros:
ocio tienen los golfos más severos;
ocio goza el bajel, ocio el piloto.
Cesa de la borrasca la milicia:
nunca cesa el despojo ni la usura
ni sabe estar ociosa su codicia.

[Eurus and Notus practise more restraint, Lichas, than do our present-day usurers. Even brutal winds do, on occasion, die down and, coming to rest, the sea no longer groans in its upheaval. Great waves of the Pontus crashing on the beach do not always agitate screaming sailors. Even the most daunting deep knows surcease, as does the vessel, as the helmsman does. Storms have a cessation of their hostilities. Profiteering, however, is incessant, its greediness incapable of repose. It is oblivious of peace and insatiable, dares to call its evils equity, its robberies legal, its sickness a remedy.] (1969, 66)

This seascape of a sonnet addresses the dangers of maritime navigation in pursuit of gain through the classical polarities of *negotium* versus *otium*. It resembles Fray Luis's "Vida retirada," vv. 61–9, by directly confronting the turbulent seas of desire. But Fray Luis figures shipwreck so as to generate from it a landlubberly antonym and antidote. Quevedo, on the other hand, extracts *otium* from the eye of the storm, which is a Graeco-Roman turbulence churned up by the antagonism of the wind from the East, Eurus (Euro) and the wind from the South, Notus (Noto) on the surface of the Black Sea, Pontus. The activities that bring the voyager into peril are the ancient quest for profit over the waters of the Mediterranean, as well as militaristic expansion ("de la borrasca la milicia") with a view to wealth and empire. Those *negotia*, which the poem embraces and so is anything but "procul" from them, require no naming. But they acquire a contemporaneous pertinacity with the phrase "en nuestra edad los usureros." Blecua assigns this sonnet no date in his edition, but it could well have been written at the time of Quevedo's tract *Execración contra los judíos*, which attacks Olivares's attempt to replace the Crown's Genoese bankers with Jewish *converso* financiers from Portugal. Carlos Gutiérrez gives 20 July 1633 as the date of publication of the *Execración*, an odious work that puts Quevedo in the company of Ezra Pound, whose antisemitism and peculiar economics dim but cannot obliterate the lustre of his artistic achievement which, like Quevedo's own, emerges from a profound engagement with the classics, and in particular with Latin authors like Propertius.

Gutiérrez calls into question the "originality" of Quevedo's love poetry (2005, 185). To my mind, however, there can be no doubt as to the originality of the "Con más vergüenza" [with more shame] sonnet. Of course, Quevedo does not start afresh. He works with traditional materials, but as a whole the poem is an *aggiornamento* of these. Its rhetoric in the form of its anaphora of *otium* – "ocioso," "ocio," "ocio," "ocioso" frames a profound truth about economic activity in a new post-classical key. All the old *negotia* knew surcease, had their season. "The sailing season, marked by the festive launching of the bark of Isis (the *navigium Isidis*) on March 5, opened on March 10, and lasted until November 11" (Balsdon 2004, 226). Even armies went into winter quarters. Much of the poignance of "haec otia" in Virgil and Horace derives from the protracted waging of civil war throughout the Roman world between 44 and 31 BCE. However, Octavian finally brought this time of troubles to a close. Thus, all things have their intermittencies, their rhythm – except usury. It alone is incessant, owing to which the early modern (and the modern) world has lost its diastole and systole, the natural alternance between activity and repose. Continuity without pause characterizes especially the markets of the twenty-first century. Financial exchanges operate uninterruptedly thanks to the internet, and grocery stores remain open day and night. Quevedo is the early poet of this arrythmia "en nuestra edad" [in our time]. He also anticipated the semantic accommodation of greed to the lust for gain in the guise of economics, the basic rule of which is that desire, once heeded, is met not by satisfaction but by a new desire ad infinitum: "no sabe hallar hartura" [not to find the limits]. The "maldad" of usury becomes legitimate and can call its thievery lawful, its sickness a remedy, "growth" a cure for poverty. These *sententiae* are to some extent unjust but they are far from being inaccurate in this age, "nuestra edad," of rampant greed and excess.

The sonnet suggests that the poet abstains from depredation. But such is far from being the case with Quevedo who, among many involvements, became the *valido* of the Duke of Osuna. As Tellez Girón's gumshoe and point man, he found himself commissioned in 1615 to return from Sicily to Madrid with much money for bribes to influential persons for their help in securing the Viceroyalty of Naples for the duke. He succeeded. His mission has been seen as a paradigm of the corruption that flourished under Philip III, and so it is; but this is exactly how the very young Charles I obtained the imperial crown, through bribery of its electors, who pretty much auctioned off their votes. Corruption is native to the pursuit and exercise of power. The poetic answer to the seductions of might is a retreat into subsistence in a place in the country far from the madding crowd, and innocent of the ironic subversion of an Alfius. That richly traditional bipolarity certainly is a significant modality of Quevedo's, but in the "Con más vergüenza" sonnet there emerges a figure not distant but proximate, in the thick of things, a poet whose creative *otium* is an intermission in the action, in the *negotia* of self-enrichment, wars, government, religion.

A vigorously testimonial sonnet places the poet in the pleasure grounds of the palace that Lerma built after the court returned to Madrid from

Valladolid, his *monumento* (Quevedo 1969, 225). The poem's rubric is instructive: "A la huerta del Duque de Lerma, favorecida y ocupada muchas veces del Señor Rey Don Felipe Tercero, y olvidada hoy de igual concurso" [To the grounds [and house] of the Duke of Lerma, often honoured by the presence of his Majesty King Philip III and today bereft of any such frequentation]. In letter 150 of his *Epistolario*, one addressed to his neighbour and friend, the Duke of Medinaceli, Quevedo describes this same sonnet, which he encloses, in terms very like those of the rubric. He adds that he wrote the poem a few days ago, "on más celo que ingenio, como quien le amaba y temía" [with more devotion than wit, as one who both loved and feared him] (1964, 942a). And indeed these verses manifest more emotion than cleverness as Quevedo mourns the extinction of the house of Lerma in the death of the grandson of Philip III's once powerful minister. But even the emotion is ritualized in the letter as the love and the fear that by convention bind the ruled to the ruler. Their combination flatteringly, if not sycophantically, suggests that the dead duke was born to almost regal command. His demise conjures the downfall of his grandfather, Lerma:

Yo vi la grande y alta jerarquía
del magno, invicto y santo Rey Tercero
En esta casa, y conocí lucero
al que en sagradas púrpuras ardía.
Hoy desierta de tanta monarquía,
y del nieto, magnánimo heredero,
yare; pero arde en glorias de su acero,
como in la pompa que ostentar solía.
Menos invidia teme aventurado
que venturoso; el mérito procura;
los premios aborrece escarmentado.
¡Oh, amable si desierta arquitectura,
más hoy al que te ve desengañado
que cuando frecuentada en tu ventura!

[I myself have seen, in this house that great and lofty eminence, the third Philip, grand, triumphant, and deeply devout, and I have known the starry brilliance of him who once blazed in cardinal's robes (i.e., Lerma, first duke). Today that house lies bereft of monarchy and of its grandson, its great-souled scion, but it is alight with the glory of his sword, as it is with the splendour it once displayed. He fears envy less who courts danger than he

> who curries favour. [Such a one] pursues merit and, disabused, recoils from largesse. Today this palace is even more inviting, in its abandonment, to one who beholds it with unclouded eyes, than it was in its populous prosperity.] (1964, 942)

"A la huerta del Duque de Lerma" is less brilliant for its semantics (though the interplay in it among the senses of "aventurado," "venturoso," and the final "ventura" is masterful) than for the compression with which it reviews the career of the first duke, his son the Duke of Úceda, and the dead grandson, who according to letter 157 "salío de Madrid con el marques de Spínola" [left Madrid [for Flanders] with the Marquess of Spínola] and died quickly (letter 154) of a urinary disorder ("mal de orina"), not quite the "glorias de su acero" of the sonnet. However, since this last duke apparently died without male issue (Quevedo does mention a daughter) his decease means the fall of the house of Lerma, an event of great significance for Quevedo, and one rousing real emotion in him ("celo") since as a youth he had attached himself to Lerma and his confederates, above all his particular patron, the Duke of Osuna. Accordingly, "A la huerta" begins with the emphatic "yo," one of only two to do so in volume 1 of Quevedo's *Obra poética.* As subject of the verb "vi" it makes the poem into one of personal witness, and most appropriately so, inasmuch as by March of 1636 Quevedo had experienced profound personal and political vicissitudes in two great transitions, from the reign of Philip II to that of Philip III and from the rule of the "Rey Tercero" to that of the last Habsburg Philip. By the end of Philip III's occupancy of the throne, both the first Duke of Lerma and Quevedo's patron Osuna had fallen from favour. But it was at the height of his career that Lerma had created the establishment celebrated and lamented in the poem. In 1636, however, Quevedo had long since managed to survive the ruin of his sponsors by adhering to the party and the person of Lerma's successor, the *privado* of Philip IV, the Duke of Olivares. Quevedo's propagandizing for Olivares was opportunistic. Yet I think John Elliott entirely plausible in seeing a good measure of personal conviction in his support of the new dispensation. Nonetheless, as over the years Olivares failed to effect the reform he had first envisioned, Quevedo gradually fell away from the great minister: "I think we can detect in 1634–35 the first signs of an alienation from the Olivares regime which will soon convert Quevedo into an implacable opponent of the Count-Duke and his works" (Elliott 1989, 202). The sonnet on the death of Lerma's grandson fully supports this contention.

A change in attitude towards Philip III is key to Quevedo's shift in allegiance. In 1621 the Olivares faction tended to judge Philip as a misguided monarch. Quevedo contributed to such a view in his *Carta del Rey Don Fernando el Católico*, "which may be read both as an implied criticism of the late king as measured against the ideals of kingship exemplified by Ferdinand the Catholic, and an expression of hope that the young Philip IV would take Ferdinand as his model" (Elliott 1989, 190). Evidence of Quevedo's disaffection from Lerma and Philip around 1621 can justify Cacho Casal's assertion in his note 30 (1174): "It is well known that Quevedo considered Philip III an unworthy king who had let Spain fall into decadence." But the 1636 sonnet characterizes the king as great, "magno," in the sense of Carlomagno, "invicto" or undefeated, always victorious, and "santo" or very religious. The first two of these adjectives are almost impossible to defend though the third may pass. The verdict of the historians with respect to Philip is, despite Paul C. Allen's judicious showing in *Philip III and the Pax Hispanica, 1598–1621*, that this monarch was far less *fainéant* than has been supposed remains negative. But it is less negative, thanks to Allen and to Antonio Feros's *Kingship and Favoritism in the Spain of Philip III, 1598–1621.* Still, it is difficult to imagine Quevedo himself subscribing to the image of Philip as a great warrior king, associated as he is by Allen with the putative Pax Hispanica, a truce which occupied exactly half his reign, from 1609 to 1621.

A fair portion of the poem's hyperbole derives from one of its several modes, that of the "Ubi sunt" which nostalgically evokes the vanished grandeur of yesteryear and in this case the poet's youth. Corollary to this theme is the fall of greatness into oblivion, the disgrace of Lerma and the extinction of his ducal line, in view of which moral reflection on the vanity of human ambition is almost unavoidable and indeed does explicitly occur in the first tercet, the grammatical subject of whose three verbs, "teme," "procura," and "aborrece" is not easy to ascertain but which I take to be "nieto," dead but configured in the present tense, a feature that turns the scene back to the living and their surviving witness, the poet Quevedo. In meditation on the death of an aspiring military hero who has chosen the battlefield over the palace intrigue that doomed his grandfather and father, the poet now adopts his model's vision. Like the young duke he is "escarmentado," chastened, so that he comes to see the scheme of the palace and its gardens, its "arquitectura," not as a theatre of jealousy and envy but as a peaceful place, in its neglect, for edifying rumination on mortal delusion, the *huerta* of Fray Luis's *Vida retirada*. Thus the scheme, not now one of pride and ambition, is "amable," morally endearing because the poet, himself "escarmentado" and "desengañado," can discern its purpose and plan and meaning.

But the poem cannot remove from its architecture the character of the palace as a theatre of ambition. Fray Luis, whose first editor Quevedo had been in 1631, far more conclusively rejects all rivalry in the nine wonderful lines of 'Al salir de la cárcel':

> Aquí la envidia y mentira
> me tuvieron encerrado.
> Dichoso el humilde estado
> del sabio que se retira
> de aqueste mundo malvado
> y con pobre mesa y casa
> en el campo deleitoso
> con solo Dios su vida pasa
> ni envidiado ni envidioso.

> [Here envy and perjury kept me imprisoned. Blessed is the condition of the sage who withdraws from this evil world and in the delightful countryside, poorly housed and fed, communes with God alone, neither envied nor envious.] (Sarmiento 48)

Envy is the great negative force of this utterance, and Fray Luis completely disarms it by spiritual retreat to that locus where he is "ni envidiado ni envidioso." Quevedo's transformation of Lerma's "huerta" diminishes but does not banish the whole of striving and ambition: "*Menos* envidia teme." It is indeed the powerful psychic motivation for his art and career, one replete with conflict and rivalry, and one in which praise can be a potent weapon.

Unamuno in his brilliant *Abel Sánchez* portrays a lifelong rivalry between the painter of its title and his antagonist, Joaqúin Monegro. The consummate *mala lengua* of the novel is Federico Cuadro, who in the *casino* deconstructs praise as a manner of detraction. Whenever Federico heard one person praise another he would ask: "¿Contra quién va ese elogio?" [Whom is that praise directed against?], then explaining that "cuando se elogia mucho a uno se tiene presente a otro al que se trata de rebajar con ese elogio, a un rival del elogiado" [When one person greatly praises another, the person praising has in mind a third party whom he is trying to bring down with that praise, a rival of the person being praised] (1963, 94). This is a technique with which Quevedo is entirely familiar. He used Don

Fernando el Católico to discredit Philip III in his *Carta del Rey*. Now, Victor Hugo of the seventeenth century, he implausibly lauds a notably undistinguished monarch, and by extension Philip's *valido* Lerma, so as to create an unfavourable evocation of Lerma's successor under Philip IV, the Count-Duke of Olivares, the tacit target of those three fulsome adjectives.

The location of the sonnet in Lerma's deserted grounds and house itself conjures a less implicit competition than does the eulogy of the monarch ministered to by the first duke, whose palace in what were then the exurbs of Madrid, the Carrera de San Jerónimo, stood out in a concentration of estates belonging to the *títulos*, or high Spanish nobility. When the Count-Duke resolved to have a grandiose pleasure palace built for Philip IV and sited it "along the Prado de San Jerónimo ... one house in particular would have been seen as a challenge to Olivares's power as a builder. Right across the road from San Jerónimo was the large estate consisting of house and gardens created by the Duke of Lerma after the return of the court from Valladolid [1606]. Lerma had been a builder on the grand scale, but Olivares was determined to outbuild him. The Retiro, once expanded, would cut down Lerma and his palace by size" (Brown and Elliott 1980, 62). Similarly, the sonnet of 1636 is in part meant to cut Olivares down to size, a task not accomplished in Quevedo's lifetime.

By brandishing his mastery of the adversarial art of polemical praise, Quevedo constructs his poem with the integument of external rivalries. Matching it is an inner competition, that between the material and the moral. If in no other way, Lerma did distinguish himself by his architectonics, his palaces. They, and the edifice in the Carrera de San Jerónimo, would then constitute his memorial, a notion strengthened by the poet's reading of the estate as an epigram. In that epigram, we experience a retreat from the *vita activa* of *negotia* to a landscape of *otium* that fosters meditation and *litterae*. In Lerma's garden, itself a semi-retreat from business in Madrid, ambition confronts extinction. Ambition faints and fades but does not altogether vanish. "Non omnis moriar." The estate is a vacancy of rivalrous striving, a mausoleum for dead hopes that express their ghostly being in the recognition of their vanity and so invite the *caminante* in the garden to sepulchral ponderation in a "campo deleitoso," thus effecting a transformation of the material into the spiritual without annihilating the material, a very rich and exceedingly dangerous sublimation.

A cognate sublimation occurs in the *silva* on the death of the Duke of Osuna, Pedro Téllez Girón, in 1624. His bond with Quevedo may have begun as early as 1599 (Gutiérrez 2005, 222) but became intense in the period of the duke's major exercise of power first as viceroy of Sicily and then of Naples. A letter of April 1617 describes Quevedo upon his arrival in Rome to confer with the pope as a "caballero de muchas partes, muy entendido, y muy privado del virrey de Nápoles [Osuna]" [a gentleman of many attainments, savvy, and very much the favourite of the viceroy] (Gutiérrez 2005, 221). In this *silva* and the sonnets about Osuna and his death, the quality that the poet celebrates most is his patron's military and naval prowess. The *silva*'s orthography is that of the autograph manuscript as reproduced in Blecua. Line 4 has in "imitas" an error of Quevedo's. Grammar and sense call for *imita*:

No con estatuas duras
en que el mármor ocioso
i el arte perezoso,
difunto, imita fixas las figures,
detendré tu semblante
que el mundo teme i llora;
ni emulo de Lisipo i Policleto,
¡o grande, ia inmortal Duque de Osuna!,
para contradezir a tu fortuna
procuraré con tus facione reales
animar los metales:
que los dorados bultos
más doctos i más cultos
lisonxa muerta son sin movimiento.
Valdréme del açento
de la lira i del canto
que, disfrazando mi sonoro llanto,
tu nombre llevará de xente en xente
i a la tumba del sol desde el Oriente.
Razonarále el Noto por las gavias
i el mar, que tanto honor deve a tu quillas,
hará que le pronuncien sus orillas;
i sus golfos, que fueron
teatro a tus hazañas,
aplaudiendo sus sañas
las pirámides tres de tus Xirones,
que hizieron callar en tus pendones
las bárbaras de Exipto,
hoy, lastimados de tu ausencia [eterna],
de lágrimas seran borrasca ticrna.

[I will not arrest your likeness (with which time at that ultimate moment which all fear and mourn stole away) in hard statues where indolent marble and malingering deathly craft imitate form as a fixity. Nor will I, following Lysippus and Polyclitus, undertake, O grand and now immortal duke, to reverse your fate by quickening bronze with your regal features, for even the most skilled and refined gilt castings are but a lifeless and immobile form of flattery. I will avail myself of the strains of the lyre and of song which, overcoming my sounding dirge, will transport your name from nation to nation and from the sun's cradle to its grave. Notus will proclaim it in the rigging, and the sea, which owes so great a debt of honour to your ships [keels], will cause its shores to articulate it. And the high seas (which were the theatre of your exploits, applauding the wrath of the three pyramids of the arms of the Téllez Girón which, flown in your pennants, outdid [silenced] their piratical Egyptian models) today, aggrieved at your everlasting absence, will be a tender tempest of tears.] (Quevedo 1969, 289)

In *Abel Sánchez*, Federico Cuadro goes so far as to assert, "Nadie elogia con buena intención" [Nobody praises disinterestedly] (Unamuno 1963, 94) and in fact nearly all of Quevedo's encomia serve a dual purpose, to shore up the subject of his admiration and to subvert that subject's rivals. So he published a poet whom it is extremely difficult not to admire, Fray Luis, on his merits but also with a view to diminishing the *culterano* school, so close to his own poetic as to make them unbearable. However, it is not easy to discern a second and polemical object in the "No con estatuas duras" eulogy and elegy. In 1624 the poet was still in the first flush of his enthusiasm for Olivares's reform movement, which had brought about the duke's fall and prosecution. Quevedo was, as Osuna's right-hand man, naturally implicated in any allegation of viceregal misconduct. So the poem may be an effort by Quevedo to clear himself through a resounding vindication of his former patron, although to do so could have put him in an awkward position with his then-current sponsor. That problem may explain the non-publication of the poem which, to judge by Blecua's comments on the manuscript, was at best in semi-final form. It is, nonetheless, a notable composition, especially for its personal tenor, as in the "yo vi" sonnet. Indeed, the first-person anaphora structures the *silva*: "detendré," "procuraré," and "Valdréme."

Quevedo had many occupations, several of them unsavoury, but he had one profession, that of poet. In the elegy on Osuna he is a poet very much and very visibly in command. His power with words enabled him in the sonnet on Lerma's trophy estate to transform an empty theatre of insolent display into a Thebaid, a hermitage,[9] not severe but one beckoning to rumination on the point of it all. Here, there is even more wonderful alchemy as, Orpheus with Aeolian harp, he transmutes the hard base matter – metal and stone – of memory and fame into wind and storm driving ships over the Mediterranean Sea, and so making the waters and the gale and the masts and the rigging one huge instrument of wild lamentation over Osuna, a storm of grief but an intimate personal one, "borrasca tierna." Moreover, in this elegy the decried incessancy of the profit motive in the "Con mas Vergüenza" sonnet is exploited so as to modulate Mediterranean gales into a never-ending *planctus* for the dead duke, *negotia* raised to infinity, where there is no *otium*.

## NOTES

1 All translations are my own unless otherwise cited.

2 The passage I quote appears in Ruskin's volume *The Seven Lamps of Architecture*, chapter 6, "The Lamp of Memory." The editor of this collection, Joan Evans, calls her volume of excerpts from the various writings of Ruskin *The Lamp of Beauty*. All references to this work here come from this edited text.

3 The text is that of Paul Alpers in his invaluable, *The Singer of the Eclogues* (1979, 10–14).

4 "*Otium* is a keyword in the discussion of the pastoral" (Rosenmeyer 1973, 67).

5 In a discussion of Quintilian's sense of *genus* David Halperin cites that author's opinion of Theocritus, an assessment that brings out the notable contrast between the *Idylls* and the *Eclogues*: "Theocritus is much to be admired ... but his rustic and pastoral poetry shuns not only the marketplace and politics, but even the very City [i.e., the financial district, Wall Street] itself" (1983, 11).

6 Bowditch compellingly places Horace's dealings with Maecenas and Augustus in the context of a gift economy whose largesse conceals the fundamental exchange of land for verse. The gift economy also can provide, I think, a better account of Quevedo's transactions with the magnates of his country than does Gutiérrez's sense of "field," which is better suited to the year 1800 in Europe than to 1600 in Spain.

7 I cite Epode II from Shorey and Laing's edition of Horace.

8 This account of the painting owes a great deal to Jonathan Brown's understanding of it as expressed in his *Images & Ideas in Seventeenth-Century Spanish Painting*, as well as in his *Velázquez*.

9 The grounds of the Retiro had six hermitages. They "were the most distinctive feature of the park and appear to have been purely Spanish in origin.

Hermitages had been incorporated into the park on the estate at Lerma, built by the Duke of Lerma in the 1600s" (Brown and Elliott 1980, 77).

## WORKS CITED

Allen, Paul C. 2000. *Philip III and the Pax Hispanica, 1598–1621*. New Haven: Yale University Press.

Alpers, Paul. 1979. *The Singer of the Eclogues*. Berkeley: University of California Press.

Balsdon, J.P.V.D. 2004. *Life and Leisure in Ancient Rome*. London: Phoenix.

Bailey, D.R. Shackleton. 1982. Profile of Horace. Cambridge, MA: Harvard University Press.

Bowditch, Phebe Lowell. 2001. *Horace and the Gift Economy of Patronage*. Berkeley: University of California Press.

Brown, Jonathan. 1978. *Images & Ideas in Seventeenth-Century Spanish Painting*. Princeton: Princeton University Press.

Brown, Jonathan, and J.H. Elliott. 1980. *A Palace for a King*. New Haven: Yale University Press.

Cacho Casal, Rodrigo. 2009. "'The Memory of Ruins': Quevedo's Silva to 'Roma Antigua, y Moderna.'" *Renaissance Quarterly* 62 (4): 1167–203. http://dx.doi .org/10.1086/650026.

Cervantes, Miguel de. 1981. *Novelas ejemplares II*. Edited by Harry Sieber. Madrid: Cátedra.

Elliott, J.H. 1989. *Spain and Its World*. New Haven: Yale University Press.

Feros, Antonio. 2000. *Kingship and Favoritism in the Spain of Philip III, 1598–1621*. Cambridge: Cambridge University Press.

Gutiérrez, Carlos M. 2005. *La espada, el rayo y La pluma*. West Lafayette, IN: Purdue University Press.

Hadas, Moses. 1950. *A History of Greek Literature*. New York: Columbia University Press.

Hadas, Moses. 1952. *A History of Latin Literature*. New York: Columbia University Press.

Halperin, David M. 1983. *Before Pastoral*. New Haven: Yale University Press.

Horace. 1960. *Odes & Epodes*. Edited by Paul Shorey and Gordon J. Laing. Facsimile Reprint. Pittsburgh: University of Pittsburgh Press.

Lemprière, John. 1984. Lemprière's *Classical Dictionary*. London: Bracken Books.

Lichtheim, Miriam. 1976. *Ancient Egyptian Literature II*. Berkeley: University of California Press.

Panofsky, Erwin. 1969. *Problems in Titian*. New York: New York University Press.

Paton, W.R. 1917. *The Greek Anthology*. 5 vols. Loeb Classical Library. Cambridge, MA: Harvard University Press.

Putnam, Michael C.J. 1982. *Essays on Latin Lyric, Elegy, and Epic*. Princeton: Princeton University Press.
Quevedo, Francisco de. 1964. *Epistolario*. In *Obras completas II: Verso*. Madrid: Aguilar.
Quevedo, Francisco de. 1969. *Obra poética I*. Edited by José Manuel Blecua. Madrid: Castalia.
Rosenmeyer, Thomas G. 1973. *The Green Cabinet: Theocritus and the European Pastoral Lyric*. Berkeley: University of California Press.
Ruskin, John. 1980. *The Lamp of Beauty: Writings on Art by John Ruskin*. Edited by Joan Evans. Ithaca, NY: Cornell University Press.
Unamuno, Miguel de. 1963. *Abel Sánchez*. Madrid: Espasa Calpe.

# PART THREE

# Objects against Culture

# 10 Transformation and Transgression at the Banquet Scene in *La Celestina*[1]

CAROLYN A. NADEAU

In early modern Spain no novel more masterfully constructs a world moved by materialism or commodifies more thoroughly every aspect of life than Fernando de Rojas's *La Celestina.* From the opening act in which Calisto purchases Celestina's skills to secure love to the final lament in which Pleberio shares his materialist vision of the universe, all the characters fully embrace a world defined by consumption and the commerce that surrounds it. Central to this commodified vision of the universe is the banquet scene of Act IX. At this point in the novel, Celestina is fully involved in manipulating the star-crossed lovers, Calisto and Melibea, and Calisto's once faithful servant, Pármeno, has recently surrendered his loyalty to the old bawd demonstrating his conversion with a banquet. By contextualizing Rojas's work with historical accounts of banquets and other literary markers such as cookbooks and dietary manuals, we begin to get a fuller picture of how food culture reflects social identity and what roles the characters play in shaping that very identity.

Twenty-first-century criticism is becoming increasingly aware of the fundamental role that material culture and, I would argue, food as a material artefact, have in expressing positions of social difference. Looking back, we know from the generative work of Claude Lévi-Strauss and Mary Douglas, who both draw consistent analogies between food and culture, that food categories encode social events and that from the mundane act of preparing food and eating it we can learn about social values.[2] Pierre Bourdieu added to the discussion that food habits, as an indicator of cultural consumption, legitimized social differences.

> Social subjects, classified by their classifications, distinguish themselves by the distinctions they make, between the beautiful and the ugly, the distinguished

> and the vulgar, in which their position in the objective classifications is expressed or betrayed. And statistical analysis does show that oppositions similar in structure to those found in cultural practices also appear in eating habits. The antithesis between quantity and quality, substance and form, corresponds to the opposition – linked to different distances from necessity – between the taste of necessity, which favours the most "filling," and most economical foods, and the taste of liberty – or luxury – which shifts the emphasis to the manner (of presenting, serving, eating, etc.) and tends to use stylized forms to deny function. (1984, 6)

In the case of the banquet, subjects can project an image they want to present, for example, Pármeno who provides the food and invites the people, projects himself as host of the event and therefore, not just one of the group but a key figure. But, the banquet, as Bourdieu argues, is also "the systematic expression of a system of factors including, in addition to the indicators of the position occupied in the economic and cultural hierarchies, economic trajectory, social trajectory and cultural trajectory" (1984, 79). With this concept in mind, we can examine the reason the banquet was organized, the food Pármeno "acquires," and the actions and words of those present, to understand the "trajectories" at play in the text.

Consumption is an act of material culture, one that allows us to gain insight into social relations.[3] In early modern Spain, from the royal court to the pueblo, people celebrated rites of passage – birth, baptism, marriage, death – religious holidays, and public events with a banquet. Historiography recounts in detail aristocratic banquets like the one the president of the court in Valladolid hosted for the arrival of the new king Charles I.

> Hablaros a lo largo de los diversos platos y servicios con que fue servido sería largo de narrar, ya que tantas viandas exquisitas había allí. Por esta causa, el Rey, Su Alteza y toda la nobleza fueron muy bien festejados y abundantemente servidos; y lo fueron todos, desde los grandes dignatarios hasta nosotros, los criados, que comimos en la cámara de retiro, en la que fuimos servidos con tantos y tan buenos platos que no había nada mejor.
>
> [To speak in length of the many dishes and courses which we were served would take too much time, as there were so many exquisite delicacies there. The king, His Highness, and all nobility present were so well honoured and abundantly served, as all of us were, from the grand dignitaries to us, the servants, who ate in a side room where we were served so many and such excellent dishes that there was nothing better.] (Vital 1958, 352)[4]

Like this feast that honours Carlos I on his arrival in Spain, banquets confirm and celebrate the established social order.[5] They are ritual sites of solidarity and communication that take the biological need for eating as survival and convert it into a site of feasting, social pleasure, and social order. Covarrubias defines *banquete* in the following way:

> vale tanto como un festín, convite y comida espléndida, abundante de manjares y rica en aparato. Tomó nombre de las bancas, o mesas sobre que se ponen las viandas, como llamamos mesa franca el dar de comer a cuantos quieren sentarse a la mesa, que sean de las calidades que se requieren; y hacer plato el admitir un señor a su mesa de ordinario, el número de caballeros competente; de manera que debajo destos nombres banco, mesa y plato, se entienda el convidar en la forma sobredicha.
>
> [It is equal to a feast, a dinner party with splendid food, abundant in delicacies beautifully displayed. The name comes from benches or tables on which food was placed; in the same way we say "open table" when anyone who wants to sit at the table is fed, as long as he has the necessary social standing, and "to make a plate for" when a nobleman admits the appropriate number of gentlemen to his everyday table; so that from these names "bench," "table," and "dish," it is understood that one invites in the way explained above.] (1994, 162)

As Covarrubias explains, the table is the centre of the banquet and is as much defined by the food placed on it as it is by the people seated around it. Furthermore, the spectacle is filled with rules of presentation, etiquette, service, seating plans, and bodily censorship. Yet, at the same time it is a site of excess and ostentation that easily leads to opposing outcomes such as a breakdown of rules and corporal improprieties. In this way, the banquet is order and chaos, refinement and bacchanalia, bodily censorship and sensual gratification. The table brings community together but also forces hierarchies, webs of inclusion and exclusion. It is this disparate dimension that makes the banquet a perfect place for transformation and transgression. Comparing contemporary cookbooks, dietary manuals, and classical representations of banquets with that in *La Celestina*, we can understand more fully how Fernando de Rojas parodies the event of the banquet, its host, food, and even language in Act IX of *Celestina*. Here, he unravels the bonds of servant-master that might have been, exposes the materiality of love, and exploits the tensions that define class divisions. In his novel, the banquet becomes the site of transformation that ultimately leads to the tragic destruction of the text's main characters.

## The Host

If we consider the responsibilities of the banquet host – arranging the event, inviting the guests, procuring the food – there remains little doubt that Pármeno casts himself as host to the affair. The idea of the banquet is his alone. After spending his first evening with Areúsa, he is desperate to create a space where the two lovers can meet again: "Y aun porque más nos veamos, reciba de ti esta gracia, que te vayas hoy a las doce del día a comer con nosotros a su casa de Celestina," [And so – that we may see more of each other – please accept my invitation to dine today at 12 at Celestina's] (2004, 212; 1958, 130).[6]

But, the meal he plans is not only to regale Areúsa with another kind of oral delight; it is also the agency of recognition and celebration of Pármeno's new identity. He understands that his passage into manhood must be shared with others. On his way home he muses:

> Quál hombre es ... más dichoso y bienandante, ¡que un tan excellente don sea por mí posseýdo, y quan presto pedido tan presto alcançado! .... ¿Con qué pagaré yo esto? O alto Dios, ¿a quién contaría yo este gozo? ¿A quién descobriría tan gran secreto? ¿A quién daré parte de mi gloria? Bien me dezía la vieja que de ninguna prosperidad es buena la possessión sin compañía. El plazer no comunicado no es plazer.
>
> [What man is ... happier or more fortunate? I cannot believe that so excellent a treasure should have fallen into my hands. No sooner asked for than possessed! .... How shall I repay all this? Almighty God! To whom shall I recount my joy? To whom uncover so great a secret? With whom share my glory? The old one was quite right to say that, in all justice, prosperity should be shared, for pleasure uncommunicated is not really pleasure at all.] (2004, 212; 1958, 130–1)

His fortune will not only be shared verbally as he recounts his exploits to Sempronio but also celebrated through food and drink and community with his newly bonded associates. In fact, the banquet also celebrates Pármeno's decision to join the ranks of Celestina's *cofradía* [association], and the society of con artists, thieves, and prostitutes that she epitomizes. María de los Ángeles Pérez Samper tells us,

> El banquete tenía un importante papel de cohesión social, comer juntos indicaba formar parte del mismo colectivo, ya fuese un grupo de cortesanos o

un grupo de personas que compartían el mismo oficio o profesión o pertenecían a la misma corporación o institución. Muy representativos de los banquetes de consolidación de grupo, clara expresión comunitaria, resultaban las comidas de las cofradías.

[The banquet played an important role of social cohesion; eating together meant that you were par t of the same collective, whether it be a group of courtesans, a group of people from the same trade or profession or the same institution or corporation. A clear expression of community, association meals turned out to be very representative of banquets of consolidated groups.] (1997, 76–7)

The banquet, then, is the site of multiple recognitions, most important among them, Pármeno's self-identification as a member of Celestina's *cofradía*.

As host, Pármeno is responsible for inviting the guests. After leaving Areúsa's house, Pármeno first invites Sempronio and is sure to include Elicia as well: "Tú y ella [Areúsa] y allá está la vieja y Elicia; avremos plazer" [Oh, you and Areúsa … and of course Mother and Elicia, who are already there. We can have a lot of fun] (2004, 217; 1958, 135).[7] Later in the text, as she drinks more than her usual share of wine, even Celestina recognizes herself as a guest at the feast: "no me harán pasar de allí salvo si no soy conbidada como agora" [I cannot be prevailed on to exceed that intake – unless, of course, I happen to be invited to dinner, as on this present occasion] (2004, 225; 1958, 143). As Pármeno plans to send the food in advance so that it will be prepared upon his arrival, Sempronio inquires what they will eat while at the same time implicitly acknowledging the reason for the social event: "¿Qué has pensado embiar, para que aquellas loquillas te tengan por hombre complido, biencriado y franco?" [What have you planned to send? You will certainly want the girls to think you are quite a man of the world – well-bred and free with your money] (2004, 217; 1958, 135). The idea of an accomplished, gracious, and generous host is a topos of banquet history. Perhaps the best literary model for Pármeno can be found in Trimalchio, the ex-slave of Petronius's *Satyricon*, who is married to a former prostitute and throws lavish banquets to write himself into affluent society. But to understand more fully his decision to break his bond with Calisto and return to Celestina, we turn to contemporary cookbooks and dietary treatises, in which we find lessons on how to be virtuous and serve one's master; these reveal key absences in Pármeno's upbringing.

In 1423 Enrique de Villena authored *Arte cisoria* [The art of carving] at the request of Sancho de Jarava, official carver for Juan II of Castille.[8] In his treatise Villena describes in detail the performance of carving and, drawing from the juridical authority of the day, Alfonso el Sabio's *Siete Partidas* [Seven Partidas] (specifically, the Second Partida, title IX, law XI), Villena includes a chapter on the instruction of good servants: "Cómo deven ser criados moços de buen linaje acostunbrados, para tomar dellos para el ofiçio del cortar" [How boys of good lineage should be raised in order to be selected for the office of carving]. Villena asserts that both the boy's unquestionable lineage ("de fidalguez non dudoso") and apprenticeship are key to becoming an excellent servant. It is clear that Pármeno's lineage is stained and, as such, he will need to rely all the more on good instruction. For Villena and, more generally, for aristocrats of fifteenth-century Spain, the master was responsible for instructing apprentices and fledgling servants in the necessary virtues: "onde por tales demostraçiones e criança ... serán fechos por buen uso leales, entendidos, discretos, non cobdiçiosos, non enbidiosos, non yrados, que son las siete condiçiones que han menester" [where by such reason and upbringing ... they will become with good practice loyal, knowledgeable, discreet, not greedy or envious or angry, which are the seven required conditions] (1984, 123).[9] The first virtue, loyalty, should be modelled, praised, and rewarded: "que sean abezados a mantener lealtad, loándola simpre ante ellos, e contándoles de aquéllos que la mantovieron quánto prez por ello ganaron, e quán buen nonbre dellos quedó" [they should be praised for remaining loyal, continually extolling (its virtue) in front of them and reminding them of others who have remained loyal and were promptly rewarded and what estimation they earned because of it] (1984, 121). These instructions for being virtuous servants continue throughout the sixteenth and seventeenth centuries in the cookbooks of Ruperto de Nola, Diego Granado, and Francisco Martínez Montiño.

In the case of Calisto and his servants, the modelling is misdirected.[10] Calisto praises Sempronio for what Pármeno (and the reader) know to be greedy motivations and reproaches Pármeno, whose efforts to remain loyal are interpreted as strains of envy. "Quanto remedio Sempronio acarrea con sus pies, tanto apartas tú con tu lengua, con tus vanas palabras; fingiéndote fiel, eres un terrón de lisonja, bote de malicias, el mismo mesón y aposentamiento de la embidia" [All that Sempronio achieves with his feet in running about on my missions you nullify with your tongue and your vain and idle words. Pretending to be loyal, you are a mass of deceptions, a receptacle of malice, the very inn and lodging-place of envy] (2004,

136; 1958, 57). Pármeno continues to advise Calisto but feels trapped between his desire to serve well and the frustrations he encounters by doing so: "por ser leal padezco mal. Otros se ganan por malos, yo me pierdo por bueno. El mundo es tal; quiero yrme al hilo de la gente, pues a los traydores llaman discretos, a los fieles necios" [I am suffering now for being so loyal. Other people get ahead by being bad, but I – I lose because I try so hard to be good. Well, so goes the world. I must do what everyone else does, for the discreet are called traitors, and the faithful, fools] (2004, 137; 1958, 58). He recognizes the absence of sound council from his master: "Mas esto me porná escarmiento daquí adelante con él. Que si dixere comamos, yo tanbién; si quisiere derrocar la casa, aprovarlo; si quemar su hazienda, yr por huego. Destruya, rompa, quiebre, dañe; dé a alcahuetas lo suyo, que mi parte me cabrá" [But this will forewarn me forever against him. If he says, "Let us eat," I will say, "Let us eat." If he wants to tear down the house, I will say it is a fine idea. If he wants to burn down his property, I'll run and bring him the fire to start it with. Let him break, destroy, damage, shatter! You may, sir, give your wealth away to go-betweens, but I can tell you that I intend to get my share of it] (2004, 137; 1958, 58). Beyond stealing from his master's pantry, Pármeno formulates lies to explain the loss: "haréle creer que los ha comido … diré que hedían" [I will make him think he has eaten them … I'll say they spoiled on us] (2004, 818; 1958, 136), and expresses his desire to distance himself from Calisto and further his betrayal for his own benefit, "y allá hablaremos más largamente en su daño y nuestro provecho" [There we'll talk at great length about his troubles and the profit we are to share] (2004, 218; 1958, 136). With no lineage to stand on and no proper modelling from his master, Pármeno's decision to organize a banquet, pilfer food, and celebrate a return to his roots is the ritualistic act that signifies his transgressions.

## The Food

But what do we know of the food that Pármeno steals? He is specific in the quality and quantity that he will provide: "pan blanco, vino de Monviedro; un pernil de toçino … seys pares de pollos … [y] las tórtolas" [white bread, Monviedro wine, a gammon of pork … six pair of chickens … and the turtledoves] (2004, 218; 1958, 136). By distinguishing the bread by its colour, Pármeno reveals its quality. Piero Camporesi explains: "The hierarchy of breads and their qualities in reality sanctioned social distinctions. Bread represented a status symbol that defined human condition and class according to its particular color" (1980, 120). White bread was reserved for the upper classes while millet, rye, barley, and other supposedly "inferior" grains were used to make bread for the lower classes. Philip III's doctor wrote that the best bread was one that was "más fácil de partir con los dientes, y partido se mostrare por dentro más blanco que rubio" [easier on the teeth and when broken the inside reveals a colour that is more white than blonde] (cited in Sánchez Meco 1998, 131). In early modern Spain, and generally throughout Europe, quality wine was tied to the name of the town from which it came.[11] In other words, the fact that the wine Pármeno stole was labelled "de Monviedro" signified quality (and still does today). In addition, and just a few years later, Luis Lobera de Ávila, personal doctor to Carlos I, cited the wine of Monviedro as having specific medicinal properties in his dietary treatise *Banquete de nobles caballeros* [Banquet of noble gentlemen] (1996, 63). Beyond these social markers, bread and wine carry with them obvious spiritual significance as well. But at every turn in *La Celestina*, the sacred has been replaced with the material. The bread and wine at the last supper that Celestina shares with her followers no longer symbolize a sacred sacrifice but rather transgression (stolen food) and commercial enterprise (payment for sexual favours).

Meat, the third main food group of the early modern period, together with bread and wine, was consumed by those with money. By introducing "*seis pares* de pollos" [*six* pairs of chickens] (emphasis added) Rojas reiterates both the number of guests at the banquet, and the coupling of guests. Sempronio / Elicia and Pármeno / Areúsa are obvious but Celestina / Lucrecia are another pair as both stand witness to, but do not directly participate in, the sexual games around the table. *Tórtola* or turtledove, the bird that symbolizes amorous fidelity, is one of the many displaced signifiers in Rojas's text. Covarrubias explains that this bird is "símbolo de la mujer viuda, que muerto su marido no se vuelve a casar y guarda castidad" [symbol of a widow, who, after her husband has died, does not marry again and remains chaste] (1994, 928–9). Seen through this lens, the readers can perceive Rojas's sense of irony as fidelity and chastity certainly have no place at this table. Beyond these misfired signifiers, fowl was highly valued as was mutton, beef, veal, and pork (Valles Rojo 2007, 237–8). Like the white bread and labelled wine, its presence at the banquet, along with the *pernil de tocino* [high-quality ham] indicated excellence. Pork, consumed at all social levels, marked social differences by the different cuts and the *pernil de tocino* was among the most valued. Many authors signal the importance of this cut; for example, in *Guzmán de Alfarache*, "jamas dejó mi señor de tener gallina, pollo, capón o palomino a comida o cena, y *pernil de tocino entero*, cocido en vino, cada domingo"[my master never stopped having hen, chicken or capon at lunch or dinner and a *whole, high-quality ham*, cooked in wine, every Sunday] (Alemán 1969, 153; emphasis added).

For workers and the poor, meat was consumed in small quantities and lower grades: fat back and bones in stews, offal, and cured meat – as opposed to a whole ham or a dozen chickens – were mainstays throughout the year for the lower classes. In fact, an entire gastronomic social hierarchy existed that regulated certain types of food, including meat and fowl, for certain classes. Doctors of the day, for example Lobera de Ávila, claimed that eating food inappropriate to one's rank would cause illness. In categorizing meats, he draws from several medical authorities and concludes that the best are mutton, veal, and kid (1996, 73). Although most of his decisions are based on the physiology of the humours, social class also plays a role: "Y por lo dicho, las personas de negocios, grandes señores o de muy alto estado, débense evitar del mucho uso de comer vaca o buey, máxime viejo; o si lo comieren, sea pocas veces y poco en cuantidad o con alguna salsa de mostaza, en que entre algo que reprima el humor melancónico" [And with that said, businessmen, grandees, and men of high rank should avoid eating much beef or ox that is particularly old, or if they did eat it, that it be infrequent and in small quantities or with some mustard sauce so that it is eaten with something that represses the melancholic humour] (1996, 74). According to this theory of nutritional privilege, "the relationship between 'quality of person' and 'quality of food' was not a simple fact tied to the chances of wealth or need, but rather a basic and ontological postulate: to eat well or poorly was an intrinsic individual characteristic (and hopefully unalterable), just as was social class"(Montanari 1996, 87). Later, during the festivities, the class divisions that the food items represent will be central to the conversations of the guests.

Although the food Pármeno supplies for the banquet reflects the wealth and abundance of the upper class, the actual event of its consumption is framed by images of hunger and punctuated with complaints of poverty. Upon arrival Pármeno speaks of the transformative power of hunger. "La necessitad y pobreza, la hambre, que no ay mejor maestra en el mundo, no ay mejor despertadora y abivadora de ingenios" [poverty, and need. And hunger too – the greatest teacher in the world. There's nothing better to whet the mind than hunger] (2004, 224; 1958, 141). This hunger drives Pármeno's transformation. It is not virtue or salvation that motivates him, or any other character in the text for that matter, but rather, hunger and carnal appetite.

Throughout the meal, Celestina is often described as gnawing on and gumming her food. Before her arrival Sempronio reminds Pármeno, "Quando ay que roer en casa, sanos están los santos" [When she is well-provisioned at home and has something to gnaw on, she leaves the saints alone] (2004, 223; 1958, 140). When recalling Calisto's fast at the Church of Saint Magdalene, Pármeno reminds Celestina, "que puedas bien roer los huessos destos pollos" [you might enjoy gnawing on the bones of these chickens] (2004, 230; 1958, 145), comparing her physical gnawing with Calisto's figurative gnawing of saints' bones while he spirals deeper into his fit of love madness.[12] Celestina herself suggests that she is all too familiar with the art of survival: "un cortezón de pan ratonado me basta para tres días" [(w)ith ... only a crust of mouse-nibbled bread I can get along very nicely for three whole days] (2004, 225; 1958, 142), and that what remains of her capacity to enjoy food has been reduced to gumming leftovers of what the others have devoured: "la vieja Celestina maxcará de dentera con sus botas enzías las migajas de los manteles" [And old Celestina will with her empty gums greedily lap up the crumbs you leave upon your tablecloth] (2004, 232; 1958, 147). Beyond these images of meagre scraps of bones and stale bread, the meal that the servants and prostitutes share is best characterized by its absence. There are no references to the delicacies Pármeno and Semprono had previously pilfered, no elaborate courses, no staging of dishes, no homage paid to the exotic tastes and smells or the ostentatious surroundings of the meal, no desserts. In fact, the biggest event of the meal is Elicia's refusal to eat, a physical manifestation of the nausea she feels provoked by Sempronio's comment on Melibea's grace and beauty.

## The Language

The third element of any banquet, apart from the people and the food itself, is the language that shapes it. Often the strength of the banquet lies not so much in the food's physical presence but rather the description of it. In early modern Spain there are abundant references to famous banquets including a Christmas celebration Francisco Martínez Montiño records in his 1611 cookbook, *Arte de Cocina, pastelería, vizcochería y conservería* [The art of cooking, pie making, pastry making and preserving]. Martínez Montiño spent his entire life in royal kitchens, beginning with the kitchen of the Infanta Juana in Portugal in 1553 and working his way up through the kitchen of Philip II to the position of *cocinero de servilleta* [personal cook] for Philip III and IV. In his description he, too, makes clear that the food itself is not enough, but that how it is presented is equally, if not even more, important. "Y daré á entender, como se han de servir porque en los banquetes, todo el toque está es saberlos servir; porque aunque se gaste mucho dinero en un banquete, si no se sirve bien no luce" [And I will explain how one should serve, because at banquets the difference is in knowing how to serve; even though one might spend a lot of money on the banquet, if it is not well served, it does not stand out] (1997, 9–10). After he finishes his instructions on how to serve a banquet, he proceeds with a list of dishes appropriate for a Christmas banquet that includes both *pollos* [chicken] and *perniles* [ham] as well as the following:

> Olla podridas.
> Pabos asados con su salsa.
> Pastelillos saboyanos de ternera ojaldrados.
> Pichones, y torreznos asados.
> Platillo de Arteletes de aves sobre sopas de natas.
> Bollos de vacia.
> Perdizes asadas con salsa de limones.
> Capirotada con solomo, y salchicas, y perdizes.
> Lechones asados con sopas de queso, y azucar, y canela.
> Ojaldres de masa de levadura con enxundia de Puerco.
> Pollas asadas.
>
> [Spanish stew.
> Roasted peacock in its sauce.
> Pastry-wrapped veal with Sabayon sauce.
> Roasted pigeon and bacon.
> Grilled poultry in a cream sauce.
> Hollow rolls.
> Roasted partridge with lemon sauce.
> Cured pork loin, sausage, and partridge stew.
> Roasted lamb in a cheese, cinnamon, and sugar sauce.
> Puff pastry from leavened dough and pork fat.
> Roasted chickens.] (1997, 14)

The very titles of these dishes (only the first of four courses) stimulate the appetite and underscore the importance of language in the enjoyment of food.

The absence in Rojas's text of these types of descriptions that are so vital to the pleasure of food parallels that of food's primary role in creating community and strengthening fellowship. Without descriptions of the food, the centre of the feast is missing. It destabilizes the feast and signals the collapse of friendship much like other linguistic absences in the text. Like Melibea's coy denial to Calisto, Elicia's lies to Sempronio about another lover, Celestina's contrived sympathies for Calisto's circumstances, and Pármeno's excuses for the food he stole, genuine descriptions of the characters' feelings and motivations are absent. Because the central focus of the banquet is missing, the situation becomes unstable and sets up a space in which a threat to the order of the state develops. The banquet, a spectacle that traditionally reaffirms political power, here serves to destabilize it as this scene sets the stage for unravelling the accepted social order. It is no surprise, then, that this social affront be accompanied by Elicia's jealousy, Areúsa's anger, and Celestina's frustration and acknowledgment of lost indulgences; as we will see momentarily this is the very direction the discourse takes that afternoon as their conversations break down and the seeds of destruction begin to grow.

Laurent Vital, the valet of Carlos I who recorded details of the king's arrival in the capital, does take careful note of one important aspect of the banquet: the wine. In fact, similar to Celestina's opening elegy to wine, in Vital's account, it is the first and most visual element of the spectacle.

> [H]abía mandado construir y edificar en medio de su casa una hermosa fuente sobre el suelo, de la cual salía vino por dos caños, a saber: por uno vino blanco, y por otro vino tinto; y tan bien estaba hecha la separación, que duró tanto tiempo como el Rey estuvo allí. A esta fuente todos podían ir a beber lo que querían y lo que no se bebía caía en una gran pila, por un conducto, iba a dar a una gran vasija en la bodega de este presidente… hubo mucha apretura por la multitud de gente que de todos lados abordaba allí y se adelantaba para beber en ella, a causa de lo cual hubo entonces tanto vino derramado como bebido, pero, pasada esa afluencia, todos bebían allí a su gusto.
>
> [A beautiful fountain was ordered to be built and staged on the floor in the centre of the house from which wine poured forth from two spouts in the following way: white wine from one and red wine from the other. The separation was done so well that it lasted for as long as the king was there. Everyone could drink as much as they wanted from the fountain and what wasn't consumed continued on into a basin, via a canal, and ended up in a great vessel in the president's wine cellar … Among the multitude of people there was plenty of pushing around the entire fountain as all approached to drink from it and due to this there was as much wine spilled as drunk but after this influx, everyone there drank as they pleased.] (1958, 349–50)

While both Vital and Rojas privilege wine in its primary sequence in the banquet description and thus exemplify its central role in celebratory occasions at each end of the class spectrum, the sources for Celestina's extended praise of wine are many and varied.[13] From Hippocrates and Galen to Arnaldo de Villanueva and Lobera de Ávila, medical doctors throughout time have elaborated on its benefits (and detriments). Celestina begins her monologue on the warm nature of wine: "Pues de noche en invierno no ay tal escalentador de cama ... esto me callenta la sangre" [On a cold winter night there's no better bed-warmer ... it warms my blood] (2004, 225; 1958, 142). Likewise, Lobera, drawing from Galen, begins his chapter on the warm nature of wine: "vinos hay blancos de una tierra, que son más calientes que tintos de otra, y tintos de otra, menos calientes que blancos de otra. Así como vinos de Pelayos y de San Martín, blancos, son más calientes que tintos de Escalona y de otras partes; y tintos de Pelayos y de San Martín son más calientes que blancos de Madrid" [there are white wines from some regions that are warmer than reds from another and red from another (region) that are not as warm as whites from another. For example, wines from Pelayo and San Martin, whites, are warmer than reds from Escalona and other regions; reds from Pelayo and San Martin are warmer than whites from Madrid] (1996, 61). It goes without saying that all wines, white and red, are characterized by their warm nature.

Celestina continues with a myriad of advantages that drinking wine offers:

> esto me sostiene contino en un ser; esto me haze andar siempre alegre; esto me para fresca ... Esto da esfuerço al moço, y al viejo fuerça, pone color al descolorido ... saca el frío del stómago, quita el hedor del aliento, haze potentes los fríos, haze sofrir los afanes de las labranças a los cansados segadores, haze sudar toda agua mala, sana el romadizo y las muelas.
>
> [it keeps me all together; it lets me get about merrily; it keeps me fresh ... it imparts verve to youth and strength to age; it gives colour to the pallid ... drives coldness from the stomach, erases the odours on the breath, makes potent the frigid, alleviates the toil of tillage, causes weary reapers to sweat out their noisome humours, and cures our colds and toothaches.] (2004, 225; 1958, 142)

Lobera also continues with multiple benefits of wine consumption, this time acknowledging as his authoritative text Aristotle's *De secretis secretorum*.

> [B]ebido el vino moderadamente, siendo bueno, claro y odorífico, no muy viejo ni nuevo, conforta el estómago, esfuerça el calor natural … ayuda contra la putrefación de los humores, que no se podrezcan tan aína; aprovecha a la cabeça, alegra el coraçon, causa bien color, hace experta la lengua, es de buen mantenimiento y de buena sustancia, engendra buenos espíritus y claros.
>
> [Wine drunk in moderation, if it is good, clear, and with a pleasant bouquet, neither too old nor new, brings comfort to the stomach, improves natural colour … aids against the deterioration of the humours so they do not decay as quickly, improves the head, lightens the heart, gives good colour, makes the tongue sharp, and helps maintain good health and substance, breeds good and clear spirits.] (1996, 62–3)

Both Celestina and Lobera point to wine's positive effect on one's physical and mental health. It is clear that Rojas and Lobera draw from a long tradition of medical treatises. Of course all medical treatises and later moral and juridical ones include the dangers of drinking wine and the problems excessive drinking can cause, elements that Celestina sums up in one passing reference: "No tiene sino una tacha, que lo bueno vale caro y lo malo haze daño. Assí que con lo que sana el hígado, enferma la bolsa" [There is about it one disadvantage only, as far as I can see: which is that the good variety comes high and the poor kind is hurtful. Thus it is that – "Wine's for the liver a soothing nurse, but it wreaks deep ravages on your purse"] (2004, 225; 1958, 142). Even one of the last remaining pleasures for Celestina, drinking wine, is reduced to an economic paradigm. If it is good wine, it is expensive.

As the banquet comes to a close, Celestina returns to the topic of wine. This time, in her nostalgic glance back to her glory days of fame and fortune, she recalls with pride the excellent wines she drank.

> Pues vino, ¿no me sobraba? De lo mejor que se bevía en la ciudad, venido de diversas partes: de Monviedro, de Luque, de Toro, de Madrigal, de San Martín, y de otros muchos lugares, y tantos que aunque tengo la differencia de los gustos y sabor en la boca, no tengo la diversidad de sus tierras en la memoria, que harto es que una vieja como yo en oliendo qualquiera vino diga de dónde es.
>
> [Had I not also wine in great abundance? I did indeed; the best ever drunk in this town. Many kinds of it, too, from all over: Monviedro, Luque, Toro, Madrigal, San Martín, and many other places too – so many, indeed, that

> though I still know them from the memory I have of their taste and bouquet, I no longer recall where they came from. It is too much to expect an old thing like me, when she smells wine, to tell you where it comes from] (2004, 236; 1958, 151–2)

Celestina, like Sancho in *Don Quijote*, had an expert nose and could tell where a wine was from simply by inhaling its aroma. Her wine list holds prestige with multiple authors of the day. Several *Cancionero* poets, Arcipreste de Hita, Lope de Vega, Góngora, and Tirso all cite "vino de Toro" [wine from Toro] as an outstanding wine (Valles Rojo 2007, 315). The same is true with the wine of San Martín to which Miguel Herrero-García, in his *La vida española del siglo XVII* [Spanish lifestyles of the seventeenth century], dedicates an entire chapter (1933, 6–12). Lobera de Ávila writes about the excellent white wines specifically from Madrigal and Monviedro, and the reds from Toro and San Martín (1996, 63). Wine from Luque, as well as most of the others, is included in the poem, "Coplas hechas por Alonso de Toro, cojo, sobre la abundancia del vino que Dios ha dado, en el año de XXXI y el el año de XXXII" [Stanzas written by Alonso de Toro, lame, on the abundance of wine God has provided in the 31st and 32nd years] (cited in Valles Rojo 2007, 298–300).

The power of language is not limited to the mere description of food and drink but extends to the conversation and stories Celestina, Pármeno, Sempronio, Elisia, and Areúsa share. Bearing in mind the classical tradition, we know that the banquet King Alkinoös hosts for Ulysses on his return to Ithaca is best known for the hero's stories, not the food served. Likewise Plato's *Symposium* is remembered for the guests' speeches on the nature of love.[14] The site of the banquet is a natural space for the power of language to explode as the primacy of orality, eating, speaking, and in the case of *La Celestina*, sexual activity, blend together. Pármeno's sexual exploits lead to the feast of food. Celestina's extended elegy on wine prompts Sempronio to remind her that they need to eat and not just talk. Words about Melibea's beauty disrupt Elicia's pleasure of eating and so on. One act of orality instigates another and becomes a destabilizing force in the text. A passing comment transforms into an argument on the nature of beauty and love, and the arrival of Melibea's servant, Lucrecia, instigates an invective against the upper class. Far from the dialogue of love in Plato's *Symposium*, here the lovers exhibit jealousy and anger while nausea and vomit become the dominant images the food provokes.

The discussion of beauty and love that the characters of *La Celestina* sustain during the banquet recalls the humanist debate on the banquet of senses. Some critics argue that Rojas would not have been familiar with Marsilio Ficino's *Commentary on Plato's Symposium* (1496) or Lorenzo Valla's *De Voluptate* [On pleasure] (1431) or Platina's *De honesta voluptate et valetudine* [On right pleasure and good health] (1474), but others have already noted the connections between them.[15] Whether or not Rojas read these works, he was certainly familiar with the ideas of love, beauty, and the pursuit of pleasure that they addressed.

The very first book published on food, Platina's *De honesta voluptate et valetudine* contains 10 books that deal with such diverse topics as the science of cooking, diet, exercise, the nature of food, and the best ways to prepare and season one's meal.[16] His work draws from Valla's theory that pleasure is the guiding principle of moral behaviour. It also responds to and in part corrects Ficino's theory on divine, natural, and bestial love and how the first two can lead to a contemplative life while the third leads to dishonour as the senses take priority over the contemplative realm of reason. The importance of Platina, and humanists in general, is that his work defends the pleasure of eating as an honest virtue. In his introduction Platina writes: "Who is so stolid … that he is not suffused by some pleasure of body or mind if he has held to temperance in eating, from which comes good health, and to integrity and consistency in action, from which happiness arises? … I have written to help any citizen seeking health, moderation and elegance of food rather than debauchery" (1998, 101–3). For the first time, Platina defends what Nestor Luján calls "la honestidad de un placer discreto y deleitoso como es el del paladar" [the honesty of a delightful, discreet pleasure like that of the palate] (1997, 96).

In *La Celestina* no one ever ascends the Platonic rungs of the ladder in pursuit of beauty, or advances into the contemplative realm Ficino imagines. Rather, the characters indulge in a purely physical and material universe that embraces pleasure but surely not in the moderate terms Platina outlines in his text. After Sempronio's comment, "aquella graciosa y gentil Melibea" [that gracious and lovely lady, Melibea] (2004, 226; 1958, 143), instead of contemplating a higher beauty or a more noble soul, Elicia responds violently. Her jealousy and rage are couched in terms of regurgitating food: "¡mal provecho te haga lo que comes, tal comida me as dado! Por mi alma, revessar quiero quanto tengo en el cuerpo de asco de oýrte llamar a aquélla gentil" [I hope you get indigestion for saying that. You have certainly spoiled my dinner. Honestly, I feel like throwing up everything I've got in my body – it makes me so sick at my stomach to hear you call her "lovely lady"] (2004, 226; 1958, 143). No longer able to stomach food from the table at which her lover is seated, words become Elicia's food. She refutes Melibea's beauty by stating that it is artificial, a product bought cheaply. In her commodification of beauty, Elicia compares Melibea with neighbours and finally asserts that she herself is more beautiful. Elicia's food for thought prompts Areúsa to respond with more food metaphors of disgust: "Si en ayunas la topasses, si aquel día pudiesses comer de asco" [If you had ever seen her before you had had breakfast, you would get so sick at your stomach you couldn't eat all day long] (2004, 226; 1958, 143). Areúsa exploits the economic argument and reiterates that women's wealth can purchase beauty.

She draws on typical ingredients for cosmetics that provoke grotesque images, for example, her references to *hiel* and *higas pasadas* [bile and overripe figs]. In the anonymous *Manual de mujeres en el cual se contienen muchas y diversas recetas muy buenas* [The manual for women in which is contained many, very good and diverse recipes], written between 1475 and 1525, the main ingredient of "mudas para rostro y manos" [cosmetics for the face and hands] is a half pound of black figs and "para el paño del rostro" [for spots on the face], honey and bile are mixed together with other ingredients.[17] But these commonly known beauty recipes do not allay the disgust that Areúsa communicates in her description.

Elicia begins to calm down and takes her seat at the table when the conversation changes to Calisto's love sicknesses and his presence at Saint Magdalene's Church. The contrast between those at the feast engrossed in carnal pleasures with the star-crossed lover fasting at the Church of Saint Magdalene, the repentant prostitute who sacrifices all carnal pleasure in pursuit of divine grace, exemplifies once again Rojas's use of irony in the banquet scene. Celestina couches Calisto's lovesickness in terms of the denial of food: "ni comen ni beven … que comiendo se olvida la mano de llevar la vianda a la boca" [They eat not, nor drink … their hands forget to bear their victuals to their mouths] (2004, 230; 1958, 146), sprinkling the central feast of the text with images of food's absence.

As the afternoon wears on, Sempronio tries to appease Elicia by reminding her of sacrifices he endured to win her love: "Pero todo lo doy por bienempleado, pues tal joya gané" [But now I consider it was all for the best, for look what a jewel I have won!] (2004, 231; 1958, 146). But her rage continues and Celestina tries to cool her violent outburst with images of appetites both biological and sexual. Her suggestions to indulge in the culinary and sexual pleasures at hand lead to her own voyeuristic pleasures. Celestina must take up her sexual pleasure as a voyeur of the younger couples much in the same way that she can only gum the crumbs of their banquet. "Besaos y abraçaos, que a mí no me queda otra cosa sino gozarme de vello" [Oh, kiss and hug, you frisky young things! I'll delight in watching you – for that's all there's left that I can do: just look on] (2004, 232; 1958, 147). Celestina's rhetorical prowess is all that remains of her oral skills. No longer able to eat or engage in sexual exploits like the more youthful characters of the text, her language is able to kindle the flames of the lovers' argument and pushes them to return to the pursuit of their bodily appetites.[18]

Lucrecia's arrival at Celestina's house sets off Areúsa's diatribe on the upper class and how they treat those who serve them. Areúsa's soliloquy at the banquet on how the wealthy treat their servants is the reader's first sign of her vindictive, scornful personality that will be fully exploited as she plots the revenge for Sempronio and Pármeno's death later in the text. For now, she concludes that her modest freedoms far outweigh the repression and captivity those who serve must endure. Celestina agrees with Areúsa and uses food metaphors to bring closure to the topic: "Que los sabios dizen que vale más una migaja de pan con paz que toda la casa llena de viandas con renzilla" [Wise men tell us that peace and a bit of bread are worth more than a house filled with quarrelling and victuals] (2004, 233; 1958, 149). However, Areúsa will later choose *rencilla* [quarrelling] over *paz* [peace] as she returns to images of poison, vomiting, and bitterness to describe her future interactions with others in the novel.

The food and sexual exploits shift to a remote past as Celestina recalls with nostalgia twenty years earlier when she ruled the world. Acknowledging the fickle nature of fortune, she describes the respect and control over others she exercised at the pinnacle of her career. She then turns to food images that magnify her success and describe the type of payments she regularly received for services rendered: "entravan por mi puerta muchos pollos y gallinas, anserones, anadones, perdizes, tórtolas, perniles de toçino, tortas de trigo, lechones … para que comiesse yo y aquellas sus devotas" [I began to receive presents of chickens and hens, geese and ducks, partridges and turtledoves, gammons of pork and wheatcakes, and sucking pigs … so that the lasses they loved, and I, should dine well] (2004, 236; 1958, 151). Celestina's past banquets, clearly more gratifying that the current one, are directly tied to her profession. She proves that her gift of orality is still fresh enough to captivate as Lucrecia responds, "Y assí me estuviera un año sin comer, escuchándote y pensando en aquella vida buena" [I could go without eating for a whole long year just to listen to you and imagine what a good life those girls must have enjoyed] (2004, 237; 1958, 152). But, this rhetorical prowess is also slipping away as the very next evening, when she struggles to talk her way out of her impending doom, the last of her oral skills will fail her.

In the banquet scene of Act IX, we witness the destructive force of materiality as Rojas's description begins with optimism and a wealth of food before digressing into images of poverty and sickness. While the planning of the banquet anticipates abundance and fulfilment, the actual event is marked by the guests' association of food with hunger, gnawing, and vomiting. The description of food's allure is relegated to a distant past that can only be recovered through Celestina's linguistic magic. But the banquet scene is more than just a collection of food metaphors that suggest social ills. It is a textual centre for Rojas's examination of a repressive power structure and social injustice. It provides the only textual space where all the servants meet and carve their trajectories. Pármeno manifests his moral transgression by organizing the celebration and Sempronio is consumed by self-indulgent pleasures without regard for its effects on others. The banquet brings out Elicia's volatile nature. Her responses to Sempronio's understanding of beauty turn the event from one of camaraderie to verbal attacks that Areúsa continues and reveals what will later surface as her vindictive, violent nature. Finally, the banquet becomes Celestina's last supper where she is portrayed as the drunk old bawd she is, whose oral indulgences are only enjoyed vicariously and whose power of language will soon fail her as well. The banquet celebration in Act IX does not reveal the lofty ideals of virtue recorded in the cooking manuals of the day, nor the pursuit of the Platonic banquet to which Ficino aspires, but rather it shows that the hunger to belong, to survive, to purge oneself of the repressive social structures, drives these characters and moves the text forward.

## NOTES

1 Research for this article was inspired by my participation in a 2009 NEH Summer Seminar at the University of Virginia, directed by E. Michael Gerli, called "Celestina and the Threshold of Modernity." I am most grateful for Professor Gerli's careful reading and helpful suggestions. Support for this article also came from an Artistic and Scholarly Development grant from Illinois Wesleyan University.

2 Since the groundbreaking work of Levi Strauss and Douglas, anthropologists have continued to examine food production and distribution, food's relationship to health, its role in human relationships, and its effects on human relationship with the environment, social relations, and social structures. More recently, "modes of identification," that is, the roles, motivations, and actions of agents in the identification process have begun to take on greater significance. Marcus and Fischer (1986) term these accounts "experimental

ethnography" as they highlight the role of ethnographer in the *problematique* and exposition.

3 Miller, in his work on consumption and material culture, argues that a material culture approach does not reduce humanity by focusing on the object but rather the focus on the object helps us understand more deeply humanity and social relations, particularly by understanding the balance between what we acquire and what we relinquish (2006).

4 Except for selections from *La Celestina*, all translations are my own.

5 Some of the outstanding banquets recorded from the Habsburg dynasty include the banquet that Luis XIV's ambassador, the Duke of Agramont, held for the king's petition of the hand of María Teresa de Austria y Borbón in 1659, in which they serve 500 meat dishes and 300 starters and desserts (Cubillo de Aragón 1659), the Duke of Lerma's banquet in Valladolid 1605 to honour Lord Nottingham, England's ambassador at the court of Spain (Pinheiro da Veiga 1989, 117–18), or the banquet at Doñana that the Duke of Medina Sidonia organized in honour of Philip IV's ascension to the Crown (Alonso 1995). For more on the history of the banquet and its social significance, see Jeanneret (1991).

6 All citations from *La Celestina* are from the Severin edition (2004). All translations from *La Celestina* are from the Singleton edition (1958).

7 Wilhite argues that Pármeno organizes the banquet to befriend Sempronio: "The final step in Parmeno's transformation into a pícaro and a member of Celestina's confederation is to confirm his friendship with Sempronio" (1976, 141).

8 As the son of Doña Juana, the illegitimate daughter of Enrique II, and of Don Pedro, a direct descendent of Jaime II of Aragon, Villena's preoccupation with lineage is directly tied to his own history. In her article, "Chivalric Identity in Enrique de Villena's *Arte Ciscria*," Miguel-Prendes argues that the treatise was a manifestation of Villena's desire to exert his influence in the political arena (2003).

9 While only six virtues are outlined here, another, sound upbringing, is laid out in detail earlier in the text.

10 Alison Weber examines both late fifteenth-century economic conditions and legal and moral discourses that explain the changing relationship between master and servant (1997). These misguided relationships were also rampant in other parts of early modern Europe. Fumerton, in her study on servants and apprentices in early modern London, explains that "[t]he master-servant bond was thus at best insecure and at worst subject to gross violation, unmooring apprentices and servants from any secure social, economic or physical place" (2000, 211).

11 For more on the quality of wine and the names of villages, see Valles Rojo (2007, 290–309).

12 In Act XI, Sempronio reproaches his master's public behaviour. "Por Dios, que huygas de ser traydo en lenguas, que al muy devoto llaman ypócrita. ¿Qué dirán sino que andas royendo los santos?" [I beg you, do not become the subject of gossip. One who is too obviously pious is always deemed a hypocrite. It will be said that the saints are all weary of your presence here] (2004, 249; 1958, 165).

13 Piñero Ramírez suggests that the medical treatise by Bernardo de Gordonio, *Lilio de medicina* [Lily of medicine], may have been available to Rojas at Salamanca as well as many other scientific and philosophical treatises on the nature of wine (1995, 212). For more on the role of wine in the banquet scene, see Cull (2009).

14 Parilla and others have noted the classical sources for the banquet feast in *La Celestina*. She includes Cicero as a source for his treatment on the dignity of old age (2000, 71). For the treatment of Plato's *Symposium*, see Larsen (1994) and for arguments on why Plato is not a source for Rojas, see Round (1993).

15 Burke discusses the five senses in *La Celestina* and how they relate to the humanist banquet of senses (2000, 103–20). He writes, "We certainly cannot be sure that Rojas would have known Ficino's commentary on the *Symposium*, which was not finished until 1474–75, and many scholars have doubted that the author(s) of *Celestina* could have had much familiarity with the ideas of Plato" (2000, 115). Other critics – Larsen, Round, Brocato – are convinced that Rojas was familiar with Plato's work (cited in Burke 2000, 115).

16 Although many cooking manuscripts exist from antiquity, the first printed publication that systematically treats food and cooking belongs to Platina.

17 Like Areúsa's catalogue of edible cosmetic ingredients, the recipe also contains honey; another uses bile for removing blemishes. For more recipes, see Martínez Crespo (1995).

18 Palafox persuasively argues that during the banquet Celestina urges the guests to awaken their appetites for food and sex so that Pármeno and Sempronio might forget their desire to collect on their share of the 100 escudos (2007).

## WORKS CITED

Alemán, Mateo. 1969. *Guzmán de Alfarache*. Vol. 2. Edited by Samuel Gili Gaya. Madrid: Espasa-Calpe.

Alonso, Juan Carlos. 1995. *El tan célebre banquete de Doñana*. Huelva, Spain: Parque Nacional de Doñana y Diputación Provincial de Huelva.

Bourdieu, Pierre. 1984. *Distinction: A Social Critique of the Judgement of Taste*. Translated by Richard Nice. Cambridge, MA: Harvard University Press.

Burke, James F. 2000. *Vision, the Gaze, and the Function of the Senses in Celestina*. University Park, PA: Penn State Press.

Camporesi, Piero. 1980. *Bread of Dreams: Food and Fantasy in Early Modern Europe*. Translated by David Gentilcore. Cambridge: Polity Press.

Covarrubias Orozco, Sebastián de. (1611) 1994. *Tesoro de la lengua castellana o española*. Edited by Felipe Maldonado. Madrid: Castalia.

Cubillo de Aragón, Álvaro. 1659. *Relación del Combite y Real Banquete, que a imitación de los Persas hizo en la Corte de España el Excmo. Sr. D. Juan Alfonso Enríquez de Cabrera al duque de Agramont. Embajador del Rey de Francia Luis XIV en ocasión de pedir la mano de la Infanta Dña. Maria Teresa de Austria y Borbón*. Madrid: Andrés García de la Iglesia.

Cull, Jonathan. 2009. "Celestina's *veritas*: Fetishizing the Salve / *salve* of Healing Wine." *Celestinesca* 33: 39–56.

Fumerton, Patricia. 2000. "London's Vagrant Economy: Making Space for 'Low' Subjectivity." In *Material London ca. 1600*, edited by Lena Cowen Orlin, 206–25. Philadelphia: University of Pennsylvania Press.

Herrero-García, Miguel. 1933. *La vida española del siglo XVII. I Las bebidas*. Madrid: SELE.

Jeanneret, Michel. 1991. *A Feast of Words: Banquets and Table Talk in the Renaissance*. Translated by Jeremy Whiteley and Enna Hughes. Chicago: University of Chicago Press.

Larsen, Kevin S. 1994. "Bed and Board: Significant Parallels between Plato's *Symposium* and Rojas' *La Celestina*." *Neohelicon: Acta Comparationis Litterarum Universarum* 22 (1): 247–68.

Lobera de Ávila, Luis. 1996. *El banquete de nobles caballeros*. San Sebastián, Spain: R & B Ediciones.

Luján, Nestor. 1997. *Historia de la gastronomía*. Barcelona: Folio.

Marcus, George, and Michael Fischer. 1986. *Anthropology as Cultural Critique: An Experimental Moment in the Human Sciences*. Chicago: University of Chicago Press.

Martínez Crespo, Alicia, ed. 1995. *Manual de mugeres en el qual se contienen muchas y diversas reçeutas muy buenas*. Salamanca, Spain: Ediciones Universidad de Salamanca.

Martínez Montiño, Francisco. 1997. *Arte de Cocina, pastelería, vizcochería y conservería* (1611). Valencia: Librerías París-Valencia.

Miguel-Prendes, Sol. 2003. "Chivalric Identity in Enrique de Villena's *Arte Ciscria.*" *La Corónica* 32 (1): 307–42.

Miller, Daniel. 2006. "Consumption." In *Handbook of Material Culture*, edited by Christopher Y. Tilley, 341–54. London: Sage.

Montanari, Massimo. 1996. *The Culture of Food*. Translated by Carl Ipsen. Oxford: Blackwell.

Palafox, Eloísa. 2007. "Celestina y su retórica de seducción: comida, vino y amor en el texto de la *Tragicomedia*." *Revista canadiense de estudios hispánicos* 32 (1): 71–88.

Parilla, Carmen. 2000. "El convite de los 'locos porfiados.'" In *El mundo como contienda: Estudios sobre La Celestina*, edited by Pilar Carrasco, 67–76. Málaga, Spain: Universidad de Málaga.

Pérez Samper, María de los Ángeles. 1997. "Fiesta y alimentación en la España moderna: el banquete como imagen festiva de abundancia y refinamiento." *Espacio, Tiempo y Forma, Serie IV, Historia Moderna* 10: 53–98.

Piñero Ramírez, Pedro. 1995. "*In Taberna Quando Sumus: De Berceo al Lazarillo.*" In *Historia y cultura del vino en Andalucía*, edited by Juan José Iglesias Rodríguez, 201–20. Seville, Spain: Universidad de Sevilla.

Pinheiro da Veiga, Tomé. 1989. *Fastiginia: Vida cotidiana en la corte de Valladolid.* Valladolid: Ayuntamiento de Valladolid.

Platina. 1998. *On Right Pleasure and Good Health*. Edited and translated by Mary Ella Milham. Tempe, AZ: Medieval and Renaissance Texts and Studies.

Rojas, Fernando de. 2004. *La Celestina*. Edited by Dorothy Sherman Severin. Madrid: Cátedra, Letras hispánicas.

Rojas, Fernando de. 1958. *Celestina: A Play in Twenty-one Acts Attributed to Fernando de Rojas*. Translated by Mack Henricks Singleton. Madison, WI: Univeristy of Wisconsin Press.

Round, Nicholas C. 1993. "Celestina, Aucto I: A Platonic Echo and Its Resonances." In *Fernando de Rojas and "Celestina": Approaching the Fifth Centenary. Proceedings of an International Conference in Commemoration of the 450th Anniversary of the Death of Fernando de Rojas. Purdue University, West Lafayette, Indiana, 21–24 November, 1991*, edited by Ivy A. Corfis and Joseph Snow, 93–112. Madison, WI: Hispanic Seminar of Medieval Studies.

Sánchez Meco, Gregorio. 1998. *El arte de la cocina en tiempos de Felipe II*. El Escorial: Consejalía de cultura.

Valles Rojo, Julio. 2007. *Cocina y alimentación en los siglos XVI y XVII*. [Valladolid]: Junta de Castilla y León.

Villena, Enrique de. 1984. *Arte cisoria*. Edited by Russell Brown. Barcelona: Editorial Humanitas.

Vital, Laurent. 1958. *Relación del primer viaje de Carlos V a España.* Translated by Bernabé Herrero. Madrid: Artes gráficas.

Weber, Alison P. 1997. "Celestina and the Discourses of Servitude." In *Negotiating Past and Present: Studies in Spanish Literature for Javier Herrero*, edited by David T. Gies, 127–44. Charlottesville, VA: Rookwood Press.

Wilhite, John F. 1976. "Fernando De Rojas' Pármeno: The Making of a Pícaro." *South Atlantic Bulletin* 41 (2): 137–44. http://dx.doi.org/10.2307/3198811.

# 11 The Prayer of the Immured Woman and the Matter of *Lazarillo de Tormes*

RYAN D. GILES

In 1996, construction workers in the Spanish town of Barcarrota in Extremadura discovered a bundle of books and a *nómina* or paper amulet that had been concealed in a wall for over four and half centuries. Intended to be carried or worn on the body, the *nómina* is inscribed with a prayer and blessings meant to heal and protecting against evil forces and ill fortune.[1] During the sixteenth century, Spanish reformers like Pedro Ciruelo sought to restrict the use of such objects and expose superstitious abuses (1978, chap. 4). The Barcarrota *nómina* was hidden together with equally controversial literary works, including Antonio Vignali's homoerotic *Cazzaria*, the satirical poetry of Clément Marot, and a previously unknown edition of the picaresque masterpiece *Lazarillo de Tormes* (from Medina del Campo dated 1554).[2] Only one book discovered at the site can be directly linked to both the story of *Lazarillo* and the power of textual amulets, and for this reason will be of primary concern in the pages that follow: a Portuguese translation of the popular prayer entitled *Oración de la Emparedada* [Prayer of the immured nun].[3] As we will see, it provides evidence of how the presence and supposed efficacy of amuletic texts can be used to interpret the kind of narrative structure that led to the picaresque novel, a topic that has not been considered in studies of literature and material culture during the early modern period.

The *Oración* is a sixteenth-century printed amulet that begins with the legend of an immured or "walled-in" woman living in a mountain retreat outside of Rome, who fervently prayed that the number of wounds Christ received during his Passion would be known to her (see fig. 1).[4] This unnamed nun was associated with St Bridget of Sweden, a widow who experienced visions of the five *stigmata* wounds suffered during the Crucifixion (in the hands, feet, and side) that are reflected in her calls to

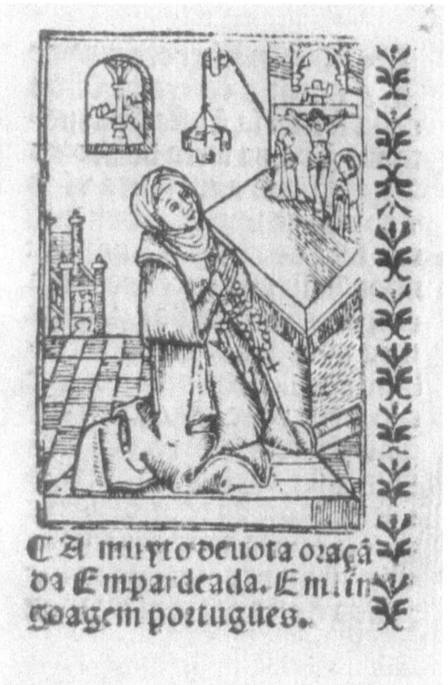
¶ A muyto deuota oraçã
da Emparedada. Em lin
goagem portugues.

Figure 1 Title page of the mid sixteenth-century Portuguese translation of the *Oración de la Emparedada* found at Barcarrota. Biblioteca de Extremadura – FA 263.

prayer: "say five Our Fathers and five Hail Marys in remembrance of the wounds of our Lord ... say this prayer ... 'I ask you, gracious Jesus ... by your five wounds ... deign to keep me safe'" (Birgitta 2008, 155, 167).[5] The elaboration on St Bridget's formula in the *Oración* consists of fifteen petitions for mercy and reflections on the suffering of Christ meant to be read every day of the year in conjunction with the same number of Ave Marias and Pater Nosters, forming a kind of threefold or Trinitarian representation of the Five Wounds. Because this number was used to factor the Measure of Christ's body (the *mensura* or *longitudo Christi*), and the drops of blood shed during his martyrdom, multiples of fifteen were believed to possess apotropaic power and widely used in the production of textual amulets (Skemer 2006, 142–3, 178).[6] The Saviour promises the immured woman that this symbolic formula will liberate fifteen souls from purgatory in the hereafter, and in this world protect and bring happiness ("prazer") and the good life ("boa vida") to any mortal sinner who freely confesses (2008, fols 2–3).[7] Like the Barcarrota *nómina* and other examples from the period, the amuletic powers of the *Oración* are derived not soley from the inscribed efficacy of prayer, but from its material presence: "E o que a rezar ... ou a trouxer consigo ... onde quer que esta oração estever ... eu guardarei aquella casa e livrarei aquella companha ... por pouco trabalho haverás grande galardão" [He who prays or carries it with him ... wherever this prayer is ... I will protect that house and deliver these people ... and with little work you will obtain great gifts] (2008, fol. 4v). The conclusion of the *Oración* explains how a hermit transcribed the text of the *Oración*, shared it with the abbess of a convent, and finally witnessed a raucous company of demons being tortured by the incessant praying of the walled-in woman, who is now described as an "encantadeira e mui palavreira" [sorceress and chatterbox] (2008, fol. 15r).

Scholars have noticed a reference to this prayer in the 1554 Alcalá de Henares edition of *Lazarillo de Tormes*. The rogue's first master is a blind man who partly makes his living by reciting prayers for women of ill-repute, "mesoneras y por bodegoneras y turroneras y rameras, y ansí por semejantes mujercillas, que por hombre casi nunca le vi decir oración" [wives of innkeepers, tavern keepers, confectioners, prostitutes, and other such lowly women, as I almost never saw him saying prayers for a man] (1987, 37).[8] In a crucial scene that foreshadows Lazarillo's final destiny as a wine-peddling town crier and a domesticated cuckold (who is provided for by his wife's lover, the archpriest of Sant Salvador), the blind man comes to Escalona, where horns are mounted on the wall of an inn:

> Iba tentando si era allí el mesón adonde él rezaba cada día por la mesonera la oración de la emparedada, asío de un cuerno y con un gran sospiro dixo ... "algún día te dará este que de la mano tengo alguna mala comida y cena." (1987, 37)
>
> [he was feeling if this was the inn where he recited the prayer of the immured woman every day for the innkeeper's wife, and took hold of one of the horns (a symbol of duped husbands) and said with a great sigh ... "one day this thing that I've got in my hand will give you an ill-deserved day's meals."][9]

While the scene is traditionally viewed as one of four interpolations, Manuel Ferrer-Chivite has more recently suggested that these could have been removed from the author's original text (2000).[10] Whatever the case, critics like Jack Weiner have found that the Alcalá version creates a more tightly connected structure in which the blind man's Escalona prophesies are comically fulfilled through the corruption of Lazarillo, ultimately leading him to consent to a dishonourable marriage. In this essay, I will show how connotations of the amuletic prayer of the walled-in woman in sixteenth-century Spain contribute to this narrative sequence.

Like *Lazarillo de Tormes*, the *Oración de la emparedada* was placed on the 1559 Index of Forbidden Books compiled by Fernando de Valdés (Reusch 1961, 237). Not surprisingly, the pamphlet found in Barcarrota was not just hidden in a wall, but also rebound in a liturgical folio so that its contents could not be readily identified.[11] Inquisitors continued to condemn the *Oración* for what the later 1581 Index of Gaspar de Quiroga classifies as its "promesas y esperanças temerarias y vanas" [vain and reckless promises and hopes], not to mention the inclusion at the end of the prayer of an apocryphal indulgence attributed to "Nicolao papa v" claiming to reveal how many drops of blood were shed during the Passion (Reusch 1961, 383).[12] Even more problematic, as María Cruz García de Enterría has pointed out, the prohibited text likens meditations on the Passion to exorcizing "conjuros" or incantations. Scholars have found that vernacular versions first appeared in fifteenth-century books of hours of the kind that were also listed in the Index of Valdés: "Mandanse quitar las Horas siguientes porque contienen muchas cosas curiosas y supersticiosas" [It is ordered that the following Hours be removed as they contain many strange and superstitious things] (Bujanda 1984, 5:671). From the 1520s on, printing houses continued to disseminate the prayer throughout the Peninsula as "cordel" literature, or cheaply reproduced broadsides that could be sold by street vendors and tied with string to be hung around the neck like *nóminas*.[13]

*Lazarillo de Tormes* provides evidence of how the *Oración* also circulated in sixteenth-century Spain as part of the oral repertoire of blind men who supported themselves by reciting such popular prayers. Additional evidence of this tradition can be found in other satirical texts from the period, some of which García de Enterría lists in her introduction. For example, in Sánchez de Badajoz's *Farsa del Molinero* [Farce of the miller, ca. 1550] a blind man calls out "¡Ayudá, fieles hermanos / al ciego lleno de males! … si mandáis rezar, christianos / ¡Dios os guarde pies y manos, / vuestra vista conservada! / la oración de la enparedada" [Help faithful brothers, the blind man full of maladies! … if you would have me pray, good Christians / May God bless your feet and hands, and your sight be preserved! The prayer of the immured woman] (1886, vv. 249–55). It would seem that the blasphemous street performer in this way associates the *stigmata* commemorated in the prayer with "males" representing his moral failings and bodily maladies.[14] Other literary citations are more concerned with the problem of superstition than the disrepute of blind men. In the *Crónica burlesca del emperador Carlos V* [Burlesque chronicle of the emperor Charles V, ca. 1528], a nobleman crossing a flooded river is said to carry seven *nóminas* and a copy of the *Oración* (Zuñiga 1981, 120–1).[15] The scene can be compared to the second chapter of Juan de Luna's *Segunda parte del Lazarillo* [Part Two of Lazarillo, 1555], when the protagonist of the sequel recites the same prayer after being cast into the sea – bringing to mind the superstitious prayers exposed in Erasmus's *Colloquy* of the Shipwreck.[16] Even more striking is Alejo de Venegas's earlier Erasmian satire in *Agonía del tránsito de la muerte* [Agony of the passage to death, 1537]: "los llevan en el sermón ... dicen que tienen bulas ... la oración del la emparedada. Item, traen consigo una nómina" [they trick them during the sermon ... they say they have pardons ... the prayer of the immured woman. Also, they have with them a textual amulet] (1571, 165; 156).[17] The Alcalá *Lazarillo de Tormes* includes a similar scene in which the rogue helps a pardoner sell phony indulgences, "con cinco paternostres y cinco avemarías ... aun también aprovechan para los padres y hermanos y deudos que tenéis en el purgatorio" [with five Pater Nosters and five Ave Marias ... they will even help your parents and brothers and sisters and other relatives who are in purgatory] (1987, 123).[18] As Weiner has noticed, this is the first time Lazarillo actively participates in such a deception, and it thus anticipates his complicity in a materially beneficial ménage à trois. The episode also recalls the *Oración* evoked in the scene of the blind man's prediction, with its sequence of Our Fathers and Hail Marys in amuletic multiples of fives and its promise to release family members from their purgatorial sentence.

The comic efficacy of the *Oración* in the life of Lazarillo cannot be fully understood without also considering how female characters invoked the walled-in visionary. For instance, in Feliciano de Silva's *Segunda comedia de Celestina* [Second Celestina, 1534], the go-between offers to teach a girl named Poncia the prayer of the "Emparedada" (1988, *cena* 20, p. 314). Poncia becomes alarmed at the suggestion that she wall herself off from the world: "madre, nunca tuve desseo de ser emparedada; por tu vida, que no me lo muestres" [mother, I never had the desire to be immured; on your life, swear you won't teach it to me]. The wordplay continues as Celestina responds with a peal of devious laughter, realizing that the girl has not yet learned how to disguise carnal desires in sacred language: "Hija, pues demparedar has tu voluntad para yr al cielo, que la vía de salvación estrecha es" [Well, daughter, to get to heaven you must unwall your will, for the way of salvation is narrow]. Just as the old bawd's joke is lost on Poncia, Lazarillo fails to see how his blind master's prophesy and recitation of the *Oración de la emparedada* at the inn can be interpreted as a premonition of the "unwalled" sexuality of his future wife. She is, in this sense, comparable to what Particia Parker has characterized as the "dilatory" woman overcoming the "partitions" of Renaissance society and narrative discourse – so that her eroticized verbal and corporal uncontainability "stands as figure" for the deferred closure of the text (11–13).[19]

This connection between the immured woman and uncontrollable wives can be most clearly seen in a surviving fragment of Juan Lorenzo Palmireno's *Comedia Octavia* (Comedy of Octavia, 1564). In the Latin play, a husband is beaten and publicly humiliated after his wife Marcelia insults him, "coniugalem thorum fugiat" [flees from the wedding bed], and arranges for cloistered virgins to celebrate a novena in which they pray for her freedom from the obligation of marital sex by intoning a novena prayer "quæ uulgo *de la emparedada* uocantur" [that is vulgarly called *de la emparedada*] (Palmireno 1566, 117). In this way, promises in the *Oración* of a happy life and the release of souls from purgatory are reinterpreted as a plea for deliverance from the unhappy confines of marriage. Instead of contemplating the Passion, Marcelia's novena celebrates the suffering of an unworthy husband. In addition to the *Oración* text, her revenge humorously counteracts the traditional threat of husbands consigning unruly brides to confinement. For instance, the medieval historian Gregorio Cavero Domínguez documents the case of a Valencian "casa de reclusión que un caballero mandó construir para encerrar a su esposa y que hiciera penitencia por la vida licenciosa que hasta entonces había llevado" [house of reclusion that a gentlemen had constructed to enclose his wife so that she would do penance for the licentious life that she had led until then] (2006, 110).[20] In *Lazarillo de Tormes*, the blind man's clientele of "wives of innkeepers, tavern keepers, confectioners" and "other such lowly women" might have requested this *Oración* for much the same reason as Marcelia. More important, the inversion of prayer in the *Comedia Octavia* sheds light on the characterization of the rogue's unruly spouse in the preordained conclusion of the Alcalá edition. The rumour has spread that she abandons her wedding bed to spend the night with the archpriest, and Lazarillo remembers the horns of the innkeeper in Escalona whose wife paid the blind man to recite the *Oración de la emparedada* (1987,

132). When the cuckold brings up the subject of her adultery, she responds with a barrage of oaths and curses that he fears will bring down the walls of their house, reminiscent of the duplicitous efficacy of the pardoner's oath-taking. Also reminded of the archpriest's generosity, Lazarillo then promises to be content with her coming and going as she pleases: "Entonces mi mujer echó juramentos sobre sí, que yo pensé la casa se hundiera con nosotros; y después tomóse a llorar y a echar maldiciones … y había por bien de que ella entrase y saliese, de noche y de día" [Then my wife swore such oaths that I thought the house would cave in on us; and after that she broke into tears and curses … and I was content that she could go in and out of the house, night or day] (1987, 134). In accordance with the power of the *Oración de la emparedada*, to protect the "home," and bestow a happy life with "little work," and plenty to eat and drink, Lazarillo ironically claims to have arrived at "la cumbre de buena fortuna" [the height of good fortune] in the last *tratado* – in fulfilment of the blind man's prediction of an "ill-deserved day's meals" (1987, 135, 137). This parody at the same time implicates the inversion at the end of the *Oración* mentioned above, as a demon portrays the petitions of the immured woman as the cursed incantations of a "sorceress and chatterbox." When the blind man's prediction at the inn "where he recited the prayer" finally comes to pass, the blessings of the bride of Christ in the *Oración* are transformed into the oaths, curses, and extramural sexuality of Lazarillo's wife.

Such an association reflects medieval and early modern anxieties over controlling the speech and sexuality of walled-in women, leading to what Peter Stallybrass has identified as the "*topos* that presents woman as that treasure which, however locked up, always escapes. She is the gaping mouth, the open window, the body that transgresses its own limits" (128). These kinds of preoccupations can already be seen in Gonzalo de Berceo's thirteenth-century *Poema de Santa Oria* (Poem of St Aurea), where an anchoress shuts herself off from the temptations of fallen language and the urges of the flesh, and her body becomes an enclosure worthy to receive the Bridegroom: "ovo con su carne baraja e contienda … que non salliessen dende vierbos desconvenientes … un rencón angosto entró emparedada … esta reclusa vaso de caridat" [with her body she clashed and battled … to hold back indiscreet words … she entered a narrow corner to be walled-in … this enclosed vessel of God's love] (1981, stanzas 16c, 18d, 20b, 25a). Julian Weiss has shown how Berceo portrays St Aurea as at once physically confined and spiritually opened up.[21] It is also worth noting that this contrast is reflected in the dual meaning of the term *reclusum* in medieval Latin as *clausum* (closed) and / or *apertum* (open). In the fourteenth-century *Revelations* that informed the *Oración de la emparedada*, St Bridget similarly identifies herself as an enclosed *sponsa Christi* receiving the espousals of the Saviour prefigured in the Song of Songs: "I have chosen you and taken you as my bride ... you ought to be ready for the wedding to my divinity, in which there is no carnal lust but the sweetest spiritual delight" (2008, 1.2.3–4, 1.20.7). According to Alfonso of Jaén, the Spanish anchorite who recorded and defended her *Revelations* – and seems to have inspired the unnamed hermit in the *Oración* – Bridget's detractors were sometimes punished with horrible afflictions.[22] Nonetheless, denunciations persisted into the fifteenth century, when Jean Gerson casts doubt on the visions of ascetic women who engage their confessors in "continual conversations" and "lengthy accounts," displaying what he views as an "unhealthy curiosity which leads to gazing about and talking, not to mention touching," indicative of a "harmful love toward God or toward holy persons, rather than being moved by true, holy, and sincere charity" (Sahlin 2001, 165).[23] During the same period, Spanish penitential writers and church synods repeatedly warned against the scandal of *emparedadas* breaking their vows of silence, receiving frequent visitors, and brazenly entering and leaving their cells.[24] As Stallybrass puts it in his study of feminine enclosure, "the mouth, chastity, the threshold ... these three areas were frequently collapsed into each other" (126). It is in this context that demons in the *Oración* depict an immured scandalizer, the bawd in the *Segunda Celestina* describes an unwalling of female desire, and Lazarillo relates the story of the unconfined libido and unleashed tongue of his wife. Her carnal relationship with the aptly named archpriest of the "Holy Saviour" can be understood as a travesty of the divine love that Christ visits upon his *sponsa* in the alleged visions of saints like Bridget of Sweden and her legendary, heterodox offshoot, the *emparedada*.[25]

During her lifetime, Bridget was repeatedly accused of witchcraft and threatened with prosecution for heresy. Sixteenth-century Spanish women who followed her example could expect to face the same kind of suspicions, and were in some cases punished with ecclesiastical confinement. For instance, the nun Magdalena de la Cruz claimed to have experienced visions after making an opening in her cell wall to contemplate the sacred host, later confessed to having carnal relations with a demon, and was sentenced by the Inquisition in 1544 to "emparedamiento ... mandamos que esté encerrada perpetuamente en un monasterio" [immurement ... we order that she be perpetually confined in a monastery] (Imirizaldu 1977, 61).[26] The same condition of enclosure or *reclusum* that had enabled her to open up to the Divine, and helped give credence to her revelations, was ultimately used to shut off and silence her. Later mystics were also subjected to this penance or *murus strictus*, as in the case of María de la Visitación, who was condemned in the 1580s for falsely claiming to have received the five *stigmata* from her Bridegroom for fifteen days – the same talismanic number used in the *Oración de la emparedada* and other amuletic texts. Such rulings bring to mind the demonic characterization of the walled-in woman as a scandalous conjurer, as well as the revelations of her prayer. A particularly revealing example can be found in proceedings brought against the early seventeenth-century prophetess known as Juana de la Cruz or the "Enbustera" or Trickster, denouncing her as a heretic:

> Tocada de los herrores de los alumbradoss, engañadora, escandalossa ... diçiendo que a tenido muchas pláticas con ... Jesús ... es mentira aver dicho que es doncella y que avía hecho boto de castidad y tanbien su marido y que la verdad es averse comunicado carnalmente y confiesa ... mentirossa, enbelecadora. (Imirizaldu 1977, 97, 104, 111)

> [Influenced by Illuminist errors, a scandalous deceiver ... saying that she has often spoken with ... Jesus ... she lies by claiming to be a maiden and having made a vow of chastity, as does her husband, for the truth is they have had carnal relations and she confesses ... she is a liar, a fraud.][27]

These kind of investigations suggest that early audiences could have interpreted connotations of the *emparedada* in *Lazarillo de Tormes* as alluding to the adultery of Lazarillo's wife in a parodic vision of mystical marriage. The idea of immurement might have also brought to mind the Inquisitorial penalization of women, whether for masquerading as visionary brides of Christ, or for other crimes.

The sentence passed against María de la Visitación orders the walled-in penitent to fast on bread and water, receive further unspecified mortifications, and recite the Psalm "miserere mei" [Have mercy on me] (Imirizaldu 1977, 196).[28] Consonant with the treatment of other false visionaries, the Inquisition mandates that all writings and relics related to her cult should be gathered and burned in public. The penance of this visionary is distinctly reminiscent of the penance of St Thais, a popular reformed sinner in late medieval and early modern hagiographic collections that present her *vita eremitica* as the mirror image of her former life, when she was closed off from faith and open to the world. Thais confessed to an abbot who entered the innermost chamber of her brothel to convert her, an enclosure where no man had ever been received and only God could see her sins. She expresses her contrition in the public square, throwing all of the goods earned from her sin into a bonfire. The abbot then mandates that Thais immure herself in a "cella pequeñuela," the entrance of which is sealed with molten iron, leaving only a small opening to receive "un poco de pan e de agua" [a little bread and water] (Beresford 2007, 135). When the repentant prostitute asks where she should relieve herself, the confessor harshly chastises her: "¡aquí en tu celda como tú lo meresciste! ... tú no eres digna de rogar a Dios nin de tomarle en tu boca suzia ... mas solamente ... di muchas vezes esta palabra ... 'ave mercet de mí'" [here in your cell as you have deserved! ... you are not worthy to pray to God or speak his name in your filthy mouth ... so only ... say these words repeatedly... *miserere mei*] (Beresford 2007, 134–5). Following a vision of three virgins on a celestial bed representing the immured woman's fear of God, shame for her past life, and newly found love of virtue, the abbot releases her and Thais lives for a period of fifteen days, a number that associates her triumph over evil and purified body with the apotropaic *mensura Christi*.

By the time *Lazarillo de Tormes* was published, this long-standing connection between visionary reclusion and the punishing and absolving of prostitutes and other promiscuous women had become something of running joke. In the *Lozana Andaluza* (1528), a prostitute known as the "emparedada" seems to be making a burlesque allusion to the filthy cell of St Thais when she asks her madam, "¿por qué no entró? ... ¿pensó que estaba al potro?" [Why didn't you come in? ... Did you think I was on the pot?] (Delicado 1985, 312). An earlier commentary in the *Carajicomedia* (1519) portrays a walled-in prostitute known as Cáceres who remains in her chamber for thirty years: "es su costumbre estar a su puerta muy devota enclavijadas sus manos cantando lamentaciones muchas vezes, recibiendo el precio de su persona" [she is customarily found at the door with her hands crossed and nailed, very devoutly singing lamentations over and over, receiving a price for her person] (1981, st. 73).[29] As I have shown elsewhere, the *Carajicomedia* parodies Ambrosio de Montesino's 1514 translation of the *Vita Christi* of Ludolph of Saxony, in addition to the fifteenth-century *Laberinto de Fortuna*.[30] In the gloss on Cáceres, the poet appears to be subverting Montesino's depiction of "una venerable matrona emparedada ... que desseava saber el cuento de todas las llagas de Jesú Cristo e que por este desseo avia gastado muchos tiempos y lagrimas" [a venerable walled-in matron ... who wished to know the number of all the wounds of Jesus Christ and for this desire spent long periods in tears] (Ludolph 1551, fol. 40r). While the *Cartuxano* goes on to describe a numerological revelation and the prayer found in the *Oración de la emparedada*, the *Carajicomedia* features an unrepentant sex worker who, instead of praying for the visitation of her mystical husband, continues to receive customers and moan mournfully within the walls of her enclosure. Instead of imitating the wounds of Christ, she graphically exhibits the stigma of a fallen woman. In keeping with these precedents, *Lazarillo de Tormes* links the immured woman with prostitutes and female clientele of the blind man, along with a wife whose adulterous affair with the archpriest of San Salvador marks the high point in a life of wounding humiliation.

Significantly, this affair occurs at a time when the Spanish church was redoubling its efforts to enforce discipline among the clergy, partly in reaction to dangerous reform movements that, as Thomas Hanrahan notes, proposed "the abolition of clerical celibacy" (1983, 335). Lazarillo's precarious situation is first mentioned in the prologue as the "caso" or matter that he has been asked to relate "muy por extenso … por que se tenga entera noticia de mi persona" [very extensively … to have a full report of who I am] for an audience identified only as "Vuestra Merced" [Your Honour] (1987, 89, 130).[31] Lazarillo responds by justifying and incriminating himself with a tongue-in-cheek account that conceals and exposes, alternating between reflections on his formerly naive point of view and his cynical perspective in the final *tratado.* David Gitlitz has compared the narrator's strategies to Inquisitorial confessions in which *conversos* or new Christians were compelled to give reports of their own experiences, as well as the lives of others, and appear to have engaged in comparable "rhetorical techniques of disclosure and evasion" (2000, 54).[32] Other scholars have emphasized the narrator's use of euphemism and preterition in anticipation of the sexual corruption of his "caso," as when Lazarillo takes refuge with spinner "mujercillas" [little women], "wears out his shoes" and other "cosillas" [little things] with a lecherous and apparently bisexual Mercedarian, and "grinds colours" for a painter of tambourines (Thompson and Walsh 1988, Shipley 1982; *Lazarillo* 1987, 93, 110–11, 125). I have found that the *Oración de la emparedada* invoked in the Alcalá edition plays into this sort of pseudo-confessional rhetoric. In sixteenth-century Spain, the prayer was linked with transgressions of the flesh and the Inquisitorial menace that Gitlitz and others have shown to be moulding and casting a shadow over the narrative. The banned *Oración* raised suspicions by offering the kind of "happiness in this world" that Lazarillo seeks, together with extravagant promises of perfect contrition, confession, redemption through the Eucharist, and deliverance from evil forces and the pains of purgatory:

> Ho que a rezar ou a fezer rezar ou ha trouxer consigo … darlhej … a comer o meu sanctisimo corpo, o qual o liurara da fome pa sempre. E darlhej a beber ho meu precioso sangue con o qual nunca auera sede … darlhey a beber hũ singular beber da fonte da minha diuindad. Outrosi, qualquer pessoa que esteuer em pecado mortal ainda que aja trinta annos que se nan aja confessado, e se confessar con amarga contriçam e esta oraçam conprir, lhe perdoarey todos seus pecados, e o liurarey do poderio de justiça e do diabo. ("A muyto devota oração da Empardeada em linguagem português" 2008, fol. 3)
>
> [He who prays it or has it recited or carries it with him … I will feed him with my holiest body, which will free him from hunger forever; and I will quench his thirst with my precious blood, so that he is never again thirsty … I will give him an incomparable drink from the fountain of my Divinity … whosoever finds himself in mortal sin, though he has not confessed for thirty years, if he confesses with bitter contrition, and fulfills this prayer, I will pardon all sins, and I will free him from the forces of judgment and the devil]

These benefits can be meaningfully contrasted with the decidedly uncontrite disclosures and quasi-Eucharistic redemption that characterize *Lazarillo de Tormes*. In fact, the narrator first recounts his early experiences of thirst and starvation as a kind of parodic excommunication in which the blind man bashes his head with a wine jug, deprives him of its "fuentecilla" [little fountain] – and, while cleaning his wounds with the fruit of the vine, entertains the innkeeper's wife and her friends by predicting that the same substance that now heals his wounds will someday bless him (1987, 31, 42–3). In the next *tratado*, a miserly priest refuses to share a store of bread that the starving rogue worships like the Corpus Christi: "por consolarme, abro el arca, como vi el pan, comencé de adorar, no osando rescebillo … contemplar en aquella cara de Dios" [to console myself, I open the trunk; as I looked upon the bread, I began to adore it, not daring to receive it … contemplating in it the face of God] (1987, 58). As we have seen, Lazarillo finally arrives at the "height of all good fortune" promised in the *Oración*, and foretold by the blind man, by earning an "ill deserved day's meals" as a town crier selling wines and profiting from his wife's extramarital affair with a salvific archpriest – though he swears to her honesty "sobre la hostia sagrada" [on the sacred Host] (1987, 135, 37, 134).[33] In this way, the conclusion to the Alcalá narrative with its "happy ending" comically subverts the alleged efficacy of the prayer to grant even the most obstinate sinners absolution and admittance to the Lord's Supper.

The promise of forgiveness and penance made in the blind man's heterodox *Oración* can be fruitfully compared to Inquisitorial proceedings against walled-in women. These sinners could be readmitted to the *Coena Domini* only after confessing and receiving their sentence at an auto de fé where they were often expected to wear nooses around their necks and face a range of other public humiliations. For instance, when Magdalena de la Cruz was sentenced to immurement for a series of alleged crimes – including the earlier-mentioned use of sorcery to view the blessed sacrament through a hole in her cell – the tribunal specified that she appear with "una bela encendida en las manos y una mordaza a la lengua y una soga" [with a lit candle in her hand, a gag in her mouth, and a rope around her neck] (Imirizaldu 1977, 61). Juana the Illuminist "Trickster" was similarly paraded with "una bela de çera en la mano y una soga a la garganta y una coroça en la caveça … sea sacada en una bestia … con voz de pregonero que manifeste su delito" [a wax candle in her hand, a rope around her neck, and a conical hat on her head … may she appear on the back of a beast … with a town crier's voice declaring her crime] (Imirizaldu 1977, 118). The practice of condemning prisoners to *murus strictus*, escorted by town criers and wearing esparto collars and gags corresponds to another prophecy that the blind man makes just before arriving at the Escalona inn, when he touches the "sogas" that hang at a shoemaker's shop: "mochacho, salgamos de entre tan mal manjar, que ahoga sin comerlo … según las mañas que llevas, lo sabrás y verás cómo digo verdad" [boy, let us flee from such bad fare, for it suffocates without even being eaten … with all of your tricks, you will come to know and see how I speak the truth] (1987, 37). In the Alcalá text, Lazarillo reflects on this divination after finding work as a town crier who, apart from peddling wines, accompanies criminals through the streets of Toledo:

> Tengo cargo de … acompañar los que padecen persecuciones por justicia y declarar a voces sus delictos, pregonero … En el cual oficio, un día que ahorcábamos a un apañador … llevaba una buena soga de esparto, conoscí y caí en la cuenta de la sentencia que aquel mi ciego amo había dicho … Teniendo noticia de mi persona el señor arcipreste de Sant Salvador … procuró casarme con un criada suya … y hasta ahora no estoy arrepentido … tengo de mi señor arcipreste todo favor y ayuda … mas malas lenguas … no nos dejan vivir diciendo no sé qué y sí sé qué de que ven mi mujer irle a hacer la cama y guisalle de comer … y habido algunas malas cenas por esperalla algunas noches hasta las laudes, y aún más, y se me ha venido a la memoria lo que mi amo el ciego me dijo en Escalona, estando asido del cuerno

> ... Mi señor ... me habló un día ... delante de ella ... "quien ha de mirar a dichos de malas lenguas nunca medrará." (1987, 129–32)[34]
>
> [I am charged with ... following those who suffer persecution for the sake of justice and calling out their crimes, a town crier ... one day we hung a thief ... he wore a course noose, and I recognized and fell under the sentence that that blind master of mine had pronounced ... The reverend archpriest of the Holy Saviour having heard reports of me... arranged a marriage for me with a servant of his ... and I have repented to this day ... I have all the favours and help from my lord the archpriest ... yet malicious tongues ... will not leave us be, saying I don't know what, and I do know what about having seen my wife go and make his bed and cook his food ... I have had some bad meals waiting up for her some nights until morning prayers, or even later, and I recalled what my master the blind man said to me in Escalona, when he was holding the horn ... My reverend Lord ... spoke to me one day ... in her presence ... "you'll never get on in life if you take notice of malicious tongues."]

In keeping with the oracular horns and prayer of a walled-in "chatterbox" at the Escalona inn, the meaning of the shoemaker's ropes becomes increasingly clear in subsequent episodes. First, when Lazarillo wears down the soles of his shoes – presumably made of esparto – in the company of the errant Mercedarian. This link between sexual corruption and worn out ropes anticipates the rogue's role in promoting the wines of his wife's lover while at the same time proclaiming the misdeeds of criminals bound with *sogas*. The rogue at once speaks as a town crier announcing his own crimes along with those of his associates, and as a haltered criminal gagged and suffocated by what the blind man calls "bad fare." The narrator's discourse is stifled, euphemistic, marked by preterition and passing allusion, and yet it has the effect of loudly disclosing unsavoury truths in spite of the threat of censorship and the spectre of Inquisitorial punishment. He claims to have put a lid on the scandal of his wife by blasphemously swearing to her honesty, but instead succeeds in amplifying the clamour of "malicious tongues": "desta manera no me dicen nada, y you tengo paz en mi casa" [this way they tell me nothing, and I have peace in my house] (1987, 135). His pronouncement brings to mind the last words of benediction, "in pace," from the *Ordo Inclusorum* or ritual of immurement, that were also used by the Holy Office to designate the walled-in chambers of penitents.[35] While Lazarillo's unfaithful, cursing wife cannot be contained, he remains trapped. The "peaceable" confines of his house are ironically foreshadowed by the *Oración de la emparedada*'s power to protect the home of "he who prays or carries it with him," and also recalls the tomblike quarters that Lazarillo shares with the squire, "tener cerrada la puerta con llave ni sentir arriba ni abajo pasos de viva persona ... Todo lo que yo había visto eran paredes" [having the door closed and locked without a sign of any living person above or below ... All I had seen were walls] (1987, 73). Later in the same episode Lazarillo hears a widow in a funeral procession crying out that her husband must now live in a dark and mournful dwelling, and becomes convinced that the dead man will be brought to his house to rest *in pace*.[36] Like recurrent noose imagery, the squire's sepulchral dwelling takes on an especially ironic significance in the Alcalá narrative.

As I hope to have demonstrated, this version of *Lazarillo de Tormes* invokes the *Oración de la emparedada* to reveal key elements of the prophesized "matter" of the rogue's marriage and ultimate occupation. The amuletic prayer correlates with the pardoner's appeal to say five Hail Marys and Our Fathers for relatives in purgatory, and how the "unwalling" of the immured woman in other literary texts coincides with the revelation of the archpriest of Sant Salvador's "dilatory" lover. She too parodies visions of mystical espousal, wounds of the Passion, and vows of silence taken by walled-in female saints, subjecting her husband to a cuckold's martyrdom in the tradition of unruly women punished with immurement. Accordingly, the benefits of the prayer are comically fulfilled through Lazarillo's adulterous arrangement: material contentment is granted, the palate quenched, the belly filled, and an incorrigible sinner's confession leads to a mock Eucharistic supper. Denied the bread and cup of life by a string of abusive earlier masters, the town crier's meals and the wine he sells are now provided by the concubinary archpriest. Finally, we have seen how the apotropaic potency to safeguard the houses of those who say, hear, or wear the *Oración* is inverted by the "peace" of Lazarillo's house, and the connections between worn ropes, lost innocence, and the noosing and muzzling of prisoners condemned to *murus strictus*.

These findings suggest that the Lazarillo character is, in a sense, bound by the amuletic text that the blind man recites, as it seems to exert an ironic force over the course of his fictional life, equivalent to the binding physical presence of a *nómina* or *cordel* prayer hung around the neck or otherwise carried on the body. The stakes of the proleptic, intertextual relationship between *Lazarillo* and the *Oración* that has concerned me can be further illuminated by turning to one last work from the Barcarrota cache, *De Lingua* (On language, 1525). A Spanish translation of the text went through several editions during the first half of the sixteenth century, until "Lengua de Erasmo, en Romance y en Latin" was placed on the 1559 Index, along with the two books from Barcarrota discussed in this study. In this treatise, Erasmus takes on his detractors by contrasting an uncontrolled torrent of printed books, many of them full of "indiscreet chattering, headlong lying" and the product of a "beguiling, impious and blaspheming tongue," with the restrained "new tongue" of true Christianity curing "men's souls with holy incantations" and offering "instead of accusation against our neighbor, confession of our own evils" (1989, 403–10). As Carla Mazzio points out, this torrent of escaping words can be related to "genital and lingual dilation" as an "analogue to the activity of narration itself ... to spread abroad or make large, to amplify, to tell" (101). Lazarillo demonstrates that he cannot control his tongue and speak the *lingua nova* any more than demons can understand the prayers of the immured woman as anything other than incantatory chatter. His story both denies and verifies the allegations of "malas lenguas," illustrating what Erasmus sees as a linguistic duplicity that breaks through the bounds of propriety represented by the tongue's natural, censoring enclosure behind its barrier of teeth. In spite of the rogue narrator's gestures of discretion and dissimulation, he remains incapable of controlling or walling-in his own tongue.[37]

## NOTES

1 This prayer was known as the Trisagion or *sanctus*. The *nómina* is also inscribed with a blessing from Christ's apocryphal letter to Abgarus, promising to cure the king of Edessa of an illness (see Skemer 2006, 96–104). Inside the circle is the word "thethagramathon" signifying the ineffable name of God, as well as an anchor cross and a star of David.

2 The other sixteenth-century texts found in the wall are two works of chiromancy (*Super Chyromantiam* and *Chyromantia del Tricasso*), two polemics against *conversos* and Muslims (the *Alborayque* and *Confusione della Setta Machumetana* translated from the work of Juan Andrés), a manual for exorcism (*Exorcismo mirabile da disfare ogni sorte di maleficii*), a collection of prayers in Hebrew, Latin, and Greek (*Precationes aliquot celebriores, e sacris Biblijs desumptae, ac in studiosorum gratiam lingua Hebraica, Graeca, & Latina*), and a treatise that will be discussed later, Erasmus's *Lingua*. Marot's work is often anticlerical, and one of his more well-known poems concerns a wily servant or "valet."

3 It is clear that the prayer was translated from Castilian (Carrasco González 2005, 51–2) to the 1500 Portuguese version that appears in a book of hours; it has been studied by Arthur Askins, and closely relates to the later Barcarrota text.

4 In the *Oración*, Jesus appears and reveals that his wounds totaled 6,676, a number symbolically linked to exorcism (the belief that 6,666 demons comprised the legion in Luke 8:36), the Apocalypse (three sixes as the number of the Beast), subsequent prayers in memory of the Seven Wounds (the Scourging and Crown of Thorns combined with the five *stigmata*), and the Seven Last Words or utterances of Christ (Mark 15:34, Matt. 27:46, Luke 23:34, 43, 46, and John 19:26–30). Other versions of the so-called *Quindecim Orationes* (The Fifteen Prayers or "O's") give the number as 6666, or multiply fifteen by the number of days in the year (either 365 or 366) to arrive at the total number of wounds, as in the case of Ambrosio de Montesino's sixteenth-century translation of the *Vita Christi* of Ludolph of Saxony (the 1514 *Cartuxano*), and the examples discussed by Robin Flowers.

5 Translation by Denis Searby. Subsequent translations in this discussion are mine unless otherwise noted. This fivefold formula is repeated elsewhere in the *Revelations* (Birgitta 2008, 154). A striking description of Bridget's visions of the stigmata can be found earlier in the text: "I felt almost comforted to be able to touch his body as it was taken down from the cross, and take it in my arms, and explore his wounds" (2008, 127). Graphic representations of the wounds and drops of blood also appear in amulets and were believed to increase their power (see Skemer 2006, 143, 248, 265).

6 Uses of the number fifteen to calculate the length of Christ's body were based on the measurements of the Golden Cross relic in the Hagia Sophia and specifically believed to protect "against evil, misfortune, and sudden death," in keeping with the promises of the *Oración* (Skemer 2006, 143). Fifteen Mysteries were sometimes used in rosary prayers (consisting of Joyful, Sorrowful, and Glorious sets of five), though this was not yet standardized during the period (see Winston-Allen 1997). Fifteen can also refer to the number of steps of the Temple, or the cubits needed to build the ark – the latter was interpreted by Ambrose as a threefold (Trinitarian) product of the five senses (Hopper 1938, 1115–16). See also Arthur Askins, who notes fifteen is "the talisman number in a variety of legends," and thus frequently used in these kind of prayers (2007, 243). Fittingly, the number is twice associated with healing in *Lazarillo de Tormes*, after the rogue is beaten by the priest (1987, 70, 71).

7 "Sejam livradas das penas do purgatório quinze almas … Outrossi, qualquer pessoa que estever em pecado mortal ainda que haja trinta anos que se não

haja confessado: e se confessar ... será outorgada ... boa vida ... darei em este mundo prazer" (2008, fols 2–3).

8 In my translation of *Lazarillo*, I have consulted the English text of Michael Alpert, *"Lazarillo De Tormes" and "The Swindler": Two Spanish Picaresque Novels*, rev. ed. (New York: Penguin, 2003). Spanish citations of *Lazarillo* are from the edition of Francisco Rico.

9 The prayer is to be said every day, presumably, to arrive at a numerological formula for the counting of Christ's wounds (see note 4).

10 As opposed to scholars and editors like Alberto Blecua (*Lazarillo* 1974, 58), Ferrer-Chivite wonders whether the interpolations were not expurgated parts of the original text. The Alcalá printer, Salcedo, specifically presents the book as follows: "nuevamente impresa, corregida y de nuevo añadido en esta segunda impresión ... a veinte y seis de Febrero" [newly printed, corrected and again amended in this second edition ... on 26 February] (*Lazarillo* 1987, 13). In addition to this reissue, and the newly discovered Medina del Campo, 1554 versions were published in Burgos and Amberes. While Rico and others have proposed a plausible stemma, the sequence remains impossible to definitively determine, as Jesús Cañas Murillo has pointed out (92–3). The authorship of *Lazarillo* also remains a mystery, although candidates continue to be proposed. Mercedes Agulló has most recently found suggestive evidence supporting the theory that Diego Hurtado de Mendoza contributed in some way to the 1573 expurgated edition of *Lazarillo*.

11 María Cruz García de Enterría notes that such prayers first appeared in books of hours, and Askins discusses versions dating prior to the association with St Bridget. García de Enterría documents a manuscript possessed by María de Aragón in the mid fifteenth century, mentioned in an inventory as "*De la dona emparedada*" (1997, xi).

12 The prayer had already been banned in the 1551 index (García de Enterría 1997, xv). While the indulgence of Pope Nicholas V is particular to the Barcarrota prayer, the amuletic count of blood drops spilled during the Passion can be found in versions outside the Peninsula. Unlike the Trinitarian number given in the *Oración*, 39,330, Skemer notes that the count was sometimes calculated using multiples of 365, similar to the totals of Christ's wounds (2006, 143).

13 García de Enterría notes early printed copies of *Oracions de la Emparedada* listed by book dealer in Barcelona in 1524 (1997), and Askins documents a number of other sixteenth-century editions in Catalan and Castilian (2007, 238).

14 The sightless performer could also be equating his condition to the blindfolding of Christ during the Passion, as an image that is evoked in such prayers.

15 This text was composed by the court fool of Carlos V, Francesillo de Zúñiga. The character of the fearful nobleman is on his way to the king's wedding, together with a catalogue of other satirized figures.

16 The prayer – showing how the sequel attributed to Juan de Luna drew on the Alcalá version of *Lazarillo* – is listed in a litany of others supposedly taught to him by the blind man, "tienen virtud contra los peligros del agua" [because they had power against the dangers of water] Luna 1988, 55). This claim correlates with the alleged promise made to the immured woman to protect against sudden death, "como livrey a são pedro das ondas do mar" [like I saved Peter from the waves of the sea] ("A muyto devota oração da Empardeada em linguagem português" 2008, fol. 3v).

17 Marcel Bataillon has related this text to Erasmian thinking, in particular the *Modus orandi* (Manner of Prayer). The *nómina* has an inscription reading "si ergo me quaeritis" [if therefore you seek me]. This phrase is from the Gospel of John, a favourite source for textual amulets due its hymn to the word (Skemer 2006, 87–9). When Jesus is about to be arrested he says: "I have told you that I am he. If therefore you seek me, let these go their way that the word might be fulfilled" [dixi vobis quia ego sum si ergo me quaeritis sinite hos abire ut impleretur sermo] (1994, 1941, 18:8–9)

18 Lazarillo also helps stage a fake exorcism in this episode, and, as Weiner points out, the Alcalá interpolation stresses his complicity when the pardoner asks him not to reveal the deception of the burning cross (1985, 828; *Lazarillo* 1987, 123–4).

19 Her subversion can also be compared with that of later female rogue characters or *pícaras*. In her discussion of Francisco López de Ubeda's *Pícara Justina* (1605), Anne Cruz points out that early modern manuals such as Fray Luis de León's *La perfecta casada* explicitly compared the virtue of a wife's "closed mouth" with the "enclosed state in which she should ideally remain" (1999, 154).

20 In the fifteenth-century *Arcipreste de Talavera o Corbacho*, a wife complains that her controlling husband would have her immured (Martínez de Toledo 1970, 128). Centuries later, the idea of immuring unfortunate brides provides the subject matter for "La inocencia castigada" in María de Zayas's 1647 *Desengaños amorosos* (1989).

21 In accordance with the *Summa theologica* of Thomas Aquinas, the legend demonstrates how visions properly come to Christian women in private (1948, II–II, Q. 177, art. 2). Shari Horner has examined a hagiographic "discourse of enclosure" in medieval English works (2001).

22 For example, a warden is described by Alfonso of Jaén as suffering from a painful swelling of the groin after making false accusations against Bridget (Sahlin 2001, 155).

23 Three of Gerson's works deal with the discernment of divine versus malevolent spirits, including *De distinctione verarum revelationum a falsis* [On distinguishing true and false revelations, 1401], *De probatione spirituum* [On testing the spirits, 1415], *De examinatione doctrinarum* [On investigating teachings, 1423]. On the question of *discretio spirituum*, see the study of Rosalynn Voaden (1999).

24 For example, in the *Libro de confesions* Martín Pérez urges "enparedadas" to maintain their enclosure at all times, so as to avoid the grave scandal that arises from "las entradas a ellas o de las sus salidas" [entering to visit them or their leaving] (2002, 416).

25 As Rico notes in his edition, the Sant Salvador parish in Toledo had no archpriest (1987, 130). This suggests that the title was meant to allude to the unsavoury reputation of archpriests, legendary by this time, in contrast to the meaning of "Holy Saviour."

26 Henry Kamen points out that, in such cases, perpetual sentences could be shortened considerably (1998, 88, 201).

27 Prior to her condemnation in 1588, the cult of María de la Visitación had spread far and wide, to the extent that Luis de Granada penned an account of her life (see Imirizaldu 1977, 122–75). Another visionary sentenced to reclusion, Lucrecia de León, was linked with the court of Philip II and brought before the Inquisition for prophesying the defeat of the Armada and collapse of the Empire (Imirizaldu 1977, 63–9). On the story of Lucrecia, see Richard Kagan's *Lucrecia's Dreams* (1990).

28 The sentence specifies "cárcel perpetua ... en una celda o apossento ... cada semana saldrá para recibir una disciplina que durará en quanto dixere un miserere mei" [perpetual imprisonment ... in a cell or chamber ... once a week she will emerge to receive a discipline that will last until she says a *misere*] (Imirizaldu 1977, 196).

29 This poem appeared at the end of an expanded reprint of the *Cancionero de obras de burla provocantes a risa* and was published in Valencia. It recently inspired the title of a novel by Juan Goytisolo.

30 See *The Laughter of the Saints* (25–32).

31 "Your Honour" refers to an authority figure identified in the text only as a "friend" of the archpriest (1987, 130).

32 This view is also supported by sixteenth-century proceedings against heretical women, like the case of Juana the "Trickster" discussed above, that investigate husbands and other men found to be complicit in the concealment of illicit activities (Imirizaldu 1977, 104).

33 Elsewhere I have linked this imagery to Lazarillo's simultaneous, parodic imitation of the life of John the Baptist and festive aspects of his cult (2009). See

also Javier Herrero's study of this water and wine pattern. Not surprisingly, the rogue's final oath was censored from expurgated editions printed after the appearance of the 1554 *Lazarillo* on the Index.

34 The image from the Beatitudes, "los que padecen persecuciones por la justicia" [those who suffer persecutions for the sake of justice], recalls the arrest of Lazarillo's father, "confesó y no negó, y padesció persecución por la justicia" [he confessed and did not deny, and suffered persecution for the sake of justice], evoking the biblical phrase applied to John the Baptist, "confessus est et non negavit" (1987, 129, 14; Matt 5:6, John 1:20).

35 The phrase forms part of the Office of the Dead. The association of the quarters of walled-in visionaries with tombs can be seen in an account of the fifteenth-century mystic María de Toledo, "tomó un aposentillo tan estrecho y oscuro que 'más parecía sepultura de muertos que aposento de vivos'" [she took a small room so narrow and dark that "it more closely resembled a tomb for the dead than a room for the living"] (Cavero Domínguez 2006, 117).

36 The rogue complains: "'¡Oh desdichado de mí, Para mi casa llevan este muerto!'" ("Oh woe is me, they are taking this dead man to my house!") (1987, 73)

37 Eliciting the question: "Tongue, where have you gone?" (22). This aspect of Erasmus's *Lingua* has been studied by Shane Gasbarra. The final Alcalá interpolation hints at Lazarillo's continued chattiness (inviting a sequelization of "casos"), "de lo que de aquí adelante me suscediere, avisaré a Vuestra Merced" [concerning what has happened from here on, I will give Your Honour notice] (1987, 136).

## WORKS CITED

"A muyto devota oração da Empardeada em linguagem português." 2008. *Artifara: Revista de lenguas y literaturas ibéricas y latinoamericanas* 7 (14). March, 2010. http://www.artifara.unito.it/Nuova%20serie/Artifara-n--7-/Editiones/default.aspx?oid=242&oalias=.

*La muy devota oración de la emparedada*. 1997. Edited and translated by Juan M. Carrasco González. Extremadura: Junta de Extremadura; Consejería de Cultura y Patrimonio.

Agulló, Mercedes. 2010. *A vueltas con el autor de Lazarillo*. Madrid: Calambur.

Aquinas, Thomas. 1948. *Summa theologica*. Translated by Fathers of the English Dominican Province. 3 vols. New York: Benziger Bros.

Askins, Arthur Lee-Francis. 2007. "Notes on Three Prayers in Late 15th Century Portuguese (the *Oração da Empardeada*, the *Oração de S. Leão, Papa*, and the *Justo Juiz*): Text History and Inquisitorial Interdictions." *Península: Revista de Estudos Ibéricos* 4: 235–66.

Bataillon, Marcel. 1950. *Erasmo y España: Estudios sobre la historia espiritual del siglo XVI*. 2 vols. Translated by Antonio Alatorre. México, DF: Fondo de Cultura Económica.

Berceo, Gonzalo de. 1981. *Poema de Santa Oria*. Edited by Isabel Uría Maqua. Madrid: Castalia.

Beresford, Andrew M. 2007. *The Legends of the Holy Harlots: Thais and Pelagia in Medieval Spanish Literature*. Woodbridge, Suffolk, UK, and Rochester, NY: Tamesis.

Bible. 1941. Douay-Rheims Version. New York: Benziger Brothers.

Biblia Sacra. 1994. Iuxta Vulgatam Versionem. Edited by Robert Weber. 4th ed. Stuttgart: Bibelgesellschaft.

Birgitta of Sweden. 2008. *Revelations*. Translated by Denis Searby. Edited by Bridget Morris. 2 vols. Oxford: Oxford University Press.

Bujanda, J.M. de, ed. 1984. *Index de l'Inquisition espagnole, 1551, 1554, 1559*. Vol. 5 of *Index des livres interdits*. Centre d'études de la Renaissance, Editions de l'Université de Sherbrooke. 11 vols. Geneva: Droz.

*Carajicomedia*. 1981. Edited by Carlos Varo. Madrid: Playor.

Carrasco González, Juan M. 2005. "Portugal en la biblioteca de Barcarrota: la *Oración de la Emparedada*." *Anuario de estudios filológicos* 28: 21–34.

Cavero Domínguez, Gregoria. 2006. "Fuentes para el estudio del emparedamiento en la España medieval (siglos XII–XV)." *Revue Mabillon* 17: 105–26.

Ciruelo, Pedro. 1978. *Reprovación de las supersticiones y hechizerías*. Edited by Alva V. Ebersole. Valencia: Albatros Hispanófila.

Cruz, Anne J. 1999. *Discourses of Poverty: Social Reform and the Picaresque Novel in Early Modern Spain*. Toronto: University of Toronto Press.

Delicado, Francisco. 1985. *La Lozana andaluza*. Edited by Claude Allaigre. Madrid: Cátedra.

Erasmus. *Lingua*. 1989. Edited and translated by Elaine Fantham. In *Collected Works of Erasmus*, 29: 247–412. Toronto: University of Toronto Press.

Erasmus. 1990. "Shipwreck (*Naufragium*)." In *Erasmus Reader*, translated by Craig R. Thompson, edited by Erika Rummel, 239–48. Toronto: University of Toronto Press.

Ferrer-Chivite, Manuel. 2000. "Sobre las así llamadas interpolaciones de Alcalá." In *Actas del XIII Congreso de la Asociación Internacional de Hispanistas, Madrid 6–11 de julio de 1998*. 4 vols. Edited by Florencio Sevilla Arroyo and Carlos Alvar Ezquerra, 1: 318–26. Madrid: Castalia; Fundación Duques de Soria.

Flowers, Robin. 1927. "The Revelation of Christ's Wounds." *Béaloideas* 1 (1): 38–45. http://dx.doi.org/10.2307/20521419.

García de Enterría, María Cruz. 1997. "Una devoción prohibida: la *Oración de la Emparedada*." In *La muy devota Oración de la Emparedada*, edited by Juan

M. Carrasco González, IX–XLV. La Biblioteca de Barcarrota 2. Badajoz: Junta de Extremadura.

Gasbarra, Shane. 1991. "'Lingua quo vadis?' Language and Community in Erasmus's *Lingua.*" *Viator* 22: 343–55.

Giles, Ryan D. 2009. *The Laughter of the Saints: Parodies of Holiness in Late Medieval and Renaissance Spain.* Toronto: University of Toronto Press.

Gitlitz, David. 2000. "Inquisition Confessions and *Lazarillo de Tormes.*" *Hispanic Review* 68 (1): 53–74. http://dx.doi.org/10.2307/474356.

Hanrahan, Thomas. 1983. "Lazarillo de Tormes: Erasmian Satire or Protestant Reform?" *Hispania* 66 (3): 333–9. http://dx.doi.org/10.2307/342304.

Herrero, Javier. 1978. "The Ending of Lazarillo: The Wine against the Water." *Modern Language Notes* 93 (2): 313–19.

Hopper, Vincent Foster. 1938. *Medieval Number Symbolism: Its Sources, Meaning and Influence on Thought and Expression.* New York: Columbia University Press.

Horner, Shari. 2001. *The Discourse of Enclosure: Representing Women in Old English Literature.* University Park: Pennsylvania State University Press.

Imirizaldu, Jesús, ed. 1977. *Monjas y beatas embaucadoras.* Madrid: Nacional.

Kagan, Richard L. 1990. *Lucrecia's Dreams: Politics and Prophecy in Sixteenth-Century Spain.* Berkeley: University of California Press.

*Lazarillo de Tormes.* 1974. Edited by Alberto Blecua. 2nd ed. Clásicos Castalia 58. Madrid: Castalia.

*Lazarillo de Tormes.* 1987. Edited by Francisco Rico. 2nd ed. Letras hispánicas 44. Madrid: Cátedra.

*"Lazarillo De Tormes" and "The Swindler": Two Spanish Picaresque Novels.* 2003. Revised, edited, and translated by Michael Alpert. New York: Penguin.

León, Luis de. 1987. *La perfecta casada.* Edited by Mercedes Etreros. Madrid: Taurus.

Ludolph of Saxony. 1551. *Vita Christi Cartuxano.* 4 vols. Translated by Ambrosio Montesino. Seville: Casa de Jacobo Cromberger.

Ludolph of Saxony. 1976. *Praying the Life of Christ.* Edited by Mary Immaculate Bodenstedt. Analecta Cartusiana 15. Salzburg: Institut für Englische Sprache und Literatur, University of Salzburg.

Luna, Juan de. 1988. *Segunda parte del Lazarillo.* Edited by Pedro M. Piñero Ramírez. Madrid: Cátedra.

Martínez de Toledo, Alonso. 1970. *Arcipreste de Talavera o Corbacho.* Edited by J. González Muela. Clásicos Castalia 24. Madrid: Castalia.

Mazzio, Carla. 1998. "Sins of the Tongue in Early Modern England." *Modern Language Studies* 28 (3/4): 93–124. http://dx.doi.org/10.2307/3195467.

Murrillo, Jesús Cañas. 1996. "Un Lazarillo de Medina del Campo: peculiaridades y variantes de una edición desconocida de 1554." *Anuario de estudios filológicos* 19: 91–134.

Palmireno. 1566. *Fragmentum ex Comœdia Octauia.* In *Rhetoric' Laurentii Palmyreni: Tertia et ultima pars*, 117–37. Valencia: J. Mey.

Parker, Patricia. 1987. *Literary Fate Ladies: Rhetoric, Gender, Property*. London: Methuen.

Pérez, Martín. 2002. *Libro de las confesiones: una radiografía de la sociedad medieval española.* Edited by Antonio García y García, Bernardo Alonso Rodríguez, and Francisco Cantelar Rodríguez. Madrid: Biblioteca de Autores Cristianos.

Reusch, F.H., ed. 1961. *Die Indices Librorum prohibitorum des sechzehnten Jahrhunderts.* Nieuwkoop: Graaf.

Sahlin, Claire L. 2001. *Birgitta of Sweden and the Voice of Prophecy*. Woodbridge, Suffolk, and Rochester, NY: Boydell.

Sánchez de Bajadoz, Diego. 1886. *Farsa del matrimonio.* In *Recopilación en metro*, edited by Vicente Barrantes, 105–16 Madrid: Librería de los bibliófilos.

Shipley, George. 1982. "A Case of Functional Obscurity: The Master Tambourine-Painter of *Lazarillo*, 'Tratado' VI." *Modern Language Notes* 97: 225–53.

Silva, Feliciano de. 1988. *Segunda comedia de Celestina.* Edited by Consolación Baranda. Madrid: Cátedra.

Skemer, Don C. 2006. *Binding Words: Textual Amulets in the Middle Ages.* University Park: Pennsylvania State University Press.

Stallybrass, Peter. 1986. "Patriarchal Territories: The Body Enclosed." In *Rewriting the Renaissance: The Discourses of Sexual Difference in Early Modern Europe*, edited by Margaret W. Ferguson, Maureen Quilligan, and Nancy J. Vickers, 123–142. Chicago: University of Chicago Press.

Thompson, B. Bussell, and J.K. Walsh. 1988. "The Mercedarian's Shoes (Perambulations on the Fourth *Tratado* of *Lazarillo de Tormes*)." *Modern Language Notes* 103 (2): 440–8.

Ubeda, López de. 2010. *La pícara Justina*. Edited by Luc Torres. Madrid: Castalia.

Voaden, Rosalynn. 1999. *God's Words, Women's Voices: The Discernment of Spirits in the Writing of Late-Medieval Women Visionaries*. York, UK; Rochester, NY: York Medieval Press.

Weiner, Jack. 1985. "Las interpolaciones en *El Lazarillo de Tormes* (Alcalá de Henares, 1554) con énfasis especial sobre las del ciego." *Hispanófila* 29 (1): 827–33.

Weiss, Julian. 1996. "Writing, Sanctity, and Gender in Berceo's *Poema de Santa Oria.*" *Hispanic Review* 64 (4): 47–65. http://dx.doi.org/10.2307/474882.

Winston-Allen, Anne. 1997. *Stories of the Rose: The Making of the Rosary in the Middle Ages*. University Park: Pennsylvania State University Press.

Zayas y Sotomayor, María. 1989. "La inocencia castigada." In *Tres novelas amorosas y tres desengaños amorosos*, edited by Alicia Redondo Goicoechea, 272–312. Madrid: Castalia.

Zuñiga, Francesillo de. 1981. *Crónica burlesca del emperador Carlos V*. Edited by Diane Pamp de Avalle-Arce. Barcelona: Crítica.

# 12 War and the Material Conditions for Suffering in Cervantes' *Numancia*

LUIS F. AVILÉS

The drama *El cerco de Numancia*, written by Miguel de Cervantes between the years 1581 and 1587, is a tragedy that explores some of the fundamental ethical problems related to war and the tradition of *jus ad bellum*. These problems include the status of civil populations during war, the limits that need to be imposed on violence, the uses of technology, and the possibility of dialogue in order to achieve peace. As a former soldier who participated in some of the most significant battles of his time, Cervantes shows a marked interest in exploring these topics through his fictional writing. He chooses to depict what I would call a "limit situation" in *Numancia*, one that I would define as an unusual living condition in which human agency and freedom are lost. In such a context, it becomes extremely difficult for characters in a text to manage effectively material and spiritual resources in order to survive such experiences. My interest is to focus on the extreme repercussions such conditions have on both material life and human dignity. I will argue that the scenes of pathos in *Numancia* are designed to reflect upon the possibilities of deliverance from total annihilation and the complex relationships between human beings and the values and objects they cherish the most within a tightly knit community on the verge of total destruction.

In order to understand this limit situation, I will focus on the way in which unreasonable restrictions to action brought about by extreme uses of technology on the part of an invading army produce unforeseeable behaviours and intense displays of emotion on the part of the victims. In my analysis of the play, I will concentrate on three distinct features of materiality. In the initial section of the paper I will first explore the material uses of military resources by the general Scipio, and their relationship to cleverness, friction, and force in the drama. His strategy will be understood within the context of an unjust war that promotes the use of all available resources against the city. The end result of this war will be the unanticipated death of the entire population of Numancia. In a second section, I will explore the negative repercussions of Scipio's military strategy on the way of life of a number of key characters in the play. I will focus on the complex relationships that the victims will establish with material objects, in particular with bread as their most significant possession at a time of extreme necessity. A third aspect of materiality that I will focus on deals with the relationship between friction in war and a persistent shift at the level of signification of both the sense of self and the meanings assigned to material possessions. My contention is that the relationships to material objects reveal deep explorations on the part of the author of how to behave when the spectre of a dishonourable death looms on the horizon of a community. In his drama, Cervantes deals with such questions as what to do when confronted with a limit situation, how to ethically approach death, and what to give or receive from others in the instance when the body is about to expire. It is in such scenes that most of the ethical content of the work is fully manifested, and the sorrow of death is brought to bear with the greatest intensity.

## Clever Solutions to War: Force and Friction

> war turns into something quite different from
> what it should be according to theory – turns into
> something incoherent and incomplete.
> Carl Von Clausewitz

The central ethical problems posed by Cervantes in *Numancia* are related specifically to the principles that govern conduct during war (*jus in bello*).[1] That is why it is important to focus on the way in which the military decisions are made, the purpose behind them, and the repercussions of those decisions for the rest of the characters in the play. At the beginning of the drama, the general Scipio is confronted by his inability to conquer Numancia despite having at his disposal superior resources both in terms of arms and number of men. The persistent pressures wrought by the long war on him are evident. The resistance on the part of the *numantinos* has made the captain very irritable. He interprets his duties as a "difícil y pesada carga/… /tanto me aprieta, me fatiga y carga,/que *ya sale de quicio mi cuidado*" [difficult and heavy task which/…weighs me down/and wearies me till my attention almost/becomes unhinged] (1995, 1.vv.1–4; 1959,

101; emphasis added).[2] There is no question that Scipio is not dealing very well with the pressures of command and is angry and resentful towards Numancia (an argument sustained by Zimic 1979, 123; Maglione 2000, 179 and 182; and Vivar 2004, 30). Immediately after trying to correct the behaviour of his troops, Scipio is depicted as making a serious tactical error when he does not accept a peace proposal presented to him by two emissaries of the city.[3] Even though he follows one of the central precepts of war, which recommends listening to the enemy during a conflict ("Oír al enemigo es cosa cierta / que siempre aprovechó más que dañase" [To give an audience to one's enemy / has always done more good than harm] (1995, 1.vv.221–2; 1959, 106), he ends up rejecting an opportunity that would bring about the end to the conflict in very favourable terms for the Romans (the envoy from Numancia states: "y a cualquiera partido nos ponemos" [we will accept any agreement], *partido* meaning here "convenio," "concierto," or mutual agreements for peace [1995, 1.v.256; 1959, 107]).[4] In other words, he misses the *kairós* or opportune moment ("ocasión"), the favourable circumstances that define *praxis*, especially in the context of military and political actions.[5] Scipio's response to the emissaries is deceitful since he has already decided that his army will wage war without the need for the soldiers to go to battle and without any physical confrontation that will demonstrate "lo que la mía [diestra] hace" [I wish to see what mine [right hand] can do] (1995, 1.v.270; 1959, 107).[6] Instead, the hands will be used only to construct the ditch that will surround the city ("Ejercítense agora vuestras manos / en romper y a cavar la dura tierra" [Now let us all exert our hands in breaking / And digging this hard earth] (1995, 1.vv.325–6; 1959, 108–9). He rejects the peace proposal by proposing a return to the traditional ways of engagement in battle, but in reality he has made plans that contradict such statements. That is why even though he says that he wants to see both armies in the field, in reality the armies will not confront each other in the drama.

The ultimate purpose of such a decision is to solve conflict by means of new, clever, and astute strategies that will expedite a resolution in Scipio's favour. In order to satiate his desire for honour and glory, he decides to deploy new uses of technology that are perceived as unprecedented within the drama. He encircles the city by constructing a ditch designed to finish off the enemy by starving them: "Pienso de un hondo foso rodeallos / y por hambre insufrible he de acaballos" [I intend to dig a deep ditch / and with insufferable famine finish / them off] (1995, 1.vv.319–21; 1959, 108).[7] The introduction of the "nueva traza" [new plan] (1995, 1.v.348; 1959, 109) is seen as an individual decision, as a new and more effective way of conquering Numancia, as a strategy that avoids the suffering of casualties on the Roman side, and as an event that will increase Scipio's honour and fame.[8] In fact, Scipio sacrifices the traditional, more honourable way to wage war associated with a chivalric ethos.[9]

Cervantes' main interest is to provide a comment on the prevailing practices of warfare at the time he was writing the drama. In the temporal overlapping he is making between the distant past and the present he is reflecting upon the proper or improper ways of waging war, in particular as it relates to the tradition of *ius in bello*. The drama exemplifies an improper way of using material resources against a city, and the character responsible for such an idea is Scipio, the Roman commander. Scipio's decision would have seemed callous to anyone who viewed the play in Cervantes' time, not only because the peace offered by the *numantinos* is generous, but also because Scipio rejects an acceptable political solution that would have avoided an undesirable (and even unnecessary) return to armed conflict. Furthermore, the new strategy does transform a limited war into what could be called a war of annihilation or total war, one that does not follow the principle of discrimination (distinguishing the legitimate enemy from the civilian population) and consequently converts all inhabitants into targets, since hunger will affect the entire population, including women and children.[10]

The central ethical problem presented in the drama stems directly from Scipio's clever use of his material resources. This effectively intensifies what Clausewitz called "friction" in war (1993, Book I, 138–40), a concept that I find very useful in order to understand the repercussions of increased tension in the drama. According to Clausewitz, friction is characterized by the correlation between action and the confrontation of a resistance (Numancia's long and effective war of defence). It is a term that helps us understand what makes events in war so difficult to predict, since friction intensifies unpredictability and also works against theoretical formulations and plans for action. Clausewitz states that friction "is everywhere in contact with chance," and is what distinguishes "real war from war on paper" (1993, 138–9). This friction is manifested on several levels in the drama, and it becomes a force that will generate unusual and unanticipated behaviour on the part of both the invading army (e.g., Scipio's construction of the ditch) and the victims.[11] It also increases the opportunities for chance to entangle any plans or strategies, leading to unpredictability. This in turn becomes the condition of possibility for an ethical error of major proportions, in the sense that the text will assign responsibility to Scipio for increasing friction and, consequently, for the devastating effects of his decisions. These effects will eventually appear in the strong feelings of despair that will be so important in the scenes of pathos. The term friction as defined by Clausewitz becomes a fundamental critical tool in order to understand the questionable use of material resources during war and its ethical repercussions in the drama.

We can profitably expand our analysis by taking into account the relationship between friction and what Simone Weil, in her famous essay on *The Iliad*, has defined as "force." There is no question that the tools of war are designed to have the most intense impact on the physical and mental being of the enemy. For Weil, force is defined as an action that effectively turns a human being into a thing (2005, 3). It is a powerful instrument that transforms a living being into a corpse, something impossible to conceive abstractly but that becomes a reality in life (2005, 8). The use of force should be limited, but this fact remains unrecognizable whenever the intensity of conflict compels humans to use extreme measures. In Cervantes' *Numancia*, Scipio decides to test the limits of warfare by implementing a strategy that will elicit another logical contradiction: a war that makes the use of arms obsolete.[12] The allegorical figure of España disapproves of these uses of technology (e.g., the ditch, towers, machines) as a means of transforming war into something else: "rehuyendo venir más a las manos / con los pocos valientes numantinos" [Although the latter are so few, refuse / anything else than stratagem and ruse] (1995, 1.vv.395–6; 1959, 110). These "intentos," "quimeras," "diligencia extraña," and "ardid nunca visto" refer to the new machines of war, denounced by the allegorical figure of the river Duero as going against nature:

> Mas, sin temor de mi veloz carrera,
> cual si fuera un arroyo, veo que intentan
> de hacer lo que tú, España, nunca veas:
> sobre mis aguas, torres y trincheas.
>
> [But with no greater heed of my swelled tides / than had I been a rill (a thing you never, / Spain, have beheld!) they've spanned my mighty river / with dykes and floating towers] (1995, 1.vv.453–6; 1959, 111–12)

In the drama the uses of technology and the material possibilities afforded by machines are meant to be understood as significant changes in the manner in which war is waged. These changes are represented as an intensification of the use of force in a way that changes the nature of war altogether. España states:

Pero en sólo mirar que están privados
de ejercitar sus fuertes brazos duros,
la guerra pediré o la muerte a voces
con horrendos acentos y feroces.

[But by realizing that they are deprived/of wielding weapons with their strong arms/I will plead for war or death/with horrendous and ferocious screams] (1995, 1.vv.413–16)[13]

Spain clamours for traditional war because she strongly believes in the ethos of chivalry (dependent upon hand to hand combat).[14] She would prefer for her people to fight using the original tools of war in order to demonstrate their valour and honour in the battlefield.

Scipio's decision to experiment with a more utilitarian and expedient use of force is significant in this context. He himself mentions the fact that his decision is not generally accepted by all, some judging it a "loco desvarío" [mad delirium] to enclose the enemy in this way. This tactic may even jeopardize the reputation of the Romans: "era mengua del romano brio / no vencellos con modos más usados" [our Roman strength/lost honour by not conquering the foe / in the outmoded, antiquated way] (1995, 3.vv.1121–2; 1959, 128).[15] But Scipio is content with the judgment of one group alone, the "pláticos soldados" [practical soldiers], a category that Cervantes is severely criticizing in the drama (see III, 1125–8). On this issue, Zimic is right when he identifies this reference to the "pláticos soldados" as a realization by Scipio himself of the problems with his own strategy (1979, 124). But even more significant is the reduction in the scope of ethical considerations, proposing a judgment of action restricted to a group of practical soldiers rather than a universal type of judgment with a wider human scope. Practicality is, without a doubt, the source of much of the anguish, despair, and, ultimately, suffering and death in the drama. I would argue that, for Cervantes, the category of the clever, practical soldier has no ethical dimensions whatsoever in the drama, with the exception of the Roman's future status as narrators of the victims' bravery, a role that assigns to the victors the task of preserving forever the memory of their victims.

Scipio's inability to foresee the possible consequences of such a use of force undermines his status as an ethical figure. He prefers to be clever rather than prudent, if we follow the classical definition of prudence in Aristotle's ethics (1985) as a way of acting that always depends on a notion of the good, one that is able to better anticipate the future and thus avoid excess and the introduction of uncertainty and chance into human action.[16] By not recognizing the limits of the use of force, the Roman general has in fact extended both force and chance, with unfortunate consequences for the vanquished as well as the victorious side. Excessive force thus has a common bond with intense friction because in both instances a closer, more dangerous relationship to chance always works its effects upon human action. We can illustrate this relationship with a quote from Weil:

> they [soldiers] exceed the measure of the force that is actually at their disposal. Inevitably they exceed it, since they are not aware that it is limited. And now we see them committed irretrievably to chance; suddenly things cease to obey them. Sometimes chance is kind to them, sometimes cruel. But in any case there they are, exposed, open to misfortune; gone is the armor of power that formerly protected their naked souls; nothing, no shield, stands between them and tears. (2005, 15)

By taking war to its extreme Scipio is inviting uncertainty, unpredictability, and chance into the conflict. If prudence requires the ability to foresee the future in a contingent world by remembering not only the experiences of the past but also imagining possible scenarios in the future, by making good use of all resources available with a good outcome in view, with the help of long deliberation and consultation with advisors and friends, then what we see represented in *Numancia* is a general who rushes into action without consultation or deliberation. The union of force and chance, so important for the outcome of the drama, stems directly from the way in which Scipio, exasperated by the long years it has taken him to conquer the city, has decided to wage war. The unlimited use of force results in an intensification of friction and, hence, the unanticipated actions that stem directly from an unreasonable treatment of the enemy. Pushed on their side to a limit position, the *numantinos* will certainly react in ways that supersede expectations, simply because one cannot expect that ordinary actions will take place under such extraordinary circumstances. It is in the scenes of pathos that Cervantes explores the consequences of war taken to these extremes.

## An Impossible Gift at the Time of Death

> Que fait-on à la dernière seconde quand
> on perd la guerre? On casse la vaisselle,
> on casse les glaces à coups de pierres,
> on tue les chiens.[17]
> Marguerite Duras

In *Numancia* we can distinguish between two firmly differentiated dramatic spaces that correspond, on the one hand, to the Roman army and, on the other, to the *numantinos* that are protected within the city walls. As I have stated before, Scipio's military strategy of enclosing and starving the *numantinos* has one major ethical repercussion, which is that the war has been extended to the general population of the city. This means that Scipio does not discriminate between soldiers (legitimate targets in a war) and the civilian population (women, children, older people, all who are unable to bear arms).[18] The war waged by the Romans entails not only an unprecedented use of force, the inappropriate deployment of technology, or even the introduction of more friction with the consequential increment in unpredictability, but in a more significant way it has become de facto total war. By total war I mean that the traditional limits of warfare have been overpowered by the deployment of extreme means in order to achieve the complete surrender of the enemy. Furthermore, this total war will evolve into a war of annihilation at the end of the play.

Cervantes takes great care in producing compelling and highly emotional scenes of pathos in his drama in order to convey precisely the lack of prospective vision and prudence in the Roman general. Under the circumstances that Scipio has created, the *numantinos* will suffer extreme hunger, will need to destroy their most cherished possessions, and will have to sacrifice their lives by committing mass suicide (including killing their own children).[19] Under the pressure of impending defeat and dishonourable death, the overview of the self is fragmented and the natural world of things upset. Gender is reversed as males complain that they are made to appear more feminine because they are denied the use of arms.[20] Women propose the idea of mass suicide as a preferable solution to their dilemma and even suggest killing their own children (see III, 1251–401). This plural and, possibly, dislocated sense of self results directly from intensified (and unresolved) friction, and this same friction engenders even more tension and desperation. As a result, all relationships between the *numantinos* start to manifest new and unforeseeable disturbances directed not only towards the Romans, but towards the very members of their own community.

One of the major irregularities suffered during the experience of this kind of war manifests itself in the relationship characters have to objects and material life. My epigraph from Marguerite Duras suggests how the value of all material possessions changes dramatically the moment one anticipates that defeat is near. Even the moral compass that guides human action suffers greatly under such situations. Here the excess of friction experienced by a population on the brink of defeat produces a strategy that tries to diminish the future profit of the conquerors (destroying property so that it will not fall into the enemy's hands), but it is also part of a psychological effect that transforms the perceived value of things. In the third act (Jornada Tercera) Teógenes suggests that all *numantinos* should deposit their possessions in the central square, so that they may be burned (III, 1426–9). Later on a *numantino* will convey more directly the difficulty of destroying one's most cherished possessions:

En la plaza mayor ya levantada
queda una ardiente y cudiciosa hoguera,
que, de nuestras riquezas menistrada,
sus llamas suben a la cuarta esfera.
Allí, con toda priesa acelerada
Y con mortal y tímida carrera
Acuden todos, como santa ofrenda
A sustentar las llamas con su hacienda.

[Up in the central square they've made a huge / blazing and hungry conflagration, which, / fed with our riches, soars to the fourth sphere. / There with sad, fearful haste runs every one, / as with a sacred offering, to feast / the roaring flames with his own goods and chattels, / sustaining them with households and estates.] (1995, 3.vv.1648–55; 1959, 140)

The sacrifice of all material possessions is a difficult proposition due to the population's strong attachment to their property. The use of adjectives that qualify the haste and rush to burn everything (a mortal and timid race) is symptomatic of the pain caused by such a loss. The possessions are also compared to "sacred offerings," acquiring an elevated, religious significance. There is a recurrent sense in the drama that the misfortunes of war have arrived at an inconvenient moment. The same happens to their soon-to-be lost possessions, since their "haciendas" are "mal gozadas / pues se guardaron para ser quemadas" [the badly enjoyed *haciendas*, since they were kept in order to be burned] (1995, 3.vv.1670–1; 1959, 140).[21] The time of war is incongruous with that of the proper enjoyment of the "haciendas." The experience of approaching death transforms the present into a time of lost enjoyment and forms part of the representation of the city's defeat and the psychological impact on its inhabitants. The strong bond between objects and human beings is severed by the anticipation of death.

There are two instances in which this incongruent temporality, which exists parallel to the displacements of the self, is strongly associated with specific characters and their bonds to life. On the one hand, it is a constitutive element of Lira and Marandro's amorous relationship and, on the other, it also has an effect on young Bariato's relationship to death. For the specific purposes of this essay, I will concentrate on the first case and the relation it has with material life. I propose that the incongruity between the vital experience of life (or the particular temporal relationship to life) and the context generated by Scipio's new strategy is summarized in two crucial verses in the play: "es dolor insufrible el de la muerte/si llega cuando más vive la vida" [Insufferable is the pain of death/If it comes on us when we're most alive] (1995, 2.vv.587–8; 1959, 115). I would also argue that these verses anticipate the construction of the scenes of pathos that will be so important in the drama, since they are designed to illustrate to the spectators the extreme suffering generated by war. The communicability of suffering and pain will depend precisely upon the strong attachments to life of some of the characters. An intense bond to life will depend on affective relationships, the love one feels for the land and the city, intense relationships with friends, the always important sense of honour, attachments to one's possessions, and also the temporal experience related to a particular stage in life (e.g., being too young to die). Undoubtedly, there is a strong cultural content linked to the representation of pain and suffering, and Cervantes demonstrates a sustained sensitivity to it.[22] In the case of Lira and Marandro, their love and future marriage are represented as a stage in life that coincided with the worst possible moment. There are a number of allusions to the incongruity of their relationship and the context of war, starting with the reproach made by Marandro's best friend Leoncio:

> ¿Ves la patria consumida
> y de enemigos cercada,
> y tu memoria, burlada
> por amor, de ella se olvida?

> [You see your country half consumed, and by/her enemies shut in, yet tricked and fooled/by Love, you must forget her altogether?] (1995, 2.vv.717–20; 1959, 118)

For Leoncio, the love relationship between Marandro and Lira is inappropriate under the lived circumstances. But Marandro strongly rebukes his best friend by using effective arguments that justify the coexistence of love and the duties required from a soldier during war. But despite his proposed solution, Marandro is aware of the unfortunate timing of the situation he lives in, and is unable to solve this problem:

También sabes que llegó
en tan dulce coyuntura
esta fuerte guerra dura,
por quien mi gloria cesó.
Dilatóse el casamiento
hasta acabar esta guerra,
porque no está nuestra tierra
para fiestas y contento.

[You also know that, at this youthful juncture, / came this fierce strife by which my glorious hopes / were slain, and so the wedding was deferred / till after the cessation of the war / because our country's now no place for feasts / and happiness.] (1995, 2.vv.749–56; 1959, 118)[23]

Both quotes do illustrate the unfortunate context in which Marandro finds himself, questioned by his friend and unable to enjoy Lira as wife and lover. It is obvious that Cervantes is establishing a connection between the lack of enjoyment of the possessions that need to be sacrificed to the fire in the central square and the impossibility of enjoying a relationship that will remain unfulfilled due to the Roman siege.

But Marandro will try desperately to fight against such a rigid and imposed context. During the most difficult moments represented in the drama (the strong suffering caused by hunger), Marandro will appropriate for himself some of the responsibilities of the husband that he will not be able to become in the future. In other words, Marandro's actions (the ones that will lead him to his death) are dictated by a desire to fulfil responsibilities that will not only combine effectively his duties of soldier and lover, but also anticipate his future functions as husband and household provider. He will be able to add a new aspect to his own self not only as a reaction to the situation created by the Romans (friction), but also as one of those moments in which unexpected behaviours and chance come into play. It is a reaction to friction that will fight against a closed future by appropriating for himself the power to assume a future subjectivity in the present. This may seem complicated, but I believe that we can understand better Marandro's actions if we see them as the desire to experience an impossible-to-attain future stage in life. Aristotle's distinction between acquisition of wealth and household management in *The Politics* sheds light on Marandro's suffering. Related to his discussion on the nature of slavery, in Book I Aristotle associates the acquisition of wealth (along with the acquisition of slaves) with hunting and war (1984, I,

1255b, 35 and 1256b, 20–5). Household management, on the other hand, is defined as a limited acquisition of necessities required for the living of an honourable life (1984, 1258a, 40).[24] This is the art of acquisition associated with the household and the family that will determine Marandro's actions after he finds out that Lira is dying of hunger as a consequence of the siege. Lira states:

> Que me tiene tal la hambre,
> que de mi vital estambre
> llevará presto la palma.
> ¿Qué tálamo has de esperar
> de quien está en tal extremo,
> que te aseguro que temo
> antes de un hora expirar?

> [That with such hunger I contend / I am near vanquished in the fight / and feel my life is at its end. / What sort of nuptials can you dream / with one whom, in this fierce extreme, / such agonising pangs devour / that she must perish in an hour?] (1995, 3.vv.1479–85; 1959, 136)

In this quote Lira is still contemplating the possibility of a future marriage. However, extreme necessity is making such a future an impossibility. In his response Marandro decides to make a "most improbable" promise, one that Leoncio characterizes as a "Terrible ofrecimiento" [a terrible offer] (1995, 3.v.1574):

> de hambre no morirás
> mientras yo tuviere vida.
> Yo me ofrezco de saltar
> el foso y el muro fuerte,
> y entrar por la misma muerte
> para la tuya excusar.
> El pan que el romano toca,
> sin que el temor me destruya,
> le quitaré de la suya
> para ponello en tu boca.

> [Though hunger-stricken, / you shall not die! Across the trench / out of the Romans' hands I'll wrench / the bread for want of which you sicken, / and put the bread between your lips.] (1995, 3.vv.1504–13; 1959, 137)

I would argue that the promise of sustenance made to his lover is best understood as a desire to fulfil obligations that surpass a mere gift between lovers, even if the bread that will be taken from the Romans and brought to Lira will be later understood within an economy of gift-giving. Since it has to do with hunger and the need for food, Marandro's valiant promise and actions should be linked to the maintenance of the household and the provisions necessary for survival. Lira is aware of the unreasonable proposal made by Marandro and she responds that she is not willing to accept sustenance under such dire circumstances ("yo no quiero sustento / ganado con tu sudor" [I want nothing / that's won at cost of sweat or blood by you] (1995, 3.vv.1540–1; 1959, 137). The promise of food is a performative utterance that should be understood in the context of a desire to accomplish some of the functions associated with family responsibility. But the situation is paradoxical and tragic because the promise is made by someone who is destined never to become a husband. In this desire to fight against his own tragic fate, Marandro adds another aspect of the self to the plurality that is already experienced (lover and soldier), one that has the main social function of alleviating the corporal necessities of life (in this case, hunger).

After the promise, bread becomes a fundamental material object that adds dramatic intensity to the scenes of pathos. Bread is repeatedly preferred by characters who appear on stage and suffer extreme hunger, and who are willing to give anything in return for it. In the case of Marandro, the pursuit of bread participates in the economy of gift-giving (as a "prenda"), but is more significantly related to a household economy because gifts are not necessarily given in order to provide for necessities such as food. This link to necessity is very strong whenever bread is mentioned by characters who are dying of hunger, especially the children. The son of a woman who brings possessions to the fire expresses it well: "le daré toda esta ropa / por un pedazo de pan" [I'll trade / all of these clothes for it – just for one piece!] (1995, 3.vv.1706–7; 1959, 141). The mother is not capable of providing a piece of bread, nor is she able to breastfeed her child:

¿Qué mamas, triste criatura?
¿No sientes que, a mi despecho,
sacas ya del flaco pecho
por leche, la sangre pura?
Lleva la carne a pedazos
y procura de hartarte,
que no pueden ya llevarte
mis flacos, cansados brazos.

[Poor creature, what is that you're sucking / out of my breast? Can you not taste? It's blood, / not milk. Come, bite my breast in pieces / and eat them if it satisfies your hunger.] (1995, 3.vv.1708–15; 1959, 141)

Scenes like this make it impossible to restrict the symbolic functions of bread and nourishment solely to a gift-giving economy between lovers. In this instance the appearance of bread associated with blood and the body of the mother becomes part of a representation of the impossibility of sustaining the most basic function of parenthood. Eating has evolved into a cannibal act in which the mother offers her own flesh and blood as food, even if her body is no longer capable of fulfilling this function: "¿con qué os podré sustentar, / si apenas tengo qué os dar / de la propia sangre mía?" [What more can I provide you than my blood?] (1995, 3.vv.1717–19; 1959, 142). The scene is also designed as an extreme experience of the civilian population's suffering and the devastating effects on the innocent victims of war. It represents a point of view available to the audience of the drama, but denied to Scipio in his inability to perceive the consequences of his decision.

As the fundamental object of nourishment within an economy of extreme necessity, bread suffers the same displacements of meaning experienced by characters. As part of a system of exchange, it acquires a greater value (the child is willing to exchange all his clothing for a little piece). Such transformations become even more significant when Marandro appears on stage with a basket of bread taken from the Romans, the first instance in which a soldier has effectively used weapons against the enemy. After losing Leoncio in battle, Marandro begins to assess the true price of bread, linked now to the loss of his best friend ("¿Que es posible que ya dan / tus carnes despedazadas / señales averiguadas / de lo que cuesta este pan?" [And is it possible / that your hacked limbs bear witness to the price –/ and what a price!– this luckless bread has cost?] (1995, 4.vv.1804–7; 1959, 144). The bread was bought with the blood of two friends ("con sangre comprador / de dos sin ventura amigos" [at the cost of the unlucky blood / of two devoted friends] [1995, 4.vv.1826–7; 1959, 145]). These allusions to exchange value and price indicate that the drama does not fall prey to a representation of reduced dimensions, which would happen if the author treated bread solely as a lover's gift. The mention of its price is significant as well. Bread is something that has been bought in order to assist in the impossible tasks that characters wish to accomplish: the possibility of feeding a son or a future wife. That is why the semantic field associated with bread becomes expansive, migrating from signifier to signifier in the same way that characters are affected by a multiple sense of self. Bread also assumes a strong sacrificial content similar to the possessions destined to be burned. It is stained with blood, represents the human body, and is linked to cannibal rituals. These are all designed to intensify the limit experience of war for the audience.[25]

In the end, Marandro dies fulfilling a promise. And yet again his expansive sense of self is emphasized by Lira's words immediately after his death: "enamorado y valiente / y soldado desdichado" [a courageous lover, and an unfortunate soldier] (1995, 4.vv.1874–5). As a lover, a soldier, and a provider of food, Marandro fought hard against the friction imposed by the way in which Scipio decided to wage war. He is one of those characters that fulfils the impossible: he leaves the walls of the city and attacks the Roman encampment, killing many of them and taking away a basket of bread in order to feed Lira. That is why it should not surprise us that after Marandro's death, Lira is able to call him, for the first and only time in the drama, "esposo" [husband]; "ya está muerto mi esposo," and later calls him "esposo mío" (1995, 4.v.1869, 1877). I would like to suggest that this can only happen because of the intention on the part of Marandro to behave as a husband by bringing nourishment to his loved one. In fact, this action unites war with household maintenance, effectively unifying what in Aristotle remains distinct. His heroic battle against the Romans was in a sense part of the war, but also originated from a desire to acquire bread in order to feed a future wife. This "domestic" or household suffering is precisely what Scipio cannot sense, trapped in the desires of an economy of war and its mode of violent acquisition. The act perpetrated by Marandro and Leoncio is also part of the manifestations of unpredictability and chance in the drama, since at the beginning of the fourth act the Romans are absolutely surprised by what has happened. Even more significant, this action has begun the process of transforming the victorious Romans into spectators with the function of communicating the valour of the *numantinos* (Fabio states: "cuyo valor [Marandro's and Leoncio's] será razón se alabe" [whose valour should be praised] [1995, 4.v.1753]).

Like the expansive sense of self, bread has become another object that continuously changes meaning in the context of war and extreme necessity. It acquires a high value, its costs are enormous, the investment in its acquisition is extreme. But in the end, bread suffers a last transformation and assumes the properties of a *pharmakon*, something that problematizes its status as food. Stained with blood and the cost of human life, bread becomes a poison, a sort of impossible gift, an extreme burden unable to be incorporated or completely accepted in its intended material function:

¡Oh, pan de la sangre lleno
que por mí se derramó!
¡No te tengo en cuenta, no,
de pan, sino de veneno!
No te llegaré a mi boca
por poderme sustentar,
si no es para besar
esta sangre que te toca.

[This bread / stained with the blood that he has shed for me / is now no longer bread but deadly venom. / My lips shall never touch it, but to kiss / the dear-loved blood that spatters it.] (1995, 4.vv.1880–7; 1959, 146)

The object has finally changed from food to poison and, after that, from poison to an extension of the lover's body (the willingness to kiss the blood-stained bread, but not consume it). It has become a contaminated object caught up between the functions of nourishment and the lover's gift, an intermediate locus between food to be ingested and a precious object to be cherished and preserved. In the drama, it works as a last gift of life during the experience of death, effectively unifying two extremes of material life into what I would call an impossible gift. This gift is impossible because it cannot fulfil the functions assigned by the giver, and in fact produces opposite psychological effects on the recipient who now experiences it as poison. It also imposes a tremendous amount of burden on the structure of reciprocity, since it is a gift that cannot be returned. Its value has become impossible to assess.

In one last scene, bread will also manifest a temporal discontinuity in which the needs of the body can no longer be nourished by its presence. This happens when a young boy, Lira's brother, appears on stage and sees the bread:

¡Oh pan, y cuán tarde vienes
que no hay ya pasar bocado!
Tiene la hambre apretada
mi garganta en tal manera,
que, aunque este pan agua fuera,
no pudiera pasar nada.
(...)
veo que me sobra el pan
cuando me falta la vida.

> [Oh bread, you've come too late/since not a crumb can pass! So tight has hunger/throttled my throat, that if this bread were water/no drop could pass [...] There's bread to spare, when life cannot be spared.] (1995, 4.vv.1894–904; 1959, 146)

In the case of Lira's young brother, bread appears too late, right when the most intense scenes of pathos are taking place (mainly in the third and fourth "Jornadas"). The body has succumbed to the absolute closure of bare life, a life driven to a limit situation in which the human being has become an anticipation of a corpse, unable to feed or be fed. In this scene that unifies life and death, bread has lost any effective meaning and it becomes an object without any value (it has no place in the world, "sobra"). The scene reminds us of Simone Weil's conception of force as the power to transform a human being into a corpse. Lira's brother, to use Weil's words, is "a compromise between a man and a corpse" (2005, 8).

As part of the equation that pairs the arrival of death at a moment when life is felt at its most intense (the verses I already quoted: "es dolor insufrible el de la muerte/si llega cuando más vive la vida"), the appearance of bread within this temporality intensifies the bonds of lovers, children, and younger persons to life. This strong bond to life is what explains Bariato's hesitation to commit suicide. In the end, he recognizes his communitarian bond only after the whole city has perished. He is able to sacrifice himself at the same time that he rejects the multiple and enticing offers of the conquering commander. In fact, such offerings are also non-coordinated temporally, and Bariato knows that they have come too late: "¡Tarde, cruel, ofreces tu clemencia,/pues no hay con quien usarla" [You, cruel man, too late have come to offer/your clemency, when there is no one left/on whom to use it] (1995, 4.vv.2342–3; 1959, 157). Once again, these riches signify nothing under the circumstances. Similar to bread, they cannot be incorporated, accepted, given, but in another sense they are different because they participate solely within an economy of war and, as such, are impossible to define as gifts. One cannot make such offerings in front of a multitude of corpses. Bariato has become a sort of commodity for Scipio, one that will reward the general, but not the young prisoner who refuses to equal the offerings he is promised with his own value as an individual self. Bariato's love and devotion to the city (the communal side of his own self) becomes strong, and he understands that death is the only path to a certain kind of victory, one that cannot be bought.

To conclude, the complex scenes of pathos represent the devastating effects of friction and force in the drama. The unreasonable circumstances that the inhabitants of the city have to endure generate scenes of rich complexity that explore the relationships characters have to objects, the strong bonds they feel to life, and the multiplicity of subject positions experienced in order to confront death with a certain degree of dignity. Specific characters and objects (such as the pieces of bread) acquire a diversity of signifying meanings, and this progressive change forms part of the desperate attempts to confront a limit situation. The drama reveals strong representations of suffering as a form of illustrating Scipio's blindness. These terrible scenes confront the spectator of the play with extreme actions: mass suicide, the killing of women and children, cannibalism, and desperate attempts to resist imposed temporalities. They all form part of an effort to indict excessive uses of violence.

I propose that Cervantes' *Numancia* is a deep exploration of the ways in which war affects human beings and their emotional relationships to life and material things. It is a strong critique of the categories of cleverness and astute military thinking whenever they are not limited or restricted. It is a call to maintain ethical limitations during conflict. The uses of excessive force generate a friction that leads to extreme forms of behaviour and consequently produces unanticipated, sometimes tragic results. However, we cannot conclude that Cervantes is a pacifist or that *Numancia* represents an indictment of war or empire. I believe that this is an untenable position, since the author is proposing models of subjectivity for the Spanish empire, and these paradigms are reflected in the way in which the *numantinos* resist the enemy and ultimately decide their own death. Furthermore, all characters operate within an ideology dominated by honour and fame, categories that function as strong incentives for violence and war. These categories are not deconstructed by the drama, since the *numantinos* died maintaining their honour and fame intact, later becoming the victors in a new empire. In other words, the desire for honour and glory is not indicted by Cervantes in the same way that Erasmus criticizes it in his *Dulce bellum inexpertis* (2001, see for example 353). But *Numancia* does represent the devastating effects of the lethal combination of hatred and cleverness in the context of armed conflict, and this combination is present in the character of Scipio. It is a form of blindness that effectively eradicates prudence and a limited understanding of force in order to privilege clever and more expedient ways of achieving what the commander really wants. The play also illustrates the need for empire to contemplate limitations to violent action and a more ethical way of treating the enemy. These are some of the most important contributions of this literary work to the ethical tradition of *jus ad bellum.*

## NOTES

1 The literature on the subject of just war theory is immense. For a very succinct and clear definition of what just war means, see Thomas Aquinas (1988, 64–5). I also recommend Michael Walzer's classic book on the subject (2006). See as well Bainton (1960) and Cahill (1994), both from a Christian perspective. See as well Russell's book on just war theory in the Middle Ages (1975). As an introduction to the subject of *jus in bello*, I highly recommend consulting Brian Orend's "War" (2005; especially the section "Just War Theory"). See as well the collection entitled *The Ethics of War: Classic and Contemporary Readings*, with excellent bibliography (Reichberg, Syse and Begby 2006). Francisco de Vitoria (1991) is one of the fundamental sixteenth-century humanists who wrote extensively on the topic.

2 I quote from Hermenegildo's edition of *Numancia* (Cervantes 1994). All quotes in the text will be followed by the corresponding *jornada* and verse numbers in parenthesis. I have also consulted Marrast's edition (Cervantes 1995). Unless otherwise indicated, I use the English translation included in the volume *The Classical Theatre*, edited by Eric Bentley (Cervantes 1959). Vivar has correctly emphasized Scipio's words, which for him already indicates his lack of moderation and anger (2004, 29).

3 The majority of scholars agree with this judgment (see Zimic 1979, 118 and 121; de Armas 1998, 74–6; Maestro 2004, 45). But there are scholars who would like to maintain the ethical integrity of Scipio and tend to pass over in silence the general's angry and unreasonable response to the ambassadors. For example, Hermenegildo believes that Cervantes honours and respects the general (1976, 59), an interpretation defended by King (1979). More recently, Aurora Egido has argued that Scipio is a prudent general with an irreproachable reputation. For a list of critics who defend Scipio, see Zimic (1979, 109).

4 I have changed the translation in order to better convey the meaning in Spanish. Francisco de Vitoria states that "for the just war it is necessary to examine the justice and causes of war with great care, and also to listen to the arguments of the opponents, if they are prepared to negotiate genuinely and fairly" (1991, 307). Although this statement is made in reference to *ius ad bellum* (prior to war), it is relevant to the particular scene of the envoys in *Numancia* because it takes place just before Scipio employs his new strategic approach to war. Thus, this moment represents an opportunity to listen to the enemy and try to work out a non-hostile, political solution. Vitoria quotes a significant phrase from Terence: "In every endeavor the seemly course for the wise man is to try persuasion before turning to force" (1991, 307). It is obvious that Scipio's decision not to accept the offer of peace is the fundamental cause of the disasters that follow.

5 For a full discussion of *kairós*, see Aubenque (1999, 112–22) and Kerkhoff (1997, in particular his discussion of the concept in Aristotelean terms, 10–21).

6 He will tell Quinto Fabio that "yo pienso hacer que el numantino / nunca a las manos con nosotros venga" [I think I can prevent that any / Numantines come to grips with us] (1995, 1.vv.313–14; 1959, 108).

7 I have modified the translation slightly.

8 The manuscript Sancho Rayón reads "mi nueva poco usada hazaña" (this is the version chosen by Marrast in his edition). This version places particular emphasis on the newness of the strategy, corroborated by later statements in the drama. For example, the figure of Spain will refer to this strategy as an "ardid nunca visto" [never seen before ruse] (1995, 1.v.408).

9 I am referring here to the transition towards modern warfare (the increase in military discipline, the professionalization of the soldiers, and a more practical view of war). For an excellent analysis of the conflicts between the chivalric ethos and the practical view of war exemplified by the *soldados pláticos*, see González de León's excellent article (2003), later on expanded in his book 2009). See also Simerka (2003, 101–2), who argues correctly that in the siege there is an implied loss of epic heroism.

10 I borrow the concepts of war of annihilation and total war from Arendt (2005; see especially 159–60). She uses these phrases not only to refer to the kind of war introduced by totalitarian regimes in the twentieth century, but also in her discussion of the Trojan war in Homer's *Iliad*.

11 I will discuss these forms of behaviour on the victims' side in a subsequent section of the essay.

12 I am unable to agree with Avalle-Arce's interpretation of Scipio's decision as an expression of a "teoría humanitaria de la Guerra" [a humanitarian theory of war] (1975, 263). On the contrary, the drama does represent Scipio's non-humanitarian posture, which should be considered his mistake. A true humanitarian theory of war would need to contemplate avoiding casualties and the loss of life on both sides of the conflict.

13 I have slightly altered the translation.

14 I would agree that Cervantes seems to defend this ethos against the new practices of warfare characteristic of the sixteenth century and cemented upon questionable moral ground. See Avalle-Arce (1975, 251 and note 4); see also Simerka (2003, 102), who mentions the anachronistic depiction of chivalric and heroic combat. There could be a critique of what has been called The School of Alba, in reference to Juan de Austria's preferred means to wage war. The duke "avoided field battles and preferred … to wear out the enemy with dilatory maneuvers, harassing skirmishes, frequent ambushes and sneak attacks under cover of darkness" (González de León 2003, 241; and 2009, 71).

I hesitate to make a stronger claim, however, since Cervantes will use the Duke of Alba as a paradigm of magnanimity during the invasion of Rome in 1556–7 (see 1995, 1.vv. 489–96; 1959, 112–13). For a more direct reference to a relationship between the drama and the context of imperial politics in Flanders, see Johnson (1980, 88–9). See also Simerka (2003) on imperial power and literary genre. I agree with de Armas's statement that Cervantes "may be warning the rising Spanish Empire of its *arrogancia*" (1998, 89). King argues that the drama is a "meditation about the trajectory, legitimacy, power, burden, and mistakes of empire" (1979, 217). Hermenegildo postulates a link between the drama and the severe response of Juan de Austria to the rebellion of the Alpujarras (1976, 47). What is certain is that time and time again Cervantes includes characters in his works that defend honour and glory from the perspective of traditional warfare. Such is the case of the famous debate between arms and letters voiced by Don Quijote, or the way in which Ricaredo behaves as a commander in *La española inglesa*, to name just a few examples.

15 Similar arguments were made against the Duke of Alba. See González de León (2003, 241; 2009, Part One).

16 In the *Nicomachean Ethics*, Aristotle (1985) defines prudence as "a true disposition accompanied by rational prescription, relating to action in the sphere of what is good and bad for human beings" (VI. 5 1140b 5). Later on in the *Ethics*, Aristotle will distinguish between prudence and cleverness (see VI. 12, 1144a 25). My point here is that Scipio does not demonstrate an ability to recognize what is good or bad in human action. This is his error. What he does demonstrate is an ability to be clever, but without a notion of the good (a notion that must include a consideration for the enemy). That is why I am unable to agree with Egido's judgment of Scipio: "A Cipión nada se le puede reprochar, desde la perspectiva del buen estratega" [From the perspective of the good strategist, there is nothing to reproach in the figure of Scipio] (2003, 119). For a clear distinction between prudence and cleverness, see Aubenque (1999, 74, note 133).

17 "What do you do at the last moment when you are losing a war? You break the china, you throw stones and smash windows, you kill dogs" (in *The War*, English translation of *La douleur*).

18 For clear limitations to conduct during war, especially the guiding points on how to act against the enemy, see Vitoria (1991, 314–21).

19 See Simerka (2003), who states that "the emphasis upon the personal lives of the vanquished provides a 'humanizing' element that is central to the counter-hegemonic ideological dimension" of the play (111). Friedman also sees in the depiction of suffering a way of making visible "the human aspect of the historical event" (1977, 84).

20 Caravino tells his men: “estamos como damas encerrados” [Like women kept inside the house] (1995, 2.v. 570; 1959, 114). Another example is the Romans’ tendency to animalize their enemy.
21 This is another instance in which the translation is inaccurate.
22 For the relationship between culture and the experience of suffering and pain, see Dijkhuizen and Enenkel (2009).
23 Leoncio responds with assurances that he will enjoy his wife in the future, something that will not happen in the drama.
24 Usury is another mode of acquisition, but Aristotle censures it because it is an unnatural way of getting wealth (1984, 1258b, 5).
25 For the relationships between this and other scenes to cannibalism, see Greer’s article on the subject (2006).

## WORKS CITED

Aquinas, Thomas. 1988. *St. Thomas Aquinas on Politics and Ethics.* Translated and edited by Paul E. Sigmund. New York and London: W.W. Norton.

Arendt, Hannah. 2005. “Introduction into Politics.” In *The Promise of Politics*, edited by Jerome Kohn, 93–204. New York: Schocken Books.

Aristotle. 1984. *The Politics.* Translated by Carnes Lord. Chicago and London: University of Chicago Press.

Aristotle. 1985. *Nichomachean Ethics.* Translated by Terence Irwin. Indianapolis and Cambridge: Hackett.

Aubenque, Pierre. 1999. *La prudencia en Aristóteles.* Translated by José Torres Gómez-Pallete María. Barcelona: Editorial Crítica.

Avalle-Arce, Juan Bautista. 1975. *Nuevos deslindes cervantinos.* Barcelona: Ariel.

Bainton, Roland H. 1960. *Christian Attitudes toward War & Peace.* Nashville, TN: Abingdon Press.

Cahill, Lisa Sowle. 1994. *Love Your Enemies: Discipleship, Pacifism, and Just War Theory.* Minneapolis, MN: Fortress Press.

Cervantes, Miguel de. 1959. “The Siege of Numantia.” In *The Classical Theatre*, edited by Eric Bentley, and translated by Roy Campbell, 3: 7–160. New York: Doubleday Anchor Books.

Cervantes, Miguel de. 1994. *La destrucción de Numancia.* Edited by Alfredo Hermenegildo. Madrid: Castalia.

Cervantes, Miguel de. 1995. *El cerco de Numancia.* Edited by Robert Marrast. Madrid: Cátedra.

Clausewitz, Carl von. 1993. *On War.* Translated by Michael Howard and Peter Paret. New York: Everyman’s Library.

de Armas, Frederick. 1998. *Cervantes, Raphael and the Classics*. Cambridge: Cambridge University Press.

Dijkhuizen, Jan Frans van, and Karl Enenkel. 2009. "Introduction: Constructions of Physical Pain in Early Modern Culture." In *The Sense of Suffering: Construction of Physical Pain in Early Modern Culture*, edited by Jan Frans van Dijkhuizen and Karl Enenkel, 1–17. Leiden & Boston: Brill.

Duras, Marguerite. 1986. *The War*. Translated by Barbara Bray. New York: The New York Press.

Egido, Aurora. 2003. "La discreción y la prudencia en el teatro de Cervantes." In *Theatralia* (El teatro de Cervantes ante el IV centenario de la edición del *Quijote* 1605–2005), edited by Jesús G. Maestro, 89–121. Vilagarcía de Arousa and Vanderbilt: Mirabel Editorial.

Erasmus, Desiderius. 2001. *The Adages of Erasmus*. Translated by Margaret Mann Phillips. Toronto: University of Toronto Press.

Friedman, Edward H. 1977. "*La Numancia* within Structural Patterns of Sixteenth-century Spanish Tragedy." *Neophilologus* 61 (1): 74–89. http://dx.doi.org/10.1007/BF01511546.

González de León, Fernando. 2003. "*Soldados platicos* and *caballeros*: The Social Dimensions of Ethics in the Early Modern Spanish Army." In *The Chivalric Ethos and the Development of Military Professionalism*, edited by D.J.B. Trim, 235–68. Leiden and Boston: Brill.

González de León, Fernando. 2009. *The Road to Rocroi: Class, Culture and Command in the Spanish Army of Flanders, 1567–1659*. Leiden and Boston: Brill.

Greer, Margaret. 2006. "Imperialism and Anthropophagy in Early Modern Spanish Tragedy: The Unthought Known." In *Reason and Its Others: Italy, Spain, and the New World*, edited by David R. Castillo and Massimo Lollini, 279–95. Nashville, TN: Vanderbilt University Press.

Hermenegildo, Alfredo. 1976. *La Numancia de Cervantes*. Madrid: Sociedad General Española de Librería.

Johnson, Carroll. 1980. "*La Numancia* and the Structure of Cervantine Ambiguity." *Ideologies and Literature* 3: 75–95.

Kerkhoff, Manfred. 1997. *Kairos: Exploraciones ocasionales en torno a tiempo y destiempo*. San Juan: Editorial de la Universidad de Puerto Rico.

King, Willard F. 1979. "Cervantes' *Numancia* and Imperial Spain." *Modern Language Notes* 94: 200–21.

Maestro, Jesús G. 2004. *La secularización de la tragedia: Cervantes y* La Numancia. Madrid: Ediciones Clásicas; Ediciones del Orto.

Maglione, Sabatino G. 2000. "Amity and Enmity in Cervantes's *La Numancia.*" *Hispania* 83 (2): 179–88. http://dx.doi.org/10.2307/346160.

Orend, Brian. 2005. "War." In *The Stanford Encyclopedia of Philosophy*. Edited by Edward N. Zalta. Winter edition. http://plato.stanford.edu/entries/war/#2.

Reichberg, Gregory M., Henrik Syse, and Endre Begby, eds. 2006. *The Ethics of War: Classic and Contemporary Readings*. Malden: Blackwell.

Russell, Frederick H. 1975. *The Just War in the Middle Ages*. Cambridge: Cambridge University Press.

Simerka, Barbara. 2003. *Discourses of Empire: Counter-Epic Literature in Early Modern Spain*. University Park: Pennsylvania State University Press.

Vitoria, Francisco de. 1991. *Political Writings*. Edited by Anthony Pagden and Jeremy Lawrance. Cambridge: Cambridge University Press.

Vivar, Francisco. 2004. *La Numancia de Cervantes y la memoria de un mito*. Madrid: Biblioteca Nueva.

Walzer, Michael. 2006. *Just and Unjust Wars: A Moral Argument with Historical Illustrations*. 4th ed. New York: Basic Books.

Weil, Simone. 2005. *War and the Iliad*. Translated by Mary McCarthy. New York: New York Review Books.

Zimic, Stanislav. 1979. "Visión política y moral de Cervantes en *Numancia*." *Anales Cervantinos* 18: 107–50.

# 13 The Goddess, Dionysus, and the Material World in *Don Quijote*

TIMOTHY AMBROSE

In this essay, I will discuss, among other things, three material objects that either appear in or may be connected to the novel *Don Quijote*: 1) an enchanted talking bronze head that appears in chapter 62 of *Don Quijote*, Part II, 2) a painting by Titian entitled *Bacchus and Ariadne*, and 3) a labyrinth, the ruins of which may still be found on the island of Crete. Linked to these three material objects, the essay's overarching theme will be that of something non-material: an ancient feminine divinity known by many names,[1] as well as the connections between this feminine divinity and the equally ancient god Dionysus, for Dionysus and the Great Goddess of antiquity were intimately related. My essay will suggest the presence of a number of signs of Dionysus and the Goddess in Cervantes' novel.

The possible interrelatedness of the three objects mentioned above suggests a matrix of which they are a part or out of which they emerge. An archaic meaning of the word "matrix" is womb. This word, "womb," points to the origin of the word "matrix": etymologically, "matrix" originates in the same root as the word "matter," as does the latter's derivative "material"; the etymological source of "matrix," "matter," and "material" – as well as of "maternal," "matriarchy," and "matrimony" – is the Indo-European root *mater*, meaning mother.[2] It would seem, therefore, appropriate that an investigation and interpretation of three material objects be contained within an essay that speaks about the Great Mother Goddess whose cult extends beyond the limits of written history.

Helmut Jaskolski, studying the feminine divinity worshipped in the Near East and the Mediterranean world in ancient times, finds that "the Great Mother was venerated – *natura naturans*, the embodiment of the eternally constant primordial force of nature, the source or ground of life ... one of the many manifestations of the Magna Mater, Mother Earth

… In the Mediterranean region at that time, there existed a feminine, maternal culture. It was not a male god who ruled the world, but the Great Goddess, the mother of all life" (1997, 39). The Great Goddess spoken of by Jaskolski was closely connected to the material world. In this regard, Jean Markale makes the following observation: "We must not ignore the fact that the concept of divine mother is linked to *matter*, thus to the earth, and that, consequently, this telluric aspect necessarily leads to a search for special places supposedly favorable to a privileged relationship between mother and child, between the 'creator' and the creature. At Delphi, the sanctuary of the Great Goddess, an underground *womblike* sanctuary is marked by the *omphalos*, the world's navel" (1999, 31).

A special place, like those referred to by Markale, which is connected to the Goddess in *Don Quijote*, Part I, is the Sierra Morena, and I will discuss this connection more fully below. For now, let us simply note that the Sierra Morena is a metaphorical labyrinth.[3] This analogy between the Sierra Morena and the Cretan labyrinth leads us to Ariadne, the name by which the Great Goddess was known on the island of Crete, and thence to Titian's painting, which depicts the famed meeting of Ariadne and Bacchus (Dionysus for the Greeks) on the island of Naxos (see fig. 1). In addition to being the source or ground of the material world, the Goddess was also intimately linked to other ancient divinities. We will see her as Cybele, also known as Goddess of the Mountain.[4] Dulcinea, then will have dominion over the labyrinth of Sierra Morena, and more importantly, over the labyrinth of Don Quijote's mind.

The enchanted head that I have mentioned above will turn out to be that of Orpheus, the mythical musician and singer, Dionysus's priest and founder of the mystical cult of Orphism. The ancient Greek and Roman gods were fundamental to the Italian Renaissance. Joscelyn Godwin elucidates the relationship between the gods and Renaissance art, suggesting that during the Renaissance there existed an unspoken, perhaps even unconscious, "dream" of dwelling in the realm of the gods. Outlawed in almost every form, this impulse found expression in "the favorite language of the unconscious, of dreams: that of images. [Thus,] the dream of an alternative, pagan cosmos entered the European imagination through the visual and performing arts" (2002, 2).[5] Titian was one of many Renaissance artists who depicted the gods. His mythological paintings are considered by art historians to be among his finest works. A work that strikingly displays Titian's skill in bringing to life the world of the gods is his *Bacchus and Ariadne*.[6]

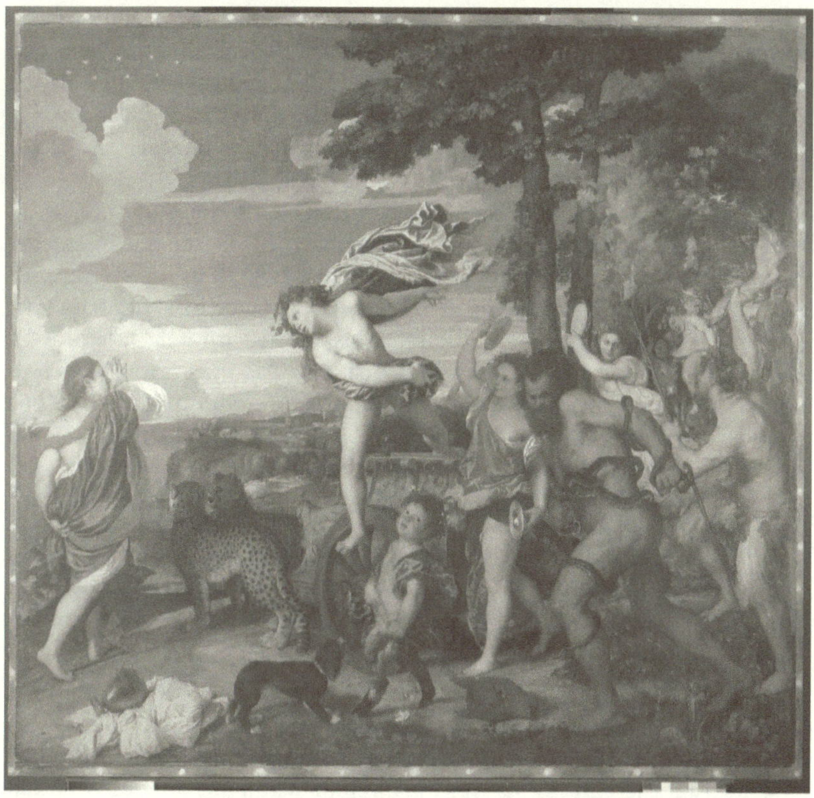

Figure 1 Titian. *Bacchus and Ariadne*, 1520–3. The National Gallery, London / Art Resource, NY.

In the first part of Cervantes' novel, we find evidence of Don Quijote's own dream of living in the world of the pagan gods when he speaks about the wonders of a primordial Golden Age,[7] a time of heaven on earth – in other words, the time of the gods: "siglos dichosos aquellos a quien los antiguos pusieron nombre de dorados" [Fortunate the age and fortunate the times called golden by the ancients] (1978, 1.11.155; 2003, 76), hence also the time of the ancients. Frederick de Armas has discussed the influence and importance of the ancient world in *Don Quijote*, as well as in other Cervantine texts. As de Armas states, "Beneath the chivalric surface, a deeper subtext can be perceived, one that derives from antiquity" (1998,

3). Dulcinea, although obviously an important part of the parody of chivalric romance, may also be located in this more ancient subtext. De Armas suggests this when he discusses how Don Quijote constructs his beloved from images found in a number of Renaissance mythological paintings (2001, 4–5), works of art that represent through their imagery the pagan world, the world of the ancients, the world of the gods.

Imagination, Godwin tells us, is the domain of the gods (2002, 2). Roberto Calasso expresses a similar notion when he states, "Whatever they may be, the gods manifest themselves above all as mental events' (2001, 169).[8] Don Quixote emphasizes the importance of mental activity, in the form of imagination and desire, in his construction of Dulcinea: "Y así, bástame a mí pensar y creer que la Buena de Aldonza Lorenzo es hermosa y honesta … para concluir con todo, yo imagino que todo lo que digo es así, sin que sobre ni falte nada, y píntola en mi imaginación como la deseo" [And therefore, it is enough for me to think and believe that my good Aldonza Lorenzo is beautiful and virtuous … And to conclude, I imagine that everything I say is true, no more and no less, and I depict her in my imagination as I wish her to be] (1978, 1.25.314; 2003, 201). This passage connects Dulcinea to both painting and the imagination, thereby suggesting her possible status as a goddess.

If there were a Graeco-Roman god we might identify with Don Quijote, it would be Dionysus,[9] who triggered the catasterism of Ariadne into a constellation. In addition, this god, like Don Quijote, is associated with madness, comedy, and tragedy, as well as with the transformation of one thing into another. Dionysus was the Olympian god not only of wine and intoxication, and consequently of joyfulness,[10] but also "of ritual madness and ecstatic liberation from everyday identity…the god of the theatre and impersonation, the mask being the symbol of the transformation of identity" (March 2001, 264).[11] The knight-errant created by Cervantes exhibits these characteristics: his madness is a sort of ritualistic liberation from everyday identity – indeed, isn't this what Alonso Quijano is seeking when he transforms himself into Don Quijote? In fact, the central theme of the entire novel might be stated as that of transformation.

Another reason that Dionysus is of importance for our present inquiry is his close association with two formidable goddesses. One is the ancient Pan-Hellenic Goddess Cybele, originally from Phrygia and often called The Mother of the Gods. The other goddess associated with Dionysus is Ariadne, best known to the modern world in her human form as a character in the story of Theseus and the Minotaur. Dulcinea, as we will see, may be associated with both Cybele and Ariadne.

Ruth El Saffar, while not using the word "goddess," does suggest Dulcinea's other-than-human, i.e., divine, dimension: "Don Quixote, like the heroes of the chivalric romances, sees the lady as a distant image of beauty and refinement, so distinct from the familiar world of men as to be not only unattainable but scarcely human" (1984, 53). Leo Spitzer emphasizes the play of opposites in the novel, but he also draws attention to what he perceives as a permanent reality that transcends the shifting surfaces of this fictional world: "And yet, beyond this perspectivism, we may sense the presence of something which is not subject to fluctuation: the immovable, immutable principle of the divine" (2005, 164). The presence of something divine that Spitzer perceives in Cervantes' novel may be associated, although Spitzer does not do so, with the Goddess and Dionysus, as well as with the gods in general, i.e., the pagan dream of the Renaissance.

The rhetoric of parody in Cervantes' novel may seem to be at odds with the presence of the gods. However, Calasso cogently argues that parody accompanies the return of the ancient gods in the modern era. As the gods make their tumultuous reappearance, "at the same time a subtle, indomitable mockery embraces everything and renders it all uncertain, ephemeral: parody" (2001, 74). Parody and the gods – or the parody of the gods, to be more precise – actually precedes modernity; it originates in ancient Greece and is linked to Dionysus. Jenny March describes this phenomenon: "At the Festival of Dionysus at Athens, in the fifth century BC, each tragedian wrote a satyr play that provided comic relief after his set of three tragedies ... the plot was taken from myth, sometimes with connections to the preceding trilogy" (2001, 688). The word "satyr," used to name these burlesques of mythical episodes, is the probable source of the words "satire" and "satirical" (2001, 1549), words intimately connected to Cervantes' novel.

Spitzer explicitly denies the existence of any Dionysian elements in Cervantes' novel, almost as though he felt the possibility of those elements being present and made haste to eradicate them: "[Cervantes'] humor is the freedom of the heights, no fate-bound Dionysiac dissolution of the individual into nothingness and night ... but a freedom beneath the dome of that religion which affirms the freedom of the will. There is, in the world of his creation ... the crystalline lucidity of an artistic Maker in its manifold reflections and refractions" (2005, 197). Spitzer's words implicitly affirm the Apollonian aspect of Cervantes' novel and identify it with Christianity, "that religion which affirms the freedom of the will." However, given the play of opposites that characterizes *Don Quijote* – a play of opposites that Spitzer himself discusses – it is likely that if there are Apollonian elements, there will also be elements that are Dionysian, and if there are Christian elements, there will be those that are pagan as well.[12]

A remarkable instance of something pagan occurs in Part II of Cervantes' novel. I am referring to the enchanted head that appears in chapter 62. This bronze head appears amid a whole constellation of signs or indicators that point to Dionysus, two of these being the greater importance given to both women and Sancho in Part II. Dionysus is the Greek god most associated with women; the maenads or female bacchants were a prominent part of his ritual worship, as we can see in Euripides' *Bacchae* (Segal 1982, 159; March 2001, 473). Because of this, the greater importance of feminine elements in Part II, noted by Ruth El Saffar,[13] suggests an increase in the Dionysian aspect of the novel. El Saffar further links this increased importance of the feminine to the more prominent role that Sancho assumes in Part II, stating that Sancho's greater prominence is a sign of, "the assertion of the body over the head" (1984, 124).[14]

This greater importance given to the body further suggests a strengthening of the Dionysian aspect of the novel, for, as Rafael López-Pedraza has pointed out, Dionysian ritual is linked to the body: "The mysteries give the soul a dimension of living religious experience which, in the case of Dionysus, means feeling oneself in the body" (2000, 43). Furthermore, the appearance of the enchanted head immediately follows the episode of the two ladies who dance with Don Quijote until he collapses. Dancing was an integral part of the revelries of Dionysian worship as we see in the *Bacchae* when Cadmus proclaims his readiness to dance all night to honour the god (Euripides 1990, 17). It is significant that these same two women, symbolic maenads as it were, are among the small group of people that Don Antonio invites to witness the spectacle of the enchanted head.

The head itself, a ruse to make fun of Don Quijote, recalls the head of Orpheus. After Orpheus was torn to pieces by the Thracian women, "his head was thrown into the River Hebrus and floated, still singing, down the stream" (March 2001, 573). The fact that Don Antonio's bronze head is able to speak, together with the Dionysian signs that surround its appearance in the novel, suggests the disembodied head of Orpheus. Orpheus was said to be Dionysus's priest and to have spread the god's worship. Ovid, for example, tells us that after Orpheus had been murdered and dismembered, Dionysus "would not leave this crime unscourged. / His grief was great." Dionysus then avenged, "the loss of Orpheus, the poet who had sung / of Bacchus' [i.e., Dionysus's] sacred mysteries" (1993, 361). Orpheus was also traditionally known as the founder of Orphism, an esoteric cult with Dionysian elements, and to have authored poems and mystical books (Tripp 1974, 436). This aspect of the mythology associated with Orpheus, i.e., the tradition of his mystical wisdom, is echoed in the phenomenon of Don Antonio's bronze head, which has the power not only to speak, but also to answer correctly any question asked of it.[15]

The episode of the enchanted head appears between the dancing scene and that of Don Quijote's defeat by the Knight of the White Moon, the moon being one of the symbolic indicators of the feminine according to El Saffar. It is, therefore, all the more appropriate that the enchanted head be associated not only with Orpheus, but also with Dionysus, a god in whose cult dancing and women play such an important part. That the enchanted head expresses something pagan is further suggested by the fact that the Inquisition orders Don Antonio to destroy it: "divulgándose por la ciudad que don Antonio tenía en su casa una cabeza encantada, que a cuantos le preguntaban respondía, temiendo no llegase a los oídos de las despiertas centinelas de nuestra Fe, habiendo declarado el caso a los señores inquisidores, le mandaron que lo deshiciese" [word spread throughout the city that Don Antonio had an enchanted head in his house that would answer every question asked of it, and fearing that the rumors would reach the ears of the alert guardians of our Faith, he informed the inquisitors of the matter and was ordered to dismantle it] (1978, 2.62.517; 2003, 872).[16]

Although Part II of the *Quijote* may signal in certain respects an intensification of the Dionysian aspect of the novel, Part I also contains many signs of the ancient mythical world. A prime example is the explicit reference to the Great Mother Goddess found in Don Quijote's discourse on the Golden Age. Of the Golden Age, Don Quijote states, "Todo era paz entonces, todo amistad, todo concordia; aún no se había atrevido la pesada reja del corvo arado a abrir ni visitar las entrañas piadosas de nuestra primera madre, que ella, sin ser forzada, ofrecía, por todas partes de su fértil y espacioso seno, lo que pudiese hartar, sustentar y deleitar a los hijos que entonces la poseían" [In that time all was peace, friendship, and harmony; the heavy curve of the plowshare had not yet dared to open or violate the merciful womb of our first mother, for she, without being forced, offered up, everywhere across her broad and fertile bosom, whatever would satisfy, sustain, and delight the children who then possessed her] (1978, 1.11.156; 2003, 76–7).

This passage suggests the ancient fertility goddess who has come down to our own day, divested to a large extent of her sacredness, with the name Mother Earth – an appellation that suggests a telluric goddess. In terms of the pagan world, Don Quijote's words evoke the feminine divinity who went by different names, but who in the Mediterranean world was most commonly known as Cybele, "the great Phrygian mother-goddess" (March 2001, 230), who either absorbed or became associated with many other goddesses, such as Diana, Gaia, Rhea, and Demeter. Cybele, as we shall see, is closely associated with Dionysus.

Satyrs are also closely related to Dionysus and his cult in ancient Greece and Rome and, therefore, when Don Quijote declares that the Golden Age was a time in which Mother Earth had not yet been violated by means of plowing, he is invoking the sacred time and place of satyrs, and therefore also of Dionysus, because, in the words of Edward Tripp, "Satyrs were spirits of the uncontrolled fertility of the woods and unplowed fields" (1974, 521). Cybele had a certain kinship with satyrs – one of her companions was Pan – and she was "a goddess of fertility and the mistress of wild nature" (March 2001, 230), the latter, that is "wild nature," being also associated with Dionysus (264). It is therefore fitting that this goddess and this god should be linked to Don Quijote, who wanders the countryside, preferring to remain in the wilderness rather than a town. This preference is most notably expressed in Part I in the affinity the knight feels for the Sierra Morena: "Así como don Quijote entró por aquellas montañas, se le alegró el corazón, pareciéndole aquellos lugares acomodados para las aventuras que buscaba. Reducíansele a la memoria los maravillosos acaecimientos que en semejantes soledades y asperezas habían sucedido a caballeros andantes" [As soon as Don Quixote entered those mountains his heart filled with joy, for it was a landscape that seemed suited to the adventures he was seeking. What he recalled were the marvellous events that had befallen knights errant in similarly desolate and wild places] (1978, 1.23.278–9; 2003, 174). Indeed, when Don Quijote finds himself fully enveloped by Sierra Morena, he intuits it as that sacred space where the Goddess and the satyrs abide: "así los ligeros y lascivos sátiros, de quien sois, aunque en vano, amadas" [loved, although in vain, by wanton and lustful satyrs] (1978, 1.25.308; 2003, 196).

One of Cybele's epithets was Mountain Mother, and in *Mother of the Gods: From Cybele to the Virgin Mary*, Philippe Borgeaud tells us that the Goddess, "loves … mountains filled with echoes, and small wooded valleys … Localized in a mountain landscape among the wild beasts, she loves a music that is frequently found in the Dionysian context" (2004, 9). Although Dulcinea is not physically present in the Sierra Morena, Don Quijote emphatically associates her with the ritualistic madness, a most Dionysian enterprise, which he intends to enact there. Thus, in the Sierra Morena, Dulcinea may be associated with the goddess Cybele and Don Quijote with Dionysus.

Cybele is, as we have said, linked to Dionysus, in whose myth she plays an important part: Zeus's jealous wife, Hera, having learned that Semele is pregnant by Zeus, forevermore bears a grudge against Semele's son Dionysus. Hera finally gets her revenge on the youthful Dionysus by driving him mad. After many wanderings, not unlike those of Don Quijote, Dionysus arrives in Phrygia. In Phrygia Cybele, "received a young Dionysus in her home to cure him of his madness and initiate him into her own rites. In fact, when Dionysus is shown in Thebes, his country of origin, he is depicted as a foreigner coming to these regions, arriving after a long voyage" (Borgeaud 2004, 2).[17] Like Cybele's cure of Dionysus, feminine elements in Part II of Cervantes' novel, as Ruth El Saffar notes, are at work in effecting the cure of Don Quijote's madness (1984, 122).

Because of the close relationship between Dionysus and Cybele, both in mythology and in ritual, signs of one of them may be taken to imply the presence of the other. As we will see, *Don Quijote*, Part I contains a number of intriguing signs of the presence of Dionysus. Dionysus is associated not only with the Goddess, but also – more than any other god – with women in general. With regard to Dionysus's association with women, Charles Segal in *Dionysiac Poetics and Euripides' Bacchae* states:

> In the *Birth of Tragedy* Nietzsche analyzed the dichotomy between the Dionysian and the Apollonian, the principle of emotional fusion and the principle of differentiation and individuation. The point was epoch-making for the understanding of Greek tragedy and Greek culture. But what is missing from Nietzsche's discussion, otherwise fruitful for the study of the *Bacchae*, is a consideration of the feminine in relation to both Dionysus and Apollo. The vehemence of Pentheus' resistance to Dionysus and the close association of Dionysus with women in the play together constitute a remarkable insight into the weaknesses of that Apollonian view of self and world that has come to dominate Western consciousness ... Dionysus's cult gives to women a power and an importance that were denied them, on the whole, in fifth-century Athens. (1982, 158–9)

Dulcinea is, in many respects the centrepiece of Cervantes' novel, and the fact that such a powerful feminine presence provokes and permeates Don Quijote's adventures suggests a fundamentally Dionysian element of his character. Dulcinea is, in Javier Herrero's words, "the center of his knightly adventure and will reign over his life as long as his madness lasts ... the interpretation of Dulcinea's place in Don Quijote's pilgrimage is essential to our understanding of the book" (1982, 42). Herrero's use of the word "pilgrimage" in this passage suggests Dulcinea's sacredness, her goddess-like quality.

James Hillman writes that Western consciousness, "has never known what to do with the dark, *material*, and passionate part of itself, except to cast it off and call it Eve. What we have come to mean by the word 'conscious' is 'light'; this light is inconceivable for this consciousness without a distaff side of something else opposed to it that is inferior and which has been called – in Greek, Jewish, and Christian contexts – female" (1978, 8; emphasis added). Hillman's remarks evoke the opposite of those attributes that Spitzer sees as dominant in *Don Quijote* – they evoke Dionysian rather than Apollonian attributes.

In certain respects, Dulcinea may be thought of as representing the marginalized – dark, material, and passionate – part of the human psyche to which Hillman refers. Roberto González Echevarría draws our attention to this phenomenon when he relates the dark side of Don Quijote's love for Dulcinea to "his prurient desire for Aldonza," who is, in a sense, a marginalized substratum of the idealized Dulcinea. Although Echevarría does not mention it specifically in the terms I am using here, he suggests this Dionysian side of Dulcinea when he asserts that she, "does not give the impression of being distant and literary; rather, she seems current with our modern conceptions of love [which are] conscious of [love's] dubious source in dark drives beyond our control" (2005, 35). Furthermore, Echevarría relates what he calls the "engendering of Dulcinea [to] dark drives beyond not only our control but more significantly also our comprehension" (2005, 52). These words evoke one of Dionysus's primary characteristics, his incomprehensibility.[18]

Dionysian elements are present not only, as we have just mentioned, at what can be considered the core or centre of Cervantes' novel, that is Dulcinea, but also in more peripheral locations. For example, in chapter 15 of Part I, Don Quijote decides to ride on Sancho's donkey, because Rocinante has been badly beaten by drovers who resent the horse's trying to mate with the mares they are pasturing. Don Quijote and Sancho are also beaten as a result of Rocinante's actions, while Sancho's donkey remains unharmed. Don Quijote explains why he does not consider it beneath him to ride on a donkey: "que no tendré a deshonra la tal caballería, porque me acuerdo haber leído que aquel buen viejo Sileno, ayo y pedagogo del alegre dios de la risa, cuando entró en la ciudad de las cien puertas iba, muy a su placer, caballero sobre un muy hermoso asno" [I shall not consider such a mount a dishonor, because I remember reading that when Silenus, the good old tutor and teacher of the merry god of laughter, entered the city of one hundred gates, he rode very happily mounted on a beautiful jackass] (1978, 1.15.196; 2003, 108).

Don Quijote identifies himself with Silenus, who according to many accounts was the youthful Dionysus's guardian, teacher, and foster-parent. Sileni, of whom Silenus is an individualized representation, were almost indistinguishable from satyrs, except that they were generally older, wiser, and drunker. Together with the satyrs, they were the male members of Dionysus's ritual entourage that was led by Silenus. Silenus was also the chief comic character in the satyr plays (Tripp 1974, 524). Don Quijote's reference to Silenus as someone worthy of imitation can only be explained by Silenus's close association with the god Dionysus, which is reinforced by his own reference to Dionysus as "Dios de la risa."[19]

Another element associated with Dionysus is the labyrinth. This is due to the god's association with Ariadne. It was Ariadne who helped the hero Theseus exit the artful construction of Daedalus after he had killed the Minotaur. When Theseus fled Crete, he took Ariadne with him, but then abandoned her. Dionysus, or Bacchus as the Romans called him, discovered her on the island of Naxos and Dionysus and Ariadne were subsequently married. The encounter between Ariadne and Dionysus / Bacchus is the subject of one of Titian's most celebrated mythological paintings, *Bacchus and Ariadne*. This work was commissioned by Alfonso d'Este, Duke of Ferrara, to be part of a group of mythological paintings.

In *Bacchus and Ariadne*, Titian used Ovid as one of his sources. Ovid's *Fasti* and *Ars Amatoria* both mention Bacchus's transformation of the jewels of Ariadne's diadem into the constellation known as Corona, visible in the upper left-hand corner of the painting (Panofsky 1969, 142). Because this incident provides an example of transformation or metamorphosis, Ovid also includes it in *The Metamorphoses*. This detail of Titian's painting draws our attention to the theme of transformation, characteristic of Dionysus / Bacchus and a theme that runs throughout Cervantes' novel. In the painting, the stunning figure of Bacchus, whose distraught visage suggests madness – perhaps the madness of his love for Ariadne – appears to either leap or fly out of his chariot. These features, together with the contortion of Bacchus's body as he moves through the air, seem to connote a metamorphosis or transformation through which the god himself is passing, again perhaps due to his sudden sight of and falling in love with Ariadne. This madness and transformation are reminiscent of Don Quijote and the transformation his madness provokes in him and all he perceives, including his sublime passion for Dulcinea. Although he does not mention Ariadne by name, this figure is not far from the novel's mythical underpinnings. In Part II, Ariadne's crown is invoked: "la corona de Ariadiana" [the crown of Aridiana] (1978, 2.38.334; 2003, 709).

Ariadne's body too is contorted: her hand waves towards the sea, towards the ship of the fleeing Theseus, while her face is turned in amazement as she locks her gaze with that of Bacchus. Silenus can be seen to the right in the background being held up on his donkey by one of Bacchus's retinue of satyrs. Charles Hope, commenting on Titian's *Bacchus and Ariadne*, speaks of the "irresistible joyfulness and vitality of the figures" (2003, 67). Of another painting, *The Worship of Venus*, commissioned by Alfonso d'Este to be part of the same group, Hope remarks that, although Titian had little knowledge of art and architecture from the ancient world, he was able for that very reason to express more freely a vitality that gives the viewer a more profound sense of what the primordial experience of the world of the gods must have been like for the ancients: "Because he had no direct experience of the overwhelming visual remains in Rome he had to rely very largely on his own imagination. If anything this proved to his advantage, for he was able to enter freely into the spirit of the ancient world without resorting to a merely pedantic restatement of the norms of classical art" (2003, 64). These words could also apply to Titian's *Bacchus and Ariadne*. Of special interest is the emphasis placed on Titian's ability to enter into that other world, the world of the gods, by means of his imagination, an attribute he shares with Don Quijote and, perhaps, with Cervantes himself.

Cervantes would have been acquainted with Titian's painting.[20] The signs of Dionysus / Bacchus and Ariadne present in Cervantes' novel suggest the possibility that Cervantes' own imagination could have been sparked by gazing at this impressive canvas.

The story of Ariadne and Theseus and of Dionysus's encounter with Ariadne and marriage to her confers an extremely high status on Ariadne, who was known in the ancient world not only as the Wife of Dionysus, but also as the Mistress of the Labyrinth. Carl Kerényi states that Ariadne, "must have been a Great Goddess" (1976, 90), and that in the well-known story about her helping Theseus, "the Great Goddess has become a king's daughter, but there can be no doubt as to her identity" (1976, 99). In addition, Walter F. Otto states that, "with Ariadne the nature of the Dionysiac woman is exalted to marvelous heights. She is the perfect image of the beauty which, when it is touched by its lover, gives life immortality" (1965, 181). Otto's words could easily be used to describe the transformation of Aldonza into Dulcinea. Due to the presence of signs of Dionysus in Cervantes' novel, as well as to Don

Quijote's possible identification with Dionysus, Ariadne, like Cybele, may be identified with Dulcinea.

Furthermore, the novel uses the labyrinth, a structure so closely associated with Ariadne, as a metaphor to represent situations and places. For example, when Don Quijote wants to remain in the Sierra Morena to act out his ritualistic madness – a Dionysian activity, as we have noted above – he sends Sancho to Dulcinea with a letter explaining the arduous penance he is undertaking on her behalf. Before Sancho's departure, Don Quijote advises him to be very careful going and coming back to this secluded spot in the mountain wilderness: "que lo más acertado será, para que no me yerres y te pierdes, que cortes algunas retamas de las muchas que por aquí hay, y las vayas poniendo de trecho a trecho, hasta salir a lo raso, las cuales te servirán de mojones y señales para que me halles cuando vuelvas, a imitación del hilo del laberinto de Perseo" [so that you will not make a mistake and lose your way, you should cut some of the broom that grows in such abundance here, and place the stalks at intervals along the way until you reach level ground, and they will serve as markers and signs, as did the thread of Perseus in the labyrinth, so that you can find me when you return] (1978, 1. 25.317; 2003, 204).

Whether we take the name of Perseus in place of Theseus to be an oversight on Cervantes' part or not, the association of the labyrinth with the wilds of the Sierra Morena evokes the goddess Ariadne, Mistress of the Labyrinth and Wife of Dionysus. Don Quijote's Dionysian, ritualistic madness in the service of Dulcinea/Ariadne in this remote place is in keeping with his use of the labyrinth as a metaphor for the Sierra Morena. Just as Ariadne has authority over the labyrinth – without her, Theseus is hopelessly lost – so too Dulcinea may be thought of as having dominion over the labyrinth of the Sierra Morena into which Don Quijote enters and from which he, like Theseus, departs. And yet, she does not leave his imagination. It is as if Dulcinea (as Ariadne and Cybele) have dominion of the knight's mind.

The most important instance of the labyrinth metaphor may perhaps be that found in chapter 28 of Part I, when the reader is told that the story he is reading follows "un hilo" that is "rastrillado, torcido y aspado" [tortuous, winding, and meandering thread] (1978, 1.28.344; 2003, 227). With these words, the narrator evokes not only the thread that Ariadne gave to Theseus but also the bewildering path that leads through the passageways of the labyrinth itself. The narrator thereby suggests to us that the labyrinth, with its connotations of the Great Goddess and Dionysus, is a metaphor encompassing the entire text of the novel.

## NOTES

1 The ancient Goddess of whom I am speaking held dominion over the European world long before the arrival of the masculine gods.

2 This etymology has been taken from *The American Heritage Dictionary*, 4th ed. (2000, 2037).

3 On Sierra Morena as labyrinth, see Herrero (1981), Fajardo (1984), and Juárez-Almendros (2004).

4 Indeed, all of the ancient gods were considered to be the offspring of the Goddess and one of her many names was Mother of the Gods.

5 Roberto Calasso echoes Godwin's point: "Long euphemized and tightly bridled in literary texts, the gods ran wild in painting" (2002, 29).

6 There were strong political links between Spain and Italy during Titian's lifetime and Titian was favoured by both Charles V and Philip II, Spain's kings during the sixteenth century. Cervantes would have been well acquainted with Titian's paintings, either from having seen the originals or from the numerous reproductions that were available. Even today, the Prado Museum in Madrid has the largest collection of Titian's paintings of any museum in Europe.

7 The age of gold was the first of five ages defined by the ancient Greek poet Hesiod in his *Works and Days*.

8 Calasso then adds a most intriguing caveat: "Yet, contrary to the modern illusion, it is the psychic powers that are fragments of the gods, not the gods that are fragments of the psychic powers" (2001, 169).

9 This is truer of Part I than Part II in which Dionysian forces, rather than being identified with Don Quijote, would seem to be involved in defeating him. The section of my essay that deals with the enchanted head discusses some, but far from all, of the Dionysian forces in Part II.

10 "Homer calls him [Dionysus] a 'joy for mortals' (*Iliad* 14.325) and Hesiod 'he of many delights' (*Theogony* 941)" (March 2001, 264). March also states that Dionysus, "was the god of all wild nature" (2001, 264).

11 The fact that Don Quixote's imagination is the primary characteristic of his madness suggests a further link between the Manchegan knight-errant and the gods. This link goes back at least to the time of Plato, who states in the *Phaedrus* that "madness is superior to temperance … because the latter has a merely human origin, while the former belongs to the divine." Roberto Calasso suggests that this remark by Plato reawakened the cult of Dionysus in both philosophy and painting at the beginning of the Renaissance (2001, 62).

12 Cervantes was undoubtedly aware of the pagan elements in his text and of the possible criticism that such elements would attract. Two examples

are found in chapters 12 and 13 of Part I. In chapter 12 the priests in Grisóstomo's village have challenged the unchristian, i.e., pagan, manner in which Grisóstomo has asked to be buried, after dying of lovesickness for Marcela. On his way to witness this most unusual burial the next day in chapter 13, Don Quijote meets a traveller named Vivaldo who echoes the priests when he questions the knight about the other-than-Christian nature of his worship of Dulcinea. Although Don Quijote gives an answer of sorts to Vivaldo's question, the matter, like so many others, is not resolved in the text. That this question should arise with regard to Dulcinea would seem to be especially appropriate given the expressions of the Goddess and Dionysus that we find in Cervantes' novel.

13 El Saffar discusses the distinction between women in *Don Quijote* Part I and Part II: "In Part I, women appeared almost exclusively in the role of nubile creatures disputed over by the men. In Part II, however, women are no longer subject to the desires of men" (1984, 122–4). El Saffar goes on to enumerate the many instances of the more imposing presence of the feminine in Part II.

14 Mikhail Bakhtin too notes this aspect of Sancho relative to Don Quijote when he comments on "Sancho's materialism" (1984, 23).

15 The enchanted head's ability to answer truthfully questions put to it perhaps suggests a connection to Apollo rather than to Dionysus, for it is the former god who is most associated with prophecy. W.C.K. Guthrie discusses the possibility that Orpheus had as many connections to Apollo as he did to Dionysus (1993, 42–7). In fact, the two gods were half-brothers and both were associated with the Oracle at Delphi (March 2001, 112).

16 On the pagan mysteries which the Inquisition wishes to censor, see Kallendorf (2004).

17 In an account that differs only slightly from Borgeaud's, Edward Tripp relates that while Dionysus was in Phrygia, "he adopted the oriental costume that he and his followers affected; there also he instituted many of his own rites, some of which resemble those of Cybele" (1974, 205).

18 W.C.K. Guthrie states, "The worship of Dionysus is something that can never be wholly explained" (1950, 145).

19 With respect to Dionysus as a god of merriment, happiness, and joy, see note 10 above. The fact that Don Quijote states that he has read about Silenus is a clear indication of the availability of texts about both Silenus and Dionysus. Both appear in Ovid and certain other Latin texts, and Cervantes would have had access to Greek texts in Latin or in summary form in the available compendia in Spanish and Italian (de Armas 1998, 87).

20 See note 6 above.

## WORKS CITED

*The American Heritage Dictionary of the English Language*. 2000. 4th ed. New York: Houghton Mifflin.

Bakhtin, Mikhail. 1984. *Rabelais and His World*. Translated by Hélène Iswolsky. Bloomington: Indiana University Press.

Borgeaud, Philippe. 2004. *Mother of the Gods: From Cybele to the Virgin Mary*. Baltimore, MD: Johns Hopkins University Press.

Calasso, Roberto. 2001 *Literature and the Gods*. Translated by Tim Parks. New York: Vintage Books.

Cervantes, Miguel de. 1978. *El ingenioso hidalgo don Quijote de la Mancha*. 2 vols. Edited by Luis Murillo. Madrid: Castalia.

Cervantes, Miguel de. 2003. *Don Quixote*. Translated by Edith Grossman. New York: HarperCollins.

de Armas, Frederick A. 1998. *Cervantes, Raphael and the Classics*. Cambridge: Cambridge University Press.

de Armas, Frederick A. 2001. "Painting Dulcinea: Italian Art and the *Art of Memory* in Cervantes' *Don Quijote*." *Yearbook of Comparative and General Literature* 49: 1–19.

El Saffar, Ruth. 1984. *Beyond Fiction: The Recovery of the Feminine in the Novels of Cervantes*. Berkeley: University of California Press.

Euripides. 1990. *The Bacchae*. Translated by C.K. Williams. New York: The Noonday Press / Farrar, Straus and Giroux.

Fajardo, Salvador J. 1984. "The Sierra Morena as Labyrinth in Don Quixote I." *MLN* 99 (2): 214–34. http://dx.doi.org/10.2307/2906185.

Godwin, Joscelyn. 2002. *The Pagan Dream of the Renaissance*. Grand Rapids, MI: Phanes Press.

González Echevarría, Roberto. 2005. *Love and the Law in Cervantes*. New Haven: Yale University Press.

Guthrie, W.C.K. 1950. *The Greeks and Their Gods*. London: Methuen.

Guthrie, W.K.C. 1993. *Orpheus and Greek Religion*. Princeton: Princeton University Press.

Herrero, Javier. 1981. "Sierra Morena as Labyrinth: From Wildness to Christian Knighthood." *Forum for Modern Language Studies* 17 (1): 55–67. http://dx.doi.org/10.1093/fmls/17.1.55.

Herrero, Javier. 1982. "Dulcinea and Her Critics." *Cervantes: Bulletin of the Cervantes Society of America* 2 (1): 23–42.

Hillman, James. 1978. *The Myths of Analysis: The Essays on Archetypal Psychology*. New York: Harper Colophon.

Hope, Charles. 2003. *Titian*. London: Chaucer Press.

Jaskolski, Helmut. 1997. *The Labyrinth: Symbol of Fear, Rebirth, and Liberation.* Translated by Michael H. Kohn. Boston: Shambala.

Juárez-Almendros, E. 2004. "Travestismo, Transferencias, Trueques e Inversiones en la Sierra Morena." *Cervantes* 24 (1): 39–64.

Kallendorf, Hilaire. 2004. "Why the Inquisition Dismantles the *Cabeza Encantada*." *Anuario de Estudios Cervantinos* 1: 149–63.

Kerényi, Carl. 1976. *Dionysus: Archetypal Image of Indestructible Life*. Princeton: Princeton University Press.

López-Pedraza, Rafael. 2000. *Dionysus in Exile: On the Repression of the Body and Emotion*. Wilmette, IL: Chiron.

March, Jennifer R. 2001. *Cassell's Dictionary of Classical Mythology*. London: Cassell.

Markale, Jean. 1999. *The Great Goddess: Reverence of the Divine Feminine from the Paleolithic to the Present*. Translated by Jody Gladding. Rochester, VT: Inner Traditions.

Otto, Walter F. 1965. *Dionysus: Myth and Cult*. Translated by Robert B. Palmer. Bloomington: Indiana University Press.

Ovid. 1993. *Metamorphoses*. Translated by Allen Mandelbaum. New York: Harcourt Brace.

Panofsky, Erwin. 1969. *Problems in Titian, Mostly Iconographic*. New York: New York University Press.

Segal, Charles. 1982. *Dionysiac Poetics and Euripides' Bacchae*. Princeton: Princeton University Press.

Spitzer, Leo. 2005. "Linguistic Perspectivism in the *Don Quijote*." In *Cervantes' Don Quixote: A Casebook*, edited by Roberto González Echevarría, 163–216. Oxford: Oxford University Press.

Tripp, Edward. 1974. *The Meridian Handbook of Classical Mythology*. New York: Penguin / Meridian.

# 14 Dismantling *Sosiego*: Undressing, Dressing, and Cross-Dressing in Mateo Alemán's *Guzmán de Alfarache*[1]

GORETTI GONZÁLEZ

> Que hubiera servido de poco alborotar tu sosiego habiéndote dicho parte de mi vida, dejando lo restante della
>
> [It would have been of little use to agitate your serenity having told you part of my life and leaving the rest of it out]
> Mateo Alemán, *Guzmán de Alfarache* (2006, 2.1.41)[2]

The protagonist and narrator of Mateo Alemán's picaresque novel calls attention to the disruption of *sosiego* that may well accompany the reading of his autobiography. In the *Tesoro de la lengua española* [The encyclopedia of the Spanish language] (1611), Sebastián de Covarrubias defines *sosegar* as "aquietar," or to calm, pacify, or placate. This *sosiego* speaks to the Spanish values of *mediocritas* and *prudentia.* Juan de Borja's *Empresas Morales* [Moral enterprises] (1581) illustrates this point. Encapsulating the resurgence of Senecan stoicism in glossing the motto, "Sapientis Animus,"[3] Borja equates prudence to an equanimity that suffers adversity with calm and *sosiego.* The neo-stoic ideals of prudence and temperance were both expressed and shaped by Spanish costume. For example, prudence and temperance are allegorically and physically engraved onto a gilded and silver-plated suit of armour made in 1585 for the seven-year-old Philip III (attributed to Lucio Marliani of Milan). Inscribing *sosiego* within the national rhetoric, Philip wears this ensemble in a 1592 full-scale portrait by Justus Tiel, (see fig. 1) titled *Alegoría de la educación de Felipe III* [Allegory of the Education of Philip III].[4] Encased within this armour, the young prince projects the virtue that Alemán's *Guzmán de Alfarache* (1599 I, 1604 II) subsequently aims to dismantle.

Américo Castro's *De la edad conflictiva* (1976) situates *sosiego* within the socio-historical context of early modern Spain. Castro defines the term

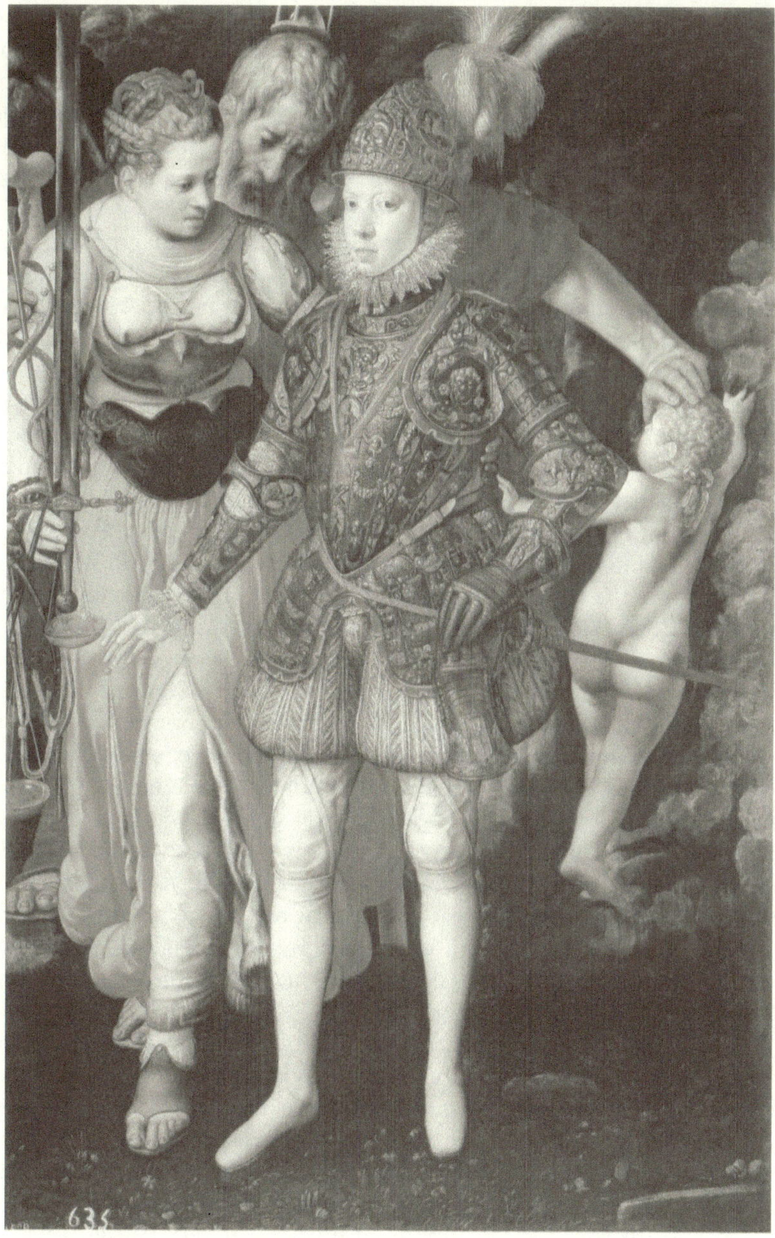

Figure 1 Justus Tiel. *Allegory of the Education of Philip III*, 1592. Museo Nacional del Prado, Madrid. ARTstor, NY.

as a sense of security that came with being an "old Christian:"[5] "Expresión de 'estar en uno mismo' fue el famoso vocablo *sosiego,* el no dejarse afectar por las circunstancias materiales, y el escaso interés por modificarlas, pues eso quedaba para moros, judíos o extranjeros" [the famous term *sosiego* was an expression of self-sufficiency, of not being affected by material circumstances and having scant interest in changing them, a task which was left to Moors, Jews, and foreigners] (1976, 68). Here, the Spanish critic extends stoic *sosiego* to the early modern Spanish ideal of integrity. A man's *entereza* signifies that he is lacking in nothing, "que no se dobla, ni tuerce, por odio, amor, o interés"[6] [that he does not bend nor twist because of hate, love, or personal interest] (1976, 68). This integrity and ease, according to Castro, could be disturbed by the mere suspected presence of foreign elements[7] (1976, 68). Mateo Alemán's disruption of *sosiego* is suggestive in light of Castro's insistence on the particular fragility of Spanish *entereza.* Is Alemán, the writer from Seville who belonged to a family of first-generation Jewish converts, thus implying that his rogue interlocutor is capable of disturbing not only the reader's, but the nation's precarious *sosiego*?

Alemán's *Guzmán de Alfarache*, published while the Spanish Crown relocated from the recently designed Madrid (1561) to the temporary capital of Valladolid (1601–5), narrates a continuously shifting life marked by incessant sartorial transformations. In *El cuerpo vestido y la construcción de la identidad en las narrativas autobiográficas del siglo de oro* [The Clothed Body and the Construction of Identity: The Autobiographical Novels of the Golden Age] Encarnación Juárez-Almendros equates Guzmán's costume changes to a "personalidad profundamente escindida, y con un sujeto totalmente abyecto" [personality profoundly divided, and with a completely abject subject] (2006, 5). This essay proposes that his undressing, dressing, and even cross-dressing, can be considered not only as the reflection of a divided and abject personality, but also as a figure that unwrites and rewrites itself. It is through the donning of material facades that Guzmán exposes the agitation of a nation which both constricts and constructs itself under the guise of *sosiego.*

The "divine Spaniard," as Alemán was dubbed, takes advantage of the existing discourses of the period, frequently incorporating emblematic, religious, mercantile, legal, medical, and inquisitorial discussions that appear in fragmentary or elliptical form in his text. Within this virtuoso amalgamation of literary codes, Alemán's protagonist and narrator alternates between ecclesiastical sermons infused with moralistic commentaries and tales of rogue antics supported by popular *refranes*. Guzmán is both the *pícaro* who narrates in the preterit, and the "Atalaya de la Vida

Humana" [watchtower of human life] who speaks in the present. Baltasar Gracián's *Agudeza y arte de ingenio* (1648) praises the superiority of Alemán's artifice and style, "que abarcó en si la invención griega, la elocuencia italiana, la erudición francesa, y la agudeza española" [because it encompassed Greek invention, Italian eloquence, French erudition, and Spanish wit] (2004, 572). Commended for his exemplary Spanish verbal skills, Alemán uses the sartorial discourse as a crucial element in dismantling the performance of Iberian serenity.

Roland Barthes's *The Fashion System* cements our understanding of clothing as a semiotic code – a sartorial discourse – that can be deciphered. The mass production of texts and textiles, which came about almost simultaneously in European history, makes references to fashion ubiquitous in early modern literature. We cannot overlook the symbolic value of Celestina's ribbon (1499); the squire's clothing in *Lazarillo de Tormes* (1554); the cape, repeatedly invoked in reference to Columbus in Oviedo's *Historia General y Natural de las Indias* (1526), in Lope's *Caballero de Olmedo* (1621), and in Quevedo's *Buscón* (1626?); the minutely detailed description of the *Caballero del Verde Gabán's* clothing in *Don Quijote* (1615); and the portrayal of Rinconete and Cortadillo (1613), to cite but a few examples. In *Don Quixote* alone, Gridley McKim-Smith and Marcia L. Welles document "thirty-five different kinds of cloth, twenty-four varieties of robes and gowns, twenty-five types of headgear, seven kinds of shirts and bodices, eleven varieties of dress as well as stockings and gaiters, thirteen types of breeches, sixteen different types of footgear, and some eighteen different colors" (2004, 67). In *Guzmán de Alfarache* the rogue's acquired skills as a tailor and the frequent description of the character's clothing transform textiles into a subtext which Alemán uses to foreground his own intentions as well as those of his rogue protagonist and narrator.

The proverbially unruffled appearance of the Spanish people was achieved through clothing. Outerwear shaped and moulded the body to the point of deformity, making it conform to a concept of beauty that sought to "mejorar el mundo por medio de la estética" [better the world through aesthetics] (Sousa Congosto 2007, 126). In rigid articles of clothing, such as the restrictive *lechugilla*[8] [ruffled collar], textiles performed the much sought-after serenity. Pierre Civil describes how the *lechugilla* isolated the head from the rest of the body, "et dans sa rigidité radicale, nié la fonction mécanique du cou" [and in its radical rigidity, denied the movement of the neck] (1990, 311). Carmen Bernis underscores the aim of male fashion to confine the body and reduce movement in order to provide a sense of "sosiego, rigidez, y empaque" [calmness, rigidity, and confinement] (2001, 203). Francisco de Sousa Congosto describes Iberian female fashion in a similar manner: "se trata de una indumentaria que determina empaque y gravedad en movimientos y actitudes, y que sistemáticamente disimula las formas del cuerpo de la mujer" [it is a type of clothing that determines confinement and graveness in movements and in attitude, and that systematically draws attention away from the woman's body] (2007, 130). Civil describes sixteenth-century courtly garments as conceived "pour des hommes et des femmes appelés à une mobilité physique limitée" [for men and women called to limited physical mobility) (312). The armourial outerwear – depicted by Alonso Sánchez Coello's *Isabella Clara Eugenia and Magdalena Ruiz* (see fig. 2) and *Portrait of Philip II of Spain* (see fig. 3) – drew attention away from the individual in order to subordinate the natural body to a uniformed appearance of serenity.

As the nation begins to deteriorate under the weight of inflation, highly decorated clothing is held responsible for economic decline and social instability. Fernández de Oviedo, the emperor's contemporary, explains: "I can testify to many changes in fashion. I have lived for seventy-seven years; and although for some time I was in other kingdoms out of Spain, among no other nation did I see so many nor so frequent changes in style of clothing as with our country."[9] In 1533, Antonio de Torquemada, the author of the *Coloquios sátiricos* and the *Jardín de flores curiosas*, affirms that when a man thinks he is dressed for ten years, not one year passes when a new fashion is not introduced "y lo que estaba muy bien hecho se torna a deshacer y enmendar, quitando y poniendo … de manera que los usos e invenciones nuevas de cada día desasosiegan a las gentes y acaban las haciendas" [and what was well made is unmade and remade, taking off and putting on … so that the customs and daily new inventions create anxiety among the people and exhaust their financial resources] (cited in Bernis 1962, 31). Fashion, like Alemán's *pícaro*, is in constant flux of fabrication and change.

These frequent shifts are mirrored in the futile, albeit incessant edicts to counteract the emerging cultural and financial anxiety. Charles V finally derides the masses who "spend the sum of their worth on clothing, and thus cause the ruin of their country."[10] Earlier in 1534 Charles V imposed a new law prohibiting his subjects "osados de traer ni vestir brocado … no echar guarniciones en las dichas ropas ni en otra cosa, de hilo de oro ni de plata ni hilado ni tirado, ni pudiesen traer bordado ni recamado de seda ni cosa hecha en bastidor" [from daring to wear brocade … and not to add decoration to their clothes or other accessories, of gold or silver thread, nor could they have embroidery of silk or anything made in this fashion] (cited in Bernis 1962, 13). This is especially remarkable in light of

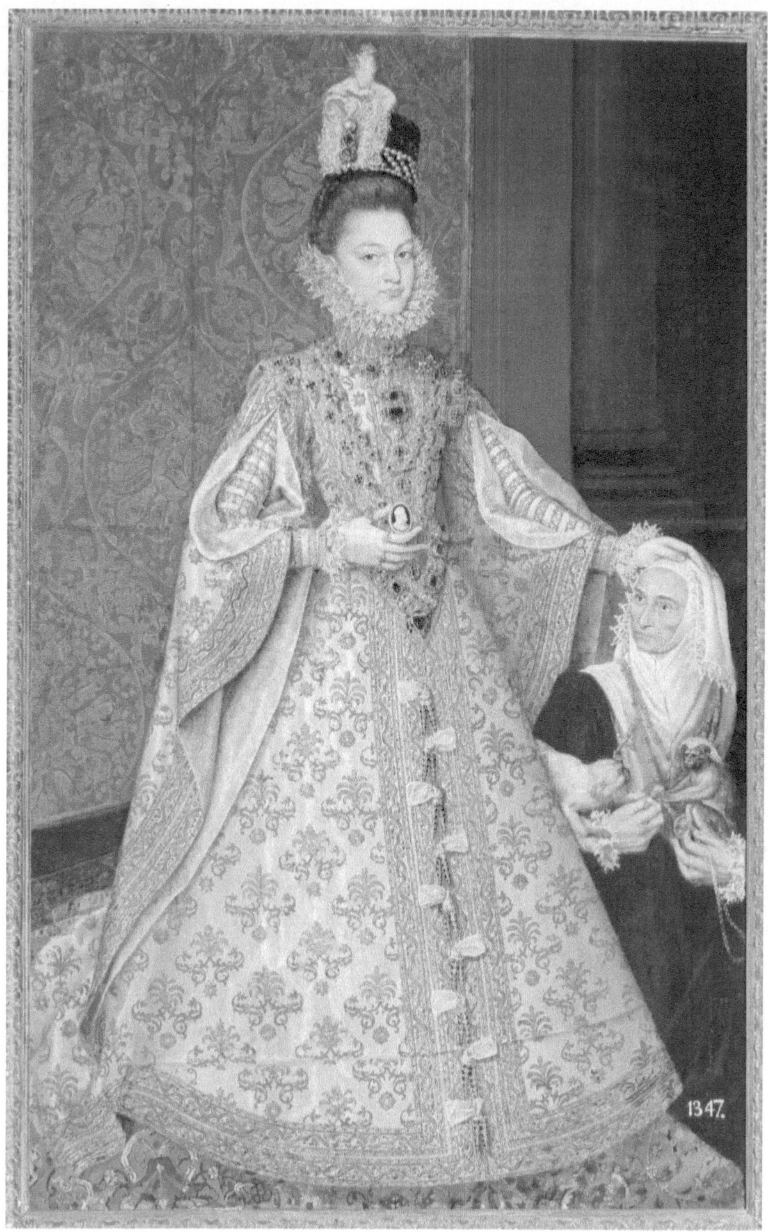


Figure 2 Alfonso Sánchez Coello, *Isabella Clara Eugenia and Magdalena Ruiz*, 1580. Museo Nacional del Prado, Madrid. Art Resource, NY.

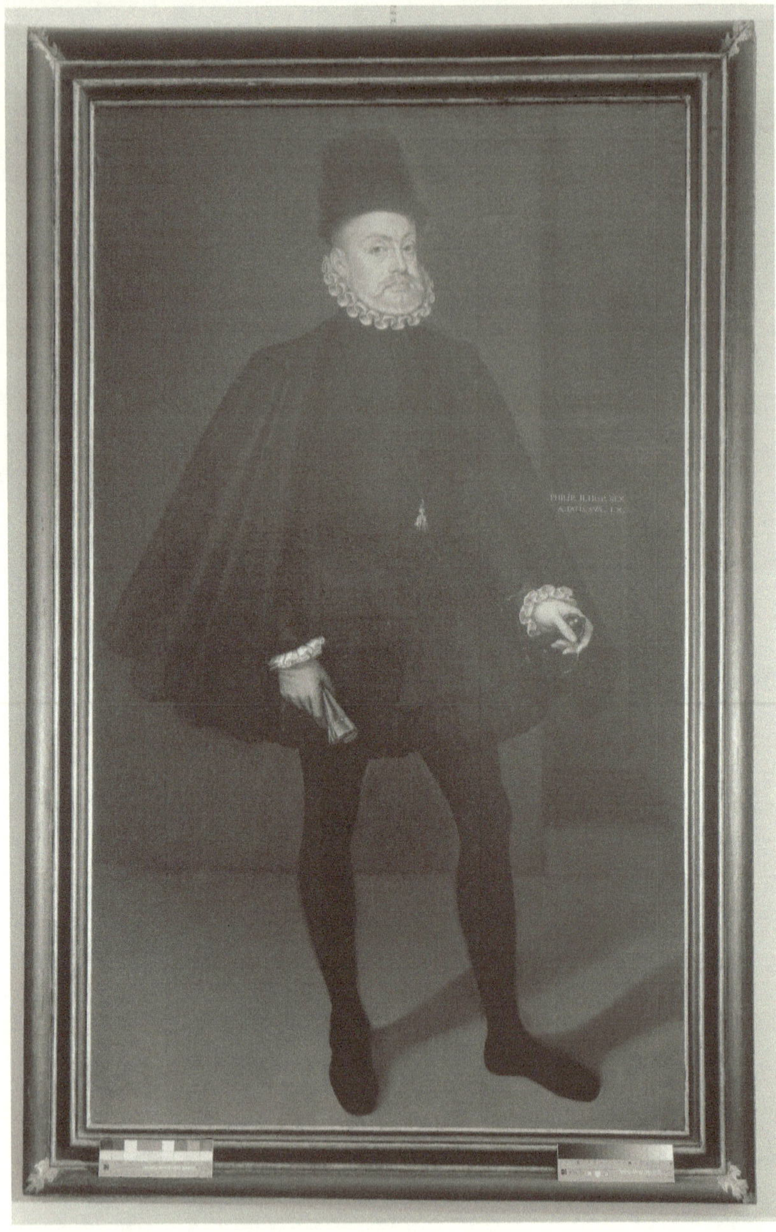

Figure 3 Alfonso Sánchez Coello, *Portrait of Philip II of Spain*, 1587. Galleria dell'Accademia, Florence. Scala / Ministero per i Beni e le Attività culturali / Art Resource, NY.

the blatant contradiction with the king's own clothing. As can be seen in period portraiture, the Spanish court used outerwear in order to project the rising prestige of the nation. When the proclaimed "Holy Roman Emperor" entered Bologna, a court historian recounts:

> Y salió del palacio por el pasadizo su Magestad muy acompañado de todas naciones ... que el que llevaba solamente tela de ora o de plata no era mirado si no llevaba bordadura de perlas y piedras. De estos bien vestidos hubo pocos italianos y flamencos. Los españoles hicieron toda la fiesta y de tal manera que todos quedaban espantados de haber visto tanta riqueza, y fueron los españoles más de ciento cincuenta.
>
> [His Majesty came out of the covered corridor accompanied by men of every nation ... he who wore only cloth of gold or silver was not admired if he did not wear embroidered pearls and stones. Among these well-dressed men were few Italians and Flemish. The Spaniards made the festivities and everyone was astounded to see such wealth, and they numbered more than 150.] (cited in Bernis 1962, 8)

With an empire so vast that it was said that the sun never set in his domains, the court of Charles I, who came to be known as Emperor Charles V, put forth an impressive show of opulent clothing. He wore an Iberian cape in the Santiago *cortes* of 1520. This garment introduced the emergent Spanish identity of a monarch born in Flanders. In 1520 the bishop of Badajoz supports his evolving image: "this is how he learned your language and has dressed in your attire."[11] Paradoxically, Alemán's protagonist will lose his cape as he learns the language and embodies the gestures of the *pícaro*.

The desire to dress fashionably and the excessive money spent on outerwear were topics of discussion each time that *cortes* were called.[12] By 1552, Emperor Charles V explores the consequences of these obviously failed laws, pointing to the previously noted overproduction and decoration of clothing inside and outside his court. This consumption, he complains, is the "causa de que muchos gasten sus haciendas y haya mucho desorden y nuestros reinos se destruyen y empobrecen" [reason why so many waste away their wealth, and why there is such unrest, and why our kingdoms are falling apart and impoverished] (cited in Bernis 1962, 14). Alemán's novel also delineates the crippling results of expenditure. Guzmán's first wife's disproportionate penchant for shopping is recorded as the cause of the affluent merchant family's financial ruin (Alemán 2006, 2.3.377–431). When asked for restitution of her sizable dowry upon her sudden death, Guzmán flees, disguised as a scholar of divinity at the recently formed University of Alcalá de Henares. Conspicuous consumption thwarts the *pícaro*'s attempt to gain social status through an advantageous marriage.

In blaming consumption, Charles V scapegoats clothing for the nation's soaring inflation, and garments become the subtext of Spain's decline. In fact, it was in this disastrous year of 1552 that the state of Spain as a fledgling hegemonic power became clear. Although in 1547 Charles assumed he had secured domination over Germany with his victory at the battle of Muhlberg, by March of 1552, as he was driven out of Innsbruck by Maurice of Saxony, the bleak future of his empire became a painful reality. Furthermore, in that same year the emperor had finally lost all credibility with the royal financiers keeping the country afloat for a decade (Elliott 2002, 209–10). In the years to follow, the signs of a recession that forced commerce to live by credit became more visible. It is not until 1600, with such publications as that of the *arbitrista* Martín González de Cellorigo's *Memorial*, that the nobles would target fiscal policy as the root of Spain's debacle. As Elliott explains, "González de Cellorigo was almost alone in appreciating that the fundamental problem lay not so much in heavy spending by the Crown and upper classes – since this spending created a valuable demand for goods and services – as in the disproportion between expenditure and investment" (2002, 317). Spain's reversal of fortune is exposed in the economic terms of inflation, which turned Europe's wealthiest country into the poorest. It is within these circumstances of actual inflation that Alemán's protagonist and narrator negotiates the denial of Spain's economic reality through sartorial *sosiego.*

Even with the *arbitrista*'s revelation, early modern Spaniards continued to express anxiety through the more tangible target of decoration and clothing. Iberian society perceived effeminate embellishments donned by males, and its greatest extreme, cross-dressing, as the root of social and economic turmoil. Although the concern remained rooted in clothing and decoration, it also pointed to the social construct of gender. Sancho de Moncada, who in the seventeenth-century founded the first university centre for the study of politics, contested the idea that the economic crisis resulted from inflation, claiming instead that Spain finds itself in such dire straits because "la gente anda toda tan regalada y afeminada" [people are all dressed up and effeminate] (cited in Maravall 1986, 94). José Pellicer de Ossau Salas y Tovar, historian of Castile and later of Aragón as well as commentator of Góngora, also noted "regalos y afeminaciones" [luxury and effeminacy] as the cause of the nation's distress (cited in Maravall

1986, 94). In a sermon delivered in 1635, Fray Francisco de León, prior of Guadalupe, points to the same root of the Spanish problem: "los hombres convertidos en mujeres, de soldados en afeminados, llenos de tufos, melenas y copetes" [the men converted into women, from soldiers to sissies, full of frills, long hair, and bangs] (cited in Maravall 1986, 94). Marjorie Garber argues that cross-dressing and transvestism are the markers of societal shifts that result from the "dissolution of boundaries and of the arbitrariness of social law and custom" (1992, 25).[13] The transvestite, according to Garber, causes anxiety by calling into question the "set of social codes – already demonstrably under attack – by which such categories were policed and maintained" (1992, 32).[14] Here cross-dressing and effeminacy carry the mark of a scapegoat that Guzmán will use to his advantage through Alemán's pen.

On the other hand, seen from outside the Iberian Peninsula, idealized Spanish identity was equated with a darkly dressed and somber nation that projected composure and solemnity (see fig. 4). In 1534 Boscán, translating Castiglione's *Book of the Courtier* (1528), already emphasized the *gravitas* and decorum that marked the black clothing of the Spanish nation: "por eso me parece que tiene más gracia el vestido negro que el de otro color ... pero en lo demás querría que mostrasen el sosiego y la gravedad de la nación española" [that is why it seems to me that the black attire has more elegance than any other ... but in everything else I would prefer that they show the calm and solemnity of the Spanish nation] (Castiglione 1942, 161). The Italian Cesare Vecellio's *Habiti Antichi et Moderni* (1590) depicts the Spanish people as "grave by nature" and dressing "in black more than in any other color" (Rosenthal and Jones 2008, 281). Amedeo Quondam's *Tutti i colori Del Nero: Moda e cultura del gentiluomo del Rinascimento* (2007) focuses on the importance of dark clothing in the representation of sixteenth-century Italian selfhood. Pointing to Castiglione's text as a cultivator of the Italian "migliore forma" – ethical and aesthetic beauty, elegance, and restraint that are "made in Italy" – Quondam describes the arrival of a fashionably late gentleman dressed entirely in black. This grave man's persona and clothing project the harmony of the classical *aurea mediocritas* and the dignity of a magnanimous sovereign. Remarkably, the prime example of Italian *sprezzatura* turns out to be a vassal of the Spanish Emperor Charles V. The black clothing of the Spanish Marchese di Pescara contrasts starkly with the ostentatious golden hue donned by the Italian nobles. John Harvey affirms that "it was Spain, more than any other nation, that was to be responsible for the major propagation of solid black both throughout

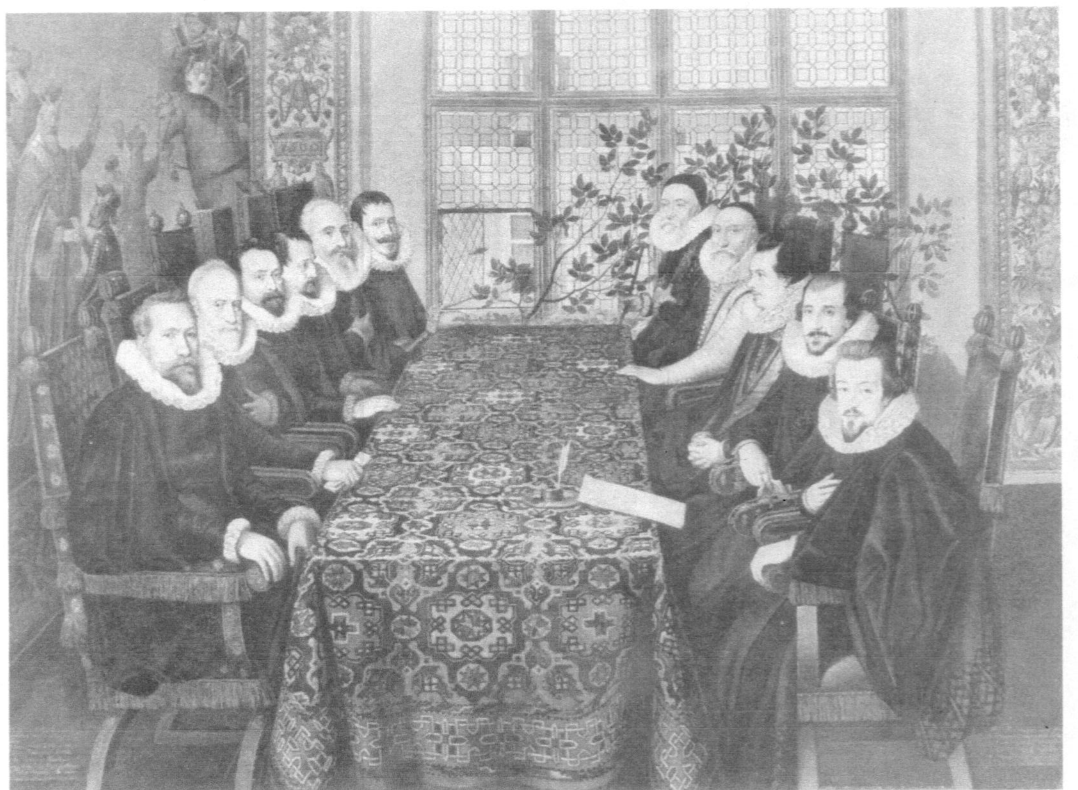

Figure 4 Juan Pantoja de la Cruz (attributed to). *The Somerset House Conference*, c. 1604. National Portrait Gallery, London. Art Resource, NY.

Europe, and in the New World" (1995, 72). Although recent scholarship shows that in fact the colour palette for personal attire may have been much broader, and that Spaniards were even dressing *a la morisca,*[15] *sosiego* is projected by somber outerwear.

In *Anotaciones* to Garcilaso (1580) Fernando de Herrera uses the same rhetoric of containment to invoke the Spanish language when he underscores the difference between the lascivious Tuscan and the grave Spanish tongue. As an introduction to his commentary on Garcilaso de la Vega's first poem, Herrera carves out a space for the production of a new Spanish poetry by assigning *sosiego* to his mother tongue: "Porque la toscana es muy florida, abundosa ... lasciva ... Pero la nuestra es grave, religiosa, onesta, alta, manifica ... toda entera y perpetua muestra su castidad y cultura y admirable grandeza y espíritu ... Finalmente la española se debe tratar con más onra i reverencia" [Because Tuscan is more florid, abundant ... lascivious ... all integral and perpetually showing her chastity and culture and admirable greatness of spirit ... But ours is grave, religious, honest, tall, magnificent ... Finally Spanish should be treated with more honour and reverence ...] (2001, 278). Even as her Tuscan counterpart's abundance casts restraint aside, Castilian speech embodies pure composure. This religious and moral foundation provides her with a gravity that demands respect. Although Herrera does not employ the term, he dresses Castilian in the very trappings of *sosiego:* Herrera's mother tongue carries herself well.

The much-debated anonymous writer of the first picaresque novel, *Lazarillo de Tormes* (1554), already incorporates the sartorial nature of Iberian "serenity" into his narrative. The squire adopts the semblance of *sosiego* in order to simulate a noble facade that anticipates Alemán's later dismantling.[16] The impoverished *escudero* from old Castile who relocates to Toledo walks with a "paso sosegado y el cuerpo derecho, haciendo con él y con la cabeza muy gentiles meneos, echando el cabo de la capa sobre el hombre" [serene stroll and a very straight back, making genteel movements with both body and head, placing the tip of his cape over his shoulder] which makes him appear to be of "tan gentil semblante y continente, que quien no le conosciera pensara ser muy cercano pariente al Conde de Arcos o a lo menos camarero que le daba de vestir" [such noble visage and composure that those who did not know him would think he was a close relative of the Count of Arcos or at least the one who dressed him] (2003, 82). Fed up with the behavioural custom of social address – doffing one's hat first to persons of higher social status – he abandons old Castile in defiance of imposed decorum. This apparent simple gesture unleashes a meditation on Spanish *honra* [honour], which according to the squire constitutes the entire social capital of contemporary gentlemen of his class. While in Toledo, his honour is safeguarded by his ever-present cape and with elaborate performances of public tooth-pickings in lieu of actual meals. By 1617 *sosiego* had become such an indicator of the Spanish persona that Carlos García uses it to register the differences between a Frenchman and a Spaniard. García, who wrote *La desordenada codicia de los bienes ajenos* [The Uncontrolled Desire for the Property of Others] (1619), calls attention to "aquella acción mesurada y denuedo ... aquel sosiego en el andar" [that controlled action ... that *sosiego* in his manner of walking] (cited in Bernis 2001, 204). Thus García observes in an ascetic treatise what the *Lazarillo* already notes in fiction and what Alemán then exposes.

Within a country aiming to project national *sosiego*, sons of wealthy bourgeois families, very much like the fictional Guzmán de Alfarache, reject their prescribed social roles and refashion themselves as *pícaros*. In *La cultura del barroco*, José Antonio Maravall depicts an ironclad social order that constrains, reorganizes, and deforms the liberating forces of individualism (1986, 91). In this same study, he chronicles the historical flight of "jóvenes de casas nobles y acomodadas que huyen a perderse en medios de picaresca" [young men of noble and wealthy households who escape in order to lose themselves in the picaresque environment] (1986, 111).[17] The rogue lifestyle carves out a space where the self can be altered and refurbished.[18]

The definition of *pícaro* suggests a generic reading of these rascals. The *pícaro* appears in Covarrubias's *Tesoro de la lengua* as "vil y de baja suerte, que anda mal vestido y en semblante de poco honor" [vile and of a low sort, who is poorly dressed and has an appearance of very little honour] as well as a continuation of pícaño, "el andrajoso y despedazado" [the tattered and torn] (http://www.cervantesvirtual.com/servlet/SirveObras/80250529545703831976613/index.htm). Carroll Johnson observes that "in the honor-mad society he is striving to enter, appearance quite literally makes the man. The progression is inevitable: tattered clothing means *pícaro ladroncillo*, which in turn means unemployable" (1978, 58). While searching for employment in Madrid, Guzmán's prospective masters describe him as "algún pícaro ladroncillo que los había de robar" [some *pícaro* thief who would surely steal from them] (Alemán 2006, 2.2.2).

The recently created capital Madrid sets the stage for Guzmán's entrance into his new mode of being. On the road that takes him from an "hijo de viuda y de ocio" [son of a widow and of leisure] to the world of constant shifting, Guzmán systematically rids himself of the garments which mark him as bourgeois: "Fuime valiendo del vestidillo que llevaba puesto" [I made use of the clothing that I was wearing] (Alemán 2006, 1.2.2). Using clothing as barter, by the time he enters Madrid he is "hecho un gentil galeote, bien a la ligera, en calzas y en camisa: eso muy sucio, roto, y viejo, porque para el gasto fue todo menester" [made into a genteel galley slave, wearing only stockings and a shirt: all of it very dirty, ragged, and old, because it all had to be used to cover the costs] (Alemán 2006, 1.2.2). He sheds the composure of bourgeois outerwear and dons the soiled threadbare garments of the *pícaro.* In a capital that is still in the process of creating its own identity – soon to be provisionally superseded by Valladolid – Guzmán forges a temporary self that both refutes and assumes branding.

While *sosiego* calls for clearly identifying rhetoric and garments, Guzmán constantly makes himself unrecognizable. His roguish persona provides a tabula rasa on which many subsequent identities will be inscribed. The underworld of the picaresque is described as a space devoid of social regulations and free of the very instruments with which tailors create garments. Guzmán meditates on his recently acquired modus operandi: "¡Qué linda cosa era y que regalada! Sin dedal, hilo, ni aguja, tenaza, martillo, ni barena ni otro algún instrumento más de una sola capacha, como los hermanos de Antón Martín" [What a beautiful thing it was and how luxurious! Without a thimble, thread, or a needle, pliers, a hammer, ruler, or any other instrument more than a wicker basket] (Alemán 2006, 1.2.2). As an *esportillero* (porter), and without a master, the self-employed rogue is free of the complications imposed by society. Guzmán finds such delight in this lifestyle that he would not change it "por lo mejor que tuvieron mis pasados" [for the best that my ancestors had] (Alemán 2006, 1.2.2).

Alemán's picaresque novel affords a reification of the trade of the tailor. Guzmán's chosen last name, Alfarache, closely resembles the Arabic term for tailor, *alfayate.*[19] The customizer of clothing's soiled reputation was a staple of early modern Iberian satirical literature. Texts such as Francisco de Quevedo's *Sueños* (1605–22) and *Hora de todos* (1645), and Cervantes' *Rinconete y Cortadillo* (1613), feature the dubious sartor. Cervantes' *pícaro*, *Cortadillo*, whose name literally means "cut," is in fact the son of a garment maker. When Alemán's narrator speaks of the dishonesty of many professions, the reformed galley slave Guzmán focuses specifically on the tailor's trade: "Considera el de un sastre" [consider that of the tailor] he tells us, "todos roban, todos mienten, todos trampean; ninguno cumple con lo que debe, y es lo peor que se precian dello" [they all steal, they all lie, they all cheat; not one carries out what he should, and what is worse is that they pride themselves on this] (Alemán 2006, 1.2.4). Yet, Guzmánillo offers many accounts of his own tailoring.[20] In the early days as a rogue, he acts as a dressmaker in order to adopt the persona of a nobleman: "Fuime de allí a la tienda de un mercader ... corté un vestido" [I went from there to a merchant's shop ... I cut an outfit] (Alemán 2006, 1.2.8). It is important to remember that Guzmán admonishes these crafters of garments from the vantage point of the galleys. Mateo Alemán, a lawyer by training whose research on galley slaves brought to light many injustices suffered by prisoners,[21] would have been familiar with the edicts that could land a sartor in the galleys. Bernis informs us that "la pena mayor que podía recibir el que no se ajustase en sus vestidos a la pragmática era ser desterrado por cinco años; pero el sastre, jubetero o guarnicionero que cortare, cosiere, o bordase lo prohibido, a la segunda vez que desobedeciese la pragmática, sería condenado a servir perpetuamente en galeras" [the greatest sentence administered for those who did not adhere to the sartorial edicts was to be exiled for five years; but the tailor who cut, sewed, or stitched what was forbidden, the second time that he disobeyed the edict, would be condemned to perpetual service as a galley slave] (1962, 14). Although Guzmán is never specifically linked to the violation of a sartorial edict, the rogue, who is referred to as a "gentil galeote" [genteel galley slave] when he first comes into the picaresque lifestyle, narrates his autobiography from the galleys.

The movement of Alemán's *pícaro* into the world of roguery is marked by frequent undressing and dressing and by a systematic dismantling of his bourgeois identity.[22] The "hijo de algo" [son of something] makes himself into a temporary "hijo de nada" [son of nothing], from which the many desired personas can emerge. As he abandons his birthplace and shifts into the life of the rogue, Guzmanillo performs a striptease that involves both identity and clothing. After the death of his Genoese father, he leaves Seville and his mother. The young Guzmán explains that "para no ser conocido, no me quise valer del apellido de mi padre, púseme el Guzmán de mi madre y Alfarache de la heredad, adonde tuve mi principio" [as I couldn't be recognized, I did not want to use my father's last name, so I took Guzmán from my mother and Alfarache from the inherited property where I had my beginning] (Alemán 2006, 1.1.2). The protagonist eliminates his paternal surname, which is never shared with the reader, and thus begins the complete eradication of his lineage. Given both his mother and his grandmother's avowed promiscuity,[23] his claim to a name famously used to invoke a fictitious Gothic origin is certainly questionable (footnote 90 in Alemán 2006, 1.1.2). The last vestige of Guzmán's former life, his cape, disappears without a trace: "como azogue al fuego o humo al viento, se desapareció entre las manos" [like mercury in the fire or smoke in the wind, it slipped through my hands] (Alemán 2006, 1.1.6). The vanishing cape also serves to symbolically sever ties to the old *caballero* of the Alfarache estate.

While newfound freedom affords him the ability to travel, his role as a tailor permits Guzmán to differentiate himself according to his whims. The rogue underscores the importance of customizing his clothes: "tú sabes mejor si te aprieta, si te aflige, si te angustia o cómo te viene" [you know best if it is too tight, if it bothers you, if it distresses you, or how it suits you best] (Alemán 2006, 1.2.4). The repentant rogue turned galley prisoner justifies his itinerant and impulsive fashioning: "ibame por donde quería, según me lo pedía el gusto y primero se me antojaba: hoy aquí, mañana en Francia, sin parar en alguna parte, y siempre trocando de vestidos, pues a parte no llegué donde lo pudiese diferenciar, que no lo hiciese: que todo era cien escudos más o menos" [I went everywhere I wanted, as my taste and desire dictated; here today, tomorrow in France, without stopping anywhere, and always changing clothing, for I never got to a place where my clothing could not be altered that I would [take the opportunity] to do it: it all cost one hundred escudos more or less] (Alemán 2006, 2.3.1). As a creator of personalized clothing, everywhere he goes he cuts himself new outerwear that in turn custom-tailors novel identities.

Guzmán shapes the first of his many future personas when confronted with a mirror image of his past incarnation.[24] Alemán's novel addresses the picaresque phenomenon through its main character as well as in his exchange of clothing with a youth described as a mirror image of himself (Alemán 2006, 1.2.7). In yet another allusion to a wealthy young man's flight into roguish freedom, as the adolescent Guzmán first leaves his birthplace he is mistaken for a page recently accused of theft: "Por las señas que les dieron debía ser otro yo" [By the description they were given he must have been another me] (Alemán 2006, 1.1.7). Outside the city walls of Toledo, which also served as the seat of Lazarillo de Tormes's self-fashioning, he meets a boy who represents the pre-*pícaro* Guzmán. Our protagonist is well aware that the current state of his own clothing causes his young friend to "misread" his lineage. His shabby dress warrants assurance from his better-dressed new acquaintance. Guzmanillo states that he is "tan buen hijo y de tan buenos padres como vos" [as good a son and of parents as good as yours] (Alemán 2006, 1.2.7). To this pledge he adds a claim for "limpieza de sangre" [purity of blood]. In an effort to deny a possible mixed heritage that comes from living in Andalucía, and specifically in the very porous Seville, he claims to be from the birthplace of the most Christian and Castilian of "Spaniards," Rodrigo Díaz de Vivar, el Cid. After inventing a noble heritage, Guzmán continues his artful manipulation of language. He convinces his alter ego to sell him his clothing: "el mozo deshizo su lío, sacó dél un herreruelo, calzones, ropilla, dos camisas y unas medias de seda" [the young man undid his purse, took out a short cape, breeches, two shirts, and some silk stockings] (Alemán 2006, 1.2.7). In the enumeration of the garments, Guzmanillo appropriates both clothing and identity.[25] This clothing fits him so well, causing him to exclaim that it is "como si todo se hubiera hecho para mí" [it was as if everything had been made for me]. When Guzmanillo dons his alter ego's clothing, he effects an immediate *translatio* of character.

Guzmán then recreates himself as a nobleman using the language of emblematic colours and fabrics. He embellishes and reconstructs himself: "al cuello del herreruelo le hice quitar el tafetán que tenía y echar otro de otra color. Trastejé la ropilla de botones nuevos, quitéle las mangas de paños y púseselas de seda, con que a poca costa lo desconocí todo" [I made him take off the taffeta collar and change the colour. I put new buttons on the *ropilla* and I took away the sleeves made of cotton, and I replaced them with silk, and with very little money I was able to make it all unrecognizable] (Alemán 2006, 1.2.8). Lacking suitable material, he switches some fabrics for others: "Por no hallar buen ante para el coleto, lo hice de raso morado, guarnecido con trencillas de oro" [Not having good suede for the *coleto,* I made it with common purple cloth, garnished with braids of gold] (Alemán 2006, 1.2.8). In other words, his new clothing is an adulterated version of a nobleman's outfit.

Having dressed up in fabricated nobility, Guzmán then uses his body to accentuate the costume – a complete reversal of the restraint of *sosiego*. His newly created persona imposes an alternate line of vision. This man of twists and turns takes his frugally fashioned nobleman to church and visits "las capillas donde acudía más gente" [the chapels where more people were present] (Alemán 2006, 1.1.1).[26] He exhibits himself in the most visible of spaces and controls the many onlookers' perspective:

> Estiréme de cuello, comencé a hinchar la barriga y atiesar las piernas. Tanto me desvanecía, que de mis visajes y meneos todos tenían que notar, burlándose de mi necedad; mas como me miraban, yo no miraba en ellos ni echaba de ver mis faltas, que era de lo que los otros formaban risas. Antes me pareció que los admiraba mi curiosidad y gallardía.

[I strained my neck, I began to expand my belly and plant my legs firmly. I swooned so much that everyone had to note my facial contortions and my body movements, poking fun at my stubbornness; but since they were looking at me I didn't look at them, nor did I see my faults, which caused others to laugh. It seemed to me that they admired my curiosity and gallantry.] (Alemán 2006, 1.2.8)

Guzmán stretches, swells, and moves vigorously, giving his gawking public the greatest amount of body surface area to scrutinize. He indeed controls their line of vision and then averts his own gaze; he chooses not to be troubled by the onlookers' negative judgments and laughter. In another of Alemán's parodies of temperance, the decorated *pícaro* explains that he felt as if he were "el rey de los gallos y el que llevaba la gala y como pastor lozano hice plaza de todo el vestido, deseando que me vieran y enseñar aun hasta las cintas, que eran del tudesco" [the king of the cocks and the one that wore the festive clothing, and like a handsome shepherd I made a show of my dress, hoping that they would see me exposing even the shoelaces that were German] (Alemán 2006, 1.2.8). In his recapitulation, the young Guzmán makes public show of a *pícaro,* who not long ago looked like a galley slave, pulling himself up by his German shoelaces (*tudesco cintas*) through thriftily bought clothing. [27] Instead of following suitable church behaviour, in the spirit of *Carnaval,* Alemán's Guzmanillo defies social decorum while revealing Alemán's tacit attack of Charles V's critique of consumption.

Guzmán further complicates these tenuous social markers through a sequence of cross-dressing performances riddled with contradictions. In the first chapters, our *pícaro* appears ready to denounce his father as homosexual if his use of cosmetics can be proven. Instead he replicates the pattern set forth by Lazarillo de Tormes, who denounces his mother and father and ends up reenacting their lives. Evoking Achilles, whose mother, Thetis, dresses him as a woman and hides him in the court of King Likomidos,[28] Guzmán cross-dresses as he attempts to flee incarceration. The rogue feigns illness and takes to his bed: "Híceme por quince días enfermo. No salí del calabozo, ni me levanté de la cama" [I pretended I was ill for fifteen days. I did not leave the cell, nor did I get out of bed] (Alemán 2006, 2.3.7). Without revealing his sartorial secrets, in the same line we are told that "al fin dellos ya tenía prevenido un vestido de mujer" [at the end of that time I had readied a woman's dress] (Alemán 2006, 2.3.7). In two weeks and one textual paragraph, he manages to recreate and present himself as a woman, and thus, to reconfigure the established borders of masculinity, passing, and national composure.

Guzmán completes the illusion through actions summarized by the verb "afeitar,"[29] which means not only to shave but also to apply cosmetics, connoting something fake and unnatural. The beard, a visual symbol of his manhood, is removed: "Con una navaja me quité la barba" [with a razor knife I shaved off my beard] (Alemán 2006, 2.3.7). We might suggest that he metaphorically becomes a *castrato,* or at least that he commits a symbolic act of emasculation. The procedure continues with the adding of a "tocado," a covering for the head that might hide some of the face, until the sartorial conversion is complete: "vestido, tocado, y afeitado el rostro" [dressed, with a head covering, and having shaved my face] (Alemán 2006, 2.3.7). He adds the *afeites* [cosmetics]: "mi blanco y poco de color" [my white powder and a bit of colour] (Alemán 2006, 2.3.7). Paradoxically, in this negotiation Guzmán bares his face only to mask it with makeup.

As with the entrance into Toledo, the night's darkness affords him a brief triumph while cross-dressing, only to be identified by a man appearing to have double vision. In spite of this sartorial and cosmetic feat, a porter who is ironically blind in one eye, sees, recognizes, and ultimately detains our protagonist. Cervantes' picaresque character, Ginés de Pasamonte, who according to Agustín Redondo is another Guzmán de Alfarache (2008, 255), has the same visual "impairment." Roberto González Echevarría has analysed the figure of the one-eyed Ginés "as the very image of the man with imagination, with the ability to singularize and synthesize the images he perceives" (2005, 231). This porter, like Cervantes' Ginés, sees what those with perfect vision are incapable of discerning. Guzmán deceives the first two gatekeepers, who are trained as expert observers: "ninguno de los porteros me habló palabra" [neither one of the porters spoke a word to me] (Alemán 2006, 2.3.7). The narrator emphasizes their vision: "tenían ambos buena vista, y sus ojos claros" [they both had good eyesight and clear eyes] (Alemán 2006, 2.3.7). This clarity of sight impedes them from seeing beyond an imposed superficial layer of temporary identity. It is a third porter, who is "tuerto de un ojo, ¡Qué a Dios pluguiera y del otro fuera ciego! Detúvome y miróme, Reconocióme luego y dio el golpe a la puerta" [blind in one eye, God willing he were blind in the other eye as well! He recognized me and alerted them at the door] (Alemán 2006, 2.3.7). This state of being "tuerto," defined by Covarrubias as "todo lo que no está derecho" [everything that is not straight], allows the one-eyed or cross-eyed porter to single in on the individual layers of the rogue's outfit and point to what has gone astray in Guzmán's dressing. His crossed vision unravels Guzmán's cross-dressing and un-writes Guzmán's female persona.

At the end of the text Guzmán is finally caught and punished for thievery with an imposed uniform and the removal of all visible hair, putting a halt to the rogue's incessant costume changes. We remember that Guzmán is already equated through Alemán's syntax to a "gentil galeote" [gallant galley slave] when he is first mistaken as a *pícaro.* Like the rogues, these historical galley men – many of whom were captured Muslim and Christian slaves – are recognized by their clothing: "Por ello, el vestido de un galeote cristiano que remaba en una galera turca y el de uno musulmán que remaba en una cristiana eran semejantes ... los cautivos podían ser reconocidos como tales por su traje" [For this reason the dress of a Christian galley slave who rowed in a Turkish galley and that of a Muslim who rowed in a Christian galley were similar ... the captives could be recognized as such by their outerwear] (Bernis 2001, 451). Guzmán resigns himself to his given role: "Galeote[30] soy, rematado me veo, vida tengo de hacer con los de mi suerte" [I am a galley slave, I see myself knocked down, I have to make a life among those that suffer the same lot] (Alemán 2006, 2.3.8). As a true galley slave, he wears the uniform assigned by the king: "dos camisas, dos pares de calzones de lienzo, almilla colorada, capote de jerga y bonete colorado" [two shirts, two pairs of canvas trousers, a red bodice, a small cape made of *jerga* and a red bonnet] (Alemán 2006, 2.3.8). Once more his hair is shorn: "Vino el barberote, rapóme la cabeza y barba, que sentí mucho por lo mucho en que lo estimaba" [The big barber came and shaved my head and beard, a loss I felt keenly for all that I loved it] (Alemán 2006, 2.3.8). Having lost the cape mentioned earlier that served to exemplify Emperor Charles V's Spanish essence and identified Guzmanillo's privileged birth, he is invested with a cape of rough fibre, a shaved head, and identifying garments that take away his *pícaro* individuality and mark his place within this *galeote* group.

Nevertheless, Guzmán will not adhere to the specifications of his uniform. Bernis provides a detailed description of the dress worn by all galley prisoners and slaves. We will focus here on the garment that covered their naked torso and is referred to as an "almilla." Covarrubias describes it as "cierta vestidura militar, corta y cerrada por todas partes, escotada y con sólo mangas que no llegan al codo. Ellas llevaban debajo de las armas, de donde tomaron el nombre armilla ... corrompidamente dixeron almilla" [a certain military dress, short and closed on all sides, low-cut and with sleeves that don't quite reach the elbows. It was worn under the weapons, from which they took the name "small arm or weapon" ... then corrupted to "little soul"]. It is precisely this garment whose etymology comes from a little weapon and evolves into a "little soul" (almilla) that Guzmán decides to reinterpret. When his "almilla" is almost stolen, the mere thought of being without it moves Guzmán to exclaim: "mejor la pudiera llamar alma, pues con aquel calor vivificaba la sangre con que la sustentaba" [it might be more fitting to call it a soul because with that heat it revived the blood with which it was sustained] (Alemán 2006, 3.3.8). Even though earlier he had resigned himself to the loss of his cape, the older Guzmán plays with the idea that this "almilla" is indeed his own soul, and he will guard it at all costs. Echoing the manner in which he attempts to mend his life and become a good Christian, Guzmán literally creates a new "almilla" [soul] that will also act as his protective outermost covering, or cape.

Despite enforced uniformity, Guzmán refashions himself in preparation for his magnum opus, his autobiography. As Benito Brancaforte explains, "Desde la perspectiva de la psicología existencialista – Sartre en particular – querer ser otro significa para Guzmán no aceptar la imagen de él establecida por la sociedad, no conformarse con los límites impuestos por los otros" [From the perspective of existentialist psychology – Sartre in particular – wanting to be someone else means that Guzmán will not accept the image that society has imposed for him and will not conform to the limits imposed by others] (1980, 171). What little money he earns, he invests it all in refashioning himself, body and soul: "Hice, con licencia de mi amo, de aquella ganancia un vestidillo a uso de forzado viejo; calzón y almilla de lienzo negro ribeteado, que por ser verano era más fresca y a propósito" [I made, with my master's approval, with that sum a dress in the style of the old galley slaves: trousers and an *almilla* of black ribbed canvas, that since it was summer was much cooler and appropriate] (Alemán 2006, 3.3.8). In place of restrictive clothing, Guzmán keeps to the confines of the prescribed colour scheme but opts for a focus on comfort and easy fit, the ultimate dismantling of *sosiego's* restrictive clothing. The distinction lies in the fact that it is his own composition. In this way he is only partially satisfying given norms, and in fact talking out of both sides of his mouth. Guzmán can thus promote his own serenity and provide an example of individuality for the other prisoners. It is from the most restricted of quarters, the galley, that the young rogue finds his voice and crafts his cape as the narrator and protagonist of *Guzmán de Alfarache*.

Alemán's vested interest in clothing and identity reaches beyond the scope of the *pícaro's* itinerant narrative. The embedded novellas of Momo (1.7) and Ozmín and Daraja (1.8) concurrently shift the sequence of the novel's plotline and enlarge the subject at hand. While the pairing of exotic and allegorical novellas is common in early modern literature, here they serve to point to and cement the novel's sartorial discourse. Momo's tale is preceded by Guzmán's discussion of dressed meats and the theft of his cape:

> Quejéme ayer de mañana de un poco de cansancio y dos semipollos que comí disfrazados en hábito de romeros para ser desconocidos. Vine después a cenar el hediondo vientre de un machuelo y, lo peor, comer de la carne y sesos, que casi era comer de mis propias carnes, por la parte que a todos toca la de su padre; y, para final de desdichas, hurtarme la capa.
>
> [I complained yesterday morning of being tired and of two semi-chickens that I ate disguised as pilgrims in order to be unrecognized. I later came to eat the putrid stomach of a mule, and the worst thing was that it was almost like eating my own flesh, on account of what we must all take on from our father; and, as a final punishment, to steal my cape.] (1.1.7)

The gastronomic jargon of this episode further expands and complicates the constant costuming. Within the fleshy nature of Guzmán's images, chickens are cloaked in the same pilgrim's outfit that Cervantes will later employ to smuggle his Moor back into Spain (*Don Quixote*, 2.54), the theme of racial passing is associated with the banned meat of the mixed-race mule, and the rogue's outer covering is stolen. The very next paragraph introduces Momo's story of mythological gods,[31] in which their anger over the earthlings' sole devotion to *contento* [contentment] triggers an exchange for his identical brother *descontento* [discontent]. Yet, this replacement is not a mere substitution: "Donde creíste que el contento estaba, no fue más del vestido y el descontento en él" [Where you thought that contentment lay, there was no more than clothing and discontent inside of it] (Alemán 2006, 1.1.7). *Descontento* is merely dressed up in his brother's trappings. Borrowing from *La historia del Abencerraje y la hermosa Jarifa* (1561), Alemán then documents the tale of the Muslim Ozmín, who is able to personify Christians without being detected, and Daraja who is dressed "a la castellana."[32] Alemán speaks to the larger imperial projects of Spain, using his novel, novellas, and protagonist to expose a precarious social world that cloaks itself in clothing and performance.

As the novel that cemented the picaresque genre, *Guzmán de Alfarche* is instrumental in shaping a literary type that both emerges from and reflects Spain. In the early modern Spain of Mateo Alemán, moralists, edicts, sumptuary laws, literature, court manuals, and costume books document the desire for *sosiego* to mask a society torn by internal factions. "Lingering political divisions and conflicting cultural identities spawned an 'invertebrate' Spain, to invoke Ortega y Gassett's adroit term – invertebrate, in the sense of its geographical and political fragmentation" (Ruiz 2001, 17). This invertebrate state calls for rigid outerwear designed to shape and secure national identity. In this restrictive milieu, *sosiego* both outfits the Spanish body and protects the body politic at the expense of the individual. Without an intermediary point between *sosiego* and *desasosiego,* emphasis falls on an outward projection of the self that goes beyond Aristotle's *giusto mezzo*, Horace's *aurea mediocritas*, or *Il Cortegiano*'s famous *sprezzatura.* Alemán's *pícaro* protagonist both exposes and dismantles the self-possession that the Spanish nation performs through clothing. Although the bourgeois *pícaro* is made a galley slave, like the "divine Spaniard" in his various discourses and disguises, he will continuously ruffle the darkly clad Spanish nation and his readers with his protean textiles and the shifting folds of his text.

## NOTES

1 I would like to express my gratitude to Professor Mary Gaylord for her generosity in the editing of this essay. I would also like to tip my hat in honour of Professor Carroll B. Johnson, in whose last class on the *Guzmán* these paragraphs took their first shape.

2 Unless otherwise noted translations are mine.

3 In *Seneca in Spain*, Alfred Bluher notes the "stoic" nature of the glossed motto.

4 Ken Johnson, cited in the Art Review article "It's a great fit, but can you breathe in there your majesty," *New York Times*, 3 July 2009.

5 Curiously, although Castro does not equate this to Alemán's novel, they both use the term "alborotar" in relation to *sosiego.*

6 Defined by Sebastián de Covarrubias in the *Tesoro de la lengua española* (1611).

7 In the sentences preceding the introductory quote, Guzmán disturbs his reader's *sosiego* and requests that they consume, digest, and regurgitate his autobiography in the fashion of animals. In this way Guzmán facilitates the insertion of strange elements into the very centre of their bodies (Alemán 2006, 2.1.41).

8 Juan Ruiz de Alarcón's *La verdad sospechosa* (1634) describes a woman whose collar masked prior illnesses. She is instantly abandoned by her lover when he sees her bare neck (Act I, vv 1–16).

9 Ibid.

10 Charles V, Edict of 1552, ibid.

11 Cited in *Indumentaria española en tiempos de Carlos V* (Bernis 1962).

12 As an indicative sample of a thirty-year span, *cortes* to create laws that would control consumption were called in 1515, 1518, 1523, 1532, 1537, 1548, 1551, 1552, 1555 (Bernis 1962). Carol Collier Frick tells us that "in clothing, there would be new styles, new ornaments, new everything, to keep one step ahead of being the target for the clothing categories available for the sumptuary fashion police" (2002, 183).

13 Interestingly, although cross-dressing is heavily chastised in society, it is a common topos in early modern literature. See Ana Felix, Claudia Jerónima, and Dorotea in Cervantes' *Quijote* and Tirso de Molina's *Don Gil de las calzas verdes*. It is primarily associated with women, even if in Cervantes' *Don Quijote* (1605 I, 1615 II) we find a *copia* of men who disguise themselves as women. Augustin Redondo, in "Nuevas consideraciones sobre el travestismo en El Quijote," informs us that there are at least five cases of male cross-dressing: the priest (1.28), the duke's assistant transformed as the "Dueña Dolorida" along with the twelve disguised men who accompany him (2.36–8), the page who dresses as Dulcinea (2.35), Don Gaspar Gregorio (2.63), and the young woman's brother in Barataria (2.49).

14 There is the curious case of Catalina de Erauso, known as the Monja Alférez. As recounted by Sherry Velasco and José Cartagena Calderón, a few years after escaping from a nunnery, she is seen fighting, dressed as a male *conquistador* in the Americas, under the name of Alonso Díaz Ramírez de Guzmán. She is eventually discovered and given royal permission by Philip IV to live as a man and change her name to Antonio de Erauso.

15 See Barbara Fuchs's *Exotic Nation* (2009), and for an earlier (and less exhaustive) study, see Gridley McKim-Smith and Márcia L. Welles (1994).

16 *Lazarillo de Tormes*, chapter 3.

17 This phenomenon, which is at the centre of Alemán's novel, is also relayed in Cervantes' *Ilustre fregona* (1611).

18 Greenblatt's *Renaissance Self-Fashioning* shapes our contemporary understanding of the early modern self and the complexities of manipulating identity, arguing that this self-creation was both personal and imposed by inflexible social institutions that controlled the middle and upper classes (1980).

19 The term *alfayate* is used in the novel: "no seamos el alfayate de la esquina, que ponía hasta el hilo de su casa" [let us not be like the corner tailor that employed even his house's own thread] (Alemán 2006, 2.3.442).

20 Although the *pícaro* Guzmanillo can appreciate a tailor's ability to create new personas through clothing, Guzmán, the moralizer, admonishes their craft. Guzmán is the *pícaro* who employs the preterit, coupled with the "Atalaya de la Vida Humana" [watchtower of human life] who speaks in the present. Barbara Davis emphasizes Alemán's "contradictory devices," positing that they "suit well a work whose form seems antithetical to its purpose and whose narrator is a hybrid creature relishing the telling of the very sins he is in the process of condemning" (1975, 213). As Davis explains, "there are times when Guzmán, the 'famosísimo ladrón' [very famous thief] and *pícaro* of old determines the language and tone of the writing, and others when Guzmán, the 'muy buen estudiante latino retórico y griego' [very good student in rhetorical Latin and Greek] predominantes" (1975, 200). Yet, as Francisco Rico has

noted, and Davis reminds us "Guzmán está en Guzmanillo [Guzmán is inside of little Guzmanillo], and the two sides of Guzmán's character often merge into a unique combination of seemingly antithetical elements" (1975, 200).

21 See Guillén (1960), Bleiberg (1966), and Bleiberg (1985).

22 Benito Brancaforte suggests that "desde el comienzo de la novela se observa la importancia del nombre, conforme a la obsesión de la sociedad española por el linaje y la limpieza de sangre. El rasgo psicológico que se identifica más estrechamente con Guzmán, es el querer ser otro. La novela comienza con el no de Guzmán respecto a su nombre y a su linaje" [from the beginning of the novel the importance of the name can be seen, conforming to Spanish society's obsession for lineage and purity of blood. The psychological attribute most linked to Guzmán is the wanting to be someone else. The novel begins with Guzmán's "no" in respect to his name and lineage] (1980, 171).

23 Guzmán exclaims: "Si mi madre enredó a dos, mi abuela a dos docenas … Con esta hija enredó a cien linajes, diciendo y jurando a cada padre que era suya" [If my mother embroiled two, my grandmother did so with two dozen … With this daughter she embroiled one hundred lineages, telling and swearing to each father that she was their own] (Alemán 2006, 1.1.2).

24 He will dress up and dress down, changing his identity and making *ricos* and *hidalgos* (the rich and the sons of something) and the *pobres* and *pecheros* (the poor and the taxed) indistinguishable. Michel Cavillac explains that in Mateo Alemán's novel, "on voit aussi s'organiser un système discursif articulé sur une série de formules dichotomiques opposant le 'verdadero mercader' au 'mercader fingido,' le 'pobre legítimo' au 'pobre fingido,' et la 'verdadera nobleza' à la 'nobleza fingida'" [one sees the organization of a discursive system articulated on a series of formulaic dichotomies that oppose the "true merchant" to the "feigned merchant," the "legitimate poor" to the "feigned poor," and the "true nobility" to the "feigned nobility"] (1983, 245). These dichotomies, which blur social boundaries, permit the rogue to overstep the sartorial regulations and cause further social unrest.

25 Jones and Stallybrass argue, "In the transfer of clothes, identities are transformed, from an aristocrat to an actor, from an actor to a master, from a master to an apprentice" (2000, 204).

26 In Book 1, chapter 1, Guzmán's Genoese father plays the part of a faithful Catholic. As if he were reading from a script, we are told that "cada mañana oía su misa, sentadas ambas rodillas en el suelo, juntas las manos, levantadas del pecho arriba, el sombrero encima dellas" [every morning he heard mass, with both knees placed on the floor, hands together, lifted up from his chest, and his hat on top of them] (Alemán 2006, 1.1.1). Even with such a consistent display of religious fervour, this *converso* is accused of questionable behaviour

in church: “Arguyéronle maldicientes que estaba de aquella manera rezando para no oír y el sombrero alto para no ver” [Evil sayers said that he was praying in this way so he could not hear, and that he placed the hat so high so that he could not see] (Alemán 2006, 1.1.1).

27 This might be a reference to the Fuggers, the German moneylenders to the Spanish monarchy.

28 In her study “Achilles: Gender Ambiguity and Destiny in Golden Age Drama,” Anita K. Stoll tells us that we find Achilles or his prototype in Tirso’s *El Aquiles*, Cristobal y Monroy’s *El caballero dama* and *Hector y Achilles*, and Calderón’s *El monstro de los jardines* and *Las manos blancas no ofenden* (1998).

29 Covarrubias explains what was understood as *afeite*: “El adereçco que se ponga a alguna cosa para que parezca bien, y particularmente el que las mugeres se ponen en la cara, manos y pechos, para parecer blancas y roxas, aunque sean negras y descoloridas. Afeitar se toma muchas veces por quitarse los hombres el cabello” [The make-up that is put on something so that it seems in a good state, and particularly the one that women wear on their faces, hands, and chest in order to appear white and pink, even if they are black and discoloured. It is often used to describe the shaving away of men’s hair].

30 This “galeote” seems also to reference the “galateo” from Lucas Gracián Dantisco’s *Galateo Español*, a manual of decorum in the tradition of *El Cortesano*. Interestingly, Margarita Morreale, in her introduction, informs us that it was often published with *Lazarillo*. Dantisco condemns effeminate decoration: “Pues por esto hallo que no se deve el hombre adereçar a manera de mujer, pues no ha de ser el ornamento uno, y la persona otra … Y ansí toda desproporción parece mal … sin cuidado de abrocharse y entallarse bien” [That is why I find that a man should not dress himself in the manner of a woman, for the decoration should not be one thing, and the person another … And in this manner all lack of proportion seems wrong … without the care of buttoning and fitting the suit well to the body] (1968, 179–80).

31 Francisco de Quevedo uses this story as the frame to *La hora de todos* (1645).

32 Noted by Fuchs (2009, 130).

## WORKS CITED

Alarcón, Juan Ruiz de. 1999. *La verdad sospechosa.* Edited by José Montero Reguera. Madrid: Cátedra.

Alemán, Mateo. 2006. *Guzmán de Alfarache* I. II. Edited by José María Mico. Madrid: Cátedra.

Barthes, Roland. 1985. *The Fashion System.* Translated by Matthew Ward and Richard Howard. London: Cape.

Bernis, Carmen. 1962. *Indumentaria española en tiempos de Carlos V*. Madrid: Instituto Diego Velázquez.

Bernis, Carmen. 2001. *El traje y los tipos sociales en El Quijote*. Madrid: Ediciones El Viso.

Brancaforte, Benito. 1980. *Guzmán de Alfarache: ¿Conversión o proceso de degradación?* Madison, WI: Hispanic Seminary of Medieval Studies.

Cartagena Calderón, José R. 2008. *Masculinidades en obras: El drama de la hombría en la España imperial*. Newark: Juan de la Cuesta.

Castiglione, Baldasarre. 1942. *El Cortesano*. Translated by Juan de Boscán. Madrid: S. Aguirre.

Castro, Americo. 1976. *De la edad conflictiva*. Madrid: Taurus.

Cavillac, Michel. 1983. *Gueux et Marchands dans le "Guzmán de Alfarache": Roman picaresque et mentalité bourgeoise dans l'Espagne du Siècle d'Or*. Bordeaux: Institut d'Etudes Ibériques et Ibéro-américaines.

Cavillac, Michel. 2002. "Alemán y Guzmán ante la Reformación de los vagabundos ociosos." In *Atalayas del Guzmán de Alfarache: Seminario Internacional sobre Mateo Alemán*, edited by Pedro M. Piñero-Ramírez, 141–66. Seville: Universidad de Sevilla.

Cervantes, Miguel de. 2004. *Don Quijote de la Mancha*. Edited by Francisco Rico. Sao Paolo: Real Academia Española.

Civil, Pierre. 1990. "'Corps, vêtement et société: le costume aristocratique espagnol dans la deuxième moitié du XVIe siècle." In *Le corps dans la société espagnole des XVIe et XVIIe siècles*, edited by Agustín Redondo, 307–19. Paris: Sorbonne.

Collier Frick, Carole. 2002. *Dressing Renaissance Florence*. Baltimore: Johns Hopkins University Press.

Covarrubias, de Sebastian. *Tesoro de la lengua castellana*. URL: http://www.cervantesvirtual.com/servlet/SirveObras/80250529545703831976613/index.htm.

Davis, Barbara. 1975. "The Style of Mateo Alemán's Guzmán de Alfarache." *Romance Review* 66: 199–213.

Elliott, J.H. 2002. *Imperial Spain 1469–1716*. London: Penguin.

Fernández de Oviedo, Gonzalo. 1959. *Historia General y Natural de las Indias*. Madrid: Atlas.

Fuchs, Barbara. 2003. *Passing for Spain: Cervantes and the Fictions of Identity*. Chicago: University of Illinois Press.

Fuchs, Barbara. 2009. *Exotic Nation*. Philadelphia: University of Pennsylvania Press.

Garber, Marjorie. 1992. *Vested Interests: Cross Dressing and Cultural Anxiety*. New York: Routledge Chapman and Hall.

Gracián, Baltasar. 2004. *Agudeza y arte de ingenio*. Edited by Ceferino Peralta. Zaragoza: Prensas Universitarias de Zaragoza.

Gracían Dantisco, Lucas. 1968. *Galateo Español.* Introduction by Margarita Morreale. Valencia: Soler.

Greenblatt, Stephen. 1980. *Renaissance Self-Fashioning*. Chicago: University of Chicago Press.

Harvey, John. 1995. *Men in Black*. London: Reaktion Books.

Herrera, Fernando de. 2001. *Anotaciones a la poesía de Garcilaso.* Madrid: Cátedra.

Johnson, Carroll B. 1978. *Inside Guzmán de Alfarache*. Berkeley: University of California Press.

Jones, Ann Rosalind, and Peter Stallybrass. 2000. *Renaissance Clothing and the Materials of Memory*. Cambridge: Cambridge University Press.

Juárez Almendros, Encarnación. 2006. *El cuerpo vestido y la construcción de la identidad en las narrativas autobiográficas del siglo de oro*. New York: Tamesis.

*Lazarillo de Tormes*. 2003. Edited by Francisco Rico. Madrid: Cátedra.

Maravall, José Antonio. 1986. *La Cultura del Barroco*. Barcelona: Editorial Ariel.

McKim-Smith, Gridley, and Marcia L. Welles. 2004. "Material Girls-and Boys: Dressing Up in Cervantes." *Cervantes* 24 (1): 65–104.

Quevedo y Villegas, Francisco. 1987. *La Hora de todos y La Fortuna con seso*. Madrid: Cátedra.

Quevedo y Villegas, Francisco. 2001. *La vida de Buscón*. Edited by Fernando Cabo Aseguinolaza. Barcelona: Editorial Crítica.

Quevedo y Villegas, Francisco. 2007. *Los Sueños: Edición de Ignacio Arellano*. Madrid: Cátedra.

Quondam, Amedeo. 2007. *Tutti i colori Del Nero: Moda e cultura del gentiluomo del Rinascimento*. Vicenza: A. Colla.

Redondo, Agustín. 1997. *Otra manera de leer el Quijote*. Madrid: Castalia.

Redondo, Agustín. 2008. "Nuevas consideraciones sobre el travestismo en El Quijote." In *Traditions and Innovations in Early modern Studies*, edited by Sherry Velasco, 273–92. Delaware: Juan de La Cuesta.

Rosenthal, Margaret F., and Ann Rosalind Jones. 2008. *The Clothing of the Renaissance World: Europe, Asia, Africa, The Americas*. New York: Thames & Hudson.

Ruiz, Teófilo. 2001. *Spanish Society, 1400–1600*. Essex: Longman.

Sousa Congosto, Francisco de. 2007. *Introducción a la historia de la indumentaria en España*. Madrid: Istmo.

Stoll, Anita K. 1998. "Achilles: Gender Ambiguity and Destiny in Golden Age Drama." In *A Star-Crossed Golden Age*, edited by Frederick de Armas, 112–25. Lewisburg: Bucknell University Press.

Velasco, Sherry. 2001. *The Lieutenant Nun: Lesbianism, Desire, and Catalina de Erauso*. Austin: University of Texas Press.

# Contributors

**Heather Allen** is Assistant Professor of Spanish in the University of Mississippi's Department of Modern Languages. She has held a Tinker fellowship at the University of Chicago, Nahuatl study scholarships through Yale/IDIEZ-UAZ, and a visiting assistant professorship at the University of Texas at Austin in the Department of Spanish and Portuguese. Her research interests include the symbolic dimensions of literacy in colonial Spanish American historiography, the early modern cultural history of print, and Nahuatl studies.

**Timothy Ambrose** is Associate Professor of Spanish at Indiana University Southeast. He has published articles on Golden Age literature, twentieth-century Spanish poetry, and the fiction and poetry of twentieth-century Latin America. He is currently at work on a book that investigates how Lope de Vega, Cervantes, and Titian express in their works different aspects of the goddesses of antiquity.

**Luis F. Avilés** is Associate Professor in the Department of Spanish and Portuguese at the University of California, Irvine. He has published a book entitled *Lenguaje y crisis: las alegorías del Criticón*, and has also written a number of articles on Gracián, Garcilaso de la Vega, Cervantes, and Sor Juana Inés de la Cruz. He is presently finishing a book project entitled *Juegos visuales: espacio y mirada en la cultura literaria de los Siglos de Oro*. He is also working on another project that studies the relationships between ethics, war, captivity, and politics in early modern Spain.

**Mary E. Barnard** is Associate Professor of Spanish and Comparative Literature at the Pennsylvania State University. She is the author of *The*

*Myth of Apollo and Daphne from Ovid to Quevedo: Love, Agon, and the Grotesque* (Duke University Press). She works on early modern lyric poetry and its relations to the visual arts, classical mythology, and material culture. Her essays have appeared in *PMLA*, *Hispanic Review*, *Romanic Review*, *Revista de Estudios Hispánicos*, among others, and in edited collections. Her book *Garcilaso and Material Culture* is forthcoming.

**Emilie L. Bergmann** is Professor of Spanish at the University of California, Berkeley. Her research focuses on visual culture, gender, sexuality, and the maternal in early modern Hispanic literature. Her most recent publications focus on optics and musical culture in the poetry of Sor Juana Inés de la Cruz and Luis de Góngora. She is co-editor (with Stacey Schlau) of *Approaches to Teaching the Works of Sor Juana Inés de la Cruz* (2007) and *Mirrors and Echoes: Women's Writing in Twentieth-Century Spain* (with Richard Herr, 2007).

**Marsha S. Collins** is Marcel Bataillon Distinguished Term Professor of Comparative Literature at the University of North Carolina at Chapel Hill. She is the author of *The 'Soledades,' Góngora's Masque of the Imagination* (Missouri, 2002), a book on Pío Baroja, and articles on Cervantes, Lope, Galdós, and Unamuno, among others. She has a special interest in the relationship between early modern literature and the visual arts, and is currently writing a book on visions of Arcadia in sixteenth-century pastoral romance.

**Frederick A. de Armas** is Andrew W. Mellon Distinguished Service Professor in Humanities and Professor in Romance Languages and Comparative Literature at the University of Chicago. His books include *The Invisible Mistress: Aspects of Feminism and Fantasy in the Golden Age* (1976); *The Return of Astraea: An Astral-Imperial Myth in Calderón* (1986); *Cervantes, Raphael and the Classics* (1998); *Quixotic Frescoes: Cervantes and Italian Renaissance Art* (2006); and *Don Quixote among the Saracens: A Clash of Civilizations & Literary Genres* (2011). The latter received the PROSE award in literature, honorary mention.

**Edward H. Friedman** is Gertrude Conaway Vanderbilt Professor of Spanish, Professor of Comparative Literature, and director of the Robert Penn Warren Center for the Humanities at Vanderbilt University. He is editor of the *Bulletin of the Comediantes*. His primary field of research is early modern Spanish literature, and his work also covers contemporary narrative and drama.

**Ryan D. Giles** is Associate Professor at Indiana University, Bloomington and the author of *The Laughter of the Saints: Parodies of Holiness in Late Medieval and Renaissance Spain* (University of Toronto Press, 2009). Recent articles and book chapters have dealt with a variety of works, from the *Libro de buen amor*, to the *Corbacho*, cancionero poetry, *Celestina*, *Lozana andaluza*, and Calderón's *Devoción de la Cruz*. He is currently working on a book that explores the way in which prayers and incantations were simultaneously employed in literature and used as textual amulets in medieval and early modern Spain.

**Goretti González** is a doctoral student in the Department of Romance Languages and Literature at Harvard University. Goretti earned a Master's degree from UCLA in Hispanic Languages and Literature and a Bachelor's degree from Scripps College in nineteenth-century French, Italian, and Latin-American literature. She spent a semester as a Graduate Fellow at the Villa I Tatti. Goretti works on cultural and literary production in early modern Spain with a special emphasis on visual and material culture and the construction of identity through the clothed body. She is also interested in Iberian-Italian exchanges and transatlantic studies.

**Carolyn A. Nadeau** is the Byron S. Tucci Professor of Spanish at Illinois Wesleyan University where she teaches courses on medieval and early modern literature and culture. She has authored a monograph on *Don Quijote* and a critical edition of *El buscón*, and published articles on mythological female figures in the comedia, the role of the wife and mother in sixteenth-century advice manuals, and food representation in Spanish texts. Her current project, *Alonso Quijano's Diet and the Discourse of Food in Early Modern Spain*, explores the representations of food consumption and etiquette in the literature of early modern Spain and examines how food informs and intersects with social constructs of identity.

**María Cristina Quintero** is Professor of Spanish at Bryn Mawr College. She is the author of the forthcoming *Gendering the Crown in the Baroque Comedia* (Ashgate 2012) and of *Poetry As Play: Gongorismo and the Comedia* (Purdue 1991). She is also the editor of *Luis de Góngora*, a special issue of *Calíope: Journal of the Society for Renaissance and Baroque Hispanic Poetry*, and has published numerous reviews and articles on Renaissance theories of translation, gender, and lyric poetry, and the politics of the *comedia* in Hapsburg Spain. Her articles have appeared in *MLN*, *Hispanic Review*, *Revista de Estudios Hispánicos*, *Bulletin of Hispanic Studies*, *Bulletin of the Comediantes*, and *Cervantes*.

**Robert ter Horst** is Professor Emeritus of Spanish and Comparative Literature in the University of Rochester, New York. He is the author of *Calderon: The Secular Plays* (1982), *The Fortunes of the Novel* (2003), and *Literary Tectonics* (in preparation) as well as an editor of *Studies in Honor of Bruce W. Wardropper*. He has published some fifty scholarly articles, most of them dealing with the poetry, drama, and prose fiction of the Hispanic Golden Age. He is a corresponding member of the Hispanic Society of America.

**Christopher B. Weimer** is Professor of Spanish at Oklahoma State University. With Barbara Simerka, he is co-editor of *Echoes and Inscriptions: Comparative Approaches to Early Modern Spanish Literatures* (2000) and co-founder of *Laberinto: An Electronic Journal of Early Modern Hispanic Literatures and Cultures*. His essays on both early modern and contemporary Hispanic theatre have appeared in journals including *Anuario de estudios cervantinos, Bulletin of the Comediantes, Calíope, Estreno, Hispanic Review, Hispanófila, Latin American Theater Review,* and *Modern Drama*.

# TORONTO IBERIC



1 Anthony J. Cascardi, *Cervantes, Literature, and the Discourse of Politics*

2 Jessica A. Boon, *The Mystical Science of the Soul: Medieval Cognition in Bernardino de Laredo's Recollection Method*

3 Susan Byrne, *Law and History in Cervantes' Don Quixote*

4 Mary E. Barnard and Frederick A. de Armas (eds), *Objects of Culture in the Literature of Imperial Spain*

www.ingramcontent.com/pod-product-compliance
Lightning Source LLC
LaVergne TN
LVHW090804070826
844660LV00022B/1071

* 9 7 8 1 4 8 7 5 4 7 6 9 1 *